CANADIAN SOCIETY
A Macro Analysis

Fourth Edition

Harry H. Hiller
University of Calgary

Prentice
Hall
Canada

A Pearson Company

Toronto

To Nathan and Drew, sons and friends

Canadian Cataloguing in Publication Data

Hiller, Harry H., 1942–
    Canadian society: a macro analysis

4th ed.
Includes bibliographical references and index.
ISBN 0-13-086405-6

1. Nationalism – Canada. 2. National characteristics, Canadian.
3. Multiculturalism – Canada. 4. Regionalism – Canada. I. Title.

FC97.H55 2000   971   C00-930308-1
F1021.H55 2000

ISBN 0-13-086405-6

Vice President, Editorial Director: Michael Young
Acquisitions Editor: Jessica Mosher
Developmental Editor: Laura Paterson Forbes
Production Editor: Avivah Wargon
Copy Editor: Imogen Brian
Production Coordinator: Peggy Brown
Art Director: Mary Opper
Cover Design/Image: Lisa Lapointe, PhotoDisc
Page Layout: Janette Thompson (Jansom)

1 2 3 4 5   04 03 02 01 00

Printed and bound in Canada

Statistics Canada information is used with permission of the Minister of Industry, as Minister responsible for Statistics Canada. Information on the availability of the wide range of data from Statistics Canada can be obtained from Statistics Canada's Regional Offices, its World Wide Web site at **http://www.statcan.ca** *and its toll-free access number, 1-800-263-1136.*

Visit the Pearson Education Canada Web site! Send us your comments, browse our catalogues, and more at **www.pearsoned.ca**.

Prentice
Hall
Canada

A Pearson Company

Contents

Chapter 3: The Issue of Inequality 83

Chapter 4: The Issue of Regionalism 127

Chapter 5: The Issue of Ethnicity 165

Chapter 6: The Question of Uniqueness 217

Chapter 7: The Question of Identity   258

Preface

In some ways, the subject of this book may appear old-fashioned. Globalization has reduced the power of the nation-state to rubble. Decisions made by supra-national organizations like the World Bank, trading blocks or transnational corporations, in conjunction with the free flow of ideas and information through telecommunications and the Internet, as well as the mobility and migration of people, may have made the study of national societies anathema. Political states are being pressured by these external factors as well as by internal demands from sub-state units for more autonomy. Sovereignty and defended borders sometimes seem to represent obsolete ideas. So why study a national society such as Canadian society?

There is no evidence that the world will not continue to be organized into political states. Increasing interconnectedness may be assumed but the national state still remains the basic location for democratic politics from which institutions are created and established to organize human life among people sharing a territory. It is important to study Canadian society because the Canadian political state continues to exist as the mechanism of organizing the life of people sharing the geographic territory called Canada. The important thing to remember is that societies are not fixed or immutable but are constantly in change in response to the pressures and conflicts which they face. Therefore the study of Canadian society should not be expected to be the study of some enduring monolithic entity preoccupied with the preservation of tradition and the maintenance of tranquility and harmony; Rather the study of Canadian society must be understood as the study of a negotiated entity in continual transformation as its constituent populations struggle over their collective life together.

The approach taken in this analysis could be called constructionist, not in the post-modern sense that there are no historical facts or that everything is contingent,[1] but in the sense that the realities that a resident of this society encounters are the result of on-going human activity.[2] This means that we might begin as children with appropriating or internalizing the substance and structure of this society as though it was always there and could be taken-for-granted, but that we soon learn that human activity means that people propose, debate, and create new structures in response to changing conditions. Therefore, it is very useful to understand how and why Canadian society is contingent, fluctuating, and always in process, i.e., continually being constructed and reconstructed. It is the purpose of this book to provide some sense of the forces that are contributing to this societal change.

This perspective is consistent with the work of Michael Mann who argues that it would be a mistake to consider that new globalization forces mean that the nation-state is dying.[3] Instead, he notes, the emphasis needs to be placed on how the nation-state is changing. The mistake is in seeing the nation-state as either hegemonic or obsolete. On the contrary, the analytical focus should be placed on transformation.

One of these transformations is away from the old idea present in classic nationalism that the ideal for which political states must strive is to establish a single and homogeneous national identity. In the contemporary era, there has been a change to both plural and shifting national identities which David McCrone refers to as the new nationalism or neo-nationalism. Of course, such a situation is plagued with problems and debates of which McCrone argues that the goal is not to recover the past but to "debate with the past about who we are now and who we want to become".[4]

It is in this spirit that this book has been written and should be read. The objective of the book is to provide the reader with a sense of the transformations which Canadian society is facing and to sketch the forces producing these outcomes, as well as to provide a sense of the debates and options available in eventual outcomes. Such a goal may be overly ambitious but five objectives can be listed. First, I wanted to provide an overview of Canadian society that would be useful to a beginning analyst, but to do so with some depth and comprehensiveness. Often we understand a society primarily in terms of some small segment but do not see the whole, and this book attempts to place issues in their macro context. Second, I wanted to bring a wide range of scattered literature together to provide this integrated portrait and to do so in a "state of the art" review. Third, there may be too many footnotes and references for a general overview, but the presentation of these footnotes and references is done so that the book can serve as a reasonable reference work on the topic of Canadian society for those interested in further reading and reflection. For this reason, earlier editions of this book have been useful to both undergraduate and graduate students, as well as the general public and others looking for references on topics presented. This tradition has been continued. Fourth, I have highlighted key concepts in my discussions as a useful way of pointing out prominent themes and to serve as key buzzwords in the recollection of important processes. Fifth, I have tried to present the material in such a way as to convey the liveliness of debate and controversy in addition to the more substantive content. The boxed inserts, the Real People segments, and the Research Clips found throughout the text are meant to contribute to that objective. The quotation at the beginning of each chapter is taken from some classic work on Canadian society in order to give the reader a sense of history or tradition of the themes discussed in that chapter. A new feature has been added called "Differing Perspectives" which attempts to show how theory can be applied to the chapter topic with different outcomes in points of view.

Readers often look for a point of view in the material they are reading and I have enjoyed hearing about readers attempting to give this work a theoretical label. Strangely enough, this is often done after reading one chapter. In attempting to provide a reasonably comprehensive overview of Canadian society, I have deliberately tried not to limit myself to one theoretical perspective, and the new section in each chapter called Differing Perspectives is my attempt to make that point clear. The goal then is for a balanced treatment of a variety of issues from a variety of viewpoints. The reader will have to determine to what extent I have succeeded in reaching the goals and objectives stated here.

Each chapter attempts to understand Canadian society from what I call *questions* and *issues* about the realities of a national society. Four questions and three issues are presented here as the most critical themes in a macro understanding of Canadian society. The four macro questions which begin and end the book are: *The Question of Society* (To what extent does the population of Canada form a society?), *The Question of Autonomy* (To what extent is Canadian society an independent societal unit?), *The Question of Uniqueness* (Are the problems of Canadian society unusual?), and *The Question of Identity* (Why is Canadian society so complex and fragmented?). The middle chapters (Chapters Three, Four, and Five) develop the issues of inequality, regionalism, and ethnicity as a way of providing the contextual information for understanding the questions framed by Chapters One and Two at the outset and Six and Seven at the end.

In using the term *Canadian society*, the orientation of the book is on society. As the author is a sociologist, the focus of the book is on the people who reside in the political unit of Canada and their relationships. One of the unique elements of the book continues to be its comparative focus (Chapter Six). I am acutely aware that this book is being read by Canadians who frequently think theirs is the only society with such problems, as well as by persons outside Canada who need some international touchstones to put things in perspective. Chapter Six provides the mechanisms to help determine the unique contours of Canadian society more clearly.

There are plenty of reasons for either a pessimistic view of national societies in general or at least the revisionist view that Canadian society has not only already changed but that the changes of the future will be even more substantial, and may even be painful for those who thought they knew what Canadian society was or should be like. The need to accommodate a multiplicity of interest groups internally and the inexorable pull of global forces are bound to produce a very different society in the future. But the process is already unfolding before our eyes—even when we are not fully conscious of its implications. This is what makes the study of Canadian society so fascinating and so exciting, and that is why this book was written—to help the reader understand the issues and processes of change more clearly.

NOTES

1   For an excellent critique of this form of constructionism, see Ian Hacking, *The Social Construction of What?* (Cambridge: Harvard University Press, 1999)

2   See Peter Berger and Thomas Luckmann, *The Social Construction of Reality* (Garden City: Doubleday, 1966) and Rogers Brubaker, *Nationalism Reframed: Nationhood and the National Question in the New Europe* (Cambridge: Cambridge University Press, 1996).

3   Michael Mann, "Nation-States In Europe And Other Continents: Diversifying, Developing, Not Dying", *Daedalus 122*(1993)3:115-140; and "Has Globalization Ended The Rise Of The Nation-State?" *Review of International Political Economy 4*(1997).

4   David McCrone, *The Sociology of Nationalism* (London: Routledge, 1998), 138.

Acknowledgments

This book is at least partially the product of over twenty-five years of teaching courses on Canadian society. Therefore one of my primary acknowledgments must be to the hundreds of students who have taken the journey with me to uncover and explore the vicissitudes of this intriguing society. Their questions and comments have helped to shape my thinking and have provoked me to explain things as clearly as possible.

I am also grateful to colleagues who have been supportive and/or encouraging in one way or another. They include Bob Stebbins, Simon Langlois, Leslie Laszlo, Rick Ponting, Jim Frideres, Cora Voyageur, Linda Di Luzio, Rebecca Chan Allen, Mark Dickerson, Gretchen MacMillan, Bohdan Harasymiw, and Don Barry, as well as reviewers Mary King, Georgian College; Bibi Laurie, Grande Prairie Regional College; Craig McKie, Carleton University; and Cora Voyageur, University of Calgary. I am also grateful for the support and assistance of the staff in the Academic Data Centre, especially Laurie Schretlen, Sharon Neary, and Helen Clarke. The good humour, splendid co-operation and team spirit of the secretarial staff in the Department of Sociology has been invaluable and I particularly want to thank Lana Westergaard, Margaret Duddy, and Diane Whitlow. The editorial assistance of Laura Paterson Forbes, Lise Creurer, Avivah Wargon, and Dove Champagne at Pearson Education Canada, plus freelance editor Imogen Brian, played a key role in expediting production of the manuscript.

This book is dedicated to Nathan and Drew in gratitude for their courage, strength, and friendship as young adults.

Harry H. Hiller

Introduction

What Is a Macro Analysis?

A macro analysis is the study of social phenomena in terms of society-wide aggregates. Whereas micro analysis takes the individual as its focus, macro analysis takes an entire society as its focus. For our purposes, the boundaries for our unit of analysis are the geopolitical borders of the country of Canada.

Early social scientists (e.g., Durkheim, Weber, Marx, Spencer) preferred the macro approach for they were interested in the broad scope of change which had occurred over time in societies and civilizations. Later, social scientists believed that the essence of human action occurred in face-to-face interpersonal micro situations. Recently, there has been a renewed interest in the macro approach to global patterns of social relations.

Social scientists refer to society as though it were a meaningful unit of analysis. Yet the careful application of scientific method requires that studies first be conducted on specifically defined components of a society at the micro level. We are then left with a series of fragmented conclusions about different aspects of a society, which, when merged, can help us see the society at a general level. Macro analysis attempts to build a broader portrait of a society so that its form and nature become clearer.

Macro analysis involves more than working from the particular to the universal. It requires that special attention be given to the structural features of a society that provide the framework or context around which the everyday life of a society is shaped. These structural features include class structure, region, the state and other institutions, and structured relationships with other societies. In other words, macro analysis implies a societal analysis which, in turn, should enable us to return the flow of analysis from the universal to the particular. Once we understand a society at the macro level, we can develop a clearer understanding of the micro aspects of the society, and the dialectic or exchange that takes place between these two levels.

As long as political states serve as a basic unit of world order, it is both useful and imperative to study societies in politico-national entities. Furthermore, if we remain aware of the fact that these national societies are not simple and homogeneous, but complex and diverse, we can look for the emergent properties of society that provide it with form and character. Macro analysis should complement the numerous micro studies available on particular aspects of society, and should also stimulate the desire for a thorough knowledge of the constituent features of society. Indeed, the macro approach is necessary both within Canada and elsewhere, if we are to understand the broader dimensions of any society.

There are *three dominant perspectives* for understanding a society. The first perspective is known as *structural functionalism*. It understands society more as an ongoing social system that seeks stability and continuity over time in spite of disruptions and change. The second perspective is known as the *conflict* perspective and understands a society as composed of social groups that are in repeated confrontation with each other due to inequalities in social position within the society. Even when conflict is not overt and is submerged, it is still possible to analyze a society in terms of the groups that have positions of dominance in relation to other groups that have less power or may even be powerless. So whereas structural functionalism attempts to ascertain how a society seeks to sustain its equilibrium over time, the conflict model understands society more in terms of change and attempts by groups within the society to retain power, exert power, or overcome their powerlessness. The third perspective is known as *symbolic interactionism* and begins with the individual rather than with society-at-large or with social groups. The focus is on how an individual creates meaning and how these meanings are shared with others.

Structural Functionalist Perspective

Structural functionalism attempts to determine how a society holds together as an entity. This perspective is known as *functionalism* because whatever aspect of society is analyzed, the object is to determine how that structural feature contributes to the integration of the society. For example, broadcasting can be assessed in terms of how it contributes to national unity, or, conversely, disunity. Do Canadian radio stations give priority to recordings by Canadian artists so that Canadian culture is developed, or does the American music industry dominate and negatively impact Canadian understanding of their own culture? Is hockey really Canada's national sport, bringing Canadians together, or, because there are more National Hockey League teams in the United States than in Canada, does hockey contribute to North American continental integration? How then does hockey or sport function to strengthen or weaken Canadian society? What function does immigration have in supplying needed labour for the society but how might it also function to create disharmony? What is the role of regionalism in creating sectionalism rather than societal unity? All of these questions focus on the function an aspect of society has in developing cohesion or integration within the society, or in preventing such consensus from occurring.

One of the problems of structural functionalism is that it assumes that all societies seek stability. While at one level this may be true, most societies exist in considerable tension and various forms of internal conflict may challenge both the form and the structure of that society. This equilibrium model of society is often thought to be conservative because it does not pay enough attention to the dynamics of change.

Conflict Perspective

The second perspective tends to see society less as an ongoing equilibrium than as a struggle between conflicting groups. This is known as the *conflict perspective* because its focus is on what groups have power within a society, what groups possess less power, and how the use of that power determines what a society is like. Terms such as *dominance* and *subordination*, *centre* and *periphery*, and *privilege* and *poverty* all express different relationships of hierarchy and inequality between people within a society. For example, the fact that persons of British descent have historically had more power in Canadian society than persons of French descent created a set of institutions in Canada expressing a British heritage and a form of communication in which English was dominant. But as numerous changes in recent years have transformed this relationship from dominance-subordination to one of greater equality, evidence of power struggles are found among both language groups regarding whose definition of Canadian society will dominate. Thus, it is useful to analyze, for example, whose conception of language (bilingualism, French unilingualism, English unilingualism) in Canada will dominate, and how differences in those conceptions will be expressed in different segments of the society.

The functional perspective usually begins with the assumption that all societies require at least a minimal amount of unity, and that such social processes are *natural*. The conflict perspective focuses on the more seamy underside of society that exposes the tensions and struggles between opposing groups, and visualizes existing inequalities as *created* through the use of power. Thus, if functionalism interprets regionalism as evidence of the natural diversity and character of a society, the conflict perspective views regionalism as created by the struggle for control and dominance of social groups within geographic units of the society. For a conflict theorist, issues of power explain how societies are shaped.

In more recent years, the emphasis in conflict analysis has shifted from conflict between groups within a society to conflict between societies. In a world systems approach, it is considered important to show how inequalities in power between national societies also help to explain a society's character because it is part of a complex global relationship.

Symbolic Interactionist Perspective

The third general perspective works from the individual to the large group in order to understand how individuals and groups relate to each other and understand each other. *Symbolic interactionism* focuses on communication, meanings, and understandings, and how they are expressed in language and symbols, and how they reflect differences in individual and group identities. At the macro level, the symbolic interactionist approach looks at how individuals project their identity to the collectivity or receive their identity from the wider group. The key point, however, is that society is fluid and is constantly being socially constructed and reconstructed or negotiated through the actions of individuals. Whereas functionalism and conflict focus on the structural nature of society, symbolic interactionism notes that what is important is the meaning or different meanings which individuals or groups give to human activity. What is important then is how people interpret their own actions and the actions of others as well as how they express those interpretations through symbols and modes of communication. Symbolic interactionism, then, stresses this more experiential and subjective aspect of society.

Perhaps the classic symbolic interactionist macro question is "What does it mean to be Canadian?" How do I understand who I am as a Canadian? For example, some people think of Canadian society as a British-type society and they place themselves in that context. Others might think of Canadian society as a bilingual or French/English dual identity type society and understand themselves in that context. Still others might think of Canadian society as essentially multicultural and view new immigrants as just as legitimately Canadian as other more entrenched groups. What is the process whereby individuals acquire the vision of Canadian society which they embrace? In what social contexts are they taught these ideas and what experiences alter them? But of even more importance, how do other people who share the same political entity (Canada) develop very different conceptions of what it means to be Canadian that may lead to sharp clashes or at least disagreements?

Symbolic interactionism focuses on how differences in meaning emerge in the context of everyday living whereby people attempt to make sense of their own life and the social group to which they belong. So, for example, the maple leaf has a very distinct meaning to one group of Canadians that is quite different from the fleur-de-lis for another group. On the one hand, a maple leaf is just a leaf from a tree, but to a Canadian it is an important symbol of collective identity that almost has sacred aspects. Or, the choice of a bilingual national anthem over a unilingual one represents a social expression of strong personal identity preferences. How is it that some people use terms like *self-government* or *distinct society* in a very positive way while others interpret these ideas very negatively as though they were threatening? How do they come to these meanings? How are these meanings related to personal identity? And what are their societal consequences?

Symbolic interactionism helps us to focus on the social construction of the worldview of individual Canadians. How do I learn who I am and to what social group(s) I belong? What words or symbols come to reflect my identity or that of the group to which I belong? Understanding an individual's viewpoint or consciousness is known as understanding their *voice*. When we try to understand the viewpoint or voice of a particular group, we try to understand how they experience reality or how they define a situation. We become aware that the voices of some groups are heard more clearly than others and we need to understand why. How do the dominant symbols of a society reflect the voice of particular groups and leave others out? For example, in some parts of Canada, francophones may feel that they have no voice because they have no input into the symbol system which is English. On the other hand, anglophones in Quebec may feel that they have no voice in the changing symbol system in that province. Aboriginal peoples represent another group who feel that their meanings of social reality are not understood nor are their cultural symbols accepted within the broader society. A symbolic interactionist perspective begins with the individual and the collectivities with which they associate, and then moves to the macro level, and for this reason makes a different contribution to a macro analysis than that obtained through functionalism or conflict theory.

There is an elaborate theoretical tradition within each of these perspectives, and there are different nuances of interpretation within each perspective but such distinctions are not the objective of this book. However, the reference to various theories such as feminist theory, world systems theory, or post-modernist theory as proposed within the book can be placed within the framework of these three base theories. Strands from each of the three perspectives will be drawn on at various points within the text. Chapters One and Seven, for example, deal with questions more typical of functionalism. Chapters Two to Four explore more of the conflict perspective. Symbolic interactionist questions are touched on in Chapters Five and Seven and in several other places as well. However, each chapter has a boxed section called "Differing Perspectives" which attempts to show how these theories can be applied to the theme of that chapter. By studying these theoretical perspectives, the reader will have a better sense of how the realities of Canadian society can be interpreted in different ways, and why the analysis of this society must be viewed dynamically rather than statically. While there is a tendency to accentuate conflict-laden issues in this book, all three perspectives provide illumination for our macro analysis of Canadian society.

THE QUESTION
OF SOCIETY

Canada is not the only society which has been created by large numbers of human beings moving into vacant areas, but it is unlikely that any other society has resembled a huge demographic railway station.

—*John Porter, a Carleton University sociologist, in his*

ground-breaking study The Vertical Mosaic *(1965, 33).*

What is it about Canadian society that is so intriguing? Is it the dilemmas and problems of a society created by wide open spaces? Is it the reality of being a relatively young society in spite of some longevity? Is it the search for common ground among a far-flung, diverse, and changing population? Is it the sense of belonging together that persists in spite of crises that threaten to tear the society apart?

It may seem ironic indeed that even though the Canadian state is over one hundred and thirty years old, the precise nature of Canadian society and its existence as an entity is still in question. In fact, the stormy years after the centennial birthday in 1967 suggested more than ever that the concept of a Canadian society could not be taken for granted. While Quebec was contemplating what degree of distance from the rest of Canadian society was most appropriate, the Symons Report was concluding that Canadians knew little about their own society, and a Federal Task Force on Canadian Unity was scouring the country for clues about ways to create a more integrated and cohesive society. More recently, the fail-

1

ure of the Meech Lake Accord and the Charlottetown Agreement with their "distinct Quebec society" ideas, as well as the anxieties produced by two Quebec referendums (and now the threat of a third referendum), continued to point out the fragility of national unity. What kind of society is this that has been problematic for so long?

The use of the term "Canadian society" implies that it can be differentiated from other societies and that it has some measure of internal coherence. Yet there seems to be evidence to suggest that internal coherence in Canadian society has been in continual question. Repeated waves of immigration and emigration, British and American influences, French–English differences, a relatively sparse but clustered population in a vast territory, and uneven economic development are only some of the factors that have contributed to fragmentation rather than societal unity.

It is, therefore, by no means certain that there really is such a thing as a Canadian society. Does the strength of the various small-scale sub-societies in Canada preclude any meaningful discussion about Canadian society as a whole? Do differences in the resident population overwhelm whatever may be held in common?

Canada exists as a nation by the political and legislative decree of the *British North America Act* passed by the British parliament in 1867. This legislative document created an independent national unit, so we are compelled to raise sociological questions regarding the nature and character of the people and their interaction within her geographic and political borders. But does merely living within these boundaries create a society? If so, why have Canadians been so preoccupied with the lack of national unity and the need for greater understanding? What is it about the people living within the political entity called Canada that contributes to a weak sense of society?

Certainly there are many things about Canada's population that make it unique among other national populations. Within the national boundaries there are various regional, ethnic, occupational, economic, and environmental distinctions which all contribute to what is known as the *national character*.[1] But in what way can we speak of the population within Canada's borders as a society?

Historically, it has been customary to describe Canada not as one society but two: French-Canadian and English-Canadian. From this perspective, the differences between the two societies were so striking that the idea of a "single society" was almost meaningless. Using multicultural or regional categories, we might conclude that Canadian society is nothing but an amalgam of numerous sub-societies which make up the whole in the manner of a jigsaw puzzle. Let us assume, however, that national political boundaries force the population within these borders to interact and to be cognizant of each other at least in some minimal way, if only because they share a common territory and political system. Thus, we use the term "Canadian society" to refer to the total population contained within the politico-national unit.[2]

DESCRIBING A HUMAN SOCIETY

Having raised the question of whether the term "society" describes Canada's population appropriately, it is important to specify the basic characteristics of a society and then to determine the degree to which Canadian society exhibits these characteristics. From a sociological point of view, a human society must possess the following characteristics: locality, organization, durability, and self-identification.

Locality

A society requires that its members share a common environment or locality. A common territory encourages and facilitates interaction that binds together the many smaller groups within the area. Thus, living together in a common environment creates the potential for the formation of a society.

Assessment

It is true that Canadians share a common territory, but perhaps the most dominant characteristics of this country are that the territory is enormous, relatively sparsely settled, and unevenly settled (see Figure 1.1). The larger the territory, the more we would expect regions and sub-regions within those regions to be significant. As we will see later in this chapter and in Chapter Four, each region has its own characteristic economy and population base in terms of occupation, ethnic background, and length of residence in Canada, as well as its own aspirations for growth and development. Clearly, geographic features such as mountains, climate, arability of the soil, and distance also affect the way the territory is inhabited, enhance the divisive nature of regionalism, and create problems for the development of a sense of society.[3]

Various forms of mass communication and transportation have reduced some of the effects of a vast territory, but other aspects of distance are much more difficult to overcome. For example, many Canadians have little understanding of life in regions of the country they have never visited and perhaps for which they have constructed negative or unrealistic stereotypes. Another tendency is to view Canadians living in other regions as competitors rather than compatriots, and each region tends to become fiercely protective of its own lifestyle and economic development. In sum, the problem of locality has meant that merely living within the geographic boundaries of Canada has not automatically knit residents into a common pattern of interaction from which a sense of society could easily develop.

Organization

For a society to survive, it must have an internal organization that draws its members together in interaction and for their mutual benefit. An internal web of interrelationships must be present that creates interdependencies. Some persons are given special roles (e.g., politicians) to protect the society and to establish guidelines that foster interaction within the national unit as well as with other units. Government agencies such as in transportation, broadcasting, and commerce regulate these activities in the national interest presumably in such a manner as to draw all members of the society together.

Assessment

In Canada, the various levels of government join with large corporations and community institutions to give organization and structure to the society. For example, everywhere you go in Canada, you will find local branches of national chartered banks, national political parties, and representatives of federal agencies which enhance our ability to recognize a locale as part of "our" society. Furthermore, members of a society learn to depend on each other for goods and services. Atlantic Canada, for instance, possesses both fishing stock and fishing tech-

FIGURE 1.1 The Canadian Ecumene

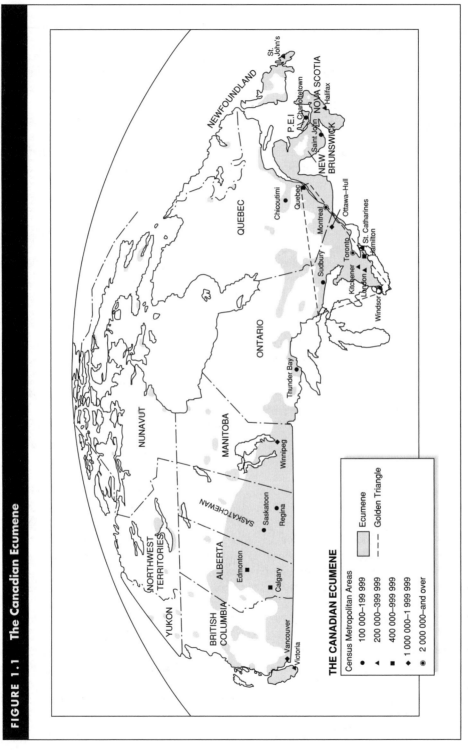

THE CANADIAN ECUMENE

Census Metropolitan Areas

●	100 000–199 999
▲	200 000–399 999
■	400 000–999 999
◆	1 000 000–1 999 999
◉	2 000 000–and over

Ecumene

Golden Triangle

Source: Based on Statistics Canada, Catalogue 98-120.

nology lacking in other parts of the country, while Saskatchewan specializes in grains, and Ontario possesses large capital pools for investment. From this perspective, a society organizes itself so that interdependencies develop.

⨉The federal government has historically used its powers to protect and expand a national societal organization as a way of reaffirming the boundaries of the society. This was necessary particularly because the distribution of the Canadian population along the southern extremities of its territory tended to encourage interaction in a north–south direction across the US border rather than in an east–west direction across Canada. Expertise, products, and knowledge were more easily exchanged with adjacent neighbours to the south than with fellow Canadians thousands of kilometres away. So in order to establish and reinforce the organizational structure of Canadian society, the federal government constructed regulatory agencies and mechanisms, such as tariffs and immigration rules, to promote greater intra-societal interaction. Tariffs force consumers to turn to Canadian industries and immigration laws monitor and control movements across national borders.

⨉While some might argue that these policy efforts tend to somewhat artificially create a sense of society, there is also a fear that the removal of some of these policies, through such agreements as free trade, potentially threatens the boundaries which help to organize a sense of society. Without incentives or regulations to ensure greater interaction within Canada, many feel that the viability of the society is at stake. In any case, with or without government controls, we are repeatedly reminded of the fragility of the society.

Durability

> *A society requires that interactive organization be relatively permanent and durable. When generations of families have inhabited an area and interacted more or less continuously over a long period of time, a heritage of common behavioural patterns and national societal coherence is likely to develop.*

Assessment

Canada is a relatively young country which has experienced considerable growth in its short history. In other words, the Canadian society in existence at the time of Confederation in 1867 was very different, and certainly had a much smaller population, than the Canadian society we know today. At that time, the population of Canada was largely confined to southern Ontario, southern Quebec, and the Atlantic provinces. Since that time, the density of this territory has increased dramatically and population has moved north as well as west. Much of this growth was accomplished by high levels of immigration coming from different source countries and arriving in different waves or time periods. The English–French balance of people typical of the early days of the society has now been obliterated through the addition of persons from other ethnic traditions. The problem of emigration has also resulted in considerable population turnover.[4]

Durability, then, has been thwarted by the changing nature of the population, which has hindered the emergence of societal traditions and a greater national societal consciousness. Furthermore, it was not until the last three or four decades that our educational system (particularly anglophone schools) had developed materials that would give Canadian youth a better understanding of their society and its heritage. Durability requires not only a stable population but the development of common reference points through which greater societal interaction can be facilitated.

Self-Identity

Finally, a society must be aware of itself as a unique and independent entity. Participants in one society must differentiate themselves from participants in another by an awareness of their society and a sense of belonging to it.

The Need to "Know Ourselves"

In the 1970s, there was a general feeling that Canadians were rather ignorant of their own country and society. One of the major issues at that time was whether Canadian educational institutions were providing students with adequate knowledge of the elements of their own society or whether they were depending too much on material emanating from other societies such as England and the United States. Thomas H.B. Symons, former President of Trent University, conducted hearings across the country and the end result was a document entitled "To Know Ourselves" published in 1975.

Instead of arguing that the need for Canadian Studies was linked to the need for a demonstration of patriotism, the Commission on Canadian Studies adopted a rationale based on the need for self-understanding as reflected in Plato's dictum "Know Thyself." The quest for self-knowledge was understood to be a basic societal need and, in its assessments, the Commission was looking for an "awareness factor" or "sensitivity" to the Canadian context or perspective within that quest.

The Report confirmed the suspicions of many that Canadian studies were being neglected in fields as diverse as art history, literature, economics, folklore, sociology, and the performing arts.

It also determined that more government and private donor support was needed for Canadian archives development and audio-visual resources, and even for the promotion of Canadian Studies abroad.

The Report argued that universities should not only be concerned with the generation of knowledge but with service to the community that supported it. Since young people were interested in learning more about Canada, educational institutions should become actively involved in fostering this goal. It was also felt that new research emphasis should be given to studying those problems which are uniquely Canadian (e.g., environmental, social) and that assumptions and methodologies should be critically investigated before being borrowed from other countries. Persons training for the professions (e.g., architecture, business) should also be assisted in relating their craft more directly to the needs and uniqueness of their own society.

Source: *To Know Ourselves: The Report of the Commission on Canadian Studies, Vol. I and II.* Ottawa: Association of Universities and Colleges of Canada, 1975. Volume III was published in 1984. An abridged version of the Symons Report, published in 1978 by the Book and Periodical Development Council, is available. Reviews of the Report appeared in many disciplinary periodicals in the time period immediately following the appearance of the Report. Six reviews (one by a sociologist) expressing a range of sentiments are contained in the Journal of Canadian Studies, 11 (1976) and 12 (1977). Also see "What Did Symons say? A Retrospective Look at the Commission on Canadian Studies," *Canadian Issues,* 2 (1977), 1.

Within the international social world, members of Canadian society must be able to locate themselves by adopting the societal identity of being "Canadian." Customs, symbols, folk heroes, and important landmarks contribute to an awareness of societal identity. For example, the display of the maple leaf in public assists Canadians in differentiating their society from other societies and helps them to establish their own national identity.

Assessment

A collective Canadian identity has been slow to develop within the society. One of the most significant retarding factors has been the presence of two distinct societies within the polity. For reasons which are discussed in Chapter Five, French-Canadian society has always had a well-developed conception of itself as a society in contrast to the more diffuse image of English-Canadian society. In addition, Québécois have been apprehensive about English-Canadian intentions regarding an emerging national society. Francophones fear that these intentions may destroy Quebec society. For this reason, even the reformulated identity of Canada as a bilingual state has produced considerable controversy and dissension.

In addition to the idea of a dual society, the so-called hyphenated Canadian (Italian-Canadian, German-Canadian) terminology has persisted. Members of the society are frequently identified in terms of the society of their origin. While these social groupings of hyphenated Canadians may have given Canada the collective identity that it does possess, and is therefore celebrated by some, others lament such pluralism because it has reduced the society's ability to establish a self-identity of its own, which all members of the society can recognize and in which they can participate.

Perhaps no national population has all of these characteristics in combination to thereby constitute the "ideal type" society. It is clear, though, that Canada has particular problems in overcoming her spatial difficulties, developing the web of social organization that binds her members together, creating durable patterns of interaction among a permanent population, and fostering a sense of identification with the socio-political unit. Many of the reasons for this will be developed in this chapter and throughout this book and will demonstrate why a sense of society is problematic and cannot be taken for granted.

THE PROBLEM OF SOCIETY WITHIN POLITICAL UNITS

Societies were traditionally identifiable because their people were living in virtual isolation from other collectivities. The boundaries and distinctive social patterns of the society were easily discernible and the network of interrelationships could be simply traced. This conception of society changed as populations expanded, and as wars and economic relations between societies resulted in an intermingling of peoples. The advent of industrialization and the breakdown of the feudal world provided the context for deep thinking by early sociologists (e.g., Durkheim, Spencer, Weber) about the nature of society and its growing complexity.[5] The breakdown of the traditionally simple society provided opportunities to examine how different peoples could be joined within a single political entity.[6]

A *state* is a political organization or structure with the power to govern. Its emergence as a primary institution with sovereignty over other institutions was a significant development in human history. The state as a complex of institutions including government, the judiciary, and civil service bureaucracies, such as public corporations and regulatory commissions, for example, creates, enforces, and interprets rules which attempt to control the behaviour of large numbers of people.

As states expanded their sphere of influence, they increasingly gathered under their governing umbrella societies which reflected ethnic, racial, class, regional, linguistic, or religious differences from the dominant group controlling the state. In its attempt to be all-encompassing, the state embraced numerous sub-societies to form what we would now call a *pluralist society*; i.e., a society consisting of many meaningful sub-units. Personal submission to the state and its authority was frequently challenged by commitments to these sub-units, some of which had links beyond the political boundaries of the country. The state was, therefore, an instrument of human power which frequently welded people into political units irrespective of their own sense of society.

The characteristics of a society mentioned earlier produce a feeling among people that they belong together. This group consciousness is heavily dependent on the concept of *nation*. The word *nation* stems from the Latin word "nasci" which means "to be born" and originally meant a group of people born in the same place.[7] Similarity of birthplace (the objective dimension) provided the basis for fellow feeling (the subjective dimension) due to the sharing of common origin, traditions, and institutions.[8] The concept of nation is related to ethnicity because of the ethnic commonality of background and sense of belonging together. For this reason we can speak of the francophone community in Quebec as a nation and legitimately refer to the existence of a Quebec society.

Native peoples have also developed an awareness of being part of the Canadian state but yet being different as Aboriginals. The designation *First Nations* (note the plural) implies not only a sense of prior occupation of the Canadian territory but a sense of cultural difference producing nationhood.[9] Different languages and cultural practices are found among different groups of Aboriginal peoples so reference is made, for example, to the Sarcee Nation, the Iroquois Nation, and to native groups in the north as the Dene Nation.

The point is that there may be many nation groups residing in the same political jurisdiction. A polity composed of only one ethnic group is considered mono-ethnic. Countries may, however, contain more than one nation due to the existence of two or more ethnic identities (Switzerland and Nigeria, for example). Nation groups can also be participants in more than one state (the French in Belgium, France, and Switzerland). When polities contain more than one ethnic nationality, they may attempt to create a new single nationality based on the political entity. In the medieval world, a multiplicity of languages and cultural traditions was common and was not incompatible with allegiance to the lord or king.[10] Only in the contemporary world has the political unit that is defined by its jurisdictional boundaries and has a globally identifiable name been inclined to demand a single allegiance so that nation and state are made to be equivalent. This demand may result in regionally based nationalist movements which may challenge the political unit and serve as the basis for secession.

When several national/ethnic groups reside within a polity, we refer to this as a *pluralist society* even though one group may dominate. Pluralist societies hold people together through a mutual commitment to abide by the regulations of the state even though the emotional dynamic of togetherness is lacking. Nevertheless, changes and adaptations over several generations may contribute to a growing sense of nationality based on the identity of a single society. As this occurs, it becomes increasingly possible to speak of a national society as circumscribed by the boundaries of the political entity.

In sum, a state is the jurisdictional apparatus that organizes people within a political unit. If there is more than one ethnic or national group within a polity, there may be difficulty in determining who controls the state. This explains why Canada has been described as

The Sense of "Nation"hood in Quebec

the fleur-de-lis—the national flag
the maple leaf—the Canadian flag
Quebec City—the national capital
Ottawa—the Canadian capital
MNA (Member of the National Assembly)—elected member of Quebec legislature
MP (Member of Parliament)—elected member of Canadian parliament

"two nations warring within one bosom" and clarifies why the idea of a single national society is problematic.

Some countries are held together more by regulation than the desire for integration.[11] The dominant anglophone model of Canadian society has been that whatever regulation was initially needed to make the society viable would eventually be replaced by the populist desire for more integration. The francophone perspective, on the other hand, has been to object to any loss of their ethnic identity in favour of a pan-Canadian identity. Clearly, the weak existence of a Canadian nationalism is rooted in the vague existence of a single Canadian society.

It may be that whatever sense of society exists at the federal level in Canada is based on a mutual acknowledgement of the authority of the state to be the final arbiter of grievances and to maximize mutual well-being.[12] It has been argued that Canada is a nationless state and can more legitimately be considered a *state nation* than a nation-state because it is the state that tries to create both a sense of society and a sense of nationhood.[13] In this sense we are an *invented community* because Canadians constantly work at "willing" themselves into existence as a community and developing a "Canadian" sense of society. This process will be the focus of Chapter Seven.

REGION AS A UNIT OF SOCIETY

The question of whether people who live within the boundaries of Canada form a society might first be examined by using region as the unit of analysis. In contrast to the state, which is a larger unit of analysis, region is a smaller unit which potentially is more reflective of local peoples, their history, and their culture. While it may be difficult to identify a society at the level of the nation-state, perhaps it is easier to observe society in the context of region. At the very least, contrasting regions as a smaller unit of analysis should enable us to determine the extent to which the society of the nation-state is fragmented.

Regionalism is a recurrent theme in Canadian society. Geographers are most likely to draw our attention to regions as places affected by physiographic, climatic, or topographical factors which are related to where and how people live.[14] Geographers may also characterize a regional society as structured around growth poles or central places which provide employment and opportunity.[15] Geographically, a region is a land area of physical territory which is in some way distinctive in contrast to other regions. Mountains, prairies, woodlands, coastal regions, and their respective supporting economies can be distinguished and boundaries established. But even geographers are aware that space is not neutral and that humans transform space into *lived space* to which they attribute specific meanings.[16]

With some exceptions, sociologists have traditionally left the regional variable to geographers.[17] Perhaps the most troublesome aspect of region is that it is difficult to locate the social boundaries of a region. Regions are seldom homogeneous social groupings, and differences within a region may be more significant than superficial similarities. To discover that the average income of the population of a region is low in comparison to other regions may be less important than to know that there are significant disparities in income within the same region. In sum, for sociological purposes, a region may be too imprecise to serve as a unit of analysis.

Yet there remains a lingering conviction that region is an important variable in understanding society. While it may be difficult to determine what aspects all residents of a region may have in common, it is clear that a combination of cultural and physical characteristics do make one area distinctive, in some measure, from another area. The sociologist looks for whatever characteristics of the population (e.g., ethnicity, occupation, income) seem to be held in common and contrasts them with other regions where population characteristics may be different. The sociologist might also look for attitudes and opinions identified with one area and then compare them with other regions. This approach suggests that a region can be considered to have a psycho-social dimension which essentially transforms the concept of region from geographic space into social space.[18] Sociologists look for *objective indicators* of region in the characteristics of the population and for *subjective indicators* in the attitude, identities, and feelings held by residents of a region.[19] In most instances, however, the identification of a region as a social construct is still largely dependent on geographic boundaries.

Differences in population characteristics or attitudes do not necessarily create regionalism.[20] It is only when these differences are specifically recognized as a differentiating feature from other regions that they can produce, reinforce, or sustain regionalism. In other words, *regionalism* has a *political dimension* that involves a consciousness of kind, a collective identity, and a defence of territorial interests.[21] It involves the politicization of regional concerns and the articulation of regional commitments. What has made region a critical factor in understanding Canadian society is not just that regional differences exist, but that the evaluation of these differences has led to the articulation of regional interests which has in turn spawned heightened regionalism.[22] An understanding of how regionalism is created will be examined in greater detail in Chapter Four.

Before the dynamic relationship between regions can be discussed, it is important to determine the extent to which there are population differences between the regions of Canada. The nature of the commitment to region (i.e., regionalism) can be understood more clearly if we develop an understanding of the population differences between regions. This exercise will also provide a comprehensive picture of the components of Canadian society.

We are still left with the problem of determining what constitutes a region. The six traditional regional units in Canada are the Atlantic provinces, Quebec, Ontario, the Prairie provinces, British Columbia, and the Territories. Other than the Atlantic and Prairie regions, and the Territories, the other regions are established provinces—which may or may not be an adequate means of determining regionalism. There are also problems with assuming that, for example, Northern and Southern Ontario are essentially the same and constitute a region. What does lend some credence to the "province as region" argument is that provinces possess the political apparatus to create a collective regional identity based on socio-political interaction within that unit. So while we cannot be totally satisfied with equating region with province, it is possible to use provincial units as the context in which regional differences in Canada can be identified. Provinces can be clustered, as long as we acknowledge that regional boundaries are more difficult to determine than simple provincial boundaries.[23]

It is possible, then, to begin with the assumption that the experiences, interests, and attitudes of Canadians will vary with the territory in which they reside. While regional differences in population and environmental factors may be identifiable, the ultimate question is whether these factors produce regional societies. Is there a Maritime or a Prairie society with unique and distinctive characteristics? If these regional societies do exist, are they obfuscated by the presence of sub-regional societies at a local or community level?

Clearly there is a hierarchy of human relationships from the simple, small-scale community to the complex large-scale society. We can expect the smallest most intimate relationship to be more important than the more distant and anonymous relationship. Society, region, sub-region, and community then form a continuum from lowest commitment to highest commitment. For that reason, we should not expect region to be a primary unit of group identity. That kind of collective consciousness is more likely to occur when region is politically transformed into regionalism.[24] For our purposes, it is only important to determine whether regional differences might serve as the basis for regional societies.

The branch of sociology that deals with the statistical study of human population is known as *demography.*[25] In a country of enormous size, it is important to look for demographic differences that might exist between regions within that political entity. Regions then are important not because of some assumed homogeneity within the region but because of differences between regions. These regional demographic differences fall under four main headings: population distribution, population composition, population change, and internal population shifts.

Population Distribution

Perhaps the most basic fact about the Canadian population is that it is unevenly dispersed over its constituent territory. While the size of the territory is vast (9 922 330 square kilometres), no permanent settlement is found in approximately 89% of that land space due to factors of climate and terrain.[26] Consequently, much of the country is uninhabited.

Demography: Fast Facts to Ponder

- Canada's population doubled in 45 years from just over 14 million in 1951.

- Big Cities Got Bigger. From 1991–1996, Toronto absorbed almost a quarter of Canada's total population increase.

- The proportion of the population with a Mother Tongue other than French or English increased from 13% of the population in 1971 to 17% in 1996. Chinese is the most common language spoken at home after French and English.

- There are more allophones (speakers of a language other than French or English) in Quebec than anglophones.

- Forty percent of francophones are French/English bilingual whereas only nine percent of anglophones are French/English bilingual.

Source: Statistics Canada

The term that is used to describe the settled areas is *ecumene*, literally meaning "inhabited space." Traditionally, population settlement took place on land supportive of agricultural pursuits. These same locations, however, were also preferred by urban dwellers. Thus the eight percent of the land surface available for farming also contains the largest urban populations. Figure 1.1 (page 4) illustrates the size of the ecumene in Canada. In general, the ecumene consists of land adjacent to the American border, with a higher northern reach in the Western provinces than elsewhere (80% of all farmland is located in the three Prairie provinces).[27] The largest cities are also located in these southern extremities of the country, with the three largest cities less than one hour's travelling time from the US border. In fact, 72% of Canada's total population lives within 150 kilometres of the Canada–US border. Thus it is clear why north–south interaction across the border has frequently been less cumbersome than east–west relationships in Canada.

In spite of the fact that the ecumene spreads across the southern boundary of Canada, it is virtually divided in two by the Canadian Shield in Ontario which separates east from west. Furthermore, some segments of the ecumene are more densely populated than others. Figure 1.2 reveals that 62% of the Canadian population of 30 301 200 (1998) live in the provinces of Ontario and Quebec, 16.8% of the population are located in the three Prairie provinces (with Alberta accounting for more than one-half), 7.9% can be found in the Atlantic provinces, and a steadily expanding 13.2% reside in British Columbia.

From a historical perspective (Figure 1.3), it is significant that the Atlantic provinces have experienced a continuous erosion of their proportion of the population from 16.6% in 1901

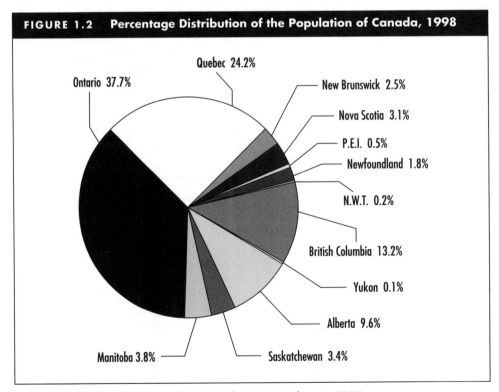

FIGURE 1.2   **Percentage Distribution of the Population of Canada, 1998**

Quebec 24.2%

Ontario 37.7%

New Brunswick 2.5%

Nova Scotia 3.1%

P.E.I. 0.5%

Newfoundland 1.8%

N.W.T. 0.2%

British Columbia 13.2%

Yukon 0.1%

Alberta 9.6%

Saskatchewan 3.4%

Manitoba 3.8%

Source: Adapted from "1991 Census of Canada, A National Overview," Catalogue No. 93-301.

to 7.9% in 1998. British Columbia, on the other hand, has experienced incremental growth from 3.3% in 1901 to 13.2% in 1998. Quebec has also experienced an erosion of its earlier population strength due to a declining birth rate, an exodus of anglophones, and the fact that this province has been a less popular destination for international immigration than Ontario. While there was large-scale settlement of the Prairie provinces during the first few decades of this century, many of these immigrants later left their farms as a response to the mechanization of agriculture and greater urbanization. Therefore, the 22.3% proportionate share of the population in 1921 was eroded in subsequent years and has been restrained from further erosion in recent years, primarily because of growth in Alberta. General tendencies throughout Canada towards industrialization and urbanization have particularly benefited Ontario where more than one in every three Canadians reside. In contrast to Quebec, where the percentage distribution of the population has been continuously eroding since 1941, Ontario's proportion of the population has been increasing with consequences which will be outlined later.

Figure 1.4 illustrates how one-sided the redistribution of the population actually is. Between 1951 and 1998, while all provinces displayed an increase in total population, some grew much more than others. The result is that all provinces reduced their proportion of the Canadian population with the exception of Ontario, British Columbia, and Alberta, which were the only provinces to increase their proportionate share.

Differences in the distribution of the population can also be illustrated another way. Table 1.1 demonstrates that size of land surface varies considerably from the smallest (Prince Edward Island) to the largest (Northwest Territories). The land area of the Atlantic provinces

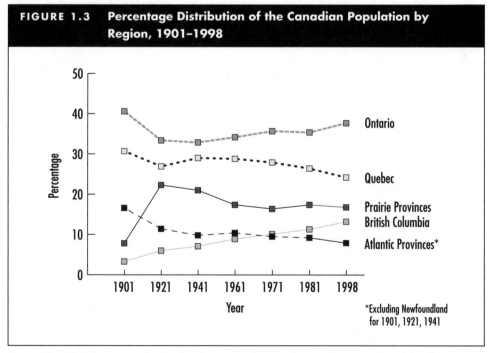

FIGURE 1.3 **Percentage Distribution of the Canadian Population by Region, 1901–1998**

Source: Adapted from Statistics Canada, *Canada's Changing Population Distribution*, 1981 Census of Canada, Catalogue 99–931, Table 2 and 91–213, Table 1.1.

REAL PEOPLE 1

Demographic Shifts: Exporting People from Saskatchewan

"Every Game Is a Home Game"

He is a big burly guy. He is a football player in the Canadian Football League. He plays for the Saskatchewan Rough-riders. People in Saskatchewan bleed green and white. They love those green Riders. The Roughriders play in Regina which is the smallest city in the CFL.

"The thing I like the most about play-ing for Saskatchewan is that the people in this province love football. Even if peo-ple don't get out to the game, you can drive down the street of any small town on game day and everybody is listening to the game or watching it on TV. But what is even better, most teams talk about how when they play at home, they like that best because they have the home fans cheer-ing for them. But not with Saskatchewan. Even when we go on the road, we have fans everywhere and they are always cheering for us. So many Saskatchewan people have moved elsewhere and left the province that it seems like every game is a home game. When we play in Calgary, it sometimes seems that there are more people cheering for us than the Stampeders. And when we played the Grey Cup in Toronto, it seemed like all the former Saskatchewan people in all of Ontario were there cheering. Same thing in Edmonton and Vancouver. That's Rider Pride for you!"

Questions to Consider:

What regions are losing population and which regions are gaining population? Why is this happening? Is this good or bad for the regions involved and what are the implications for Canadian society?

---

is particularly small in comparison to the other provinces whose individual constituent area is larger than many countries in the world. Prince Edward Island is the only province com-pletely occupied and therefore has the highest density. The large segments of unoccupied land in most other provinces, which have significant proportions of their land surface in the north (but most of their population in the south), means that population densities are unusually low.

The differences between the urban and rural distribution of the population is also quite revealing. Rural populations can be farm (primarily engaged in agriculture), or non-farm (rural but not dependent on agriculture as source of income). Figure 1.5 indicates that, while 22% of the population can be considered rural, only 2.8% is engaged in agriculture. The highest proportion of the population engaged in agriculture is found in the Prairie provinces (followed by Prince Edward Island), and, even there, mechanization has meant that fewer people are needed to farm the land. The proportionately largest group of rural non-farm residents is found in the Atlantic provinces where many people live in small fishing villages. The pref-erence for rural non-farm residence is also a phenomenon of urban growth and the desire for living space. Five provinces (Quebec, Ontario, Manitoba, Alberta, British Columbia) together contain almost 89% of the Canadian people and are also the only provinces with urban cen-tres over half a million. Thus the "Big City" category of cities over 100 000 considerably underestimates the proportion of the population in even bigger cities in contrast to other provinces where populations are found in much smaller centres.

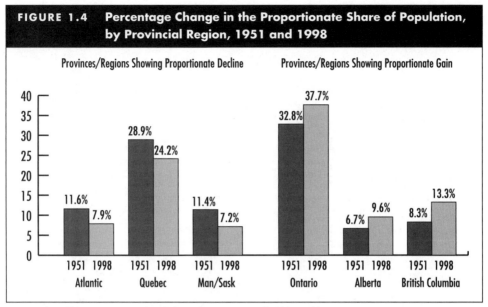

FIGURE 1.4   Percentage Change in the Proportionate Share of Population, by Provincial Region, 1951 and 1998

Source: Adapted from Statistics Canada, Catalogue 96–304E, p. 6 and 91–213, Table 1.1.

In general, the Atlantic provinces and Saskatchewan are more rural and small town, while the other provinces are more urban, in spite of a large rural component in some Western provinces. The highest level of urbanization, however, can be found in central

TABLE 1.1   Population Distribution and Land Area, by Province, 1998

	Population	Land Area (sq. km in thousands)	Density (in thousands)
Newfoundland	544 400	372	1.5
Prince Edward Island	136 400	6	22.7
Nova Scotia	934 600	53	17.6
New Brunswick	753 000	72	10.5
Quebec	7 333 300	1 358	5.4
Ontario	11 411 500	917	12.0
Manitoba	1 138 900	548	2.1
Saskatchewan	1 024 400	570	1.8
Alberta	2 914 900	638	4.6
British Columbia	4 009 900	893	4.5
Yukon	31 700	532	0.1
Northwest Territories	67 500	3 246	0.2
Canada	30 300 400	9 203	3.3

Source: Statistics Canada, *Annual Demographic Statistics,* 1998 Catalogue 91–213, Table 1.1, and Catalogue 93–301 and 93–304, Table 1.

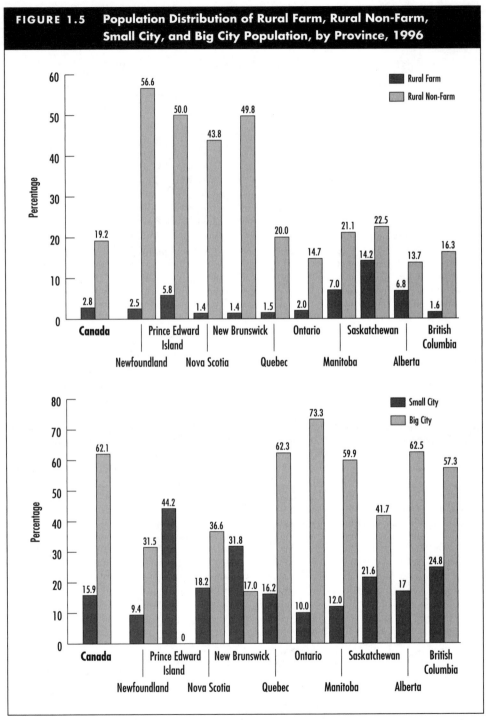

FIGURE 1.5 Population Distribution of Rural Farm, Rural Non-Farm, Small City, and Big City Population, by Province, 1996

Note: Small City refers to urban areas less than 100 000 population but more than 1000. Big City refers to urban areas of more than 100 000 population.

Source: Adapted from Statistics Canada, *The Daily*, April 26, 1999.

Canada in what is known as the Golden Triangle. The industrial heartland of Canada, the area north of the American border and south of a line extending from Quebec City to Sault Ste. Marie, contains about 60% of the Canadian population.

The demographic distribution of the population indicates an uneven dispersion of people throughout the country. We may also make the following demographic conclusions:

1. Most of the population lives adjacent to the American border and in growing cities on land suitable for agriculture.

2. History, climate, and industry have favoured the population growth and demographic dominance of Ontario and Quebec particularly as represented by their southern high density settlements.

3. The smallest provinces have the highest population densities but also more rural non-farm populations.

4. Very few Canadians are agriculturalists and most are big-city residents. The larger the provincial population, the greater the likelihood that it will be located in big cities. Conversely, the smaller the provincial population, the more likely that it will be rural but not agricultural.

5. Ontario continues to become proportionately larger and is less rivalled in population size by Quebec than it once was. British Columbia has become the new growth province followed by Alberta as a secondary population magnet in the West.

Population Composition

The uneven distribution of the population in Canada contributes to regional differences which are further compounded by other factors. Three such population characteristics are ethnicity, language, and religion.

One of the most typical characterizations of Canadian society is that it is an ethnic mosaic. What is less frequently noted is that this mosaic varies with territoriality; that is, the diversity of ethnic groups is rather unevenly dispersed throughout the nation. One of the fundamental reasons that regional cultures exist is that the ethnic composition of the population varies considerably from locale to locale in Canada.

Table 1.2 displays something of the ethnic heterogeneity found in Canadian society. Up to and including the 1981 census, it was only possible to identify a single ethnic origin. Since then, the census asked people what their ethnic origin was and did not require a single response. People could claim more than one origin ("Mother is French and Father is German"), increasing the accuracy of the responses but also making it more difficult to make a simple statement about the ethnic origins of the Canadian population. Table 1.2 presents a location index which measures the extent to which a particular ethnic origin is represented within each province, and allows for some comparison between provinces.

The use of the term "Canadian" in the 1996 Census adds a whole new dimension to understanding ethnic origin (see A Note on "Ethnic Origin" on page 19) given the significant number of people identifying their ethnic origin in that way. People from the United Kingdom (combining England, Scotland, and Ireland), and people with French ethnic origin are the two largest groups in Canada. While German is the largest other European origin, there is a mixture of other European origins as well. Since the Table combines people with single and multiple origins, it is important to note that the earlier the period of immigration, the more likely people were to report multiple ethnic origins. For example, a high proportion of persons from northern,

TABLE 1.2   Location Index by Ethnic Origin for Each Province/Territory 1996

	Canadian	English	French	Scottish	Irish	German	Italian	Aboriginal	Ukrainian	Chinese	Dutch	Polish	South Asian	Jewish	Norwegian
Canada	30.9	23.9	19.6	14.9	13.2	9.7	4.2	3.9	3.6	3.2	3.2	2.8	2.5	1.2	1.2
Newfoundland	30.7	59.8	6.8	7.0	22.2	1.4	.3	4.5	—	.3	.3	—	.2	—	.3
Prince Edward Island	29.9	38.5	23.5	42.9	29.7	4.3	.4	1.8	—	—	3.0	.4	—	—	—
Nova Scotia	36.1	37.5	19.1	32.3	20.4	11.2	1.2	3.0	.6	—	4.6	.9	—	—	—
New Brunswick	41.0	30.5	32.8	19.2	19.6	4.2	.6	2.3	.3	—	2.0	—	—	—	—
Quebec	47.2	4.1	40.7	2.7	4.5	1.5	3.5	2.0	—	.8	—	—	.7	1.3	—
Ontario	25.4	30.0	12.5	17.7	16.2	9.3	7.0	2.3	2.6	4.0	4.1	3.5	4.0	1.8	—
Manitoba	19.4	24.7	13.4	18.0	12.9	18.5	1.6	12.6	14.5	—	4.7	7.0	—	—	—
Saskatchewan	21.7	26.8	11.7	18.2	14.7	30.0	—	12.0	12.8	—	3.6	5.2	—	—	6.2
Alberta	25.8	28.3	11.5	19.3	15.4	19.9	2.2	5.8	9.7	3.7	5.1	4.7	2.1	—	4.0
British Columbia	22.2	32.8	9.2	20.4	14.5	13.5	3.2	5.0	4.6	8.5	4.8	2.8	4.5	—	2.9
Yukon	29.4	29.2	14.0	22.2	17.6	14.7	.1	21.0	4.8	—	4.0	.1	—	—	3.7
Northwest Territories	13.7	14.0	8.4	11.1	8.8	6.2	.8	62.1	2.6	—	1.6	1.4	—	—	1.2

Note: A location index measures the extent to which a particular ethnic origin is represented within an entity. It includes people who claim that origin as their only ethnic origin as well as those who claim that origin along with other ethnic origins. Therefore it counts some people twice or more and weights those of mixed origin the same as those of single origin. The purpose of the location index is to provide some sense of comparison between provinces. Read the columns downwards and compare the index for each province with the index for Canada. A number higher than the index for Canada suggests a greater representation of that ethnic origin in that province whereas a number lower than the index suggests a lower representation of that ethnic group. For example, Ukrainians are overrepresented in Manitoba and Saskatchewan but underrepresented in Nova Scotia and Quebec.

Source: Calculated by dividing total responses (single and multiple) for each ethnic group in each province by the total number of responses in each province. Adapted from Statistics Canada, *The Daily,* February 17, 1998.

A Note On "Ethnic Origin"

The census defines ethnic origin as the ethnic or cultural group(s) to which an individual's ancestors belonged. Ethnic origin does not refer to place of birth or citizenship; it is a self-reported declaration of ethnic heritage.

Prior to 1986, it was assumed that respondents would select one ethnic origin. But it became increasingly clear that many people had more than one ethnic background, so beginning in 1986, more than one response was acceptable. For the 1996 Census, the format of the ethnic origin question was modified significantly from 1991. In both censuses, respondents were asked to identify the ethnic or cultural group(s) to which their ancestors belonged. In 1991, fifteen of the most frequent origins were listed on the questionnaire, and respondents were asked to check as many as were applicable. Two blank spaces were also provided for other responses. In 1996, only blank spaces were provided but 24 examples of ethnic origins were provided for illustration. Perhaps most importantly, "Canadian" was included among the examples because it was the fifth most frequently reported origin in 1991.

The inclusion of the term "Canadian" in 1996 produced very different results and makes it difficult to compare with data from earlier censuses. Nineteen percent of the total population reported their ethnic origin as "Canadian" and an additional 12% reported both Canadian and other origins. In comparison, when "Canadian" was not listed as an example in 1991, only 3% identified their ethnic origin in that way.

Source: 1991 Census of Canada, Catalogue 93-315 and 96-304E, and Statistics Canada, *The Daily*, February 17, 1998.

western, and eastern Europe had reported multiple origins. On the other hand, persons of more recent immigration such as Koreans or Chinese had low multiple-origin reporting rates.

The Atlantic provinces have a considerable overrepresentation of persons of English, Scottish and Irish origin while Quebec and New Brunswick demonstrate a strong representation of persons of French descent. Other Europeans are weakly represented in Atlantic Canada but are much more strongly represented in western Canada (especially German, Dutch, and Polish, Norwegian and Ukrainian). South Asians and Chinese are strongly represented in Ontario and British Columbia but are weakly represented in many other provinces. Aboriginals are particularly strongly represented in Manitoba, Saskatchewan, and the Territories. Generally speaking, eastern Canada is more British whereas western Canada is more ethnically diverse—with the exception of Quebec which is strongly French. The French component of the population is weakest in the West and North, and weakest of all in Newfoundland. The Atlantic provinces show much less ethnic diversity than western provinces, which received heavy German and eastern European immigration to rural areas. Whereas Quebec was formerly essentially French and Ontario was in contrast predominantly British, Ontario has now become much more multi-ethnic, particularly in its cities. Other significant minorities, though smaller in size than those listed in Table 1.2, include Greek, Portuguese, Spanish, and Yugoslav, and are primarily found in the large metropolitan cities of Ontario, British Columbia, and Alberta. Toronto, for example, has the largest Polish, Greek, Portuguese, Jewish, and Filipino communities in Canada.

These regional variations can largely be explained through differences in settlement patterns. The Atlantic region was settled first by British and French colonists who also created what became known as Upper and Lower Canada through settlement along the St. Lawrence and Great Lakes region. By the late nineteenth century, significant settlements had also been established in the Red River area of Manitoba and on the West Coast in Victoria and Vancouver. Massive immigration from other European countries in the early twentieth century was required to populate the western plains. It was this, and subsequent immigration, which altered the dominantly bi-ethnic composition of the Canadian population and which has resulted in greater ethnic diversity. Even more significantly, different locations in Canada possess considerably different mixes of these ethnic backgrounds in their population.

If ethnicity is an important indicator of differences between people, then, clearly, the regions of Canada are very different from each other. Multiculturalism has a totally different meaning in the West than in Quebec or the Atlantic provinces. Eastern Europeans, for example, make up almost one-fifth of the population of Manitoba whereas they are virtually absent in New Brunswick. On the other hand, New Brunswick has a strong French minority (about one-third of the population) whereas British Columbia has a small proportion of this ethnic group. Being French in Quebec has a totally different meaning from being of French descent in other provinces—particularly those farther away from Quebec. The large Aboriginal population in the Northwest Territories makes that region considerably different as well, and the large Asian population found primarily in the largest metropolitan cities distinguishes regions with large metropolitan populations from regions with only small urban populations. The "old" immigration into the agricultural west at the beginning of this century is certainly different from the "new" immigration into the largest urban centres. Not only is there a rural/urban difference, but the European origins have been replaced with third world origins. It is these ethnic differences which lead to significantly different regional cultures, and which make a sense of society at the national level difficult to obtain.

In some ways, using ethnic origin as an indicator of the importance of ethnicity may exaggerate the role of ethnicity because immigrants usually eventually adapt to the dominant culture as the high response to the designation "Canadian" indicates. The data in Table 1.2 does not tell us whether the respondent was a first, third, or fifth generation immigrant, and later generations may cling to their ethnic origin only with nostalgia. For this reason, ethnic descent may not be nearly as important as current ethnic identity.

One indicator of the salience of ethnicity might be the language people choose to use (Figure 1.6). If the focus is on the language first learned in childhood (which is known as mother tongue), it becomes clear that while English is the mother tongue of the majority (59.8%) of Canadians, only 8.8% of Quebecers claim English as mother tongue. The other significant departures from the 80–90% norm of English mother tongue in other provinces are New Brunswick, where the English/French mother tongue ratio is 2:1, and the Northwest Territories where Native languages were the first spoken by 41% of the population. The difference between the Yukon and the Northwest Territories is also significant at the language level as English is the mother tongue for 86.8% of the former but only for 56.7% of the latter. The highest percentages of English mother tongue are found in the Atlantic provinces where there was little post-war immigration, with the exception of New Brunswick which possesses a significant francophone population. The multi-ethnic character of the West is demonstrated by the significance of languages other than French or English in that region. The same is true of Ontario, which has been the preferred destination for more recent international immigrants.

FIGURE 1.6 **Percentage Composition of Language First Learned in Childhood (Mother Tongue) and Language Most Often Spoken at Home (Home Language), For English, French, and Other Languages, by Province, 1996**

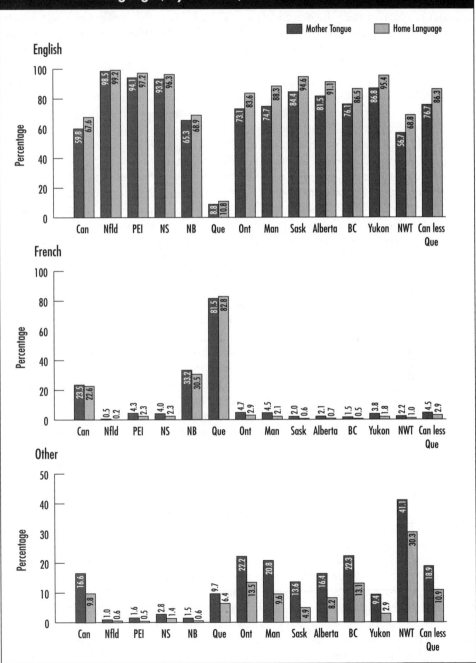

Source: Adapted from Statistics Canada, *The Daily,* December 2, 1997.

But it is not enough to just know the language learned in childhood. It is also important to know whether that language is still spoken at home. In order to see to what extent language shifts have occurred from childhood to current usage, it is useful to compare mother tongue with home language. In all provinces, the percentage using English as a home language is greater than the percentage claiming English as mother tongue—even for Quebec. In all provinces except Quebec, the percentage using French as a home language is less than the percentage claiming French as a mother tongue. Also in all provinces, the percentage speaking languages at home other than English or French is less than those claiming another language as mother tongue. The lesson is clear. English has gained importance as the language of everyday usage largely as the result of the loss of usage of "Other" languages. While 16.6% claim a mother tongue other than English or French, only 9.8% still use that language at home. Persons who claim French as their mother tongue also experienced erosion in home language usage as well, though at the national level the drop is much smaller, from 23.5% to 22.6%. The one notable exception is the province of Quebec where the proportion of the population whose mother tongue is French and who use French as their home language is almost identical. In fact, slightly more use French as a home language than possess French as a mother tongue, indicating that francophone policies there are working. Areas where English is not the overwhelmingly dominant home language in usage, then, are Quebec, New Brunswick, and the Northwest Territories. But it should not be forgotten that languages other than the two official languages are used in around 20% of the homes of Ontario, British Columbia, and Manitoba, with somewhat lower figures in the other western provinces. Very few persons use one of the non-official languages at home in Atlantic Canada. To the extent to which a language spoken at home indicates ethnic identity, it is clear that there are significant differences between various regions of Canada.

Official government policy is that Canada is a bilingual country. We will have the opportunity to discuss the meaning of this policy in Chapter Five, but Figure 1.7 indicates that only about one in six Canadians considers themselves French/English bilingual. This number, however, has grown over the last twenty-five years from 13.5% in 1971 to 17% in 1996. In fact, all provinces have seen some growth in their bilingual population over that time. The highest rate of bilingualism is found in Quebec and New Brunswick where around one third of the population considers themselves French/English bilingual. The lowest rate of bilingualism is found in Newfoundland and Saskatchewan but in general, most of the other provinces have around 10% (or less) of their population who are bilingual. English-speaking regions are most likely to speak English only, with only a small minority of persons who are able to use both official languages. In contrast, areas where French is spoken (Quebec and New Brunswick) are much more likely to contain people who speak English as well (i.e., are French/English bilingual). In Quebec, for example, although 83% of the population use French as their home language, still less than 40% of the population speak both English and French. Thus, the likelihood of being able to converse in both official languages is much greater in francophone regions than in anglophone dominated areas. The fact that French remains the dominant language in Quebec will, however, continue to distinguish that region from the rest of Canadian society.

Ottawa's increasing bilingual nature contributes to the level of bilingualism in Ontario, and historic French communities in Nova Scotia and Manitoba contribute to higher levels of bilingualism in those provinces, although it is still under 10%. But the generally low level of French/English bilingualism from Ontario west is countered by a much higher rate of bilingualism through the use of a non-official language. So, for example, only 9.4% of the population of Manitoba are French-English bilingual but 20.8% are able to use a non-official language. In sum, there is considerable variation from region to region in what languages are spoken and in the capability to speak both rather than one or the other of Canada's official languages.

Another important aspect of regional differentiation is religious affiliation (Figure 1.8). Just as there is a relationship between ethnicity and language, there is also a relationship between ethnicity and religion. Census data on religion obviously are not indicative of commitment or participation, but they do give us some measure of religious preference. In this data we find further evidence of regional differences. For example, while 86.1% of the Quebec population is Roman Catholic, only 18.6% of the population of British Columbia is Catholic. Similarly, while Saskatchewan claims 22.8% of its population as United Church members, Quebec has less than 1% affiliated with that church. The largest single religious body in Canada is the Catholic church (45.7%) and in locations where there are many people of French descent (e.g., New Brunswick), the percentage of Catholics is considerably higher. Generally, the farther west from Quebec that you go in Canada, the lower the percentage of Catholics in the population. However, the sizeable number of Catholics in other parts of Canada is usually also tied to an ethnic heritage (e.g., German Catholics in Saskatchewan). The western part of Canada has a higher proportion of persons embracing a non-Christian religion or having no religion at all. Evidence of European immigration is reflected in the significant Lutheran presence in the West and the early immigration from the United Kingdom is revealed by the comparative strength of Baptists, Presbyterians, and Anglicans in the Atlantic provinces.

Variance in ethnicity, language, and religion among Canada's population gives us further evidence of the regional differences that are present in the composition of the society. Again, differences within regions may be as important as differences between regions and we should not conclude that regions represent a homogeneous set. It is clear, however, that

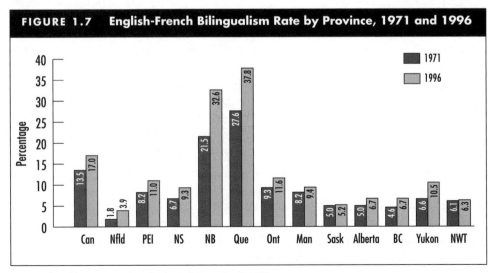

FIGURE 1.7   English-French Bilingualism Rate by Province, 1971 and 1996

Source: Adapted from Statistics Canada, *The Daily*, December 2, 1997.

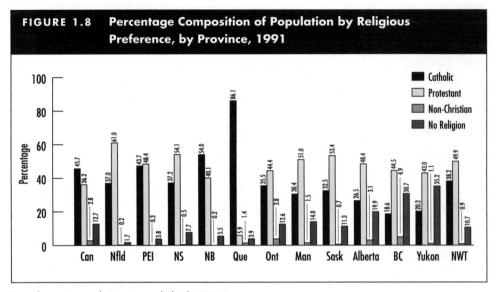

FIGURE 1.8   Percentage Composition of Population by Religious Preference, by Province, 1991

Note: The question on religion was not asked in the 1996 Census.

Source: 1991 Census of Canada Catalogue 96–304E.

different demographic patterns within the society contribute to regional patterns that distinguish parts of the society from each other. The characteristics of the population of Newfoundland, Quebec, and British Columbia, for example, are truly different on these dimensions, so regional character denotes much more than merely that conveyed by separation through enormous distances. These variations can be summarized in the following way:

1. Ethnicity, language, and religion exhibit a close regional correlation. A British heritage, Protestantism, and the English language are most likely in the Atlantic provinces, Ontario, and the West; a French heritage, Catholicism, and the French language are most likely in Quebec and the adjacent border region of northern New Brunswick. Thus, Quebec and northern New Brunswick are significantly different from the rest of Canada on these dimensions.

2. Earlier settled and more rural areas, such as those in Atlantic Canada, tend to be more ethnically homogeneous than more recently settled rural areas in the West, which are more ethnically and religiously heterogeneous. In general, the area west of Quebec is much more heterogeneous on all three of these dimensions than the area east of Quebec.

3. Native persons are found primarily in the West and the North where many maintain their own languages. They are likely to be affiliated with either the Catholic or Anglican church.

4. Asians, Africans, Italians, those who speak neither English nor French, and those who are non-Christians, are more likely to be found in provinces with large metropolitan areas.

5. Bilingualism is more likely in areas where French is spoken than in areas where English is the primary language. Persons whose mother tongue is other than English increasingly use English as the language of home except in Quebec and to a lesser extent in the Northwest Territories.

Population Change

Population Turnover

Our discussion so far has noted that ethnic diversity is a significant characteristic of the Canadian population. What is less well known is that this influx of people into the society (immigration) has historically combined with an out-migration of people (emigration). It has been estimated that even though eight million people immigrated to Canada between 1851 and 1961, more than six million emigrated or left the country during that same period.[28]

Figure 1.9 illustrates how closely emigration has shadowed immigration through much of Canada's history. A large number of the emigrants were former immigrants who used Canada as a stop-off point for later migration to the United States in what is known as a *stepping stone migration*. These and other Canadians emigrated to the United States to take advantage of employment opportunities, particularly before industrialization became stronger in Canada. Quebecers in particular migrated to the New England states where they found work while still remaining reasonably close to home.[29] However, about the same time that migration to the United States became much more difficult due to the tightening of American immigration laws, the United States became less attractive as a consequence of quality of life issues and a comfortable standard of living in Canada. More recently, government cutbacks in fields such as healthcare and a significant discrepancy between the American and Canadian dollar has sustained the emigration flow for employment in the United States.

It is also noteworthy that the source countries of immigration have changed over time. If we examine Table 1.3, we notice that persons born in the United Kingdom and southern

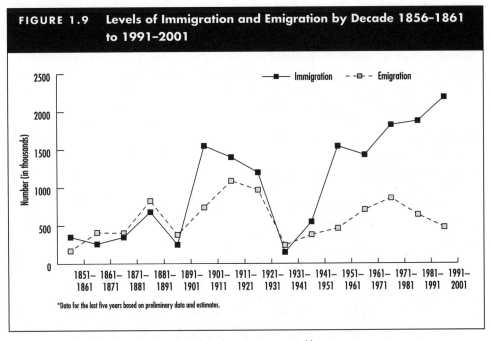

FIGURE 1.9 **Levels of Immigration and Emigration by Decade 1856–1861 to 1991–2001**

*Data for the last five years based on preliminary data and estimates.

Source: Statistics Canada, Demographic Division and Catalogue 91–213, Text Table XV.

Understanding Emigration From Canada

Between 1851 and 1991, 7.9 million people left Canada permanently whereas 12.5 million immigrated to Canada. Therefore the net migration flow has been positive. It was primarily in the time period prior to 1900 that the net migration flow was negative. From 1851–1901, 2.2 million persons left Canada and 1.9 million persons entered Canada. The decade with the largest number of persons emigrating was 1911–1921 when 1.1 million left. Emigration from Canada has largely been tied to lack of employment and economic opportunities particularly in comparison to the United States through to the Second World War. After the Second World War, immigration has been a much stronger counterbalance to emigration—though emigration continues to be a factor in Canadian society.

Persons emigrating from Canada may or may not be Canadian citizens. However, of those living abroad holding Canadian citizenship, 84% live in the United States and only 6% in the United Kingdom. Canadians are the third largest foreign born group in the United States and about one-half of them have become naturalized US citizens. Since the Second World War about 30% of all emigrants from Canada to the United States were not Canadian born. Recent data has not been collected but the 1970 US census revealed that 2.2 million persons in the United States had at least one parent born in Canada meaning that there were many persons in the United States eligible for Canadian citizenship.

Source: Craig McKie, "A History of Emigration from Canada," Adapted from Canadian Social Trends 35 (Winter) 1994: 26–29. Statistics Canada Catalogue 11-008E.

Europe provide the largest categories of foreign-born in Canada. Yet when we compare these two groups by time period of immigration, United Kingdom migrants were strongest in the pre-1961 period, southern European migration was strongest in the 1961–1971 period, but neither group was dominant from 1981 to the present. In general, as we move into the 1970s and 1980s (and 1990s), European countries (old source countries) decline in importance, and Asia and South and Central America become significant sending countries (new source countries). In fact, since 1981, about three quarters of all immigrants entering Canada have come from the new source countries/regions, and primarily Asia. It becomes evident as a result of this review that not only has immigration repeatedly injected new populations into Canada but also that each wave of immigration brought people from different countries and this has contributed to considerable societal diversity and continual change.

Immigration also has its regional components. Ontario has over one-half (54.8%) of all immigrants in Canada, with British Columbia, Quebec, and Alberta far behind (Figure 1.10). Clearly this gives Ontario a multicultural character quite unlike the other provinces, especially considering it has the largest population in the first instance. Forty-two percent of Toronto's population are immigrants and one-quarter of Ontario's population is foreign born (Figure 1.11), which indicates that the processes of absorption and adaptation continue at a high level in that province. But British Columbia is not far behind with 24.5% of its population foreign born. The smallest proportions of immigrant populations within each province are found in the Atlantic provinces, Saskatchewan, and the Territories. The regions with the largest number of foreign-born are those containing the metropolitan cities. Consequently, 91.6% of all immigrants in 1991 were located in four provinces (Ontario, Quebec, British Columbia, Alberta).

In comparison with earlier waves of immigration, the majority of the immigrants who have arrived in Canada since the 1970s are members of a visible minority group.[30] The Employment Equity Act defines persons who are non-Caucasian in race or non-white in colour, and who are not Aboriginal peoples, as *visible minorities*. While the 3.2 million persons in this group make up 11.2% of the Canadian population, Ontario contains over half of all visible minorities in Canada, with 20.7% in British Columbia, 13.6% in Quebec, and 8% in Alberta. However, as a percentage of the provincial population, British Columbia has the highest proportion of visible minorities at 18%. Almost all visible minorities live in big cities with Toronto and Vancouver the most popular destinations. Toronto is home to 42% of all visible minorities in Canada and these groups make up 32% of the population of that city. Eighteen percent of all visible minorities in Canada reside in Vancouver but as a group,

| TABLE 1.3 | Percentage of 1996 Population Born Outside Canada by Source Countries/Regions and Proportion Immigrating in Selected Time Periods |

			Time Period of Immigration to Canada (%)				
Country of Birth	% of all Foreign Born in 1996	Before 1961	1961 – 1970	1971 – 1980	1981 – 1990	1991 – 1996	Examples
OLD Source Countries/Regions							
United States	4.9	4.3	6.4	7.4	4.2	2.8	
United Kingdom	13.2	25.2	21.3	13.3	5.8	2.4	England, Ireland
Northern/ Western Europe	10.3	26.9	11.5	6.0	4.4	3.1	Norway, Germany
Eastern Europe	9.0	16.6	5.2	3.2	10.2	8.5	Poland, Russia
Southern Europe	14.4	21.6	31.0	13.2	5.3	5.0	Italy, Spain
NEW Source Countries/Regions							
Central/South America	5.5	0.6	2.2	6.8	9.7	7.3	Mexico, Brazil
Caribbean & Bermuda	5.6	0.8	5.7	9.6	6.6	5.5	Haiti, Jamaica
Africa	4.6	0.5	3.3	5.8	5.9	7.3	Nigeria, Ghana
Western Asia & Middle East	4.2	0.5	1.9	3.1	7.1	7.9	Turkey, Israel, Jordan
Eastern Asia	11.9	1.9	4.9	10.5	15.8	24.3	China, Japan, Korea
Southeast Asia	8.2	0.2	1.8	11.2	14.9	11.4	Vietnam, Philippines, Singapore
Southern Asia	7.1	0.4	3.7	8.1	9.1	13.5	India, Pakistan
Oceania	1.0	0.4	1.2	1.5	0.9	1.0	Australia, New Zealand

Source: Based on Statistics Canada, 1996 Census Nation Tables.

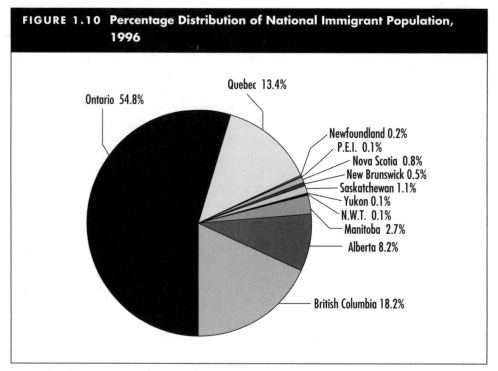

FIGURE 1.10 Percentage Distribution of National Immigrant Population, 1996

Quebec 13.4%

Ontario 54.8%

Newfoundland 0.2%
P.E.I. 0.1%
Nova Scotia 0.8%
New Brunswick 0.5%
Saskatchewan 1.1%
Yukon 0.1%
N.W.T. 0.1%
Manitoba 2.7%
Alberta 8.2%

British Columbia 18.2%

Source: Adapted from 1996 Census of Canada, Table 93F002.

they make up 31% of the population of the city. The figures are 16% for Calgary, 14% for Edmonton, 12% for Ottawa-Hull, and 11% visible minorities for Winnipeg. Whereas Chinese and South Asians are the largest visible minorities in Vancouver, blacks are the largest visible minority group in Montreal. Over two-thirds of visible minorities are foreign born but persons of Japanese descent are more likely to be Canadian born.

It is not surprising that some regions of the society are growing through immigration more than others, but what is more significant is that some regions have a rather stable population with relatively few immigrants while others have a substantial foreign-born component, indicating considerable flux and change. The largest Canadian cities have been particularly attractive to new immigrants from groups designated as visible minorities producing a very different cultural milieu from that in regions that have not experienced this kind of immigration.

Source of Growth

The movement of populations into a country or region (*immigration*) minus the movement of population out of a country or region (*emigration*) produces a rate of *net migration*. It has already been established that Canada has had a lower level of net migration because immigration has been somewhat counterbalanced by emigration. What then has been the primary source of Canada's significant population growth?

Natural increase is determined by subtracting the total number of deaths in an area from the total number of births in that same area. The data reveal that high fertility levels have been

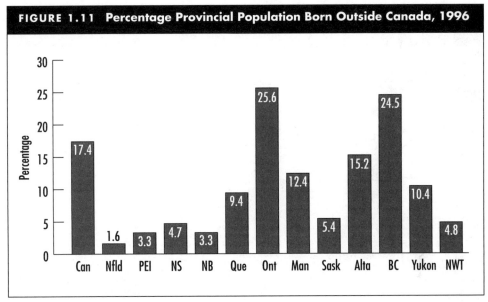

FIGURE 1.11 Percentage Provincial Population Born Outside Canada, 1996

Source: Adapted from 1996 Census of Canada, Table 93F002.

the primary source of growth. Canada has completed the *demographic transition* of high growth rates due to high fertility levels. The theory behind the demographic transition is that growth initially accelerates when improved medical care and improved nutrition cause mortality rates to decline. When this occurs, fertility rates usually also drop and natural increase becomes less important as a source of growth. The transition occurs when the period of high fertility and low mortality produce a high rate of natural increase. The traditionally high fertility rates in Quebec have been reversed in recent years and the fertility rate in Canada has dropped. It is now assumed that Canada has completed the demographic transition as both fertility rates and mortality rates have dropped.[31]

Table 1.4 shows that natural increase has been a much more important source of growth in Canada than net migration. However, even here there are regional variations. Quebec, which had a rather low level of migration, depended heavily on natural increase (see, for example, 1931–1971) to maintain the francophone share of the total Canadian population. The emphasis placed on high birth rates in Quebec has been referred to as the "revenge of the cradle"—a way of once more achieving the original balance between anglophones and francophones that had been disturbed supposedly by immigrants who were assimilating anglophone culture.

Several provinces (particularly Prince Edward Island, New Brunswick, Manitoba, and Saskatchewan) have been perpetual losers of population through net migration but these losses have been offset by gains of population through significant levels of natural increase. Ontario has gained population through both high rates of net migration and natural increase, and so has Alberta except in the 1980s when the oil boom collapsed, producing a reverse migration out of the province. British Columbia is of special interest because for much of its history that province has had both positive net migration flows and strong rates of natural increase. However, in comparison to other provinces, net migration always substantially exceeds natural

TABLE 1.4   Rates of Natural Increase and Net Migration by Province, 1931–1941 to 1991–1996

Provinces	1931–1941		1941–1951		1951–1961		1961–1971		1971–1981		1981–1991		1991–1996	
	Nat. Incr.	Net Migr.	Nat. Incr.	Net Migr.	Nat. Incr.	Net Migr.	Nat. Incr.	Net Migr.	Nat. Incr.	Net Migr.	Nat. Incr.	Net Migr.	Nat. Incr.	Net Migr.
Newfoundland	—	—	—	—	265	–29	222	–90	148	–65	90	–30	26	–28
Prince Edward Island	105	–28	121	–86	157	–96	127	–62	78	15	73	1	28	1
Nova Scotia	109	10	177	–72	183	–46	127	–59	73	–1	64	1	24	–5
New Brunswick	132	–18	184	–64	196	–49	144	–85	93	0	70	–7	25	–8
Quebec	139	8	194	2	222	36	132	4	79	–13	71	–88	33	–65
Ontario	72	27	117	76	180	123	124	86	77	36	78	146	39	–49
Manitoba	94	–53	116	–54	171	—	125	–55	85	–47	83	–37	38	–29
Saskatchewan	126	–155	107	–181	186	–80	137	–136	88	–44	100	–63	36	–30
Alberta	132	–47	139	26	236	109	162	38	113	202	136	–53	56	5
British Columbia	46	118	114	236	172	160	101	190	72	155	78	135	34	190
Yukon and					171		–2	74	—					
Northwest Territories	124	99	211	177	304	96	297	46	219	38	253	–2	126	–1

Note: Rates are per 1000 average population for the decade.

Source: Compiled and computed from Statistics Canada, 1986 Catalogue 91–1001, vol. 1 to 15, no.1, Statistics Canada, Catalogue 96–304E ., p. 98, and 91–209E, Table A.1 and Table 1.B; and 1997 Catalogue 91–209-XPE, Summary Table, p. 14–15 and Table 34, Statistics Canada, Catalogue 91–213, Table 1.1, and Catalogue 93–301 and 93–304, Table 1.

increase as a source of growth. Internal migration will be discussed further in the next section but we should recognize that net migration produced only a total population gain of 2.4 million in the first one hundred years of Canada's existence as a country, whereas growth due to natural increase was a dynamic 14.5 million.[32] Even provinces with negative or low net migration levels have depended on fertility as their primary source of growth.

Aging

The high level of population turnover coupled with high rates of fertility has meant that Canada's population has traditionally been rather youthful (Table 1.5). The drop in the percentage of those under 15 years of age in 1941 is a consequence of the Depression and the higher levels in 1961 are the result of the post-war baby boom. The lower levels in 1981, 1991, and 1996 indicate completion of the demographic transition and lower fertility rates. The implications of lower fertility become clear when we consider that the proportion of the population in each age cohort over 25 is higher in 1981 and 1991 than it was in 1921. But note also that all of the older cohorts are increasing in size, and particularly so in 1996. For example, follow the line across the page for the 65–74 age group and note how it shows steady expansion in size. In general, the proportion of the population over 35 is increasing, but specifically at both ends; the under-25 population is shrinking while the over-65 population is growing—a classic expression of population aging. In 1921, 4.7% of the Canadian population was over 65 years of age but that number had jumped to 12.2% in 1996.

The median age for the Canadian population in 1997 was the highest ever at 35.6 years, an increase of 7.6 years from 1977.[33] This is a substantial jump in only twenty years, and the median age will continue to rise.

A more graphic way of displaying population aging is revealed in Figure 1.12 in what is known as a *population pyramid*. The population pyramid gives a snapshot of the Canadian

TABLE 1.5	Percentage Distribution of the Population by Five Year Age Groups at Selected Intervals 1921–1996					
Age Group	**1921**	**1941**	**1961**	**1981**	**1991**	**1996**
0 – 4	12.0	9.1	12.4	7.3	7.0	6.6
5 – 9	12.0	9.1	11.4	7.3	7.0	6.9
10 – 14	10.4	9.6	10.2	7.9	6.9	6.9
15 – 24	17.3	18.7	14.3	19.1	14.0	13.4
25 – 34	15.3	15.7	13.6	17.3	17.8	15.6
35 – 44	13.2	12.5	13.1	12.2	16.0	16.9
45 – 54	9.1	10.7	10.3	10.3	10.9	12.9
55 – 64	5.9	7.9	7.1	8.9	8.8	8.6
65 – 74	3.3	4.6	4.9	6.1	6.9	7.1
75 – 84	1.2	1.8	2.3	2.8	3.6	3.9
85+	0.2	0.3	0.4	0.8	1.0	1.2

Source: Compiled and computed from 1991 Census of Canada, Catalogue 93-310, Table 1, and 1996 Census, Table 93F0022XDB96002.

population in 1996 by year of birth. Notice the big bulge of persons from 30–50 years of age who represent the post-war baby boom after which there is a drop in fertility and a baby boom echo. Notice also how the Depression and First World War contributed to a decline in births, and that at older ages, widowed women are a larger group than all males.

The primary contribution to demographic aging is a decline in the birth rate.[34] The replacement rate is approximately 2.1 births per woman but the fertility rate has now shrunk to 1.64 from a post-war high of 3.9 in 1959. The decision to have fewer children or to forego parenthood altogether has created some concern because the fertility rate, now at sub-replacement levels, has declined, as some have said, "from baby-boom to baby-bust." Declining fertility is of special concern to some ethnic groups, such as the Québécois or Native peoples. But low fertility is also of concern to the population at large because it suggests that immigration will be increasingly important in stabilizing the population or in producing growth (particularly since it is persons of child-bearing age who are most likely to immigrate).

What then are the consequences of population aging? Earlier we considered the problematic aspects of immigration and emigration for developing a durable society. Societal aging does have positive benefits by giving the country an opportunity to develop a sense of permanence. But if aging occurs too rapidly, an increased economic burden on the society can result and manpower needs for the basic requirements of the economy may not be met. If immigration again becomes the solution, and if that new wave of immigration is from new source countries, Canadian society could undergo more dramatic changes, which have already begun. Assuming that residents of other industrialized countries are content to stay where they are, increasing third world immigration to Canada, and concentrating immigrants in particular regions, could create new bases for intra-societal conflict.

Population change has meant that Canadian society has been rather unstable for much of its existence. The reasons for instability can be summarized as follows:

1. Both immigration and emigration have been at very high levels and this has resulted in significant population turnover. Furthermore, different waves of immigration have had different sources and this has increased ethnic diversity. Regions west of Quebec have, in this century, received considerably more growth through immigration than regions east of Quebec.

2. The significant shift of immigration streams from the old source countries of the United Kingdom and Europe to the new source countries of Asia, South America, and Africa has meant the introduction of new cultural elements into Canadian society. This is particularly so for Canada's largest cities where visible minorities have flocked and presents a very different sense of Canadian society than in those locations that have not experienced this immigration.

3. While a high rate of natural increase through the demographic transition has contributed to solid population growth in all regions, natural increase has been a more important source of growth in Quebec and the Atlantic provinces. A recent decline in the rate of natural increase below replacement levels suggests that any significant population growth in Canada may require a more active immigration policy.

4. The aging of the population has important consequences for Canadian society. On the one hand, it suggests a sense of durability. But on the other hand, it implies shrinking fertility that has great implications for the future. The fact that there are regional differences in the median age also implies an internal redistribution of the population.

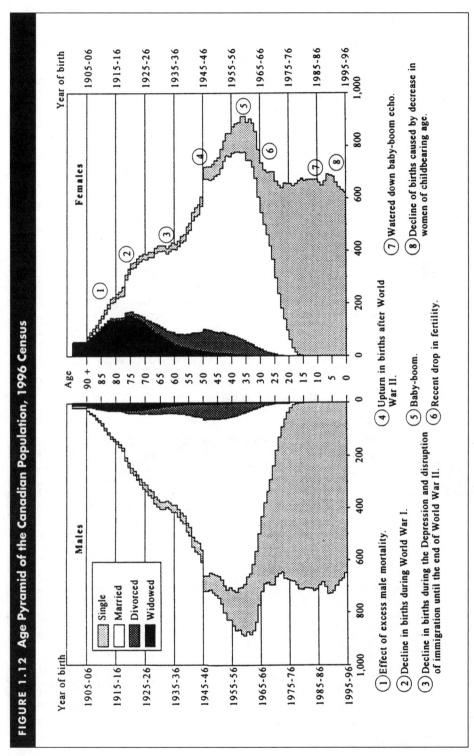

FIGURE 1.12 Age Pyramid of the Canadian Population, 1996 Census

1. Effect of excess male mortality.
2. Decline in births during World War I.
3. Decline in births during the Depression and disruption of immigration until the end of World War II.
4. Upturn in births after World War II.
5. Baby-boom.
6. Recent drop in fertility.
7. Watered down baby-boom echo.
8. Decline of births caused by decrease in women of childbearing age.

Source: Statistics Canada, *Report on the Demographic Situation in Canada 1997: Current Demographic Analysis*, Catalogue 91–209–XPE, Figure 2, p. 18.

Internal Population Shifts

The distribution and composition of the Canadian population has not been static over time for there has been a rearrangement of population within the borders of Canada. Through a voluntary form of migration known as *population drift*, individuals have chosen to relocate in more suitable surroundings. Migration might be prompted by a "push" such as the presence of a surplus population in relation to labour demands, or by the "pull" of better opportunities elsewhere. An analysis of these "push" and "pull" factors helps us to understand why population rearrangement takes place.

Many persons might decide to relocate because their current location is unsuitable as a place to earn a living, carry on a career, or just as a place to live. It also follows that immigrants who do not know the country well may try several locations before settling down permanently. Shifts in employment demands, the policy of employer-instigated transfers, and the long-term trend toward urbanization have also been important factors in internal migration. Figure 1.13 points out that the provinces with the greatest population stability of persons as residents who were born there are Newfoundland and Quebec, followed by the other Atlantic provinces and Saskatchewan. The greatest instability is in Ontario, Alberta, British Columbia, and the Yukon where many persons reside who were born elsewhere. In other words, comparatively few people move to some provinces whereas three provinces in particular contain a large population who have migrated there from elsewhere. For example, almost one-half of the residents of British Columbia were not born in that province. The migrant population of the Yukon is even higher.

Another way of measuring the internal redistribution of the population is contained in the second bar graph of Figure 1.13. It indicates the percentage of population born in a province and still living there. The Yukon and Saskatchewan show a significant tendency to lose

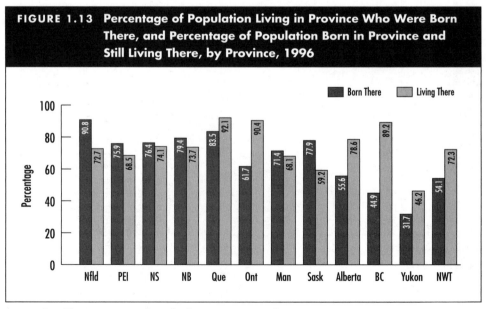

FIGURE 1.13 Percentage of Population Living in Province Who Were Born There, and Percentage of Population Born in Province and Still Living There, by Province, 1996

Source: Adapted from "1996 Census of Canada, The Nation Series," Catalogue No. 93F002.

their native-born population whereas Quebec, Ontario, and British Columbia show the highest tendency to retain their own native-born.

Table 1.4 (page 30) indicates that some provinces lost more people through out-migration than they gained through in-migration. The Atlantic provinces exhibit consistent negative emigration since 1931 with Nova Scotia at times an exception. Manitoba and Saskatchewan have also lost population through emigration. It is important to note that net migration that is negative or small does not mean that there is no in-migration to the region at all. Indeed, the in-migration may be substantial; it is only that there is also a substantial population that is leaving. Net migration to Quebec, for example, has been historically low due to a greater balance between those moving in and those moving out. On the other hand, Ontario, British Columbia, and to some extent Alberta, have been consistent recipients of positive migration flows. In short, internal rearrangement of the population is an ongoing phenomenon within the society as a whole but with some regions growing through this exchange more than others.

In most instances, population shifts have been a response to urbanization. The initial movement was from rural to urban within regions and, in later years, from urban to urban between regions. In 1871, only 19.6% of the population was considered urban whereas by 1996, 78% was urban (defined as having a minimum population of 1000). Furthermore, 61.9% of Canada's population now lives in Census Metropolitan Areas (CMAs) which are cities with populations over 100 000. This indicates the magnitude of the rural–urban shift.

RESEARCH CLIP 1	**Migration and the Transformation of Quebec**

Interprovincial migration flows are changing the nature of Quebec. The on-going confrontation between Quebec and the rest of Canada has had a clear demographic impact upon Quebec's population profile since the mid 1970s. French speakers residing in Quebec tended to remain in Quebec while the English left, and when migration into Quebec occurred, it was more likely to be French speakers rather than the non-French who moved there. Migration then has increasingly led to segregation of the two linguistic groups.

More recently, the outmigration flow from Quebec has reduced considerably but so also has the inmigration rate. Overall, however, the migration flows into Quebec are relatively small and Quebec loses population through migration. People with the highest levels of education are the most likely to leave Quebec and they are also the most likely to enter Quebec. But since the net migration flow is negative, the province has a net loss of the most highly educated. Persons with the lowest skill levels are also among the leavers but people with low skills are not among those entering Quebec. Inmigration is primarily return French-speaking migrants coming home. Approximately two-thirds of all migrants from Quebec go to Ontario.

Migration means that the linguistic duality of Canada is also leading to a territorial duality. In spite of federal policies of bilingualism, migration has made Quebec increasingly more French.

Source: K. Bruce Newbold, "The Ghettoization Of Quebec: Interprovincial Migration And Its Demographic Effects", *Canadian Studies In Population* 23(1)1996:1–21.

The relationship between urbanization and industrialization meant that population would be attracted to those locations where employment opportunities were greatest. Thus developed the *Windsor–Quebec City urban axis*, which contains the majority of the national population, most of the manufacturing employment in the country, and an average income greater than that of the rest of the nation.[35] Within this axis are the largest metropolitan cities of Toronto and Montreal and their satellite regions. Building from their initial (historical) advantage, their natural (resource base) advantage, and their central location in relation to national markets, they serve as natural magnets in population redistribution. Yet the data shows that Toronto, having passed Montreal in size, is increasingly dominating all of Canada.

The last aspect of urban-related migration has been the *counter-urbanization* trend away from the urban core and to the satellite regions of urban areas. The growth of non-metropolitan areas began in the 1970s as people moved in the opposite direction of previous decades from metropolitan to non-metropolitan areas in what has been dubbed *non-metropolitan turnaround.*[36] With the continued growth of major cities in Canada, this type of internal migration can be expected to continue.

Table 1.6 indicates that there is considerable regional variation in the rate of urbanization as it relates to Census Metropolitan Areas. Only 17% of the population of New Brunswick lives in these metropolitan areas whereas 73.3% of Ontarians reside in such cities. Furthermore some provinces (e.g., Nova Scotia), have only one such city while Ontario has ten and Quebec has five. Saskatchewan has only small cities while the neighbouring Prairie province of Manitoba has one big city that accounts for about 60% of the entire provincial population. Furthermore, some provinces have no cities over 500 000 whereas the provinces with cities of this magnitude tend to have the majority of their entire provincial population in these large metropolitan cities. Toronto (4.3 million) and Montreal (3.3 million) are unsurpassed in size in Canada with Vancouver as a distant third with 1.8 million residents. Edmonton and Calgary have experienced stunning growth since the 1960s and they are now pushing towards a million in population. So not only are there enormous variations in urbanization but there is a continuing tendency for the bigger cities to become even bigger.

Internal population movement changes the character of the society, creates regional resentments, fosters further population imbalances, and is symptomatic of underlying inequities within the society. Further, a comparison between regions with large metropolitan concentrations and regions of weak urban development suggests that the nature and substance of life varies considerably within the national society.

Internal population shifts can be summarized as follows:

1. Some regions of Canada have been more likely to attract internal migrants than others. These regions have been also more likely to retain persons born in that province/region. Ontario and British Columbia are the strongest examples of this. Conversely, provinces with comparatively fewer interprovincial migrants are obviously more likely to have a higher proportion of persons born in that province (e.g., Quebec and Newfoundland).

2. Population movements within Canada have been in the direction of large metropolitan areas. Toronto in particular has assumed a dominant position in the national landscape.

3. Regions experiencing positive net migration flows are more likely to have larger and more cities. Regions experiencing negative migration flows have smaller and fewer cities.

4. The dominance of the Windsor–Quebec City urban axis remains unchallenged, but some new growth has occurred in the Alberta urban corridor and in southwestern British Columbia.

TABLE 1.6	Percentage of Provincial Population in Census Metropolitan Areas Over 100 000, 1996			
		CMA Population	% Provincial Population	% Provincial Population over 500 000
Newfoundland	St. John's	174 051	31.5	—
Nova Scotia	Halifax	332 518	36.6	—
New Brunswick	Saint John	125 705	17.0	—
Quebec*	Montreal	3 326 510	46.6	
	Quebec City	671 889		
	Chicoutimi-Jonquiere	160 454		
	Sherbrooke	147 384		
	Trois-Rivieres	139 956		
	Total	4 446 193	62.3	56.0
Ontario	Toronto	4 263 757	39.6	
	Ottawa-Hull*	1 010 498		
	Hamilton	624 360		
	London	398 616		
	Kitchener	382 940		
	St. Catharines-Niagara	372 486		
	Windsor	278 685		
	Oshawa	268 773		
	Sudbury	160 488		
	Thunder Bay	125 562		
	Total	7 886 085	73.3	54.9
Manitoba	Winnipeg	667 209	59.9	59.9
Saskatchewan	Saskatoon	219 056		
	Regina	193 652		
	Total	412 708	41.7	—
Alberta	Edmonton	862 597		
	Calgary	821 628		
	Total	1 684 225	62.5	62.5
British Columbia	Vancouver	1 831 665		
	Victoria	304 287		
	Total	2 135 952	57.3	49.2

* While Hull is in the province of Quebec, Ottawa-Hull is identified as the national capital region with the largest part in Ontario. Statistics Canada only reports combined data.

Source: Adapted from Statistics Canada, Catalogue 93-357-XPB.

ASSESSING THE SOCIETY WITHIN CANADA'S BORDERS

A sense of society does not just happen; it requires time, structure, opportunity for interaction, and a growing collective consciousness. We can now summarize the factors that affect our perceptions of a Canadian society in evolution.

The Demographic Factor

Canadian society has experienced a large measure of population change. Population turnover through emigration and immigration; the fact that immigration came in numerous waves of different ethnic composition; the variation in the degree of assimilation of the residents; and regional differences in population characteristics have contributed to difficulties in generating a feeling of "belonging together" within Canadian society. Furthermore, the policy adaptations to these demographic differences such as bilingualism or multiculturalism, it could be argued, may be politically useful policies but they reassert old loyalties and old traditions at the expense of singular Canadian loyalties and traditions.

The Regional Factor

The national society within the state is further divided by the fact that the continuous demographic changes already noted above have a compelling regional context. The uneven distribution and redistribution of population groups; the early settlement of some areas and the recent settlement of other regions; the differences in ethnic backgrounds and language usage; and the differential in population gains and losses have produced imbalances and numerous grounds for conflict within the societal unit.

Perhaps the most critical demographic feature promoting the regionalization of Canadian society is the uneven distribution of the population whereby Ontario and Quebec contain the majority of the population of the country. As we have noted, along with this fact are other features such as the regional concentration of political, economic, and industrial power. Those regions at a distance from central Canada often feel a sense of powerlessness which often coagulates into some form of regional hostility. The second important demographic factor is the ethnic/linguistic uniqueness of Quebec in relation to the rest of Canada. As a centrally located, heavily populated province, a form of regionalization exists at the core of the country. We have also seen how sheer distance helps to promote regional feelings as regional cultures develop from the experiences of sharing a territory.

One of the ongoing debates is whether regional identities or regional feelings are more important than national feelings. Much is often made of Westerners or Atlantic residents forming a region, and certainly Quebec is often assumed to be a region. Even Ontario as the national heartland has its own sense of regional leadership which it projects to other regions. These discussions often overstate the unity that may exist in these entities for as we will see, there are both Canadian nationalists and Québécois nationalists in Quebec. Similarly, Newfoundland in the Atlantic region and British Columbia in the West are somewhat different from the other provinces in their region. On the other hand, as Canadians become more aware of each other through interaction within the national context, they do become more aware of how their regional political and economic cultures are both similar and different. Newfoundlanders, for example, have long been known for their intense loyalty and regional feeling that even carries over when they migrate to other parts of Canada for employment purposes with the eventual desire to return.[37] The sense of pride and loyalty to region is not unexpected, particularly as they encounter other regions with different cultures and agendas on the national stage. The evidence as to whether regional identities are more important than national identities is mixed and may be catalyzed by issues and political events. Most studies suggest that about three-quarters of the Canadian population think of themselves primarily in national rather than regional terms with Ontario showing the highest tendency to do so with Quebec least likely to do so followed by Atlantic Canada.[38] In other words, regional demographic differences do not necessarily minimize national attachments.

But more recently, a new phenomenon, *glocalism,* has been proposed to account for the weakening of national identities and the power of national states, with the converse effect of strengthening local identities.[39] The clear tension between local, national, and global forces, is a changing rather than static issue, and one which we will explore in more detail in Chapter Six.

The Normative Evaluation Factor

How do we interpret and evaluate the evidence provided in this chapter? In some ways, the analysis of regional differences and the identification of regional identities has been presented as a societal problem. From this perspective, it is possible to conclude that regional differences ought to be eradicated and society-wide homogeneity and equality ought to be the goal. In other words, analyzing the evidence could lead us to evaluate regional diversity and population differences as problematic. But another perspective might be that it is precisely this regional variance that gives Canadian society its unique character. From the first perspective, regional differences are viewed more negatively. From the second perspective, these differences are viewed more positively and are almost cherished. The point is that opinions may vary about how to evaluate these characteristics because of different opinions we have about *what Canadian society should be like*. It is for this reason that the interpretation and the evaluation of the facts presented (i.e., what is normative) is open to such debate. The Differing Perspectives box on the next page gives some indication of how the evidence can be interpreted differently from a theoretical point of view, but ultimately, the approach you take in evaluating the data depends on your perspective.

Another way to look at this issue is to point out that federal policies designed in the best interests of Canada may have differing or even opposing effects on regional units.[40] Several examples illustrate this point. Early federal policy may have encouraged immigration to populate the land and stimulate the economy. But to francophones, particularly in Quebec, this policy altered the bi-ethnic balance of Canada because an immigrant population would eventually embrace English culture and thereby threaten their identity and power as a "founding partner" in Confederation. So in order to protect themselves, Quebec's response in recent years has been to make it more difficult for immigrants to that province to become anglophones. Another example might be to argue that what is in the best interests of the oil producing regions (e.g., higher incomes, employment) may not be in the best interests of the oil consuming regions (e.g., higher costs). Furthermore, the industrial strength of one region may come at the expense of another region that is disadvantaged because federal policy made in the "national interest" has negative effects on their region. It is for this reason that regional differences are not always just benign facts but are charged with emotion. Clearly meeting the needs of such a diverse national society means repeated challenges from regions whose best interests frequently contradict one another.

Bell, noting that regions may be so different that their objectives may be in opposition or competition, has labelled this dimension *conflictual regionalism*.[41] But he has suggested that there is also a *co-operative regionalism*—a basic commitment to the federal state and participation in its structures (e.g., law, parliament). Thus while regional disparities may seem to hinder the viability of the nation-state, regional differences play a significant role in giving Canadian society its unique form and character, and allowances are made for this to accommodate diverse needs. In other words, while regionalism has divisive aspects for those concerned with creating a single sense of society, it is those same aspects which make the society what it is.

In addition, some persons may favour a decentralized federal system with strong regional identities while others may prefer a strong pan-Canadian society of the nation-state where

Differing Perspectives

Structural Functionalism

The structural functionalist perspective visualizes Canadian society as a giant complex organism in which its many structures work together to give the society its unique character and to sustain the whole social system. The movement of people from one region to another, for example, illustrates the self-regulating or self-correcting elements of the society whereby unemployed people seek economic opportunity in another region. Furthermore, the unique spatial distribution of the population with its varying characteristics may create certain difficulties, but over time, institutional adjustments and accommodations occur in order to maintain the viability and equilibrium of the society. In other words, the regional differences discussed in this chapter are not big problems, for the society will make adjustments to preserve itself.

Conflict

The conflict perspective emphasizes the tension inherent in Canadian society, particularly as the result of inequalities. There are vast differences and disparities between regions, and the huge variations in population size mean that regions will vary greatly in political power. Some regions will gain population but at the expense of other regions and therefore regional inequities will grow. Even international migrants to Canada tend to settle in the same few locations thereby changing the character of these locations and creating a major point of difference to areas experiencing little growth. Furthermore, ethnic and language differences make people aware of what divides them rather than what unites them as Canadians. Thus there are so many ways in which the Canadian population is in constant overt or submerged conflict, and these internal differences have persisted rather than waned over time.

Symbolic Interactionism

The symbolic interactionist perspective notes that when people interact through sharing a territory (e.g., nation, province, sub-region), they develop a particular understanding about themselves which is reflected in their unique cultural attributes (e.g., their symbols, language forms) and which sets them apart from other national societies. In a vast country, regional identities based on common experiences may be particularly strong and may produce collective definitions of situations that differ from other regions. Furthermore, immigrants bring their old loyalties and identities with them which compete with their new identities as Canadians. Language differences (particularly between English and French) help to promote linguistic identities in which the Canadian population is divided between two very different cultural worldviews. The differences pointed out in this chapter are not so much irresolvable problems but are realities that just need to be understood.

a Canadian national identity dominates over regional loyalties. Indeed, there is evidence to suggest that commitments to region and country may not be exclusive and that it is possible to maintain both allegiances at the same time.[42] We will return to region in the context of national identity in Chapter Seven but, at this point, we should recognize that the significance of region depends on a subjective assessment or evaluation as to what kind of society Canadian society should be.

CONCLUSION

Regional differences and regional disparities are not unique to Canada and are probably characteristic of all federal states. Yet in Canada, factors such as geographic size, population imbalances, ethnic commitments, and differences in economic development enhance the role that region plays in retarding the emergence of a more unitary national society. In reality, it is unreasonable to expect a national society in which all people are the same and have the same level of commitment to the federal system. We have already seen how this is impossible given a constantly changing population. But it does suggest that a sense of society cannot be taken for granted and must be constantly renegotiated. National unity strategies are constantly being proposed and evaluated.[43]

The point is that people who share a territory and a political system do strive for some sense of societal unity. Amidst population flux and diversity, there is indeed at least a core segment of the population that has made their home in Canada for generations and who view themselves ethnically as "Canadian." Public expressions of regionalism may vary, but a commitment to the federal state continues. It is from this basic commitment that a "Canadian" society struggles to continue as a meaningful reality.

FURTHER EXPLORATION

1. Do you think people in your region identify more with your region or with the nation? What events seem to alter the diversity of opinions on this issue?

2. What do you think is *the* most important reason residents of Canada form a weak sense of society? Analyze why that reason is important and suggest policies which might overcome this weakness.

3. Watch your local newspaper for concrete examples of regionalizing events and perspectives as well as nationally integrating ones. Which kind dominates the news?

4. Ask a hyphenated Canadian (e.g., Ukrainian-Canadian, Japanese-Canadian) which identity is most important to him or her. Has that identity changed over time?

SELECTED READINGS

Beaujot, Roderic. *Population Change in Canada.* Toronto: McClelland and Stewart, 1992.

Canadian Social Trends, quarterly publication of demographic trends.

McVey, Wayne W., and Warren E. Kalbach. *Canadian Population.* Scarborough: Nelson, 1995.

Statistics Canada. *Report on the Demographic Situation in Canada.* Annual publication.

ENDNOTES

1   Don Martindale, "The Sociology of National Character," *The Annals of the American Academy of Political and Social Science* 379 (1967): 30–35.

2 For a discussion of the potential of using the political or national entity as a unit of analysis in under-standing human populations as societies, see T.B. Bottomore, *Sociology: A Guide to Problems and Literature*, rev. ed. (London: Allen and Unwin, 1971), 116.

3 See David V.J. Bell, *The Roots of Disunity*, Revised Edition (Toronto: Oxford, 1992). See also A. Breton and R. Breton, *Why Disunity? An Analysis of Linguistic and Regional Cleavages in Canada* (Montreal: Institute for Research on Public Policy: 1980).

4 See Raymond Breton, Jill Armstrong, Les Kennedy, *The Social Impact of Changes in Population Size and Composition: Reactions to Patterns of Immigration* (Ottawa: Manpower and Immigration, 1974).

5 For example, see Emile Durkheim, *The Rules of Sociological Method* (New York: Free Press, 1950), chap. 4.

6 S.M. Lipset, *Political Man* (Garden City: Doubleday, 1960), 2–4.

7 Dankwart Rustow, "Nation," *International Encyclopedia of the Social Sciences*, vol. 11, 7–14.

8 Daniel Chirot, *Social Change in the Twentieth Century* (New York: Harcourt, Brace Jovanovich, 1977), 11.

9 Lilianne E. Krosenbrink-Gelissen, "First Nations, Canadians And Their Quest For Identity: An Anthropological Perspective On The Compatibility Of Nationhood Concepts", in Andre Lapierre, Patricia Smart, and Pierre Savard (eds.), *Language, Culture and Values in Canada at the Dawn of the 21st Century* (Ottawa: Carleton University Press and International Council For Canadian Studies, 1996), 329–345.

10 E.J. Hobsbaum, *Nations and Nationalism Since 1780* (Cambridge: Cambridge University Press, 1990).

11 Ali Mazrui, "Pluralism and National Integration," in Leo Kuper and M.G. Smith, eds., *Pluralism in Africa* (Berkeley: University of California Press, 1969), 345.

12 For a discussion of this type of argument, see Donald Smiley, *Canada in Question: Federalism in the Seventies*, 2nd ed. (Toronto: McGraw Hill Ryerson, 1976), 218.

13 Richard Gwyn, *Nationalism Without Walls* (Toronto: McClelland and Stewart, 1995).

14 L. McCann and Angus M. Gunn, *Heartland and Hinterland: A Regional Geography of Canada*, Third Edition (Scarborough: Prentice-Hall, 1998).

15 See N.H. Lithwick and Gilles Paquet, "Urban Growth and Regional Contagion," *Urban Studies: A Canadian Perspective* (Toronto: Methuen, 1968), 18–39.

16 E. Carter, J. Donald, and J. Squires (eds.), *Space and Place: Theories of Identity and Location* (London: Lawrence and Wishart, 1993).

17 The University of North Carolina is best known for its work in the sociology of regionalism in the 1920s to 1940s. In particular, read the work of Howard Odum, Katherine Jocher, and Rupert Vance. More recently, see the work of John Shelton Reid, particularly *One South: An Ethnic Approach to Regional Culture* (Baton Rouge: Louisiana State University Press, 1983).

18 Raymond Breton, "Regionalism in Canada" in David M. Cameron, ed., *Regionalism and Supra-nationalism* (Montreal: Institute for Research on Public Policy, 1981), 58.

19 The subjective-objective distinction is made by Ralph Matthews in *The Creation of Regional Dependency* (Toronto: University of Toronto Press, 1983), 18.

20 Matthews also argues that regionalism may be present even "when there does not appear to be much in the way of objective difference." See "Regional Differences in Canada: Social Versus Economic Interpretations," in Dennis Forcese and Stephen Richer, eds., *Social Issues: Sociological Views of Canada* (Scarborough: Prentice Hall, 1982), 86.

21 For one discussion of the political aspects of region, see Mildred A. Schwartz, *Politics and Territory: The Sociology of Regional Persistence in Canada* (Montreal: McGill-Queen's University Press, 1975), 5.

22 The comparative conception of disparities between regions is developed in Paul Phillips, Regional Disparities (Toronto: James Lorimer, 1982) and *Living Together: A Study of Regional Disparities* (Economic Council of Canada, 1977).

23 For a discussion of some of the issues associated with regionalism in Canada, see Mason Wade, ed., *Regionalism in the Canadian Community*, 1867–1967 (Toronto: University of Toronto Press, 1969); and B.Y. Card, ed., *Perspectives on Regions and Regionalism* (Edmonton: University of Alberta Press, 1969); R.J. Brym (ed), *Regionalism in Canada* (Toronto: Irwin, 1986), and Janine Brodie, *The Political Economy of Canadian Regionalism* (Toronto: Harcourt Brace and Jovanovich, 1990).

24 Alan Cairns has argued that instead of provincial governments being based on societies, the provincial governments mold their social environments to help create societies. "The Governments and Societies of Canadian Federalism," *Canadian Journal of Political Science* 10(1977): 695–725.

25 For a good review of the history of demography in Canada, see Sylvia T. Wargon, "Demography In Canada: Looking Backward, Looking Forward", *Canadian Studies in Population* 25(2)1998:199–228.

26 Canada Yearbook 1980–81, p. 1; and Rick Mitchell, *Canada's Population from Ocean to Ocean,* 1986 Census of Canada, Catalogue 98–120, 16.

27 *Canada Yearbook* 1999, p. 51.

28 Leroy Stone, *Migration in Canada: Regional Aspects* (Ottawa: Statistics Canada, 1969), 22–26.

29 Cf. Yolande Lavoie, *L'emigration des Canadiens aux Etats-Unis avant 1930* (Montreal: University of Montreal Press, 1972).

30 Statistics Canada, *The Daily,* February 17, 1998.

31 Wayne W. McVey and Warren E. Kalbach, Canadian Population (Toronto: Nelson, 1995), pp. 31–37. It is now accepted that variations in the birth rate are not solely related to industrialization and that other variables such as wars or depressions may intervene. In other words, the demographic transition theory is more complex than described here. See also Rod Beaujot and Kevin McQuillan, "The Social Effects of Demographic Change: Canada 1851–1981," *Journal of Canadian Studies,* 21(1986): 57–69.

32 T.R. Weir, "Population Changes in Canada, 1867–1967," *The Canadian Geographer* 2(1967): 198.

33 Statistics Canada, Catalogue 91-213-XPB, p. 5.

34 Jean Dumas, *Report on the Demographic Situation in Canada 1986*, Statistics Canada, Catalogue 91-209E, 51; A. Romaniuc, *Fertility in Canada: From Baby Boom to Baby Bust*, Statistics Canada Catalogue 91-524E; Leroy Stone and Hubert Frenken, *Canada's Seniors,* Catalogue 98–121; and Susan McDaniel, *Canada's Aging Population* (Toronto: Butterworths, 1986); Blossom T. Wigdor and David K. Foot, *The Over-Forty Society: Issues For Canada's Aging Population* (Toronto: James Lorimer, 1988); *A Portrait of Seniors in Canada,* Second Edition, Statistics Canada, 1997.

35 Maurice Yeates, "The Windsor-Quebec City Urban Axis" in Robert M. Irving, ed., *Readings in Canadian Geography*, 3rd ed. (Toronto: Holt, Rinehart and Winston, 1978), 68–72. See also his Main Street: Windsor to Quebec City (Toronto: Macmillan, 1975).

36 Statistics Canada, *Canadians on the Move,* Catalogue 96-309E, 47.

37 Robert D. Hiscott, "Recent Migration From Ontario To Atlantic Canada: A Comparison Of Returning And Non-Returning Migrants", *Canadian Review of Sociology and Anthropology* 24(1987):586–599.

38 There are a variety of studies on this topic. An example of an older one is Jon H. Pammett, "Public Orientation to Regions and Provinces," in David J. Bellamy, Jon H. Pammett, and Donald C. Rowat, eds., *The Provincial Political Systems: Comparative Essays* (Toronto: Methuen, 1976), 86–99. An example of a newer one is Roger Gibbins and Sonia Arrison, *Western Visions: Perspectives on the West in Canada* (Peterborough: Broadview, 1995), 59–65.

39 Carey Hill and Roger Gibbins, *Glocalism and the New Electronic Technologies: Calgary in the Global Environment*", unpublished paper, 1998.

40 For a good discussion of the issues and remedies attempted, see Garth Stevenson, *Unfulfilled Union: Canadian Federalism and National Unity*, rev. ed. (Toronto: Gage, 1982).

41 David Bell, *The Roots of Disunity: A Study of Canadian Political Culture,* Revised Edition (Toronto: Oxford University Press, 1992), 140–52.

42 David J. Elkins examined data that pointed out that Canadians may have multiple loyalties and, that with the exception of a separatist group in Quebec, loyalties to the nation-state need not necessarily erase regional attachments or vice versa. "The Sense of Place" in Elkins and Richard Simeon, eds., *Small Worlds: Provinces and Parties in Canadian Political Life* (Toronto: Methuen, 1980), 21–24.

43 Kenneth McRoberts, *Misconceiving Canada: The Struggle for National Unity* (Toronto: Oxford, 1997).

WEBLINKS

www.iom.ch/

The International Organization for Migration acts with its partners in the international community to assist in meeting the operational challenges of migration; advance understanding of migration issues; encourage social and economic development through migration; and uphold the human dignity and well-being of migrants.

www.statcan.ca/english/Pgdb/People/popula.htm

The Statistics Canada Web site on population provides information on population growth, migration, visible minorities, languages, and more.

artsci-ccwin.concordia.ca/socanth/CSAA/csaa.html

The Canadian Sociology and Anthropology Association Web site provides information about the association and links to meetings, conferences, and publications.

coombs.anu.edu.au/ResFacilities/DemographyPage.html

The CERN/ANU Demography and Population Studies home page links to 155 demographic information facilities throughout the world.

THE QUESTION
OF AUTONOMY

Canada has ceased to be a nation, but its formal political existence will not end quickly. Our social and economic blending into the empire will continue apace, but political union will probably be delayed.

> —George Grant, a social philosopher, in his
> widely read Lament for a Nation *(1965:86).*

It is often said that it is impossible to understand Canadian society without understanding that it is in many ways a product of European and American influences. Older and more dominant societies have played a formative and continuing role in the society's development but this does not occur without debate. One of the big questions is how it is possible for a society to be so open to foreign influences while at the same to develop more independently. Even in spite of the more recent trend towards global interdependence, there remain questions about how a young and less powerful society can more independently establish and control its own traditions and institutions. This chapter will describe the nature, evolution, and implications of these external influences for they provide a context in which to understand much of the conflict and cross-pressures existing in Canadian society today.

this part 4 ES

COLONIALISM AS A HISTORICAL PROCESS

Historically, Canadian society has always lived in the shadow of more powerful societies. These societies derived their power and international stature from their industrial, economic, technological, and military strength which were translated into expansionist objectives around the globe. Canadian society actually emerged as a direct response to the power and influence of European societies for they supplied the people, goods, and capital needed for what they saw as a frontier society. The early Anglo-Saxon inhabitants felt that Canadian society was in some way an extension of their own, more dominant society. As a result, it was believed that Canadian Native peoples should be pushed aside so that the society of the "new world" could be established.

Colonialism is the process whereby an imperial state maintains and extends its powers over a subordinate territory. The expansion of British and French power beyond their own national borders and around the world enabled both societies to participate in the molding of Canadian society. By initiating settlements in what is now Canada, they were able to establish and perpetuate their own national influences in a foreign land. After France lost control of Canada to Britain, British influence became more dominant in Canada.

The paternalistic relationship between the countries of origin and Canada was, therefore, established early and was perpetuated by Canada's refusal to join the American colonies in their rebellion against England. Canada thus retained her colonial ties and maintained an intricate set of dependencies. Whether these influences were economic, political, or cultural, the new society rejected autonomy in favour of sustaining colonial ties.

The first shift in colonial orientation for Canada was from France to Britain. Following World War II, however, the decline of the British Empire and the emergence of the United States as a world power prompted another shift in colonial status. Even though Canada had become an independent political entity with loose ties to the British Commonwealth, the cultural and economic strength of the neighbour country to the south (the United States) drew Canada into a new form of colonialism.[1] But where the earlier form of colonialism had been direct and formal, the new colonialism was less formal and less direct, though not necessarily any less powerful. The term *imperialism* is frequently used to describe this form of domination because the more powerful state seeks to extend its control beyond its borders by whatever means in order to retain its pre-eminent position. So, while colonialism implies political control, imperialism implies more subtle forms of influence and control (e.g., foreign corporations, resource control, fiscal indebtedness). The extent to which nations react to and participate in such control varies over time and is dependent on other global events.

The analytical approach that views national societies in the context of global power differentials is known as *world systems theory*.[2] Basic to this theory is the idea that capitalism developed a world system of economic power which consisted of core societies, peripheral societies, and semi-peripheral societies. Core societies are highly industrialized and invest in societies weaker than themselves. Peripheral and semi-peripheral societies seek to emulate core societies through the adoption of economic, technological, and political systems and processes. Despite this imitation, peripheral societies remain subordinate to the core economic powers who possess the capital needed for development. Because core societies need the markets, resources, and labour of the weaker societies, they tend to assume an expansionist posture. France, England, and Germany were core societies at the beginning of this century, but were eventually supplanted by the United States among capitalist countries and the USSR among socialist countries. Canada is considered to be semi-peripheral because it has fallen under the economic and cultural influence of the United States as a core society and is subject to economic influence by other industrialized core societies (e.g., Germany, Japan) at the same time that it has an advanced infrastructure. The world systems approach, then, ties developments within Canadian society into an international framework.

From a sociological point of view, the significance of a subordinate position within the global system is that non-core societies are the recipients of a continuous transferring process known as *diffusion*. Diffusion is the transmission of economic forms, knowledge, traditions, or technology from one society to another. The originating society shares elements of its culture with the receiving society, so that the two societies become increasingly similar. Institutional and organizational linkages (e.g., unions, business franchises, professional associations, social clubs), serve as cultural pipelines from one society to another. Theoretically, diffusion is not a one-way process; through interaction with each other, societies share cultural traits to produce a *homogenization* of culture. But because of the strength of the core society in all aspects of its culture—whether economic, political, or leisure—the direction of the flow of influence tends to be one way in what is known as *penetration*. The core society absorbs from the peripheral society what it prefers and what it needs, but the strength of the influence is dominantly one way. Because the core society possesses capital, technology, and information which other societies need, its position of dominance is retained.

The Staples Thesis

Harold Innis, writing before world systems theory was proposed, pointed out that Canadian society was founded upon staple industries established for export to empire societies.[3] Whether it was the cod fisheries, trapping, lumbering, mining, or agriculture, Canadian hinterlands were developed for exploitation by external markets. Canadian society, then, could be viewed as a series of resource-based communities centring around extractive processes and primary industries.

Innis pointed out that societal development occurred along the St. Lawrence River and on Atlantic Ocean seaports trading in staples such as fur or grain that could be shipped to European metropoles. A protégé of Innis, S.D. Clark, has described the community instability and boom and bust economies that were typical of these staple-based communities.[4] But Innis also showed how this Canada–Europe trade axis later was supplemented by a Canada–US axis as American industry and technology created new demands for Canadian staples. Innis felt that it was impossible to understand Canadian development without viewing its rich resources as a commodity in demand by more industrialized nations.

Recent years have seen a renewed interest in the staples thesis because, although considered an industrial nation, Canada possesses a truncated industrial base which is still highly dependent on natural resources. In contrast to the resources described by Innis, the new resources include minerals such as nickel, potash, hydroelectric power, and of course oil and gas. Rex Lucas has identified 636 single-industry communities in Canada.[5] Most of these communities are small (under 8000 people), are resource-based (e.g., mining towns, pulp-and-paper towns, smelting towns), and often up to 75% of the labour force works in a single industry. The dependence of many Canadians on resource-based employment means that the staples thesis is an important way of understanding the society and its dependence on external forces.

There are two aspects about a resource-based economy that are important. First, much of the impetus, capital, and technology for resource exploitation comes from core nations (par-

The Effect of Staples on Local Communities

It is possible to analyze the impact of resource extraction on local areas (and even entire societies) by distinguishing between forward linkages and backward linkages.

If new jobs and economic benefits are generated in the local area by the staple after it has been harvested through value-added activity, then the staple has created *forward linkages*. If the resource is shipped out of the area (or even the country) in its raw form immediately after harvesting and transformed into a finished product elsewhere, then the jobs that accrue from that staple occur elsewhere.

Backward linkages refer to the production of machinery and supplies needed by the staple industry in the extraction process. If these items are shipped in from elsewhere ready for use without involving benefit to the local area through employment and technology, then the staples have no backward linkages for the region.

Staples notoriously have few forward or backward linkages for the local or regional community, and sometimes even for the country as a whole because little new employment is created and little diversification occurs. That is why staples produce hinterland effects.

Note: For an application of these principles, see Patricia Marchak, *Green Gold: The Forest Industry In British Columbia* (Vancouver: University Of British Columbia Press, 1983).

ticularly now the United States but also countries like Japan), and results in a high degree of foreign ownership. Second, resource-based economies are highly vulnerable to market demand. When market demand increases, boom conditions prevail; when market conditions are poor or weak, poverty, unemployment, and displacement of population result.[6] Thus a society that is heavily dependent on resource extraction for export will require a large blue collar workforce and will lack the employment diversification necessary to maintain full industrial performance. In sum, when Canada exports raw materials needed by industry in other countries it is exporting labour-intensive industrial jobs and is said to be caught in a *staples trap*. The demands of core nations such as Japan, the United States, and Germany require natural resources to maintain their industrial base and Canada needs those markets to maintain its productivity—even though this productivity is dependent on nonrenewable resources. So while Canada reaps benefits by exporting its resources, the benefits that could accrue by using these resources in Canadian industries are lost.

The autonomy issue is not solely a matter of economic penetration or dependence; it goes beyond that to include politics, education, entertainment, and other aspects of culture. While many Canadians eagerly emulate what is occurring in core societies, others feel that such emulation is destructive of the society's own independence. Persons who are opposed to foreign influences that thwart Canadian independence and who seek to reduce those influences are called *nationalists*. *Continentalists* are people who feel that because Canada shares the North American continent with the United States, it only makes sense for Canada to be closely integrated with that country and that independence issues should be minimized. In addition, there are many residents of Canada who have ethnic or business ties outside North America, and their scope may be even more international. In Canada, the autonomy issue usually vacillates between the debates of the nationalists and the continentalists, particularly in the face of free trade.

FOCI OF THE AUTONOMY ISSUE

The Canadian dilemma is in determining how much foreign influence is acceptable. No society can be totally independent of other societies, but when is foreign influence harmful and when is it to be welcomed? Who is to decide when foreign influence is in a society's best interests? In what sectors of a society is foreign influence a more critical issue than other sectors?

A *shadow society* is a society whose sense of independence and uniqueness is obscured by the cast of continuous alien influences. In the late 1960s and early 1970s, concerted efforts were made to minimize that shadow. Most of these efforts focused on three issues: foreign ownership, manpower importation, and cultural penetration. While there has been some reduction of concern in these matters, they continue to frame public debate at various points in time.

Foreign Ownership

Foreign ownership is not a phenomenon that is unique to Canadian society, but among industrialized nations, Canada has traditionally possessed a substantially higher proportion of such ownership. Beginning with the need for venture capital to exploit Canadian staple

---

REAL PEOPLE 2	Hockey in the Heat: A New Canadian Export

Fort Worth, Texas—Reflections of a Southern Rink Rat

"When people here think about Canada, they think about two things, natural resources and hockey. We know all about oil and gas and minerals, and now we also know about hockey. They are all things you export, right?"

It's 84 degrees Fahrenheit (about 27 degrees Celsius) and humid. The Fort Worth Brahmas are in the playoffs of the Western Professional Hockey League—a league consisting mostly of Texas cities. Almost all of the players are from Canada. But then so is the game. As they say, the only ice people know about here is the ice that keeps your drinks cold.

"Hockey—a little bit of Canada in Texas. On the wall of the arena is a huge American flag. Right next to it, a small Canadian flag hangs that is less than one-tenth the size of the American flag. Nobody here knows what 'icing the puck' means. What's a power play? Nobody knows—yet.

Fort Worth was always known as 'Cowtown' because of its historic stockyards. Now the downtown is promoted as 'Wowtown' with its twenty block Sundance Square of entertainment, restaurants, shopping, theatre, and galleries. Hockey has no cultural meaning in the American South. Now it is packaged as entertainment. When you talk about sports, people here live for football. So I just tell them hockey is like football on skates—lots of body contact and a fast pace. The Canadians that come down here sure put on a great show!"

products for industrial needs in other countries, to the opening of Canadian subsidiaries of foreign corporations in sectors such as manufacturing, the issue of foreign ownership is of continued significance.

There are two main ways in which foreign investment takes place in Canada: portfolio investment and direct investment. *Portfolio investment* means that foreign money enters the country in the form of a repayable loan or a bond which promises a fixed return on the investment but does not allow direct control over the operation in which the investment is made. *Direct investment*, on the contrary, means that foreign money enters the country through ownership or control acquisition as a shareholder. Majority or minority ownership of shares can be obtained through either a controlling interest or a wholly-owned subsidiary. Through direct investment, foreign owners can possess decision-making power over a substantial proportion of the Canadian economy.

Prior to World War I, three-quarters of the foreign investment in Canada was British. Much of this investment was of the portfolio type but it has also been pointed out that there was a significant degree of direct investment.[7] By World War II and in the period immediately following the war, most investment was American—primarily direct investment through the establishment of American subsidiaries in Canada. Capital also enters Canada as portfolio investments particularly in the form of loans to finance government deficits.[8] The periodic pilgrimage of provincial premiers to the money markets in New York attests to this fact. But as we will see later, direct investment has expanded considerably in recent years.

Generally speaking, while portfolio investment may result in a distressing drain of interest payments outside the country, it is usually viewed as preferable to direct investment because ownership and control is retained within the country. Direct investment, on the other hand, is a more clearly identifiable foreign presence. Foreign control of Canadian corporations reached its peak at 37% of all assets among non-financial corporations in 1971 and then declined to 23.4% by 1985 due to government and private acquisitions primarily in mining and petroleum.[9] For example, the creation of federally-owned Petro-Canada in 1975 led to the purchase of American-owned Atlantic Richfield and Pacific Petroleum and Belgium-owned Petrofina. The BC Resources Investment Corporation bought American-owned coal producer Kaiser Resources, and Canadian Pacific bought Dominion Bridge and Algoma Steel from German owners. However, in recent years foreign ownership as measured through assets has been increasing again (29% in 1996, Figure 2.1). Foreign acquisitions such as the purchase of floundering Dome Petroleum by US-based Amoco in the late 1980s, the purchase of all Canadian Woolco stores by US Wal-Mart in the nineties, and just before the turn of the century, American corporation Weyerhaeuser's purchase of long-standing Canadian firm MacMillan Bloedel (itself with US interests) to form one of the world's largest integrated forest products company are some examples. Direct investment can also be in the form of minority shares such as the strategic investment of American Airlines in Canadian Airlines prior to their purchase by Air Canada. Since minority shares do not reflect majority ownership, the degree of foreign investment is probably underestimated in these statistics.[10] Since many Canadian corporations are listed on the New York Stock Exchange, the likelihood that there will be foreign shareholders is enhanced.

One way of measuring foreign control is to determine the nationality of assets and profits. Figure 2.1 demonstrates that foreign control is highest in the manufacturing sector including chemicals, transportation equipment, and electronics and lowest in banks, construction, and communications. About 24% of the assets of all industries are foreign owned but 31% of all profits are distributed to foreign owners, indicating that foreign-owned industries garner more than their share of the profits.[11] In 1988, almost 26% of the revenues were distributed to foreign owners so the increase to 31% is indicative of a general trend towards a more integrated economy found in other sectors as well. In every industry sector, US ownership is dominant among foreign owners with as high as 44% in transportation equipment and just under that amount for chemicals and electronics. Foreign ownership among Europeans and Others are about the same (around 5%) with the largest European ownership in chemicals and the largest Other (primarily Japanese) ownership in electronics and transportation equipment. In general, American ownership represents about two-thirds of all foreign operating revenue. It has been argued that American corporations operating in Canada are more profitable because they are equity rather than debt financed, and they are concentrated in industrial sectors where profit is highest (for example, profits are lower in utilities than manufacturing).[12] Thus, the significance of foreign control is partly its proportion but also its nationality and sector of concentration.

Why did this high level of foreign ownership occur? By stressing Canada's hinterland status as a supplier of staples to external metropolitan industrial centres, an implied power differential infers that Canada had no choice. However, one argument suggests that Canadian capitalists mediated the entry of foreign capital into Canada when domestic capital was unwilling to risk venture capital on Canadian industrial companies or when they acquiesced to the superior technology of foreign corporations.[13] The result was that Canadian commercial capital pursued those industries where profits were safest and left a vacuum for riskier ventures for foreign ownership to fill.

Gordon Laxer has noted that all arguments about foreign ownership usually end up with what he calls a "Canada-as-victim" perspective.[14] The emphasis on a staple-driven economy always accentuates external pressures and Canadian vulnerability, and, above all, the absence of a strong export market for industrial products. Laxer points out that Canada did have a high ratio

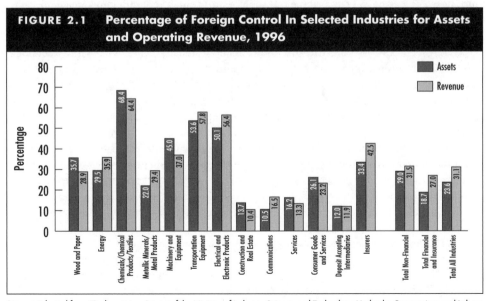

FIGURE 2.1   Percentage of Foreign Control In Selected Industries for Assets and Operating Revenue, 1996

Source: Adapted from "Parliamentary Report of the Minister of Industry, Science and Technology Under the Corporations and Labour Unions Return Act. Part I, Corporations, Preliminary ..., Foreign Control in the Canadian Economy," Statistics Canada Catalogue 61-220-XPB, Tables 1–19.

of exported manufactured goods in the late nineteenth century focusing on textiles and clothing, agricultural implements, and steel products. He notes that it was in the period prior to World War I that a regression began to take place due to the tendency for Canadian manufacturers to obtain licensing agreements with American firms for technology that would only give rights for the Canadian market. This trend ultimately led to American buyouts with stringent restrictions against subsidiaries competing with the parent company in the international marketplace.

Laxer notes that in addition to the unwillingness of the commercial banking sector to support industry, Canada did not benefit from the military industries of wartime because of the decision to remain under British military tutelage. Furthermore, the decision to build expensive railroads increased foreign indebtedness (especially British portfolio investment). But more importantly, the politics of French–English sectionalism led conservative English-speaking business interests to accentuate British dependencies in place of strategic moves to become more independent, and therefore the liberalizing effects of popular-democratic movements in Canada (particularly among farmers) were minimized. The primary contribution of Laxer's important work is to shift the focus to explain why foreign ownership occurred from external factors to the internal dynamics of actions taken within the country. Other reasons to explain how and why foreign capital entered Canada will be discussed later in the chapter. The shift in emphasis away from the role of foreign capital to indigenous capital will also be discussed in Chapter Three.

Among the reasons why foreign ownership is problematic is that large payments in the form of dividends, interest, franchise fees, management and consulting fees, and research costs are made annually to non-residents by corporations operating in Canada. The export of capital each year as payment to foreign owners affects exchange rates and removes capital from the country in which those monies were generated. So while foreign capital may initially have been needed as a stimulant for economic development, the export of profits made in Canada does not help the economy. Others would argue that the problem of foreign ownership is exacerbated by the fact that the retention of profits in the country to enlarge equity ultimately means that profits made in Canada are used to increase the size of the foreign-controlled operation in Canada. Thus retained earnings are used to increase the foreign presence.

During the latter 1960s and early 1970s a number of studies, including the Gray Report and the Task Force on the Structure of Canadian Industry, were commissioned to examine the issue of foreign ownership.[15] An organization called the Committee For An Independent Canada was established by persons interested in politics promoting economic repatriation and economic nationalism.[16] In the early seventies, the federal government established the Foreign Investment Review Agency (FIRA) to review and approve sales and transfers of corporations involving foreign capital. The Committee For An Independent Canada disbanded in 1981 and FIRA was reorganized in 1985 to be less restrictive and was renamed Investment Canada. As a government agency, Investment Canada represents a new federal approach to welcoming foreign investments while still reviewing the impact of larger investments on Canadian society. The free trade era has muted much of the public concern over foreign ownership; yet it is still an issue that is by no means forgotten. The matter continues to surface in formal and informal ways and helps to keep concerns about societal autonomy in the public eye.

Manpower Importation

For much of Canada's history, the country experienced both a *labour drain* and a *brain drain*. The industrialization of the New England states created strong employment demands in the textile and manufacturing industries in that area and led many Canadians to immigrate to the United States. Other urban opportunities that occurred elsewhere in the United States (prior to the growth of industrial opportunities in Canada) contributed to the continual drain of population to that country. Furthermore, many of Canada's best students obtained their educations at prestigious educational institutions in Britain, France, or particularly the United States and frequently remained in those countries when opportunities were lacking in Canada. Even people who were educated here took advantage of the more varied occupational possibilities in these core countries when given job offers. The same process of temporary/permanent emigration has been experienced in athletics, entertainment, the sciences, medicine, and various forms of entrepreneurship. Attracted by new challenges in the United States, Canadians such as the economist John Kenneth Galbraith, American Broadcasting Corporation's news anchorman Peter Jennings, and various entertainers left the country to pursue their careers.

The 1960s were a time of enormous change in Canadian society. The post-war industrial expansion reached its apex, universities grew rapidly and student enrollment increased dramatically. New opportunities abounded and out-migration dropped significantly. In fact, the lack of adequate manpower in Canada resulted in a government policy of liberal immigration designed to encourage skilled migration into the country. Thus university faculty, medical doctors, scientists, accountants, and others willingly migrated to Canada not only from the war-ravaged countries of Europe but also, because of the stresses created by the war in Viet Nam and urban social tensions, from the United States.[17] Throughout the rest of that decade and part of the next, Canada's manpower needs were met to a significant degree by immigration which some have nicknamed the *brain swamp* and *labour swamp*.

However, just as the foreign ownership issue heightened awareness of foreign capital intrusion, so it raised the question of whether to continue the policy of importing foreign labour. The resident population of young university graduates sought employment opportunities in Canada and they pressured the government to be much more restrictive in approving immigration as the possibilities for emigration were not as attractive and young people expressed a preference to remain in Canada.[18] During the 1970s, immigration rules were tightened considerably, and were tightened still further in the early 1980s as the recession increased unemployment. Immigration regulations now require extensive advertising for available positions in Canada first and over a protracted period of time, before employment of persons from outside the country will be permitted for anything other than short-term contracts.

Government acquiescence to public demands for restricted immigration has put to rest some of the battles and controversies of the 1970s. Yet the lack of manpower in some specialized areas and the desire to import leading people with special talents, or merely the general desire for new people with new ideas, sometimes creates controversy over whether Canadians should be by-passed for available positions. Corporations, professional sports teams, arts groups, religious organizations, and the scientific community constantly struggle with the issues raised by the availability of Canadian talent, their own organizational goals, and foreign expertise that they might like to acquire. Thus, if on the one hand it is thought that Canadian society should be self-sufficient in supplying its own manpower, public debate is often intense when others argue for a less restrictive policy in view of globalizing pressures.

Cultural Penetration

At the root of the question about who should be given employment priority within the society lies a fundamental defence of, and concern for, a national culture. The concept of *cultural penetration* suggests that more dominant core societies flood Canadian society with foreign influence against the national will and in the face of little apparent defence. While there is a real sense in which this is true, the one-way diffusion process is ironically also welcomed. For example, Canadians enjoy American movies and American entertainers and believe it is almost their right to have access to American programming on television. Restricting access to these "foreign" aspects of popular culture would clearly be resisted.[19] This creates paradoxical situations such as the Canadian Radio-television and Telecommunications Commission (CRTC) trying to increase the opportunities for "Canadian" artists and production at the same time that they also increase accessibility to cable networks which bring American television into Canada.[20]

Clearly the proximity of the United States means that American cultural influences will be strong. The real issue appears to be not so much whether these foreign components of culture should be allowed into Canada but whether their presence retards the emergence of an indigenous Canadian culture.[21] Perhaps the most visible form of this debate in Canada (where about 50% of the magazines sold in Canada are produced in the United States) has been over what is known as *split-run editions* in the magazine industry. This issue first surfaced in 1976 when Parliament passed Bill C-58 which took away the financial advantages of American-based *Time* magazine that was printing a split-run Canadian edition and gave it to the fledging Canadian news magazine *Maclean's*. The government no longer allowed Canadian advertisers to deduct their costs of advertising in *Time*. This in effect channelled those advertising dollars to the Canadian magazine, and helped it become a viable operation. While some hurled accusations of "dictatorship" and claimed loss of freedoms to the government, the government responded that *Time* was certainly still available for purchase in Canada in its American edition, but that it was important that Canadians should see themselves and others through their own eyes rather than through those of reporters and editors representing other societies with different agendas.[22]

Government policy has also attempted to encourage other aspects of Canadian culture. For example, Country Music Television (CMT), a US-based network, was available on cable in Canada in the early nineties but was ordered off the air by the CRTC and replaced by Canadian-based New Country Network, again provoking threats of retaliation under free trade policies. Another illustration of action taken by the government is the requirement that symphony orchestras receiving federal grants (which are usually required for fiscal survival) must play a proportion of "Canadian" music and use "Canadian" artists in order to retain their funding. Thus while some complain that Canadian composers do not even vaguely compare with Beethoven or Bach ("so why must we listen to Canadian music?"), others argue that unless Canadians give their own composers a chance, creative talent will be stifled within the society and Canadian culture will never be developed.

Perhaps even more threatening is digital satellite service, which will give Canadians access to a huge number of foreign television stations, or the information highway of computer networks where the issue of the protection of Canadian culture continues to be raised. In all of these instances, foreign ownership and Canadian content are recurring issues brought to the Canadian government and its agencies for action.

These are but a few examples of a counter-offensive that has become a trademark of Canadian society; i.e., government intervention even in the field of the arts and popular culture to strengthen Canadian culture in the face of foreign influence. This intervention, which

The Rationale of Split-Run Editions

American magazines are published essentially for the American market. Their news stories are selected and edited with the American market in mind. Their advertisers are largely American companies and advertisements are pitched to American readers. Their editorial policies reflect American issues and perspectives. Their revenues and expenses are predicated on their domestic sales.

A split-run edition provides a magazine the opportunity to add a small amount of Canadian news while otherwise retaining most of the American content, and then to sell the magazine as a Canadian edition. Expanded sales in Canada allow the magazine to obtain more revenues because of expanded readership from American advertisers who do business in the Canadian market. The Canadian edition may also be attractive to Canadian advertisers who may be offered lower advertising rates because the major costs of production have already been covered in the American edition. Without much additional cost, the American magazine has entry into the Canadian market with the split-run edition, and the additional revenues through sales and advertising increases profits.

From a Canadian point of view, split-run editions raise three issues. One is that Canadian magazines lose advertising revenue which would otherwise accrue to them. And related to that is the fact that their basic costs are not covered so their advertising rates must remain high which makes them uncompetitive for the advertising dollar. The second issue is that Canadians obtain their news through an American lens which may not focus on issues and persons that are specifically relevant to Canadians. The third issue is that split-run editions reduce jobs (editorial, advertising, production) in the publishing industry in Canada.

Among the most high profile split-run American magazines in Canada are *Time*, *Newsweek*, and *Sports Illustrated*.

In 1997, the World Trade Organization based in Geneva, Switzerland, ruled in response to American complaints that Canada's policy contravened international trade agreements (the General Agreement On Tariffs And Trade—GATT) that prohibits discrimination in the trade of goods. The argument was that this was not a cultural issue but was in reality protection for powerful publishing interests in Canada (e.g., Rogers Communications which publishes *Maclean's* and *Chatelaine*). Canadian representatives countered by pointing out that it was also powerful publishing interests in the United States (e.g., Time-Warner, Hearst) that were behind the opposition. In 1999, Canada proposed Bill C-55 which again attacked split-run editions but which the Americans threatened with trade sanctions in lumber, steel, and textiles. After negotiation with the American government, split-run editions were to be allowed only up to 18% Canadian advertising per issue. The Canadian government agreed to subsidize the magazine industry for their revenue loss. While the battle for Canadian culture appeared valiant, it appears that international trade agreements took precedence over the issue of defence of culture and split-run editions will now be available in Canada.

has varied among different federal governments, generally focuses on increasing Canadian content. Whether it deals with the labour component in the manufacture of an automobile or the number of songs by Canadian artists played on a radio station, *Canadian content* refers to the proportion of Canadian participation in an activity. Even though government guidelines or regulations contain an element of forced choice which is obviously controversial, there is a long history and public acceptance of this kind of intervention to maintain a significant Canadian cultural presence.

It is true that Canadian culture has traditionally been thought to be too weak and poorly organized to withstand the power of American cultural industries. Attempts to change this perpetual condition have focused on internal measures to improve cultural productivity. These internal measures, however, are largely a response to the external cultural influences of other societies (particularly the United States), which are viewed as threatening to societal autonomy.[23]

FACTORS CONSTRAINING SELF-DETERMINATION

The historical causes of dependency within Canadian society can be located in its strong linkages with core societies. As a young and expanding society possessing few indigenous traditions, Canadian society has endured repeated struggles while forging its own independence against rather formidable odds. In spite of trying to be the centre of its own universe, Canadian

Canadian Content and Canadian Culture

Almost all of the sound recording, television, and film industries in Canada with high volume sales are foreign owned. Smaller Canadian companies do produce recordings but with smaller sales.

Foreign programming accounts for about two-thirds of all television programming watched by Canadians. This percentage would be even higher if francophones were removed from the calculation, as foreign programming is more likely to be English and francophones are more likely to watch French programs. In fact, only 4% of comedy shows, 7% of dramas, and 10% of variety and game shows watched by anglophones are Canadian programming. However, news and sports programs are more likely to be Canadian—about two-thirds for anglophones but a much higher 77% (sports) and 97% (news) for francophones.

In order to encourage more Canadian content, federal regulations were established in 1971 that supported this aspect of Canadian culture. At least 30% of all music aired by Canadian AM stations must either be composed by a Canadian, the lyrics written by a Canadian, the instrumentation performed by a Canadian, or performed live or wholly recorded in Canada. Such qualifying content must be played between 6:00 a.m. and 7:00 p.m. Monday through Friday. On television, Canadian content must fill at least 60% of the overall schedule.

While many Canadians have access to American stations, the ultimate goal was to ensure that Canadian stations would have a programming difference.

Source: Jeffrey Frank and Michel Durand "Canadian Content in the Cultural Marketplace," *Canadian Social Trends* Vol. 2 (Toronto: Thompson Educational Publishing, 1994), 297–300.

society has been continually pulled like a satellite into the gravitational orbit of more dominant societies. Rocher noted that such satellite status makes a society peripheral, unbalanced, and inhibited.[24] Decisions made elsewhere and over which it has few controls impinge on the society. Efforts to exert controls are, at best, only partially effective, and feelings persist that the satellite society is inferior to the real centres of power and influence. While the way the world is organized is changing due to internationalizing forces, Canadians have repeatedly struggled with a sense of being subordinate or dependent as the result of being on the margins of power. Why is this so? Five factors explaining this dependency will be discussed.

1. The Era of the American Empire

It has already been suggested that Canada's relationship with core societies started with old-style colonialism through France and Britain and has proceeded to a neocolonialism in its ties with the United States. What all three of these countries have in common is a sequence of years in which they were a dominant global force. The concept of *empire* suggests groups of nations, people, states, or territories united under the direction of a dominant power.[25] Throughout history, groups of states have been occasionally united under the influence of a more dominant state either through direct administrative and military subordination and/or through loose allegiances and mercantile ties. The Roman Empire, for example, tied a vast territory together through a common language, technological leadership, military strength, mercantile coordination, and rule of the seas. Similarly, the French settlement around the St. Lawrence River was part of an expansion of military influence and mercantile strength that saw France establish colonial ties all over the new world. Colonials taught indigenous peoples their language and drew their marketable products into the empire economy.

The British also experienced an era of empire expansion and influence that went far beyond their small island territory. With a strong naval and mercantile fleet they "ruled the waves" and the territories beyond them. The decline of the British empire has been followed by the rise of the American empire whose military, industrial, and technological strength have made it a dominant global power, and, directly or indirectly, have brought much of the world under its influence. With the end of the Cold War, in many ways, American dominance has only increased so that, in spite of other moderating forces, the whole world has become its empire.

From a conceptual point of view, all empires have a core society that establishes and sustains directions of influence. The language of the core society becomes the major vehicle of communication among all societies within the empire. It dispatches its members to teach and train societies under its influence technologies and skills that will improve their productivity. It attracts promising leaders from other societies to be trained in its schools and absorb its culture. Through its technology and industry, it establishes interdependencies with other societies that provide markets or desired resources or products. Its marketing apparatus fosters the widespread distribution of its goods and its culture.

While some would argue that the American empire has begun to go into eclipse or that it is being replaced by huge trading blocks such as the European Community,[26] there is no doubt that the United States is a core society. It has absorbed the best technologies developed elsewhere and promises prestige and handsome financial rewards to scientists, entertainers, athletes, and other leaders in their fields who participate in that society. As a centre of capital control, decisions made in the United States automatically affect other societies. Promising students from abroad are attracted to American educational institutions; these students then return to their own society as decision-makers and frequently take American culture back with them. The distribution network is effective and elaborate, and American manufactured products are available in many countries—a process known as *cocacolonization*.[27] American influence is currently present throughout much of the world and it is particularly strong in Canada because of the geographic proximity of the two countries.

It is important to stress the current position of the United States as a dominant *world* power lest it be assumed that American influence is a uniquely Canadian concern. American cultural influence through books, films, magazines, television, and entertainers is intertwined with American capital, and technological and military influence. American presidential elections or American space launches are as newsworthy in Sweden and Germany as they are in Canada. While the current global influence of the United States is virtually a universal factor, there are clear signs that the empire is changing or breaking down under new forces of globalization. However, even in spite of this shift, Canadian society, for a variety of reasons, continues to engender specifically weak resistance to American economic and cultural penetration.

2. Continentalism

The presence of a global power (e.g., the United States) at one's border must be considered a factor of special importance. It is natural for bordering nations to establish both formal and informal patterns of interaction over common interests. Californians love Banff in the summer while Ontarians love Florida in the winter. Wheat farmers in Kansas and

---

"McDonaldization"

There is a new way to describe the global impact of Americanization and it is known as *McDonaldization*. Springing from the fast food industry which got its start in the United States, McDonaldization is different from cocacolonization in that it refers not just to exporting products but to the role of the United States in creating, producing, and exporting new means of consumption.

McDonaldization stands for a rationalization process that emphasizes efficiency, predictability, calculability, control, and homogeneity at any outlet. It emphasizes bright colours and seats that are designed to keep traffic moving. It saturates first the American market and then seeks to expand globally. McDonalds is now opening more outlets internationally on an annual basis than it is opening in the United States.

McDonaldization focuses on the globe as the unit of analysis. It exports American eating styles but makes minor adaptations to fit the local culture. For example, in Norway a grilled salmon sandwich is added to the menu called a McLak. In Uruguay, a burger with a poached egg is called a McHuevo. In the Philippines, tomato sauce with frankfurter bits makes McSpaghetti. Nevertheless the base menu is always the same and is standardized. Other retailers and food companies are seeking to follow the same model.

Source: George Ritzer, *The McDonaldization Thesis* (Thousand Oaks: Sage, 1998), Chapter 7.

RESEARCH CLIP 2.1	Analyzing Changes in North–South Interaction

The shift in Canada from being a hinterland of England to being a hinterland of the United States seems to have changed the east–west axis to a north–south axis. NAFTA adds a new dynamic to that trend. One study looked at three examples of this trend in commodity flows, air travel, and television viewing.

While there are regional differences in the flow of commodities, there has been an overwhelming increase in the flow of commodities north–south and a decrease in east–west shipments. For example, in 1989, for the first time in post-war years, Quebec exported a larger share of its manufactured goods to the United States than to Canadian provinces.

In analyzing air passenger travel, there has been a relative weakening of east–west traffic in relation to north–south traffic since 1970. But the evidence suggests that both continental traffic and Canadian traffic coexist.

Television viewing of American programs is high in Canada and increasing among anglophones, but among Quebec francophones it is not only much lower but has decreased since 1985.

Question to consider:

In addition to what this fact tells us about Canada, what does it tell us about Quebec in particular?

Source: Paul Villeneuve, "Canada, Quebec, And North American Continental Integration," *Recherches Sociographique* 39(2–3)1998:393–416.

Saskatchewan share common technologies and work styles. Religious groups interact across the border sometimes with common organizations.[28] Leisure organizations such as Shriners, Masons, and even barbershop singing groups cross the border. Americans and Canadians both drive the same brands of cars. Fast-food franchises are similar and sports leagues cross the border. There are many other examples of the ongoing integration of the two societies on the North American continent.[29]

And yet the relationship is frequently lopsided. Canadians are often appalled at American ignorance of Canada and perceptions of each other are sometimes filled with inaccurate stereotypes. Canadian society is affected by political and economic policies established in Washington where decision-makers either do not understand or minimize Canadian concerns. For example, the decision to allow interest rates to rise in the United States forces interest rates to rise even higher in Canada because of Canadian dependence on US money markets. A metaphor which has frequently been used to describe the relationship is that of the mouse and the elephant. The mouse (Canada) has an existence which is independent of the elephant (the United States), but must be ever alert to the movement of the elephant because virtually every move affects the mouse. Another metaphor is that of life with uncle (meaning the nickname for the United States—"Uncle Sam"), which suggests a paternalistic relationship between the two societies.[30]

The increasing economic interaction between the two countries (free trade will be discussed later in this chapter); the sharing of a common language (except French); the participation of both countries in common sports leagues, such as baseball and hockey; and the sharing of common defence interests (e.g., NORAD), are just some of the factors that contribute to greater continentalism and the blurring of societal boundaries, or at least increased exposure by Canadians to things American. Many Canadians prefer American television shows and are totally unaware of the nationality of the shows they are watching. Almost unconsciously, exposure to American sitcoms blends Canadian ideas and values with American values making them difficult to differentiate. Even through Canadian newspapers Canadians can read both hard news and human interest stories about the United States on a daily basis. Thus American influence is far more subtle than direct economic and political influence.

One of the most neglected aspects of continental integration is the investment of Canadian capital in the United States—a reversal of the usual expectation of American investment in Canada. Somewhat surprisingly, Jorge Niosi discovered that Canada has been a capital exporting country for many years.[31] On a per capita basis, Canadians invest almost as much outside their country as Americans do. Companies such as Alcan Aluminum, Bata Shoes, Cominco, Northern Telecom, Polysar, and Seagram are major international players. Niosi discovered that over the years the significant thing about Canadian investment was that it had little Canadian technological content. This was demonstrated by the fact that the percentage of patents registered in Canada to local residents was one of the lowest in the world. In other words, Canadian investors used technology developed elsewhere to a greater degree than expected and therefore did not own the technology they used. Thus Canadian foreign investment historically was not an application of Canadian technology in other countries but was largely the application and management of American technology (with only some exceptions). However, there are strong indications that this pattern is changing as Canadian innovations in areas such as telecommunications and software are penetrating the US market.

Because of limitations in the size of the Canadian economy and the desire for corporate growth, Canadian subsidiaries in the US have recently become quite active in cities such as Minneapolis, Denver, and growth areas in the American south.[32] For example, Montreal-based Northern Telecom expanded into the United States because it already controlled 70% of the Canadian market and was looking for new productivity gains. Canadian investments in US property and real estate developments such as shopping centres and office towers have also been significant. While such investments are sizeable, they are certainly not of the proportional magnitude of American capital flow into Canada. Nevertheless, these examples illustrate another aspect of continental integration which, as a consequence of free trade thinking, is increasing significantly.

Although continentalism, in many ways, is inevitable, it repeatedly raises the question of autonomy for a society unsure of its independence. In order to facilitate the east–west interaction across Canada rather than the north–south interaction which promotes continentalism, government intervention has again been a frequently used vehicle, particularly in earlier stages of Canadian development. For example, the Canadian Broadcasting Corporation was established by the government with the explicit mandate to foster greater national understanding and knowledge of matters of general societal interest. Railroads (CNR/Via Rail) and airlines (Air Canada) also represented a government mandate to facilitate communication within the society. Taking a *key sector approach* to the issue of foreign control, government sponsorship of communication links have always been an important mechanism in fostering societal interaction.

A significant ideological shift has occurred in recent years that debunks the role of the federal government in sustaining national unity. A fiscal reluctance to provide public sub-

The Ties That Bind: The Iron Highway

Railroads have historically played a vital role in binding Canadians together. The Canadian Pacific Railway had as its explicit mandate the linking of British Columbia with the rest of Canada. As a private venture with government support, the CPR helped bring millions of people to settle in the West.

The other main Canadian railroad, and now the largest, is the Canadian National Railroad. The CNR was formed by the merger of smaller lines in 1919 through a nationalization procedure by the federal government. As a crown corporation, the railroad was to be an instrument of national policy to help populate the country and thereby claim and integrate the territory. To put it another way, both railroads were constructed to tie together the vast distances in an east-west direction in spite of the barriers of geography. Passenger traffic was a priority for many years, and the railroad tied the dispersed population to Canadian markets, manufacturing, and raw materials.

Symptomatic of the change in times, the railroads no longer play a major role in moving people across the country. Freight has become the revenue generator but it is no longer just across the country in an east–west direction, but increasingly in a north–south direction

(a train drain?). Already in 1928, the CNR itself bought 10 small US railroads and consolidated them into one called the Grand Trunk Western Railroad to ensure access to Chicago. But in 1999, CNR made a major purchase of Illinois Central Railroad and has established an alliance with Kansas City Southern which now means that CNR spans Canada and mid-America from the Atlantic to the Pacific to the Gulf of Mexico.

As a result of its single line service in the NAFTA trade corridor with Chicago as its hub, CNR claims to be the first truly North American railroad. It first proposed a new name as CNR North America and then began using the name Powertrain: North America's Railroad. Early in 2000, another merger was proposed with US-based Burlington Northern Santa Fe to form a new entity called North American Railways.

If the railroad was initially conceived as the iron highway to tie Canadians together, ironically it has now become the vehicle to tie Canada more directly into the North American or continental economy. It is also noteworthy that this shift has taken place around the same time that the CNR was privatized from its status as a crown corporation in 1995.

sidies to enterprises such as the Canadian Broadcasting Corporation threatens this historic Canadian institution. And convictions that the private sector are more appropriate operators of crown corporations, for example, has led to the sale of Air Canada. Indeed, the general shift to privatization and the abrogation of government responsibility in these areas of historic national key-sector concern, is eroding the countervailing influences always considered necessary to thwart continentalist pressures. Thus, in spite of growing maturity as a society, Canada continues to face major questions raised by the integrating dynamic of continentalism.

3. The Multinational Corporation

The third factor accentuating the issue of autonomy for Canadian society has been the activity of huge multinational corporations. Committed to profit and to their own expansion, these corporations cross national boundaries and make decisions that affect the economies and standard of living in whichever countries they operate. Multinationals, with their conglomerates, holding companies, and subsidiaries, effectively challenge the nation-state as the type of social organization most characteristic of the post-industrial world. Their capital growth, which expands assets and profits, facilitates the growth of power which can be expressed by providing employment and handsome benefits to employees as a reward for loyalty. The primary advantage of this form of organization is that the home office of the parent company is able to manipulate its resources from country to country in order to maximize its net gain. The state attempts to establish the rules whereby it can control the multinational operation in that country, but the fact that multinationals can transfer their resources to other, more cooperative countries, considerably reduces the control of the state.[33] Thus for our purposes, the significant fact about multinational corporations is that they are *transnational*; i.e., they operate within national boundaries but follow an ethic in which profit transcends national concerns.

What are some of the ways a multinational corporation can exercise its unique flexibility? It can move its capital or use its borrowing power to establish new ventures in locations of its choosing. It can use the profits generated in one country to subsidize an operation in another country. It can move its own pool of skilled labour or management to new locations. It can bargain with governments competing against each other for the establishment or expansion of new operations. More specifically, through the use of subsidiaries, the parent company can use its massive resources to reduce or destroy competition by underpricing other domestic operations or by purchasing the products of subsidiaries below market value while domestic competitors must purchase the product at market cost.[34] Because the multinational is transnational, it can create a book loss in one country in order to reduce taxes there and shift funds and profits to a more favourable location. Thus, the desire of political units to retain or acquire the capital and technology of the corporation and the ensuing employment benefits for its citizens, can lead to a general acquiescence by the state to corporate demands and needs. Some view these corporations as the newest form of imperialism while others see them as the most practical solution to world order because of the present plurality of many small interdependent nation-states.[35] Multinational corporations have power which threatens the autonomy of, and sense of control by, national societies.

It is not surprising that, given the strength of the American economic empire, many of these multinational corporations have been American, whether operating in Canada or elsewhere in the world. Yet multinationals based in other countries are both active and growing as money is being moved to take advantage of new opportunities and as corporate strategies change.[36] But whether the corporation is Japanese or German only shifts the nationality but not the principles by which multinational corporations operate.

What problems do the multinational corporations raise for Canadian society? One problem is the tendency towards *truncation*, which occurs because a subsidiary seldom performs all the major functions which a major corporation requires for its operation. For example, scientific research, commonly referred to as R & D (research and development), or marketing are operations that are vital to the existence of the subsidiary but that are often centralized in one country by the parent firm. While the branch plant may provide employment for residents of Canada, truncation contributes to the technology gap and profession-

Self-government.

alization gap by minimizing the demand for such trained personnel in Canada. For example, a multinational American-based tire company might decide that it only needs one research site and decides to locate it in the United States closer to its head office. Truncation might be tolerated in the early stages of a subsidiary's development, but once it becomes established, truncation perpetuates restricted professional employment growth in Canada.

Another problem with the multinational corporation is that the government of the home office may attempt to put controls on the corporation's operations regardless of where it operates. This control is known as *extraterritoriality*.[37] While an internationally operating corporation may have no single national allegiance, its operation may be bound by regulations of the home country which can interfere with the interests of the country of the subsidiary. For example, the United States has had a law called the *Trading With The Enemy Act* which prohibited American companies or their subsidiaries from doing business with countries identified as enemies of the United States. Cuba was such a country for many years and the Act was invoked in order to block the sale of Canadian-made locomotives to Cuba (the Montreal firm manufacturing the locomotives was owned by a majority shareholder corporation in New Jersey). While the sale eventually went through, this is an example of how jobs and general industrial expansion can be thwarted by an extension of the laws of foreign countries. More recently, when a Canadian company called Bow Valley Energy signed an agreement with the government of Iran to build oil wells in the Persian Gulf, the United States referred to their Iran–Libya Sanctions Act which called for trade sanctions against any country that invested in Iran's petroleum sector.

A third problem with multinationals is that Canadian subsidiaries may be prevented from increasing their productivity if they are prohibited from seeking export markets. Known as *export blocking*, the parent firm may not allow the subsidiary to compete for foreign contracts because either the parent firm or another of its subsidiaries does not want competition in a market that it also wants to enter. Given the fact that increased exports mean more jobs in Canada, lost exports mean lost jobs.

The federal government has sought to counter the slipperiness of multinationals not only by creating rules and regulations, but also by establishing incentives. One such incentive is the negotiation of a *Canadian content component* in certain contracts; i.e., we will buy your product if you use a certain percentage of Canadian labour or use materials produced in the country. A second method is to give *interest subsidies* to purchasers of Canadian products. The sale of 825 subway cars made by Bombardier in Montreal to New York city was successful largely because the Canadian government offered financing to New York at interest rates which were well below the prevailing prime rate. A related method used is to require any major Canadian project receiving federal financial support to maintain a certain level of Canadian-made materials and/or labour. This is known as *industrial offsets* because it gives specialized contracts to foreign companies with the proviso that the company turn other aspects of its business into Canadian production. Ironically, the sale of subway cars to New York was subject to a US "Buy American" law which resulted in Bombardier establishing a subsidiary in Vermont.

One other possible method of controlling multinationals, at least to an extent, is a *unitary tax* that minimizes the advantages of bookkeeping shifts practised by multinationals. The government determines what percentage of a company's business is done in its territory and then taxes the company based on that percentage of the parent company's worldwide profits. In all of these methods, the goal is to exert some control, in the national interest, over the adverse effects of the practices of multinational corporations.

A fourth problem multinationals present to a society is that they often move their personnel between countries in response to the personnel requirements of the corporate structure. Transfers in and out of various countries are part of the corporate mentality of loyalty and devotion to the corporation. In her research, Levitt found that some Canadians were promoted through the ranks to managerial positions in subsidiaries around the world.[38] House, on the other hand, found that petroleum multinationals have tried to "Canadianize" their subsidiaries' management in this country as much as possible.[39] The point is that persons working for multinationals are likely to be good corporate employees who find no objections to the nature of their corporate structure as long as they are treated well. Thus, large corporations that operate transnationally establish their own set of loyalties which may or may not be in tune with national concerns and societal goals.[40]

A final dilemma presented to national societies by multinationals is their tendency to contribute to the *homogenization of culture*. The Gray Report speaks of the subsidiary as a "continuous transmission belt" of culture in general.[41] Examining the new values, beliefs, and other influences experienced by the city of Galt, Ontario, Perry discovered a "subculture of subsidiaries."[42] The duplication of products and commercials (especially advertising jingles), for example, contributes to cultural similarity. One explanation for why this has occurred will be clarified in the next section.

4. Relatively Small Population

The impact of continentalism and international corporatism is at least partially related to the fact that Canada has a population which is only one-tenth the size of that of the United States and which is dispersed throughout vast territory. This fact has produced collective feelings of comparative weakness in the presence of large-scale capital, bigger organizations, and greater diversity and specialization in the society to the south. These feelings have left many groups open to the support of linkage with American organizations, and also makes foreign penetration that much easier.

At the economic level, the relatively small Canadian population means a small domestic market in which economies of scale sometimes cannot be practised. Small Canadian industrial operations struggled to compete with American industries importing into Canada until the federal government approved the establishment of a protective tariff in 1879.[43] Regrettably, the establishment of a protective tariff did little to stimulate Canadian investment in the manufacturing sector. Canadian capitalists were reluctant to invest in relatively inefficient Canadian industries, and favoured investment in the finance, transportation, and utility sectors of the economy. This left the door open for foreign capital to establish manufacturing branch plants in Canada which brought with them their proven product lines, technology, and experience. The protective tariff ensured that foreign corporations would have to service their Canadian market, through Canadian plants, to turn out product lines identical to those in the United States. This is known as the *miniature replica effect*.

Operating on a smaller scale because of the smaller domestic market, and insulated from competition because of the tariff walls, Canadian branch plants' production costs were higher than those of their American parents. However, the tariff gave Canadian producers an additional margin (the tariff charge), by which their product's price could be increased and yet still be competitive. Canadians, then, were likely to pay more for products identical to those produced in the United States; moreover, surplus products could not enter the world market because of these higher prices. But what was provided by the branch plants was

Advertisements That Tell a Story

"Now…For your convenience. Open a USA Dollar Savings Account Here Today"
—*sign in the window of a trust company*

"Celebrate Canada Week, February 10–17"
—*ad in a Florida newspaper*

"This advertisement is directed to Canadian citizens and permanent residents only"
—*employment notice in the bulletin of a professional association*

"The Royal Visit…Get Your Souvenir Pictorial Book Today"
—*sign in a book shop*

"Here is a great buy this week. Canada No. 1 California tomatoes $1.52 a kilogram."
—*radio station ad*

employment for Canadians in the industrial sector which, as we have seen, became foreign owned with the agreement of indigenous capital.[44] In this context, Clement has referred to Canada as "a mature branch plant society."

The availability of similar products in both Canada and the United States helps to support cultural homogeneity. Smaller scale Canadian operations in the economic sector, or in social organizations or leisure activities, for example, frequently look to larger enterprises in the United States for cooperation in their mutual concerns. Emulating or modifying American procedures is frequently practised in many sectors of society, and formal or informal ties are maintained. More than that, the branch plant organizational structure produces a branch plant mentality in which initiative, ambition, and creativity are deferred to the more dominant society.[45] While there is no doubt that this perspective remains a significant element within Canadian society, it is also true that its impact has been transformed in more recent years by the forces of globalization, and especially free trade. More and more, instead of branch plants and the miniature replica effect, Canadian companies are producing a limited range of product lines for the whole continent in a process known as *continental rationalization*.[46] Of course, the corollary of that is the fact that other products may not be manufactured in Canada at all anymore as the Canadian market is serviced from the United States or elsewhere. The end result is still dependence on foreign capital.

5. Globalization

There are many forces at work promoting global integration. At the economic level, there are free trade or trading blocs, mobile international capital and multinational corporations, and global marketing of products and culture. At the communications level, there are computers, the world wide web, faxes, and all kinds of new technologies which erase the problems of distance which formerly served as enormous barriers between societies. *Globalization* means increased access to all parts of the world for whatever purposes. But globalization also means the creation of new international bodies and regulators (e.g., World Trade Organization, European Union, NAFTA) beyond the nation-state to foster such intersocietal interaction. This

Forestry as a Staple Product: Globalization and Industry Restructuring

Northern countries (including Canada) still produce most of the world's lumber, pulp, and paper but cannot meet the global demand. Therefore countries in the southern hemisphere (e.g., Brazil) have experienced rapid deforestation through industrial logging and have also provided locations for forest plantations because the climate supports more rapid tree growth and labour costs are lower.

But automation has played a key role in restructuring the industry which has reduced employment in the industry and has threatened the existence of many logging and mill communities such as in peripheral resource regions of the British Columbia interior. Whereas the forest industry had been highly labour intensive in the past, it is now more capital intensive because of its dependence on expensive machinery which means that large integrated multinational companies have taken over the industry. The interesting global effect is that the northern hemisphere has become then the supplier of both capital and technology to the southern hemisphere forestry industry which serves as a hinterland and exports wood chips with weak employment multipliers. The dual impact of both timber reserve depletion and an automated industry has meant that the capacity of sawmills and pulp mills has far exceeded the availability of raw materials both in Canada and in other parts of the world.

Japan has played a particularly important role in globalizing the forest industry due to its own small forest reserves and its needs for lumber for housing and paper and wood products. In northern Alberta and northern Quebec, for example, Japanese companies like Daishowa and Al-Pac (a conglomerate of three Japanese companies) have become more dominant actors, replacing American companies to a significant degree. Other Asian countries such as Korea and Taiwan are also competing for pulp and paper in the same global market. Thus, an old and historic staples product in Canada is experiencing both industry and globalization changes, especially in comparison to the post-war boom in the industry that ended in the early '80s, which had provided employment for many Canadians.

Source: Based on M. Patricia Marchak, *Logging the Globe* (Montreal: McGill-Queens University Press, 1995).

emphasis on globalization suggests that nation-states are facing an increased transfer of powers and loss of control, and is the other side of the glocalism or glocalization thesis presented in Chapter One.[47] The earlier discussion pointed out that regional or local identities and collective action are a response to weakened political states, and here it is argued that this is the result of the transfer of powers to supra-national structures which threatens the traditional control of the nation-state.

A strong case can be made that the future of nation-states may be at risk, or at least that their role may undergo a significant transformation. *Glocalization* suggests that the international econ-

The Impact of New Media Technologies

The role of the Canadian Radio-television and Telecommunications Commission (CRTC) is to regulate all forms of communications in Canada in the public interest and "to sustain the characteristics which make Canadians and Canada unique." For example, private television licences must achieve a yearly Canadian content level of 60% over a broadcast day to include programming about local and national events and issues. Not only is this approach supposed to help Canadians understand each other better, but it also benefits Canadian film and video industries and provides employment for writers, actors, dancers, musicians, and other artists in Canada.

However, there is a new form of media that uses digital technologies via the Internet and the world wide web and combines text, graphics, data, audio, and various video images that seems to be impervious to traditional forms of regulation. Anyone can place a product or program on the Internet and gain immediate access to a global audience. The Internet appears to be outside the control of traditional national interests because of its borderless distribution.

Forty percent of all households are expected to have access to the internet by 2001, and already 42% of connected households spend over twenty hours per month on-line with 61% connecting at least seven times per week through personal computers or television sets. What would happen if large conglomerates like Disney or MGM were to distribute their video products directly through the Internet thereby bypassing Canadian broadcasting intermediaries? Would this threaten Canadian television stations by taking away both their audiences and their revenue source?

The CRTC investigated this new media and concluded that for now it is complementary rather than a substitute for traditional media. Massive improvements in its technology would also have to occur before it could replace traditional media, but they acknowledged that the Internet does have advantages in being more interactive, unscheduled, and low cost than traditional media which is one-way and high cost in spite of its mass appeal. They also noted the existence of a strong Canadian presence on the Internet. Canadian web sites represent about 5% of all web sites and the use of search engines helps users to identify Canadian sites.

However, it is clear that the Internet demonstrates how changing technologies may make it more difficult to ensure that Canadian content is a major factor in the lives of national residents in the future.

Source: *Report on the New Media,* Canadian Radio-television and Telecommunications Commission, 1999.

omy allows local communities to become much more assertive because they no longer need the old national political structures to ensure their economic well-being as they are now directly linked to the world economy. Quebec, for example, has already argued that whatever form of independence they may seek would always be in association with the global economy and that they have no intentions of isolating themselves from their economic partners. As we will see, other places such as Scotland and Wales are experiencing the same process.

The evidence of how internationalization or globalization is transforming our lives is rather overwhelming.[48] For example, access to information whether for investment purposes or education (including courses for credit) is now available on the Internet from anywhere in the world. Of specific interest in Canadian society is the fact that in 1981, all provinces traded more with each other than they did with the rest of the world.[49] By the mid-1990s, however, only Prince Edward Island exported more to the rest of Canada than to the rest of the world, and some provinces exported more than double to the rest of the world than they exported to Canadian places. Imports showed a similar pattern indicating that trade within Canada is increasingly less important than external trade. But it also means that some regions are internationalized more in some directions (e.g., British Columbia to the Pacific Rim, Ontario to the United States) than others and therefore develop different international alliances. The increasing international role played by levels of government lower than the federal government is known as *intermesticity*.[50]

Globalization is a different phenomenon from anything we have experienced before because it means that national societies like Canada are no longer tied to only a few international partners with whom they have historic relations, but new partnerships and relationships can be established all over the globe for different purposes. As we noted above, it also means that different segments of Canadian society may establish these ties with parts of the world that are quite different from each other. Furthermore, it moves Canadian society away from those old dependency relationships and establishes new relationships with new partners, or provides the dynamic to restructure old relationships. Thus much of what has been presented in the previous four points may have been significantly altered in terms of its effect on Canadians by the new experience of globalization which encourages Canadians to interact with the new world in a more assertive fashion.

There is no better illustration of this new era than the way in which free trade is breaking down old barriers, the end result of which is still unknown. Our discussion of globalization will continue in the next section with specific reference to the role that free trade plays in this reorganization of macro societal issues. However, let it be said here that contemporary globalization is at root the world-wide expansion of capitalist forces that seeks to break down the national barriers to corporate investments and the facilitation of corporate business strategies. Globalization is clearly more complex than that but free trade as a phenomenon reflects this primary objective which happens to have social and cultural consequences.

FREE TRADE: A CASE STUDY IN SOCIETAL AUTONOMY

Background: Globalization as a New Phenomenon

The 1990s began with a series of startling events on the world stage that made us aware that inter-societal relations were changing. Perhaps the most compelling development for Canadians was the end of *bipolarity*, i.e., the end of the Cold War, which matched the Soviet Union and the United States as superpowers and which defined the rest of the world as allies with one or the other of these two political axes. There is no better evidence of the end of the Cold War than a comparison of the "space race" of the 1960s with its competition between the Soviet Union and the United States to land the first person on the moon, with the 1995 launch of a joint Russian/American space expedition. The collapse of the Berlin Wall in 1989 and the disintegration of the Soviet Union in 1991 were stunning developments that also contributed to the end of American hegemony in the West. Whereas Germany and Japan had been propped up by the United States in the post–World War II era as a strategic counterbalance to the Soviet bloc, these two nations in particular had become so strong economically by the 1980s that, at least in important respects, they rivalled the United States. Furthermore, the growth of the European Community and the openness of China suggested that a new world order was developing.

Another aspect of the process which had an impact on Canada is *deindustralization.*[51] Capitalism has moved into a new phase in which capital is highly mobile and is more readily transferred around the globe in order to maximize profits. In the previous pattern known as *Fordism*, manufacturing was domestic and foreign countries were viewed as markets for our goods. Now, with cheaper labour in less-developed countries, capital and industry have been transferred to these locations. This has led to the deindustrialization of the previous industrial countries such as Canada, turning them into service economies. But it has also meant that the Third World is now more intimately linked into the global economy. Check the labels of the clothes you wear and products you buy to verify the extent of this process of deindustrialization. Even when assembly occurs in Canada, there has usually been contracting out of parts for "just-in-time supply" to minimize inventories and costs in what is known as *vertical disintegration*. In other words, the old patterns of industrial development have been significantly restructured in a manner that is bringing the world together in a new way.

Featherstone refers to this new level of persistent international cultural interaction and exchange as the *global ecumene.*[52] Advances in communication, particularly through computers and faxes, make global interaction virtually immediate. Vast pools of capital can be transferred with the push of a button and the media can tell us about it, even with pictures, concurrently regardless of where it happens. In this context, national governments are rendered virtually helpless to control their own destinies, and national societies become more clearly part of a global network. Globalization, then, has taken on a new meaning because it has eroded national boundaries through the internationalization of the production and distribution of goods and services.[53]

Robertson has pointed out that globalization is a natural extension of the welding together of people groups into nation-states, and then the building of international linkages (a kind of "international society") through activities such as the Olympic movement, the United Nations, movements for civil rights, and ecological concerns.[54] But at the same time that these processes contribute to the making of "the-world-as-a-whole," there are also particularizing tendencies to accentuate the local as reflected by the rise of polyethnicity within national societies. Therefore localism (territorially bounded cultures) is in conflict and coexists with cosmopolitanism (transnational and global cultural networks) with considerable overlapping and intermingling.[55] From this perspective, globalization is not about uniformity or homogeneity as much as it is about diversity, but without being limited to demarcated territories.

There is one further aspect to globalization as it is being currently experienced. This is the rise of neoconservatism as the key feature of the current phase of capitalist development. *Neoconservatism* (sometimes called neo-liberalism elsewhere in the world) minimizes any form of government interventionism that impedes the free flow of capital, commodities, or any aspects of culture. The key operative word is *deregulation* of markets, trade, labour, or social policies in order to foster global competitiveness. This emphasis minimizes notions of national sovereignty and threatens to contradict much of the discussion of this chapter. In fact, it could indeed be incompatible with a unique and distinct sense of a Canadian society. If the economic and cultural nationalism of the 1960s and 1970s in

Canada came from the ideological left, then the contemporary triumph of the ideological right with its free market policies could overwhelm concerns about societal autonomy.[56] It will be interesting to observe how the forces of cosmopolitanism and localism affect the pendulum of change in the future.

Canada and Globalization

Foreign direct investment (FDI) is a significant driving force in globalization and the 1990s demonstrated remarkable annual increases in world-wide capital flows.[57] This aspect of the process of globalization has blurred the distinction between "domestic" and "foreign" companies as mergers and acquisitions as well as majority and minority shares make ownerships very complex. Global outflows of capital have increased at an unprecedented rate since 1985. The most significant development of the past decade has been the transformation of the United States from the dominant source country of worldwide direct investment to a major host country of foreign direct investment.[58] Conversely, Japan has had a dramatic increase in its share of foreign direct investment as a source country but not as a host country.

Inward FDI to Canada has doubled in the last ten years and is said to account for 1.3 million jobs, half of all exports, and three-quarters of all manufacturing exports.[59] In 1987, 66% of inward FDI came from the United States. But that share has been declining (to 52% by 1997) with increases from the European Union (but not the United Kingdom) and Asian countries. It is argued that the purpose of inward capital flows was formerly primarily to access the Canadian market but now is considered a means to access the North American market as the result of free trade. It is also argued that FDI contributes to technology transfer such as when Ericsson of Sweden brought their technology to Montreal and set up a plant hiring 800 Canadian engineers. This certainly changes the old concept of what subsidiaries do in Canada. In one case, a French vaccine manufacturer established an operation in Toronto with the explicit corporate strategy of giving it a specific project which would not be carried out anywhere else in their system. FDI is said to change the way the entire corporate community thinks and gives it an outward orientation rather than just serving the Canadian market.

Figure 2.2 shows how inward flows of capital (FDI) have increased since 1980. But it also shows that Canada is not just the recipient of inward capital flows but that Canadian companies also participate in outflows of capital known as *Canadian direct investment abroad (CDIA)*. In fact, by 1996, outflows exceeded inflows for the first time. The United States continues as the destination of the majority of the investment abroad, but its share is declining and European countries, Japan, and Mexico's share is increasing as well as numerous other countries in the world. This evidence demonstrates most clearly the globalization of capital and the fact that the traditional dependencies and linkages to the United Kingdom and the United States have been considerably modified and globalized. Canada is clearly part of the global economy in which national sovereignty has become a questionable concept. Similar patterns of increased FDI and CDIA can be found among other countries with active investment economies.

Free Trade: Context and Controversy

The collapse of the Soviet Union and the Soviet bloc, coupled with the rise of the European Community, Japan, and China, has clearly altered the position of the United States in the world. One of the key aspects of this global realignment has been the emergence of regional trading blocs which removes protectionist barriers among linked countries in the name of economic growth. Given the transformations occurring in the non-communist world, and specifically the emergence of the strength of the European Community as a trading bloc, the United States sought to cement its relationship with its continental partners, particularly Canada and Mexico. Canada, on the other hand, was aware that the United States was its largest trading partner (and vice versa) and that Canadian industries might be healthier if they had guaranteed access to American markets. *Free trade*, then, represents a special case of globalization in which countries form trading blocs to enhance economic interchanges in the face of increasing competition and to enhance access to each other's markets. Because free trade for Canada has meant lowering historic barriers to the United States, it raises once again the issue of societal autonomy and the influence of its age-old friend and American nemesis.

The matter of free trade with the United States is not a new phenomenon.[60] What is new is that after explicitly being rejected in 1891 and 1911, and considered several times since and turned aside, in 1989 free trade with the United States become law as Bill C-130. Free trade was the major issue in the 1988 federal election won by the Mulroney Conservative government. At least partly because of its alliance with business interests such as domestic manufacturers, the Conservative party, previously always the champion of Canadian protectionism, reversed course and became the champion of free trade. What reasons can be advanced for why free trade became acceptable? Some of these reasons can be listed briefly.

One of the key aspects of this decision was that the Report of the Macdonald Royal Commission released in 1985 lent considerable weight and credibility to the idea of free trade. The global realities of European and Asian trading blocs made it apparent that in the absence of international trade agreements, Canada's access to foreign markets could be reduced. Of greatest concern was the growing mood of protectionism in the United States which ostensibly threatened the trade relationship with Canada's largest trading partner. If the international trading climate was changing, then indeed, Canada needed a new trade policy in order to ensure a growing rather than a declining economy. The fact that unemployment was high in the eighties as a result of the recession only made the promise of jobs

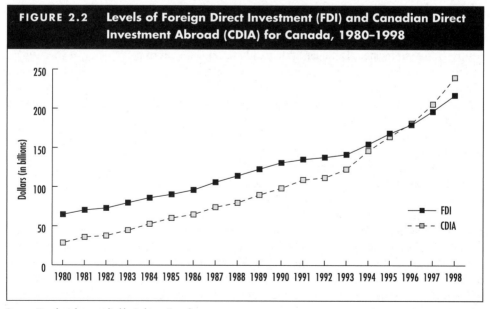

FIGURE 2.2   Levels of Foreign Direct Investment (FDI) and Canadian Direct Investment Abroad (CDIA) for Canada, 1980–1998

Source: Based on data supplied by Industry Canada.

more compelling. So the Macdonald Royal Commission recommended that adjustments be made to Canadian policies that were more adaptive to new international conditions and possessed a more market-driven and competitive approach.[61]

In view of the assumption that Canadian industries were inefficient as a consequence of protectionism, it was argued that a free trade-driven "growing" economy would result from greater access to the larger US market. Some Canadian businesses were already obtaining access to the American market by setting up subsidiaries in the US to service that market. The argument was that the new jobs created as a result of an expanded market should be created in Canada. It was also argued that the sectoral trade agreement in automotives (known as the Auto Pact) had already created significant prosperity in Ontario and Quebec, and other regions wanted to experience similar benefits.

From a different perspective, free trade could be considered the natural next step in an economy that already had a substantial foreign presence.[62] But the support of the Canadian business community, and in particular the Canadian Manufacturers' Association that had always advocated protectionism, was a significant reversal for many who now wanted to be more competitive and have "preferred access" to American markets.[63] The Business Council on National Issues (BCNI), which included the executives of the most important corporations in Canada, was a key vehicle as well in supporting free trade.

Whatever the reasons, and they are far more complex than sketched here, free trade did become acceptable to the business community which in turn made considerable efforts to convince the general public.[64] The anti-free trade forces were represented by the Pro-Canada Network, a coalition of interest groups (e.g., labour, environment, some women's groups) while the Canadian Alliance for Trade and Job Opportunities represented business as pro–free trade.

Why was free trade so controversial?[65] In the first place, there was no guarantee that a bilateral agreement would create more jobs in Canada. In fact, one fear was that companies would decide to move out of Canada to places like the American deep south or Mexico where pools of cheap labour were available, and then service the Canadian market from there. Since some American states had low minimum wage laws and there was no package of benefits (e.g., medicare) to which employers were required to contribute, Canadian firms would be more competitive if they relocated. But even if they did not relocate out of the country, it was argued that they would bargain for a "level playing field" so that Canada would have to withdraw its distinct social programs in order to be competitive with firms in the United States. So it was anticipated that the net result could be fewer jobs in Canada, particularly if US subsidiaries in Canada, without the incentives of tariff protection, closed their plants.

A second fear was that free trade might make it difficult for the Canadian state to use policy instruments (e.g., financial aid, procurement practices, subsidies, and local content rules) to accomplish certain national objectives without reprisal. For example, equalization grants to poorer regions or agricultural subsidies had been accepted aspects of Canadian life. If your trading partner perceives these as unfair subsidies, a countervailing duty could be imposed on the product entering their country which would put the sale of the product at a competitive disadvantage. Would the Canadian government then lose its sovereignty to deal with segments of its own society as it sees fit? Can the government subsidize a company to establish a plant in an economically depressed region of Canada without fear of the challenge of unfair competition? Can seasonal industries such as fishing and lumbering be subsidized without risking a reaction from the government of the importing country that the free trade agreement has been violated? Thus, among concerns about free trade were the loss (rather than gain) of jobs, the threat to social programs, and the lack of government policy control.

Third, free trade was also controversial because of its socio-cultural implications. If barriers between Canada and the United States were removed, would it mean the free exchange of labour and culture? Would it eventually mean that job opportunities in Canada, for example, could not be restricted to Canadians in the first instance? Presumably Canadians would also have access to employment in the United States as well which, potentially, would ensure more intermingling of people in both countries. Would it mean that various elements of American popular culture (e.g., magazines, films, and books) would have free entry to Canada and thereby overwhelm the fledgling Canadian cultural industry which would lose its protection? In other words, is it possible that free trade would ultimately mean the erasure of the border between the US and Canada? From this perspective, free trade was much more than an economic agreement; it raised questions about the independence, sovereignty, and distinctiveness of Canadian society in relation to the United States. How much economic integration is possible without losing cultural and policy independence?

An Evaluation

Free trade puts the emphasis on harmonization rather than sovereignty. *Sovereignty* refers to the capacity of a nation-state to control its own destiny; *harmonization* emphasizes the creation of similar rules, policies, and regulations between nation-states. Free trade, then, establishes the policies whereby nation-states encounter each other as similarly as possible—at least in matters of commerce and public policy. In this context, it becomes clear why free trade is a vital issue in societal autonomy. The problem is that it is difficult to ascertain whether harmonization and sovereignty are mutually compatible or whether, in the long run, they are in radical opposition to each other.

Currency Harmonization

Will the US dollar replace the loonie? Should there be a common currency between Canada and the United States?

The Canadian government says there is no way it would consider the elimination of a separate Canadian currency in what is called *policy dollarization*. However, *market dollarization* already exists. This is the use of the US dollar by some Canadians in everything from holding a US dollar account in a Canadian bank to corporations reporting their financial results in US dollars.

Some see the devalued Canadian dollar as giving Canadian companies a market advantage and a cost advantage because Canadian goods become cheaper in the US market, and argue that therefore policy dollarization would be a bad thing. Others say US dollars have become a worldwide standard so any company doing international business needs to find a common benchmark. Some sports teams (including the National Hockey League) and multinational corporations operating in Canada pay their employees in US dollars. If organizations increasingly have at least some of their expenses in US dollars but most of their revenue in comparatively devalued Canadian dollars, how much longer can currency harmonization be resisted?

Would monetary union with the United States mean that economic policy would really be made in the United States? Would it provide more economic stability? What about the issue of national sovereignty?

In 1994, the Canada-US free trade zone was extended to Mexico in what is known as the *North American Free Trade Agreement (NAFTA)*. It was claimed that NAFTA countries comprised the largest free trade zone in the world with 360 million people compared to the 325 million of the European Community. Mexico had been a highly regulated socialist state which, with its low wage economy, perhaps had the most to gain from NAFTA. The benefits for Canada were not considered to be substantial, though free trade with Mexico did provide some new opportunities for Canadian industries at the same time that Mexico's cheap labour also seemed a threat. But the inexorable forces of internationalism have gone beyond continentalism to include hemispherism in discussions with Latin American nations to form a future Free Trade Agreement of the Americas (FTAA). Thus the three forces of *continentalism*, *hemispherism*, and *globalism* provide a striking alternative to the isolationist–protectionist outlook that dominated Canadian thinking for so long, and which surely must have socio-cultural consequences.[66]

It is difficult to assess the impact of these free trade initiatives on Canadian society because there are so many complicating factors.[67] On the positive side, new jobs have been created and trade with the United States has grown greatly including both exports to the United States and imports from the United States. The two countries have become much closer economic partners. On the negative side is the fact that jobs have also been lost as the result of free trade and it is difficult at this point to determine the net effect on balance in employment. For example, manufacturing jobs may have been lost but knowledge industry jobs may have been created. What we do know is that the unemployment rate continues to be higher in Canada, productivity is somewhat lower, and Canada's share of global FDI has decreased somewhat. Spending on social programs has decreased and there is a higher incidence of inequality.

What is indisputable is that free trade submerges Canada in a trading bloc with the more powerful United States and renews continentalist pressures. Free trade has meant that Canada's economic dependence on the United States has grown. This fact can be interpreted both positively and negatively. Some see this trend as inevitable anyway given what is happening in the global economy and feel therefore that this linkage should be celebrated. Others view this trend as a huge step in the direction of Canada losing its sovereignty altogether as it is drawn into the American orbit where the superior economic strength of the United States prevents Canada from truly being an equal in this partnership. For example, there is increasing pressure for the lowering of tax rates in Canada to ensure that Canadian businesses are more competitive with American businesses. This could mean that the social safety nets (such as medicare) which have been characteristic of Canadian society and a deliberate attempt to make it "a kinder and gentler society" than American society could be threatened if there is not the tax base to support it.[68] We have already seen how Canada's concern to protect its cultural industries by excluding it from free trade agreements became problematic when the United States defined these industries as businesses rather than culture.

Thus the success of free trade is clearly mixed. The evaluation of free trade is also dependent on your perspective and point of view. It is also complicated by other factors such as the role the exchange rate gap has played and the role played by the European Union or the recession in Asia in contributing to restructuring. What is clear is that the Canada–US border is no longer the same economic barrier that it once was and there will be increasing pressures to make it even more permeable if not to remove it in significant ways. [69] The implications of greater economic union, whether or not it leads to greater political integration, brings us back again to the quotation from George Grant (written in 1965) on the first page of this chapter.

Differing Perspectives

Structural Functionalism

The structural functionalist perspective understands Canadian society as part of a complex international system in which different countries play different roles in the world economy. Canadian development needs to be understood as a natural result of the expansion of more dominant societies because Canada possessed raw materials needed by empire economies. Over time this role has changed somewhat, yet Canada is part of a huge global exchange system in which we must constantly search for new niches. There is little point in worrying about independence because that is not possible in the contemporary world. What is needed is to develop the society's own assets (e.g., people skills, creative technologies, cultural icons) so that Canada's contribution to the global system is obvious and important. In short, in a global economy, each society has its own role, and it is up to its residents to enhance that role through deliberate effort.

Conflict

The conflict perspective points out that the international economy is essentially one of unequal relationships. Some societies are more dominant than others because they are more powerful and are able to subordinate other societies. It is not merely a matter of economic power but also military power, cultural power, and ideological power. But it is economic power, and especially the role of the capitalist class in seeking to maximize its profits, that establishes a global dynamic.

While Canada has never seen itself as a world power, Canadians depend on societies with lower labour costs to provide many of the things that are part of their daily life. So as an intermediate society, Canadians feel exploited at the same time that they participate in the exploitation of weaker societies. However, from the point of view of Canada's attempt to sustain its own sovereignty, the globalization of the economy only draws Canada into American dependency more tightly, and the Americanization of Canada will continue unless deliberate efforts at resistance occur.

Symbolic Interactionism

The symbolic interactionist perspective focuses not so much on economic relations between societies but on how societies develop their own cultural attributes within the world. How do cultural distinctions develop and how do societies share their culture? The unique histories of each society in interaction with other societies helps to explain where elements of culture have originated but also forces us to look for ways in which local peoples modify what they have received to make it their own through a process of sifting and exchange. What is interesting is how Canadian society has indeed developed its own institutions, its heroes, and its own dialects or colloquialisms (e.g., *toque, eh*?) in spite of globalizing pressures. So while there are many instances of foreign symbols operating in Canada, there are also many ways in which these symbols have been Canadianized.

FOREIGN INFLUENCE RECONSIDERED

The extent to which foreign influence is problematic for Canadian society is open to much debate. While, occasionally, nationalist arguments provoke widespread support, the majority of Canadians have accepted the standard and quality of living that has come with at least partial continental integration. Those who felt most disadvantaged by the old order (e.g., persons outside the industrial heartland) were the most likely to support continentalism.[70] On the other hand, those clamouring most strongly for economic and cultural nationalism seemed to be those with the most to gain from protectionism (e.g., the middle class and working class). It is more than coincidental that the widest public concern for societal autonomy came during the 1960s and 1970s when a large wave of young university-educated persons were entering the workforce and wanted employment protected in Canada. It appears that many of the current new university graduates have a different view about opportunities being enlarged by opening the borders. In fact, a 1999 study showed that most Canadians are optimistic about the consequences of globalization, a situation that represents a significant change of attitude from the beginning of the 1990s. While Canada is still considerably dependent on the export of raw materials, most young Canadians think of Canada more as a high-technology economy with a major role to play on the world stage.[71]

Yet support for integration that fosters economic growth is not necessarily the same as support for complete integration, though it may be a slippery slope from one to the other. We have seen in this chapter that there are enormous pressures at the level of popular culture, for example, and Americanization may be an overwhelming force. Yet there may be other factors that resist such integration and act to sustain an indigenous Canadian culture. In other words, while we may embrace many elements of American culture, we still modify and reformulate at least some of what we do absorb in a manner which is peculiarly Canadian.[72] But an empirical study of the values of Canadians, Americans, and Mexicans concluded that along with free trade as an economic phenomenon, there has also taken place a convergence of values (for example, in how citizens view government) that suggests that political boundaries are less important and that a fundamental value shift is occurring everywhere toward a post-materialist culture.[73]

Even at the economic level, some have argued that criticizing foreign capital does not get at the root of the matter because corporations (whether Canadian or foreign) do not make decisions on the basis of the national good but, rather, on the basis of profit.[74] Others argue that the repatriation of the economy has been made a faulty panacea.[75] Still others have argued that integration theory is wrong to assert that considerable interaction will lead to the breakdown of national attributes and the creation of a single polity. Instead, when two units interact with uneven capacity, a self-regulator in the smaller nation may inhibit the integrative process.[76] In fact, what we see in Canadian–American relations is just such a partial integration. One analyst has described Canadian–American relations as a *disparate dyad* because in spite of the inequality, Canada's goal has been to rearrange the nature of the relationship rather than terminate it, for termination would be unrealistic.[77] Thus, it could be argued that in continually seeking to control the nature of that relationship, Canadian society is expressing its autonomy.

The objective struggle to maintain that precarious balance between integration and independence has had its subjective effects. The *cumulative impact hypothesis* suggests that all of the debate and controversy, as well as the realities engendered by Canada's dependent position over so many years, have produced a feeling of society *inferiority*.[78] These feelings reveal themselves in the *mixed emotions* of envy and admiration towards more dominant societies which serve as models, and also in the expression of hostility and antagonism in the struggle against subordination.

It is impossible to understand Canadian society without knowing of this perpetual search for autonomy. In fact, S.D. Clark has argued that historically in struggling to discover itself, the society attempted to discover *what it is not* by distinguishing itself from American society.[79] This resulted in a *paranoiac* form of *nationalism* based on a sense of persecution and powerlessness which sometimes had little positive content or which sought protection in Britain as mother country. Ironically now globalization has brought with it the twin themes of deregulation and privatization—both of which minimize the role of the state which had played a key role in providing protection from at least some external forces. The meaning of sovereignty in this context is thus in transition as Canadians are left to seek new methods to sustain their society on the horns of the integration–independence dilemma. The recurring attempts to take control of its own destiny is the more *positive* side of society-building which will be discussed in Chapter Seven.

FURTHER EXPLORATION

1. Some people think that one way out of the continentalism dilemma in Canadian society is to support economic continentalism alongside cultural nationalism. Assess the merits and problems of this position. Is it possible through free trade?
2. What staples are characteristic of your province? How do those staples tie your province into the world system?
3. Take a position on the foreign ownership question. Defend your position with whatever examples you can find and anticipate criticisms from people who hold other positions on the same issue.
4. What do you think the impact of free trade has been? Watch for illustrations in your newspaper and bring them to class for discussion.

SELECTED READINGS

Barry, Donald (ed.), *Toward a North American Community* (Boulder:Westview, 1995).

Flaherty, David H. and Frank E. Manning (eds), *The Beaver Bites Back? American Popular Culture in Canada* (Montreal: McGill-Queens University Press, 1993).

Hillmer, Norman, ed. *Partners Nevertheless: Canadian-American Relations in the Twentieth Century.* Toronto: Copp Clark Pitman, 1989.

Teeple, Gary. *Globalization and the Decline of Social Reform.* Toronto: Garamond Press, 1995.

ENDNOTES

1   Gordon Laxer has argued that Canada had more independence by the beginning of the Second World War when the influences of Britain and the United States were more balanced. But that balance was lost by the end of the war when the United States became a pre-eminent world power, and especially when the Cold War drew sharp battlelines between the east and west. "Constitutional Crises And Continentalism: Twin Threats To Canada's Continued Existence," *Canadian Journal of Sociology* 17(2)1992:218.

2   See Immanuel Wallerstein, *The Modern World System* (New York: Academic Press, 1976) and Daniel Chirot, *Social Change in the Twentieth Century* (New York: Harcourt, Brace, and Jovanovich, 1977) for discussions of world systems theory. For its adaptation to Canada, cf. Lorna R. Marsden and Edward B. Harvey, *Fragile Federation: Social Change in Canada* (Toronto: McGraw-Hill Ryerson, 1979).

3   H.A. Innis, *The Fur Trade in Canada* (Toronto: University of Toronto Press, 1930); *The Cod Fisheries* (Toronto: University of Toronto Press, 1940); *Problems of Staple Production in Canada* (Toronto: Ryerson Press, 1933).

4   S.D. Clark, *The Social Development of Canada* (Toronto: University of Toronto Press, 1942).

5   Rex Lucas, Minetown, Milltown, *Railtown: Life in Canadian Communities of a Single Industry* (Toronto: University of Toronto Press, 1971). For a further discussion of some of the problems pro-

duced for human populations by big industry in small towns, see Roy T. Bowles, ed., *Little Communities and Big Industries: Studies in the Social Impact of Canadian Resource Extraction* (Toronto: Butterworths, 1982).

6   For illustrations of these problems in the mining industry, see Wallace Clement, *Hardrock Mining: Industrial Relations and Technological Change at Inco* (Toronto: McClelland and Stewart, 1980).

7   Donald G. Paterson, *British Direct Investment in Canada*, 1890–1914 (Toronto: University of Toronto Press, 1983).

8   Richard Starks, *Industry in Decline* (Toronto: James Lorimer, 1978), 71.

9   Corporations and Labour Unions Act Report for 1986, Part I Corporations, Statistics Canada Catalogue #61-210, 21.

10   Note that a corporation is not reported as foreign unless it is at least 50% foreign-owned. Edward Grabb, "Who Owns Canada? Concentration of Ownership and the Distribution of Economic Assets, 1975–1985," *Journal of Canadian Studies* 25(1992): 72–93.

11   Statistics Canada Catalogue No. 61-220-XPB, 1995 and 1996.

12   See also Daniel M. Shapiro, *Foreign and Domestic Firms in Canada* (Toronto: Butterworths, 1980), 74, regarding the profitability of American firms.

13   This argument can be found in a number of places including Patricia Marchak, *In Whose Interests: An Essay on Multinational Corporations in a Canadian Context* (Toronto: McClelland and Stewart, 1979), 101; Wallace Clement, *Continental Corporate Power* (Toronto: McClelland Stewart, 1977), 79; and R.J. Richardson, "Merchants Against Industry: An Empirical Study of the Canadian Debate," *Canadian Journal of Sociology* 7(1982): 279–95, who argues that merchant capital and industrial capital merged.

14   Gordon Laxer, "Foreign Ownership and Myths About Canadian Development," *Canadian Review of Sociology and Anthropology* 22(1985): 311–45; and his *Open for Business: The Roots of Foreign Ownership in Canada* (Toronto: Oxford University Press, 1989).

15   M.H. Watkins, *Foreign Ownership and the Structure of Canadian Industry, Report of the Task Force on the Structure of Canadian Industry* (Ottawa: Privy Council, 1968); Gray Report, *Foreign Direct Investment in Canada* (Ottawa: Information Canada, 1972). See also A.E. Safarian, *Foreign Ownership of Canadian Industry* (Toronto: McGraw Hill, 1966); a good introductory discussion in Malcolm Levine and Christine Sylvester, *Foreign Ownership* (Toronto: General Publishing, 1972); and a good retrospective discussion in Michael Bliss, "American Investment," in Norman Hillmer, ed., *Partners Nevertheless: Canadian-American Relations in the Twentieth Century* (Toronto: Copp Clark Pitman, 1989), 259–70.

16   Abraham Rotstein and Gary Lax, *Independence: The Canadian Challenge* (Toronto: The Committee For An Independent Canada, 1972); and *Getting It Back: A Program for Canadian Independence* (Toronto: Clarke Irwin, 1974).

17   See Erick Jackson, ed., *The Great Canadian Debate: Foreign Ownership* (Toronto: McClelland and Stewart, 1975).

18   As manpower importation relates to universities, see Robin Matthews and James Steele, *The Struggle for Canadian Universities* (Toronto: New Press, 1969); as it relates to other areas, see Ian Lumsden, ed., *Close the 49th Parallel: The Americanization of Canada* (Toronto: University of Toronto Press, 1970).

19   John Meisel speaks of a mass-elite dichotomy on this issue with better educated high income groups more interested in indigenous cultural products. "Escaping Extinction: Cultural Defense of an Undefended Border," in D.H. Flaherty and W.R. McKercher, eds., *Southern Exposure: Canadian Perspectives on the United States* (Toronto: McGraw-Hill Ryerson, 1986), 155–56.

20   For a good review of the issues in American influences on Canadian broadcasting policy, see Bruce Feldthusen, "Awakening From The National Broadcasting Dream: Rethinking Television Regulation For National Cultural Goals", in David H. Flaherty and Frank E. Manning (eds.), *The*

Beaver Bites Back? American Popular Culture in Canada (Montreal: McGill-Queens University Press, 1993), 42–74.

21 For a good review of all of the cultural industries in Canada from newspapers to film to music, see Michael Dorland (ed.), *The Cultural Industries of Canada: Problems, Policies, and Prospects* (Toronto: Lorimer, 1996).

22 Reader's Digest was initially also the target of Bill C-58 but it was exempted on the ground that it was not news-oriented. For a discussion of some of the issues in this debate, see Isaiah Litvak and Christopher Maule, *Cultural Sovereignty: The Time and Reader's Digest Case in Canada* (New York, Praeger, 1974); and M. Patricia Hindley, Gail M. Martin and Jean McNulty, *The Tangled Net: Basic Issues in Canadian Communications* (Vancouver: J.J. Douglas, 1977), chap. 2. For a more recent discussion of cultural industries (especially film, broadcasting, and publishing) in the pre- and post-NAFTA era, see Peter Karl Kresl, "The Political Economy Of Canada's Cultural Policy", in Andre Lapierre, Patricia Smart, and Pierre Savard (eds.), *Language, Culture and Values in Canada at the dawn of the 21st Century* (Ottawa: Carleton University Press, International Council For Canadian Studies, 1996), 223–245.

23 For a good review of the issues, see Janice L. Murray, ed., *Canadian Cultural Nationalism* (New York: New York University Press, 1977); and S.M. Crean, *Who's Afraid of Canadian Culture?* (Don Mills, Ont.: General Publishing, 1976).

24 Guy Rocher, *A General Introduction to Sociology* (Toronto: Macmillan, 1972), 513–14.

25 The concept of empire developed here has been influenced by the work of George Grant who has applied it to Canada's relationship with the United States. See his *Technology and Empire: Perspectives on North America* (Toronto: House of America, 1969); and *Lament for a Nation* (Toronto: McClelland and Stewart, 1965), 8. See also John Hutcheson, *Dominance and Dependency* (Toronto: McClelland and Stewart, 1978), chap. 3, and Michael W. Doyle, *Empires* (Cornell University Press, 1986).

26 For example, see Joel Kurtzman, *The Decline and Crash of the American Economy* (New York: W.W. Norton, 1988); Pearl M. Kramer, *The US Economy in Crisis* (New York: Praeger, 1988); and Bertrand Bellon and Jorge Niosi, *The Decline of the American Economy* (Toronto: Black Rose, 1988); and "Whither The American Empire: Expansion or Contraction?" *Special Issue of The Annals of the American Academy of Political and Social Science*, 500 (1988).

27 Kari Levitt, Silent Surrender: *The Multi-National Corporation in Canada* (Toronto: Macmillan, 1971), 112.

28 See Harry H. Hiller, "Continentalism and the Third Force in Religion," *Canadian Journal of Sociology* 3 (1978): 183–207.

29   Norman Hillmer, ed., *Partners Nevertheless: Canadian-American Relations in the Twentieth Century* (Toronto: Copp Clark Pitman, 1989); and R. Lecker (ed.), *Borderlands: Essays in Canadian-American Relations* (Toronto: ECW Press, 1991).

30 John W. Holmes, *Life with Uncle: The Canadian-American Relationship* (Toronto: University of Toronto Press, 1981).

31 Jorge Niosi, *Canadian Multinationals* (Toronto: Between the Lines, 1985).

32 Susan Goldenberg, *Men of Property: The Canadian Developers Who are Buying America* (Toronto: Personal Library, 1981); Steven Globerman, *Canadian-Based Multinationals* (Calgary: University Of Calgary Press, 1994); Wendy Evans, Henry Lane, and Shawna O'Grady, *Border Crossings: Doing Business in the United States* (Scarborough, Prentice-Hall, 1992). At one point in the early 1980s, Oxford Development Group of Edmonton controlled about 40% of the downtown office space in Minneapolis. *Calgary Herald*, August 28, 1981.

33 For a discussion of these points, see George Modelski, ed., *Multinational Corporations and World Order* (Beverly Hills: Sage, 1972), 20–24.

34 Patricia Marchak, In Whose Interests, 102. See also her second edition of *Ideological Perspectives on Canada* (Toronto: McGraw-Hill Ryerson, 1981), particularly Chapter 8 expressing her pessimism about the role of multinational corporations.

35 C.S. Burchill, "The Multi-National Corporation: An Unsolved Problem in International Relations," *Queen's Quarterly* 77(1970): 3–18.

36 For a study of a Japanese transplant auto assembly plant in Ingersoll, Ontario, see James Rinehart, Christopher Huxley, and David Robertson, *Just Another Car Factory? Lean Production and its Dissidents* (Ithaca, N.Y.: ILR Press, 1997).

37 A.A. Fatouros, "Multi-National Enterprises and Extraterritoriality," *Journal of Contemporary Business* 1(1972): 36.

38 Kari Levitt, *Silent Surrender*, 108.

39 J.D. House, "The Social Organization of Multi-National Corporations: Canadian Subsidiaries in the Oil Industry," *Canadian Review of Sociology and Anthropology* 14(1977): 1–14.

40 For an interesting study of seven multinational corporations in Canada, see I.A. Litvak, C.J. Maule, and R.D. Robinson, *Dual Loyalty: Canadian-US Business Arrangements*. For a reverse study of Canadian multinational corporations, see I.A. Litvak and C.J. Maule, *The Canadian Multinationals* (Toronto: Butterworths, 1981). See also Ahmed Idris-Soven, and Mary K. Vaughan, eds., *The World as a Company Town* (The Hague: Mouton, 1978).

41 *Foreign Direct Investment in Canada*, chap. 12.

42 Robert L. Perry, Galt USA.: *The American Presence in a Canadian City* (Toronto: Maclean-Hunter, 1971), 36.

43 J.H. Dales, *The Protective Tariff in Canada's Development* (Toronto: University off Toronto Press, 1966), particularly Chapter 6.

44 This is essentially the argument of Wallace Clement, most clearly presented in his Class Power and Property: *Essays on Canadian Society* (Toronto: Methuen, 1983), chap. 3.

45 See Rex Lucas, *Minetown, Milltown, Railtown*, 338.

46 Wallace Clement and Glen Williams, "Resources And Manufacturing In Canada's Political Economy", in Wallace Clement (ed.), *Understanding Canada: Building on the New Canadian Political Economy* (Montreal: McGill-Queens University Press, 1997), 56.

47 Thomas J. Courchene, "CHASTE And Chastened: Canada's New Social Contract", in Raymond B. Blake, Penny E. Bryden, J. Frank Strain (eds.), *The Welfare State in Canada: Past, Present, and Future* (Toronto: Irwin, 1997), 11–13.

48 Ted Schrecker (ed.), *Surviving Globalism: The Social and Environmental Challenge* (New York: St. Martins, 1997).

49 Thomas J. Courchene, "CHASTE and Chastened: Canada's New Social Contract", in Raymond B.Blake, Penny E.Bryden, and J. Frank Strain (eds.), *The Welfare State in Canada* (Toronto: Irwin, 1997), 11–13.

50 Earl H. Fry, "Regional Economic Development Strategies In Canada And The United States: Linkages Between Subnational, National And Global Settings," *International Journal of Canadian Studies* 16(1997):69:91.

51 Ricardo Grinspun and Maxwell A. Cameron, *The Political Economy of North American Free Trade* (Kingston: McGill-Queens University Press, 1993).

52 Mike Featherstone, ed., *Global Culture: Nationalism, Globalization, and Modernity* (Newbury Park, CA.: Sage, 1990), 6.

53 Two excellent references on the process of globalization are M. Albrow and E. King, eds., *Globalization, Knowledge, and Society* (London: Sage, 1990); and Roland Robertson, *Globalization: Social Theory and Global Culture* (Newbury Park, CA: Sage, 1992).

54 Roland Robertson, "Mapping the Global Condition: Globalization as the Central Concept" in Mike Featherstone (ed.), *Global Culture: Nationalism, Globalization and Modernity*, 24–28.

55 Ulf Hannerz, "Cosmopolitans and Locals in World Culture," in Mike Featherstone, ed., *Global Culture: Nationalism, Globalization, and Modernity*, 237–51.

56 The notion that neoconservatism as an ideology is incompatible with the continued existence of Canada and that the damage already done is difficult to reverse is proposed by Stephen McBride and John Shields, *Dismantling a Nation: Canada and the New World Order* (Halifax: Fernwood, 1993).

57 *World Investment Report 1998.*

58 Industry Canada, *Economic Integration in North America: Trends in Foreign Direct Investment,* 1994 (Ottawa: Minister Of Supply And Services, 1995), Charts 2 and 3.

59 From a speech given by John Manley, "Who Benefits From Foreign Investment?", Industry Canada 1999. See also "Consultation Paper On WTO/FTAA Investment", Department Of Foreign Affairs And International Trade, 1999.

60 For a history of free trade as a societal issue, see J.L. Granatstein, "Free Trade Between Canada and the United States: The Issue That Will Not Go Away," in Dennis Stairs and Gilbert R. Winham, *The Politics of Canada's Economic Relationship with the United States* (Toronto: University of Toronto Press, 1985), 11–54

61 One of the key elements of the Commission's recommendations was the reduction of government ownership or federal subsidies which had been used for many years to sustain national sovereignty in various ways. For an abridged version of the report of the Royal Commission, see Rod McQueen, *Leap Of Faith* (Toronto: Gowan, 1985). See also a special issue of *Canadian Public Policy*, XII Supplement, February 1986 for a series of reviews of the final Report. Many of the critiques of free trade also assess the Report.

62 R. Jack Richardson, "Free Trade: Why Did It Happen?", *Canadian Review of Sociology and Anthropology* 29(1992): 316.

63 C. Bruce Doern and Brian W. Tomlin, *Faith and Fear: The Free Trade Story* (Toronto: Stoddart, 1991), 46–49, 103–110.

64 William G. Watson, "Canada-US Free Trade: Why Now?", *Canadian Public Policy* 13(1987): 337–49.

65 For good overviews of what was at issue at the time of the free trade negotiations, see C.D. McLachlan, A. Apuzzo, and W.A. Kerr, "The Canada-U.S Free Trade Agreement: A Canadian Perspective," *Journal of World Trade* (1988): 9–33; Robert M. Campbell and Leslie M. Pal, *The Real World of Canadian Politics* (Peterborough: Broadview, 1989), 315–68 which also includes an abridged summary of the agreement; Gordon Ritchie, *Wrestling with the Elephant: The Inside Story of the Canada-US Free Trade Negotiations* (Toronto: Macfarlane and Ross, 1997); and Michael Hart, *Decision at Midnight: Inside the Canada-US Free Trade Negotiations* (Vancouver: UBC Press, 1994).

66 These concepts are discussed in Alan K. Henrikson, "The US 'North American' Trade Concept: Continentalist, Hemispherist, or Globalist?", in Donald Barry (ed.), *Toward a North American Community? Canada, the United States, and Mexico* (Boulder: Westview, 1995), 155–184.

67 There are many attempts to assess free trade and its consequences. In addition to sources cited in this chapter, other references that take a variety of perspectives include Steven Globerman and Michael Walker, *Assessing NAFTA: A Trinational Analysis* (Vancouver: Fraser Institute, 1993); A. R. Riggs and Tom Velk, eds., *Beyond NAFTA: An Economic, Political, and Sociological Perspective* (Vancouver: Fraser Institute, 1993); Nora Lustig, Barry P. Bosworth and Robert Z. Lawrence, eds., *North American Free Trade: Assessing the Impact* (Washington, D.C.: The Brookings Institute, 1992); Ann Weston, Ada Piazze-McMahon, and Ed Dosman, *Free Trade With A Human Face? The Social Dimensions of CUFTA and NAFTA* (Ottawa: North South Institute, 1992); Andrew Jackson, *Impacts of the Free Trade Agreement (FTA) and the North America Free Trade Agreement (NAFTA) on Canadian Labour Markets and Labour and Social Standards* (Ottawa: Canadian Labour Congress, 1997); Mel Watkins, ed., *Alternatives to the Free Trade Agreement* (Ottawa: Canadian Centre For Policy Alternatives, 1988).

68 For a discussion of this issue in a global perspective, see Gary Teeple, *Globalization and the Decline of Social Reform* (Toronto: Garamond, 1995).

69 See, for example, Lawrence Martin, "Continental Union," *Annals of the American Academy of Political and Social Science* 538(1995):143–150.

70 In an earlier study, Carl Cuneo found that underprivileged groups (e.g., those with low education, low family income, older people, and residents of Atlantic Canada) were most likely to support continentalism because they presumed they had nothing to gain by retaining the old order. "The Social Basis Of Political Continentalism In Canada," *Canadian Review of Sociology and Anthropology* 13(1976): 55–70.

71 The study was done by Ekos Research Associates and was reported in the *Calgary Herald*, July 10, 1999.

72 The thesis that Canadian culture has been Americanized, at the same time that American hegemony has been resisted through a reconstitution or recontextualization of American culture in Canada rather than simply passive acceptance of it is the theme of David H. Flaherty and Frank E. Manning (eds.), *The Beaver Bites Back? American Popular Culture in Canada.*

73 Ronald Inglehart, Neil Nevitte, and Miguel Basanez, *The North American Trajectory: Cultural, Economic, and Political Ties Among the United States, Canada, and Mexico* (New York: Aldine De Gruyter, 1996).

74 See Jorge Niosi, *Canadian Capitalism: A Study of Power in the Canadian Business Establishment* (Toronto: James Lorimer, 1981); Gary Teeple, ed., *Capitalism and the National Question in Canada* (Toronto: University of Toronto Press, 1972).

75 John G. Craig, "What is a Good Corporate Citizen?", *Canadian Review of Sociology and Anthropology* 1 (1979): 181–96.

76 Denis Stairs, "North American Continentalism: Perspectives and Policies in Canada," in David M. Cameron, ed., *Regionalism and Supranationalism* (Montreal: Institute for Research on Public Policy, 1981), 95.

77 Naomi Black, "Absorptive Systems are Impossible: The Canadian-American Relationship as a Disparate Dyad," in Andrew Axline et al., *Continental Community: Independence and Integration in North America* (Toronto: McClelland and Stewart, 1974), 92–108.

78 Rocher uses both marginality and ambivalence to describe the relationship and feelings of the colonized for the colonizers. *A General Introduction to Sociology*, chap. 14.

79 "Canada and her Great Neighbor," *Canadian Review of Sociology and Anthropology* 1(1964): 197. Glen Frankfurter has argued that English-speaking Canadians created an imaginary ideal Britain to which they could be loyal as a means of distinguishing themselves from the United States. *Baneful Domination*, (Toronto: Longmans, 1971).

WEBLINKS

www.dfait-maeci.gc.ca/nafta-alena/over-e.asp

An overview of the North American Free Trade Agreement (NAFTA) provided by Canada's Department of Foreign Affairs and International Trade.

info.ic.gc.ca/cmb/welcomeic.nsf/icPages/Menu-e

The Industry Canada Web site outlines the department's initiatives to improve conditions for investment, increase Canada's share of global trade and build a fair, efficient and competitive marketplace.

www.macleans.ca

Maclean's is Canada's premiere weekly news magazine.

www.crtc.gc.ca/welcome_e.htm

The Canadian Radio-television and Telecommunications Commission is an independent agency responsible for regulating Canada's broadcasting and telecommunications systems, including Canadian content in broadcast programming.

C h a p t e r

THE ISSUE OF INEQUALITY

Many Canadians are reluctant to admit that their country has a class structure…. But this does not dismiss the other evidence of the class division of the population which exists in terms of inequality of wealth, opportunity and social recognition. These barriers are not the horizontal ones of geographical regions or distinctive ethnic cultures but the vertical ones of a socio-economic hierarchy.

—Leonard C. Marsh, one of Canada's first social researchers,

in his classic study Canadians In and Out of Work *(1940: 403).*

Now that we have some sense of how external factors play a crucial role in shaping Canadian society, we can turn our attention to how people are sorted out within the society. One of the most important means to do that is to focus on the differences that exist within the population in terms of power and access to resources. Sharing a territory does not mean that there is equality or that goods are randomly distributed. Rather, some persons have advantages that others do not have; a situation that produces both visible and less visible (but just as real) evidence of the existence of a hierarchical society.

Virtually every society has a system of *ranking* its members. We are most accustomed to thinking of this in terms of personal characteristics (e.g., income, ownership, education, personal abilities). But ranking is also related to group characteristics (e.g., gender, ethnicity, race) in which particular qualities give some groups dominance or control over other groups. Dominant groups obviously have the ability to define what is important, how things are done, and who obtains the largest rewards. The study of the structure and consequences of the ranking patterns that exist in a society is known as *social stratification* or *class analysis.*

There is no modern society in which all people are equal; some people are just more equal than others. Yet the notion of human equality is deeply imbedded in the ideology of Western democracies.[1] In the United States, for example, the preamble to the Constitution states that all men are created equal (note that women are not explicitly mentioned), and yet the long history of the subordination of blacks indicates that equality does not exist in that society. While many people like to think that the gap between rich and poor is narrower in Canada, inequality still exists along a variety of dimensions. There is a rich legacy of research on inequality in Canadian society. The purpose of this chapter is to outline the basis for this inequality, and to indicate how it contributes to the dynamics of life within the society.

INDICATORS OF INEQUALITY

The most visible indicator of inequality in everyday life is income, or wealth. You have probably established a connection between income, education, and occupation. We frequently see people with little or no education in low-paying occupations and, conversely, we see people with considerable education in high-paying positions. The relationship between income, education, and occupation is not always so clear—a real estate agent with a high income may not have a high level of education. Generally speaking, however, the three dimensions of income, education, and occupation are perceived as good objective indicators of where one might be placed in a society's ranking system. What evidence is there that a differential of these qualities exists?

Income

Because income is directly related to purchasing power—which in turn determines standard of living and lifestyle—a person's income level is an important indicator of social stratification. Table 3.1 shows how income is unequally distributed within the population. If total income were distributed equally, each quintile's share in Row A would amount to 20%. The data show, however, that the lower the quintile, the lower its share of aggregate income. For example, the quintile with the lowest earnings possesses only 4.6% of the aggregate income. Conversely, the quintile with the highest income earns 44.5% of the aggregate income—more than double its share. But there is also evidence that the middle quintile is slipping (from 18.3% in 1951 to 16.3% in 1996) while the highest quintile is gaining (from 42.8% in 1951 to 44.5% in 1996) suggesting that inequality is growing.

Table 3.1 also shows that the sources of income vary. Persons in the lowest quintile receive most of their income from transfer payments, such as old age assistance, family subsidies, unemployment insurance, and other forms of government assistance. The largest groups in this category are female single-parent families, elderly persons, and families in which the husband does not work. In contrast, the quintile with the highest income receives most

TABLE 3.1	Percentage Distribution Within Income Quintiles of Families and Unattached Individuals, Canada, 1996				
	Lowest Quintile	Second Quintile	Middle Quintile	Fourth Quintile	Highest Quintile
Income Share (A)	4.6	10.0	16.3	24.7	44.5
Source of Income (B)					
wages and salaries	23.3	42.4	65.1	75.7	79.9
self-employment	1.9	5.4	5.2	5.8	7.8
transfer payments	66.0	37.9	16.8	8.7	3.6
investments	3.3	4.6	3.8	3.3	4.2
other money income	5.5	9.7	9.2	6.6	4.5

Source: Compiled from Statistics Canada, 1996 Catalogue 13–207, Tables 55 and 56.

of its income from employment. Husband-and-wife families in which both spouses work make up a majority of this quintile, although it should be noted that such dual-income families are also becoming more common within other income quintiles as well.

The picture which emerges, then, is that of a population with a wide range of available incomes. Underemployed and unemployed persons, the elderly, and lone-parent families have the lowest incomes, while dual-income, highly professional, and well-educated salary holders have the most substantial incomes.

Education

In an industrial society, differences in the level and type of education obtained by its members are a significant factor in stratification. Because industrialization demands a high level of specialized training and job expertise, education is thought to be the key to success in the system. This perception suggests that a better education leads to a better occupation, and that this should generate higher income. Accessibility to education and actual attainment, then, become the basis for further ranking within the society.

Table 3.2 demonstrates that there is indeed a wide range of levels of educational attainment, and that these levels have changed significantly over time. When persons still likely in process of formal education are removed and only those 25 years of age and over are considered, 14.9% hold university degrees and 14.3% have less than a Grade 9 education. The largest single category (36.9%) are those who have completed some level of high school education. The most striking evidence in the top part of the table is the comparison with 1951 when over half (54.9%) of the population had less than a Grade 9 education (now shrunk to 14.3%). Also noteworthy is the significant increase of those holding university degrees, and above all the large 34% who have completed some type of post-secondary education. When comparing 1951, 1976 and 1996, it is clear that there has been a massive upgrading of educational levels within the general population. We will return to the meaning of this important shift later. At this point, however it is important to note that significant differences in educational attainment provide an important basis for hierarchical differentiation. Gender and provincial differences in education will also be discussed later.

TABLE 3.2	Population 25 Years or Older and Highest Levels of Education Attained, Canada, 1996			
	Highest Level of Schooling Attained (%)			
	Less Than Grade 9	**Grades 9–13**	**Some Post-Secondary**	**University Degree**
Total Population				
1951	54.9	42.9	—	2.3
1976	32.0	36.8	23.7	7.6
1996	14.3	36.9	34.0	14.9
By Gender 1996				
Males	14.1	35.8	33.6	16.5
Females	14.4	37.8	34.4	13.4
By Province 1996				
Newfoundland	21.7	35.7	33.4	9.2
Prince Edward Island	16.2	37.6	34.6	11.6
Nova Scotia	13.1	38.1	35.6	13.3
New Brunswick	20.0	37.4	31.3	11.2
Quebec	20.8	37.2	28.4	13.6
Ontario	12.2	36.7	34.4	16.7
Manitoba	15.0	38.7	33.4	13.0
Saskatchewan	15.9	38.7	34.3	11.1
Alberta	9.0	36.3	39.4	15.3
British Columbia	8.9	36.0	39.8	15.4
Yukon	6.8	28.9	47.4	16.8
Northwest Territories	22.9	23.0	40.7	13.3

Source: Adapted from "1996 Census of Canada, Population 15 Years and Over by Age Groups and Sex, Showing Historical Level of Schooling, for Canada, Provinces and Territories, 1976 Census, 1981 and 1996 Censuses," Catalogue No. 93F0028XDB96002.

Table 3.3 indicates that higher education is indeed linked to income. When average income of all individuals is examined (including those no longer in the labour force), the pattern is very clear; the higher the education, the higher the income. Those with university degrees earn almost three times what is earned by the poorest educated category.

Occupation

Occupation is also an important dimension of inequality because it provides clues to a whole series of facts about an individual. We know that some occupations require particular kinds of credentials while others do not, and we know that remuneration and lifestyle vary from one occupation to another.

There are two indexes that have been created in Canada which combine education and income levels of persons within occupational groupings to produce a ranking system of

TABLE 3.3	Average Income for all Individuals by Education and Sex, Canada, 1996		
Education Level	**All Individuals**	**Males**	**Females**
0–8 years schooling	$16 858	$21 509	$12 520
Some secondary education	18 449	23 503	13 097
High school graduate	24 392	30 163	18 821
Some post-secondary	20 337	24 450	16 388
Post-secondary certificate or diploma	28 297	34 316	22 013
University degree	42 747	49 703	34 423

Source: Adapted from Statistics Canada, 1996 Catalogue 13-207, Table 48.

occupational status. They are the Blishen, Carroll, and Moore index (usually referred to as the Blishen scale) and the Pineo-Porter-McRoberts scale.[2] Table 3.4 provides a modified occupational Blishen scale collapsing all occupations into general categories. It is clear from this table that education and income are correlated and are expressed in a hierarchical occupational ranking.

Table 3.5 presents a list of select occupations that shows that earnings differ greatly among occupations. Note that even within fields such as health care that there is a clear hierarchy among the various roles just as there is between management and clerical workers. There is also an important gender difference in this table which we will explore later, but the income differences between occupations is indisputable.

TABLE 3.4	Modified Occupational Scale by Average Blishen Scores, Years of Schooling, Income, and Gender					
	Blishen Score		**Years of Schooling**		**Income**	
Occupation	**Men**	**Women**	**Men**	**Women**	**Men**	**Women**
High level management	69	67	14.0	14.0	$62 555	$36 637
Professional	65	65	15.0	15.0	38 226	27 672
Middle management	52	52	13.0	13.0	36 935	21 894
Semi-professional/technician	52	51	13.6	14.0	30 784	25 732
Upper (skilled) white collar	46	42	12.7	12.9	37 334	18 005
Upper (skilled) blue collar	44	37	11.0	11.6	28 572	18 476
Lower (unskilled) white collar	33	32	12.0	12.0	23 016	13 301
Lower (unskilled) blue collar	32	28	10.5	10.0	22.186	13 444
Farmers	28	28	10.0	14.0	26 528	13 147
Farm labourers	24	24	10.0	11.0	14 774	8830

Note: the negative income reflects net losses for some farmers

Source: Adapted from Gillian Creese, Neil Guppy and Martin Meissner, *Ups and Downs on the Ladder of Success: Social Mobility in Canada*, Statistics Canada 1991 Catalogue 11–612, Table D.

TABLE 3.5	Select Occupations, Number of Earners and Average Earnings, by Sex, 1996			
	Number of Earners		Average Earnings	
	Men	**Women**	**Men**	**Women**
Senior Management	114 765	29 960	$ 86 265	$ 46 641
Bookkeepers	9 875	95 760	21 863	19 133
Secretaries	6 975	409 600	25 605	21 710
Clerical	475 130	1 161 375	24 260	20 105
Family Physicians	26 540	11 575	108 555	72 880
Registered Nurses	12 140	226 430	37 134	32 028
Dentists	12 420	3 500	102 547	61 892
Dental Assistants	355	22 575	20 046	19 170
Judges	1 960	490	122 564	112 800
Lawyers	42 565	18 585	86 141	52 926
Social Workers	9 445	29 945	37 373	31 546
Elementary School Teachers	44 305	194 440	44 046	35 255
Cashiers	40 510	248 280	9 867	8 859
Trades Labourers	118 975	7 140	17 195	10 239

Source: Adapted from "1996 Census of Canada, Population 15 Years and Over with Employment Income by Sex, Work Activity, Highest Level of Schooling, Age Groups and Detailed Occupation, Showing Number and Average Employment Income in Constant (1995) Dollars, for Canada, Provinces and Territories, 1990 and 1995," Catalogue No. 94F0009XDB96068.

INTERPRETING INEQUALITY

Now that we have established that socio-economic inequality exists in Canadian society, we need to suggest how it can be interpreted. While there are many variations of theories proposed to explain inequality, there are two core explanations: the functional and the conflict approach.[3] The *functional approach* suggests that a stratified society is not only natural but it is inevitable given the differential rewards and opportunities found within the society. The key notion here is that individuals attain the class position they deserve. In other words, individual merit or achievement explains why differences in salaries or status are generated. Inequality is viewed as a motivating factor in serving the functional needs of a society.

Criticisms of the functional view suggest that inequality is not so much natural as it is traditional or even hereditary. Merit or achievement is always qualified by where you start out. If you are born into a home with an unemployed father, living in low-cost housing, and are surrounded by family and friends who have a pessimistic view of the world, how can you be faulted if you have little ambition or feel that the odds against which you struggle are too formidable? Compare such a person to one who has parents who are both professionals, who own property, and who inculcate values of optimism and advancement. Do the two persons have an equal chance of attaining the position they deserve? What about people who have not earned their substantial rewards and yet have inherited large sums of money? Are janitors paid less than professional athletes because they are really less important to

---

RESEARCH CLIP 3.1

The Relationship Between Education and Earnings

Hunter and Lieper studied the issue of credentialism—the role of achievement through certification in enhancing earnings. They found that people with more years of schooling and a completion certification do indeed earn more money than those without. But they also found that it was not just the education or the certificate per se that produced the earnings effect but the employment position that required the schooling and the degree or certificate. In other words, the primary impact of level of education attainment was to make individuals eligible for consideration for positions which had the earnings payoff, and therefore it was the position that was the primary determinant of higher earnings.

Source: Alfred A. Hunter and Jean McKenzie Lieper, "On Formal Education, Skills, and Earnings: The Role of Educational Certificates in Earnings Determination," *Canadian Journal of Sociology*, 18(1993): 21–42.

---

the functioning of a society? In sum, the functional view more or less justifies the inequality that already exists by ignoring other factors that affect an individual's ability to respond to opportunities in the society.

While the functional approach places great emphasis on the individual, the *conflict approach* places its emphasis on the shared nature of inequality. Class formation occurs when people become aware of the characteristics they share with others in a similar condition. This usually revolves around the ownership of private property or ownership of the means of production. Those who are the owners are the bourgeoisie; the non-owners are the proletariat. Members of a society become increasingly aware of which one of the two classes they belong to (i.e., class consciousness develops). Even when the existence of an interstitial middle class is acknowledged, this group is still essentially wage labourers when working as expert or credentialled managers. The dominant ideas and beliefs in the society can be viewed as ideologies which sustain the class structure of inequality. Whether or not the labouring class eventually challenges the dominant class to overthrow it, it should be expected that there will be repeated struggles by groups that resist domination by the capitalist class.

Criticisms of the conflict view of inequality suggest that just as the functionalist approach appears to be a rationale for inequality, so the conflict view appears to be a rationale for social change. The antagonism between these two opposing groups or classes, as the original advocate of this perspective, Karl Marx, had envisioned it, has been muted by the fragmentation of the non-owners of the means of production into sub-groups or class fractions which lack unity and which may be in opposition to each other. There are also differences between owners who hire large pools of workers and small owners who hire no workers. The complexity of inequality, some argue, cannot be reduced to simple divisions, especially when large numbers of people enjoy a reasonable standard of living. It might also be argued that in a society where individualism prevails, many people resist adopting a perspective that requires class action or group views of class condition.

The functionalist view explains inequality on the basis of differences in *individual* abilities and tasks. The conflict view explains inequality in terms of *group* differences in power, capital accumulation, and the conflict which develops when groups struggle to preserve or rearrange their relationships.

Differing Perspectives

Structural Functionalism

If there is inequality in Canadian society, the structural functional perspective accepts that inequality is present in all societies, and is the result of differences in individual abilities to achieve and compete. Some individuals who share characteristics may have advantages over other individuals with different characteristics and the result may be a mosaic type society that has hierarchical dimensions. However, Canadian society as a stratified society is not necessarily permanent and fixed, as individuals can and do take advantage of opportunities to change their class position. Movement in the class structure, known as social mobility, is what is important. All societies require people at a variety of class positions in order to fulfill all of the functions required in a society from low status positions to high status positions. Inequality in Canadian society then is natural and inevitable.

Conflict

The conflict perspective understands Canadian society as essentially divided into groups in which power and ultimate authority is unequally distributed. The concentration of power in the hands of a few known as elites engenders resistance on the part of others who lack power and desire power. In a capitalist society, persons with economic power receive particularly handsome rewards and structure the society in such a way that they retain and justify their power and maximize their profits. Groups are constantly forming to challenge the distribution of power. Change in a society is best understood in terms of how people organize themselves to challenge the hegemony of dominant groups. In addition to social class, other bases for dominance may be region, gender, ethnicity, and race. Power thus produces counter-movements that attempt to rearrange the distribution of power.

Symbolic Interactionism

The symbolic interactionist perspective understands that inequality leads to different ways of understanding and communicating reality. Symbols of wealth and prestige can be contrasted with lifestyles and symbols of poverty. The experience of being poor or disadvantaged or marginalized must be understood as a social world in which there are few choices but in which life proceeds with different cultural assumptions, norms and values for those with more resources. In fact, each social class in society as well as each segmented group has its own cultural symbols and worldview which help to sustain differences within the society. Inequality leads to behavioural differences and expectations. This means that people will feel most comfortable with people who are from the same group as their own. From this perspective, it is not so much that inequality is good or bad, natural or created, as that it produces different social worlds which must be analyzed and understood.

Class Analysis

When the focus is on differences in the attributes of individuals, the concept of social class becomes a loose statistical category of persons with similar characteristics (e.g., they all have similar incomes). Higher income presumably means higher class position, and arbitrary distinctions can be made between upper middle class and middle class, for example. When the focus shifts to the basic split between, and the opposing interests of, capital and labour, the concept of social class identifies social groups which are formed as a consequence of their relation to the means of production.[4] It is not how much income or education you have that matters, but where you fit in a society structured by corporate capital.

It is important to discuss this latter concept of social class because much of the critical analysis of Canadian society has been informed by this perspective. Instead of merely comparing income levels, people in the labour force can be classified according to whether they are employers or employees. One such analysis pointed out that 2.7% of the labour force were employers and formed the capitalist class (though many of these persons ran small businesses and were a much smaller segment of the capitalist class), 6.4% were self-employed, and 90% were employees of either the private or public sector.[5] Once the basic distinction has been made between employees and employers, the employee category can be broken down further into managers and technocrats, supervisors, semi-autonomous workers, and workers.

Another analysis with a similar conclusion identifies two primary instruments of power as the ability to command the means of production and the ability to command the labour power of others.[6] The capitalist/executive class have power in both areas and make up 6.2% of the population. On the other hand, the working class have no power in either area and make up 57.6% of the population. The old middle class (11.3%) may have some capital/property but little labour power whereas the new middle class (24.9%) have no control over the means of production but some control over labour through bureaucratic power. In any case, ultimate power lies with a few.

The result of this kind of analysis is that the capitalist class is seen to be very small and interlocked through its corporate power. This analysis also shows that workers are by far the largest group in the labour force. The existence of an intermediate group between capital and labour is acknowledged, though it is most typically identified as a class fraction within the subordinate class.

The most dominant class-based interpretive model in understanding Canadian society over the last twenty years has been *political economy*.[7] Built from the conflict model, this perspective begins with how people earn their living (the economic), and then explores the conflicting social relations that develop out of this process (the political). Some people accumulate capital (the capitalist class), others work for wages (labourers), while still others are self-employed (the petite bourgeoisie). This perspective maintains that those who possess capital hold the ultimate power, and the exercise of that power will automatically be exploitative of workers unless challenged. Studies in political economy can be either liberal or Marxist. What they all have in common is a focus on how power is used or experienced in a stratified society.

The focus in the political economy paradigm is on property rights and capital accumulation, which have social consequences since economic control produces social power. Capital concentration can be viewed in a national context, but it also has international implications affecting other societies. Political economy searches for the economic basis of public and private decision-making in terms of class interests. Canadian political economy is usually rooted in the staples thesis of Harold Innis, and continues in the elite studies of

The New Political Economy

Political economy emphasizes how a society is organized for the production of goods and services, and points out how these arrangements reflect the realities and consequences of social inequality. The political consequences of this inequality is a statement about power relations within that society and is not just a matter involving government and the state. But it is true that the capitalist class seeks to mobilize the power and authority of the state for its own interests. Thus political economy takes what is known as a materialist perspective because it understands social relations in terms of their economic bases.

Because the "old" political economy often appeared too economically deterministic, the "new" political economy recognizes what is called *structure and agency*. Human beings are actors and do make choices in shaping history but they do so within the limits of the structures of society in which economic relations supply the context.

Political economy is keenly interested in societal change over time and in particular identifies tensions or contradictions which produce challenges or resistance to the established order. For example, labour may challenge the capitalist class such as in the well-known Winnipeg General Strike in 1919. More recently, political economy has shown how globalization and deregulation has strengthened the capitalist class but has weakened the power of workers and resulted in greater inequality in society.

Further Reading: Wallace Clement (ed.), *Understanding Canada: Building on the New Canadian Political Economy* (Montreal: McGill-Queens University Press, 1997) and Wallace Clement and Glen Williams (eds.), *The New Canadian Political Economy* (Montreal: McGill-Queens University Press, 1989).

Porter and Clement, but also includes numerous studies on region, gender, and ethnic conflict, as well as various forms of dependency analysis.

Does the evidence of inequality cited here support the functional or the conflict perspective? The answer revolves around whether people who share similar characteristics (on the dimensions of ranking which we have cited) are merely a statistical category, or whether they actually possess a group consciousness. If we just place individuals or families into categories based on income or education and view them as artificial constructs, there is no implication that they are anything more than a statistical aggregation of individuals. On the other hand, if groups of people can be perceived as sharing both economic interests and a similar view of the world in contrast to those with different interests and world views, there then exists the likelihood of repeated conflicts between groups seeking to retain or rearrange the structure of power. In Canadian society, notions of group or class interest are repeatedly challenged by individual ideals of reward based upon merit and achievement. However, from a macro perspective, the analysis of Canadian society is greatly enriched by examining how dominant ideas and structures are sustained and how groups emerge to challenge or resist dominant forms considered unfair or oppressive.[8]

It is important that the differences between these two conceptions of inequality be grasped at the outset since each perspective contains its own interpretive schema and proposes its own solutions. We will use both perspectives in our continuing analysis of inequality because they represent opposing streams of thought within our society. However, the conflict approach is a much more incisive tool in our understanding of the quest for human justice.

OTHER DIMENSIONS OF INEQUALITY

Thus far inequality has been discussed as essentially a socio-economic phenomenon with no cross-cutting variations. However, three other dimensions of inequality have received considerable attention in Canadian society. They are the dimensions of ethnicity, region, and gender.

Ethnic Inequality

Perhaps the earliest form of inequality acknowledged in Canadian society was that of ethnicity. Beginning with the history of French–English relations and continuing to later phases of immigration, it is clear that ethnic groups have different positions in the status hierarchy. Ethnic descent or ethnic origin, then, may be an important dimension of inequality.

In 1965, John Porter, a sociologist at Carleton University, published *The Vertical Mosaic*, which has become a Canadian classic. The underlying theme of the book was that ethnicity was intimately related to the stratification structure in Canada. The cultural mosaic of Canada was not random, argued Porter; some ethnic groups possessed a more favourable position in the society than others. Porter ties this ethnic hierarchy to the early settlement of the country and particularly to French–English relations. When the British and French first settled in Canada, there was a tendency to recreate a stratified society similar to that of the homeland. After the British defeated the French, the two culture groups existed side by side with their own individual structure of social organization; the British, however, retained the dominant position. Nevertheless, Quebec social structure remained relatively intact with doctors, lawyers, and the clergy occupying the highest levels of social standing in a largely agrarian community. British farmers also retained their rural social structure. The major hierarchical differences that could be observed were in the areas of commerce, trade, and administration where persons of British descent held overwhelming control.

With the onset of industrialization and the shift away from an agricultural economy, the entrenched English-Canadian upper class became the industrial leaders not only in English Canada, but also in Quebec. The situation was further exacerbated by the fact that the Quebec educational system emphasized classical studies and was not designed to prepare its students for technological occupations. As a result, the British were considerably overrepresented at the professional, administrative, and financial levels of the Quebec labour force. Similarly the French were overrepresented in the agricultural, primary, and unskilled occupations in that province. When the French moved to the urban areas, they formed a convenient working class or "oppressed majority" under English-Canadian control.[9] The implications of this kind of class subordination will be discussed in Chapter Five, but at this point it should be noted that, virtually from the beginning, ethnicity and class position combined in such a way that persons of French descent shared a social status which was lower than that of the English. Dofny and Rioux speak of this convergence of class consciousness and ethnic identity as ethnic class or *eth-class*.[10] This focus on ethnic differences in ranking may have ignored class differences among English-Canadians, but it did sensitize Canadians to the fact that ethnicity was an important component of the stratification of Canadian society.

The addition of other ethnic groups to the society through immigration contributed to greater complexity in ethnic stratification patterns. It is important to note that federal government policy determines which ethnic groups are preferable immigrants, and a change in qualifications for admittance can significantly affect the nature of ethnic representation.[11] The government, then, determines which ethnic groups will be admitted and what work they are likely to do. For example, when Eastern Europeans entered the country in the 1920s, they were largely rural peasants encouraged to settle remote western farmlands (e.g., the Ukrainians in northern Saskatchewan), whereas the immigration of Asians in the 1970s consisted mostly of skilled and professional persons destined for urban centres. The term used to refer to the class position at which immigrants enter a society is *entrance status*.

The key contribution of Porter's *The Vertical Mosaic*, then, was the idea that while Canadian society was a colourful kaleidoscope of ethnic groups, there was a vertical or hierarchical dimension to this patterning. Not only was there an asymmetry between English and French, but other ethnic groups as well possessed a distinct location in the hierarchy not only related to their entrance status but also related to their ability or likelihood to respond to their new environment.

Recent research has suggested that the ethnic component of stratification is now eroding.[12] It is possible that ethnicity may have been more relevant at an earlier point in the society's history or that it may primarily be an issue now only for the foreign born. Ethnic status may be increasingly irrelevant among those born in Canada regardless of ethnic origin, with some exceptions which we will note. The evidence is that ethnic stratification has been greatly attenuated among persons with European ancestry.[13] One study even found that Canadians of French ancestry now earn significantly more than Canadians of British ancestry at all educational levels when other variables are controlled.[14] When French–English differences do exist, they may be accounted for by generational factors more relevant to the older generation. In a similar manner, language first spoken at home is no longer a predictor of educational attainment in Canada either.[15] Thus the issue of being born abroad may be the most important variable in accounting for the role which ethnicity plays in inequality.

But such a conclusion is far too simple as we know that some immigrants born abroad have greater advantages than others in the host society. After reviewing the literature and completing their own analysis of the data, Lautard and Guppy argue that there has been a decline in the significance of ethnicity as measured by occupational differences but that the decline has not totally erased ethnic origin as a factor.[16] The ethnic division of labour has been reduced by about 50% and is now less prominent than the gendered division of labour. This of course is not to deny that some groups have distinctive occupational concentrations, such as British and Jewish in managerial/professional fields, or Asians in personal services or professional occupations.[17] But in general, the *"new" vertical mosaic* is understood more in racial terms than ethnic terms as aboriginals (who are native born) and visible minorities (who may or may not be native born) encounter definite barriers in the stratification system.

When measuring educational attainment, dominance by persons of British descent has clearly eroded, and there is some evidence that the children of immigrants are particularly keen to use education to change the class position of their family of origin. Furthermore, recent immigration policies giving priority to persons with professional skills has produced a more educated immigrant stream. But the question is whether similar education generates similar incomes or whether there are ethnic penalties associated with occupational position.[18] There are two conclusions here. One is that immigrants educated abroad receive lower returns on their investment in education in terms of occupational status and earnings than the native-

RESEARCH CLIP 3.2	Inequality Among Persons of Caribbean Origin in Toronto

Approximately three-quarters of all Caribbean-born persons in Canada live in the province of Ontario, with most living in Metropolitan Toronto and the surrounding areas of Mississauga and Brampton. In these cities, there is increasing residential concentration.

Inequality is expressed through what Francis Henry identifies as *differential incorporation.* Persons of Caribbean origin as a whole are not structurally integrated into the mainstream of Canadian society primarily due to their inability to gain full access to the economic, social, and cultural rewards of the society. While they are part of Canadian society in a broad sense, there are both internal and external factors which create barriers to their full participation in the society.

The most significant internal factor is that the black community is segmented by a division into two classes: working class and middle class. But there is also a growing underclass of youth born to working class parents and/or single mothers who frequently become school dropouts and who experience significant frustration with poverty and racism in the surrounding environment. While coping mechanisms such as entrepreneurship, support groups, and island associations have developed, varying degrees of marginalization and internal class divisions continue to fragment the group and prevent more cohesive political mobilization.

The major barrier to integration into Canadian society, however, is racial discrimination as expressed through various forms of exclusionary behaviour. The strongest evidence of differential incorporation is experienced in matters of employment. Persons of Caribbean origins are poorly represented in managerial and supervisory positions and are overrepresented in skilled, semi-skilled, and manual occupations.

Source: Based on Frances Henry, *The Caribbean Diaspora in Toronto: Learning to Live with Racism* (Toronto: University of Toronto Press, 1994).

born.[19] The second conclusion is that visible minorities earn less than the average of those with similar levels of education while those of European background generally receive above average income for their educational level. As groups, however, foreign-born visible minorities and aboriginal peoples have incomes considerably below the national mean with native-born visible minorities somewhat closer to the mean but not as high as caucasians (whether foreign born or native born, with the exception of Southern Europeans).[20]

It then can be asked whether it is ethnic status that serves as a barrier to equality or whether it is the structure of the society that creates discrimination against particular ethnic groups. In other words, is it the characteristics of the ethnic group that is a problem in inequality or is it the response of the host society? The answer appears to depend upon the ethnic group in question. For example, Italians and Portuguese have lower levels of education and occupational status but they have higher incomes than the first two indicators would suggest. Conversely, Chinese and South Asians have higher levels of educational attainment than their incomes would suggest. Hou and Balakrishnan argue that ethnic differences in socio-economic status still exist within Canadian society but that their manifestations are different for diverse groups.[21] In that sense, the structure of society appears to possess elements of *systemic discrimination* (institutionalized practices that are arbitrary and exclusionary) that contribute to ethnic inequality. Devaluing foreign credentials is one such practice and the lack of employment networks for top jobs may be another.

It is important that the complexity of these questions be acknowledged, for ethnicity is sometimes viewed as a cause of inequality whereas it is in reality intimately connected to other factors such as occupation, educational opportunity, gender, and age. Peter Li has concluded that in contrast to the argument of *The Vertical Mosaic*, there is not a strong relationship between ethnicity and class position but that ethnicity must be understood as combining with additional factors to give some groups advantages over others, rather than in itself causing inequality.[22] Longevity of residence in Canada or cultural accommodation are important variables, but so also is race, in determining how and whether inequality will be experienced. The importance of race and ethnicity is still an important variable in the examination of inequality but its precise role is not always clear—particularly after several generations.

Regional Inequality

Another historic dimension of inequality in Canadian society is based on regional economic differences. Mildred Schwartz has described regionalism as a form of "institutionalized inequality" between the various parts of the Canadian entity.[23] While this inequality may be a consequence of the power relationships between regions, regions may also be viewed as a consequence of the class structure that cuts across regions.

The traditional view of regional disparities stresses the importance of geographical causes, such as distance from markets or transportation problems, as the basis for inequality. Some areas of the country are less developed than others because these difficulties made the region less competitive. The point is that regional disparities were considered more or less natural. If there is a differential in power and development between regions, it is because some regions have more people, more industry, and more resources. From this perspective, it is the government's role to correct normal market forces with stimulants to create jobs and grants to equalize the standard of living across the society. However, Brym has pointed out that in spite of this government intervention, the per capita income gap between regions has actually increased.[24]

The *political economy perspective* suggests that those who own and control the means of production, the capitalist class, enlarge their activities in those locations where profit-making potential is the greatest.[25] Profit-making, in turn, is more likely to occur in places closest to markets, adjacent to large pools of labour, proximate to other members of the decision-making capitalist class, and at transportation nerve centres. These factors have encouraged *centralization* and *concentration* of business activity, which have helped produce regional differences in wealth. There are vast hinterland resources in outlying regions of Canada, and these resources are important to the industrial economy of central Canada and foreign markets. Extraction of these resources requires a hinterland working class whose employment cycle is heavily dependent on forces not only external to their region but also external to their class position. In other words, decisions by the economic elite, who have interests in other regions or countries, effectively control the nature and existence of resource-based jobs. Mine or mill shutdown, in deference to the escalation of activities in other regions from whom competitive pressure has been felt, or in the face of reduced market demand by industrialized regions, is the threat continually faced by workers in the resource industries.

Whenever the concentration of corporate capitalism occurs, an infrastructure of manual workers, a middle class of technocrats and managerial workers, and a capitalist class of owners with higher levels of income will be developed in that area. This development will effectively increase regional disparities in income. Poorer regions will experience a drain on their best people to regions with greater income potential. When hinterland economic activity requires participation by corporations from the centre, persons from the industrial heartland are sent to the hinterland as managers and supervisors, and this also limits outlying regions to providing manual labour with little opportunity for advancement. The centralization of capitalist activity, then, both reflects and contributes to regional disparities.

Just as ethnic inequalities have a strong economic basis, so also must regional inequality be grounded in economic realities. But just as we debated whether or not, and to what extent, ethnic inequality is rooted in the class structure, and indeed is the product of class relations, so regional inequality can also be debated as not just the natural result of economic differences but as a consequence of decisions made in the interests of the dominant class. Are there indeed economic differences between the regions?

Table 3.2 on page 86 points out significant differences in levels of educational attainment by province. The Northwest Territories (22.9%) has the highest level of residents with less than Grade 9 education with Newfoundland (21.7%), Quebec (20.8%) and New Brunswick (20%) not far behind. These numbers can be compared with a much lower percentage for the Yukon (6.8%), British Columbia (8.9%), and Alberta (9%). With the exception of the Northwest Territories, there is not a significant difference in levels of high school or post-secondary education. But in terms of the population holding university degrees, there is a considerable gap from Newfoundland (9.2%) to the Yukon (16.8%). Ontario (16.7%), British Columbia (15.4%), and Alberta (15.3%) also have a relatively high percentage of university degree holders. This is not to imply that the more poorly educated areas do not have good educational systems but that the better educated choose to live where employment is more certain. Therefore we would expect that regions with stronger economies would be the regions with the best educated labour force.

Table 3.6 shows that Alberta, Ontario, and British Columbia do indeed have lower unemployment rates, higher median earnings and a greater percentage of persons with incomes

TABLE 3.6	Unemployment Rates, Median Income, and Percentage of Population With Incomes Over $100 000, By Province		
	Unemployment Rate	**Median Employment Income**	**% With Incomes Over $100 000**
Newfoundland	18.0	$11 300	2.6
Prince Edward Island	15.7	12 000	2.0
Nova Scotia	12.8	16 700	4.7
New Brunswick	10.7	14.800	2.8
Quebec	12.0	19 300	3.4
Ontario	8.8	22 500	7.8
Manitoba	7.3	18 000	4.0
Saskatchewan	6.3	15 600	3.5
Alberta	7.7	20 000	5.8
British Columbia	9.0	21 000	6.0

Note: Unemployment rate is seasonally adjusted for March, 1995. Median employment income is for 1993 tax filers.
Source: *The Daily*, Statistics Canada, April 7, 1995, December 1, 1994, and Catalogue 13–207, Table 34.

over $100 000. The Atlantic region has higher unemployment rates and lower median incomes, whereas Quebec exhibits a middle position in unemployment and percentage of incomes over $100 000 but a stronger position in median earning. In the West, Alberta and British Columbia seem to be different in important ways from Manitoba and Saskatchewan, particularly in median earnings and percentages of incomes over $100 000. Ontario's pre-eminence is clear and the contrast with Quebec is striking. There is a $2861 spread in median income and Ontario has about double the number of persons with high incomes that Quebec does. It is not surprising that provinces with the biggest cities are also the provinces where these indices of economic health are the strongest, although Montreal is somewhat of an exception to this statement.[26] In general, the lack of job availability, particularly in the Atlantic provinces, dampens the median income and exacerbates regional inequalities.[27]

Core regions in Canada consist of highly urban industrial areas, and hinterland regions are peripheral to the core.[28] A *metropolis* is a centre of political and financial power, and it is from here that the elite engage in decision-making that affects the rest of the society. The *hinterland* essentially plays a supporting role, in relation to the metropolis, by providing raw materials and labour as needed. The relationship between the metropolis and hinterland is *symbiotic*: one needs the other. The relationship, however, is *unbalanced*; the metropolis tends to dominate and exploit the hinterland (to the benefit of the metropolis.) Regions may appear to be in opposition to one another but this is primarily because the decision-making elite of one region is in a position to exercise control over subordinate regions. Thus, for many subordinate regions, there is the perception that their fate is being controlled by sinister powers in dominant regions. For example, the farmers' movements of the West in the 1920s and 1930s were built out of regional perceptions of elite control identified as the "Bay Street Barons" in Toronto. Similarly, Pierre Vallieres viewed francophone Québécois as "white niggers" because of their subordination to the anglophone industrial elite.[29]

Region then can be understood not only as a demographic or territorial relationship, but as a class relationship. Regions can be analyzed in terms of their own common class basis (e.g., the petit-bourgeois farmers of the West), in opposition to elite control that happens to be located in central Canada (e.g., control of credit, markets, transport policy).[30] Or, regions

RESEARCH CLIP 3.3	Life Satisfaction in Marginal Regions

Disparities in levels of economic development does not imply superior or inferior lifestyles. In fact, one study of an underdeveloped region, the Great Northern Peninsula of Newfoundland and Labrador, found that residents had a high level of life satisfaction because they could own their own residence without a mortgage due to informal labour exchanges within the community. Leaving to go elsewhere for better work would inevitably mean a higher cost of living as well as loss of a meaningful friendship network. People therefore deal very constructively with marginal economic environments.

Source: Lawrence F. Felt and Peter R. Sinclair, "Home Sweet Home: Dimensions and Determinants of Life Satisfaction in an Underdeveloped Region," *Canadian Journal of Sociology* 16 (1991): 1–21.

might be examined in terms of their own class structure, so that interregional elite structures are discovered and accommodations are made between them which help to maintain the hierarchical relationship between regions. Struggles for control of a regional resource (e.g., fishing) by large extra-regional capitalist entrepreneurs in competition with regional capital or local residents also reflects the class context of regionalism.[31] The dynamics of regionalism will be the subject of Chapter Four, but it must be noted here that inequalities based on region are an important dimension of Canadian society.

Gender Inequality

A third dimension of inequality with great importance is that of gender. In fact, it has been argued that most of our analyses of hierarchical ranking in society virtually need to be redone in view of a traditional neglect of gender in studies of inequality.[32] It is perhaps only in the last twenty or thirty years that a consciousness-raising has taken place about the socio-economic importance of gender differences.

Whatever the biological differences between men and women may be, as referenced through the term "sex," there are also social/cultural differences between the two groups to which we attach the term "gender." By focusing on gender differences, we come to see how differences between men and women are socially constructed, that is, how our society establishes roles and expectations for people based on their gender.[33] Why is it that secretarial skills are considered a feminine domain and positions of authority a male domain? Men are just as capable of filing or typing as women and yet the structure of society traditionally defines and even restricts women to certain roles. When these societally-defined roles involve being subordinate to men, the result is gender inequality, or what is known as a *gendered division of labour*.

What evidence is there of gender inequality? Let's go back to tables presented earlier in this chapter and review the data which we deferred for discussion until now. Table 3.2 points out that there is very little gender difference in levels of educational attainment between men and women. Women were slightly more likely to have some post-secondary education as their highest level of attainment whereas men were even more likely to have a university degree than women. In spite of the fact that women make up the majority of undergraduates in universities, their proportion with degrees is not yet as strong as men's because in the past women were not as likely to obtain degrees. But it is clear that significant change is underway.

Does a similar level of education lead to equal pay? Table 3.3 suggests that at all levels of education, men earn considerably more than women. The gap is especially wide for those with university degrees. Table 3.4 makes the point even clearer. While women's schooling rate is equivalent to or higher than men's, their income is substantially lower in all occupational categories. Note that in Table 3.5 men make up the overwhelmingly largest number of earners in the highest paying professions, whereas women are the overwhelming majority in the lowest paying occupations (except labourers). In all professions, men earn more than women. The gender gap in earnings is measured by the female to male earnings ratio. In 1997, women employed full-time earned 72.5% of what men earned. Part-time women workers earned 78.6% of what men earned. For all types of workers, though, women earned 63.8% of what men earned. Figure 3.1 indicates that women have made significant progress since 1967 when they earned 46.1% of what men earned but the gender gap is still very much present. Not shown in the data presented is the fact that single women are the only group to approximate men's earnings at 91.8%.

↳ almost equal

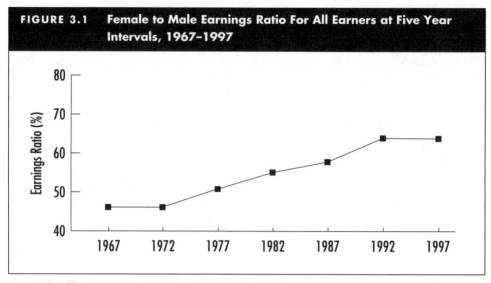

FIGURE 3.1 Female to Male Earnings Ratio For All Earners at Five Year Intervals, 1967–1997

Source: Adapted from Statistics Canada Catalogue 13–217XIB, Text Table I.

It has already been suggested that the matter of gender inequality has been a relatively recent societal issue. The reason for this is that there has been a dramatic increase in women's labour force participation. In 1901, 16% of all women participated in the labour force. That number only edged up by eight percentage points to 24% in 50 years (by 1951).[33] Since 1961, the increase of women in the labour force has been phenomenal, from 29% to 40% between 1961 and 1971, to 51% by 1981, and even further to 58% by 1991. Ironically, in recent years, the participation of men in the labour force, while still substantially higher than that of women, has declined from 78% in 1975 to 73% in 1993. Depending on how it is calculated, 60–75% of all women between the ages of 20 and 54 are employed in the labour force.[34] Clearly, the traditional view of women solely as homemakers is out of date. What is remarkable is how relatively recent these changes are!

There are two observations about this altered character of the Canadian labour force that should be noted. One fact that needs to be pointed out is that women's employment roles are concentrated in specific sectors. Men have a broader range of occupational sectors in which they work, whereas women are clustered in clerical and service industries with a smaller concentration in health and education from where they build their management and administrative roles. The concentration of females into a narrow range of occupations is known as *crowding*, which virtually indicates a *dual labour market* (i.e., that women have their spheres of employability almost distinct from men's).

The second observation about this changed labour force is that even in the relatively short time from 1982 to 1993, women have made some impressive gains. For example, while women made up 29.2% of all persons classified as managerial/administrative in 1982, women had become 42.2% of that category by 1993.[35] Other gains are noticeable in other occupational categories as well, though some are still incredibly low, e.g., in the natural sciences. It must be kept in mind that these are very broad categories and there is clearly considerable gender differentiation in traditional male domains such as engineering and transportation. The gains in female to male earnings ratio have already been noted but overall the situation is far from gender equality.[36]

Important changes are taking place, and it is true that some women have moved into traditionally male professions. But as Armstrong and Armstrong have pointed out, two-thirds of women are in jobs where 70% of the workers are women.[37] They are concentrated in 35 of the 200 occupations listed by Statistics Canada. Furthermore, the wage gap among men and women with degrees seems to be increasing, though among all workers regardless of education, the wage gap is decreasing but primarily due to a decline in male employment income. The percentage of women in clerical careers, for example, shows no sign of abatement at all and women continue to be crowded into low paying employment sectors.

Women from visible minorities also face problems related not only to the gendered division of labour but also to the racialized division of labour.[38] Immigrant women from visible minorities often deal with huge cultural differences in role expectations and often find themselves doing menial or part-time work for wage labour. These women then are doubly disadvantaged.

Explanations

How can gender inequality be explained?[39] A structural-functional type of explanation would focus on the fact that women and men each have their different roles to perform and functions to fulfill, and therefore whatever inequality exists is *natural*. For example, the fact that men are more active in the economic sphere and women are more active at home reflects a natural division of labour in which different roles are played by members of society. Yet the reality is that only one-third of married women with children under 16 are full-time housewives.[40] The economic realities of the cost of living and/or lifestyle preferences increasingly require a dual income. The evidence is, then, that the traditional family pattern has been significantly altered and that gender roles are not fixed.

A conflict type of explanation looks at the structural basis for inequality and roots it in *patriarchy*. The central idea of patriarchy is that males have supported or created a social structure in which they have greater power and economic privilege. Two consequences result from this situation. First, since men are the primary breadwinners, women's work can be trivialized into temporary, part-time, or seasonal activity. All of these jobs are low-paying and lack the security, benefits (e.g., pensions), and higher pay of full-time jobs. When the jobs are full-time, they are more likely to be found in the clerical and service sector where pay is also relatively low. The second consequence is that, to the extent that women do upgrade their skills and education, they are blocked by traditional practices and attitudes to lesser roles in those professions or occupations. Either way, men retain their position of dominance and women are (consciously or unconsciously) prohibited from reaching their potential.

Another conflict-based interpretive scheme ties women's work into the capitalist economy. While it is true that some women wish to only work part-time, it can be argued that this flexible labour pool is of significant benefit to profit-making. Women make up 72% of the part-time labour force, and employers can cut costs by hiring more part-time employees. Furthermore, women engage in domestic labour which goes unrewarded but which is essential to the maintenance of the paid labour force.[41] When women are responsible for raising the dependent children who become tomorrow's work force, as well as being caregivers to all family members, they are doing work which is considered economically valueless but is necessary to sustain the economy. Women then, remain highly dependent on men because their own work keeps them economically subservient (as a proletariat)[42] without pensions and with poor remuneration. Women play a critical role in supporting the capitalist system but are excluded from its benefits through structural subordination.[43]

As women have entered the workforce in greater numbers, and primarily of economic necessity, one thing that has shown little change is women's responsibility for domestic labour. The so-called *"second shift"* means that women who do paid work outside the home must also do unpaid work inside the home which massively increases the workload.[44] This dual segregation of women into the so-called "pink ghetto" of paid labour and the domestic ghetto of unpaid labour is called the *double ghetto*.

Transforming the Status of Women

The *feminist movement* arose as a response to gender inequalities. It has a descriptive and interpretive objective whereby evidence is evaluated and explained, but it also has an activist agenda to bring about change. Within feminism, three streams or approaches can be identified. *Liberal feminism* tends to accept the fact that men and women differ but lobby for laws and policies that eradicate inequality and promote equal opportunity to hopefully produce a more just society. *Socialist feminism* views capitalism as structuring oppression in both class and gender dimensions and therefore desires to change the capitalist structure whereby these inequities are preserved. *Radical feminism* understands the ideology of male superiority as the fundamental source of oppression and exploitation and seeks to replace this dominant ideology. Strains of all three of these approaches can be found in Canadian society and frequently are expressed in ways that are not mutually exclusive.

Roberta Hamilton has argued persuasively from a feminist perspective that the Canadian state itself has been patriarchal and that in spite of some changes, the status quo of male dominance has been sustained through things like the lack of gender equity among political decision-makers and the undervaluing of women's work.[45]

REAL PEOPLE 3	Gendered Inequality in Leadership: Selected "Occupational Firsts" for Canadian Women

1957	first woman federal cabinet minister	Ellen Fairclough
1973	first woman president of a coeducational university	Pauline Jewett
1975	first woman federal deputy minister	Sylvia Ostry
1975	first woman president of a major union	Grace Hartman
1980	first woman Speaker of the House of Commons	Jeanne Sauvé
1982	first woman appointed to the Supreme Court of Canada	Bertha Wilson
1984	first woman Governor General of Canada	Jeanne Sauvé
1991	first woman Premier	Rita Johnson
1991	first woman President of the Canadian Medical Association	Carol Guzman
1992	first woman President of the Canadian Bar Association	Paule Gauthier

Source: Compiled from *Woman in the Labour Force*, 1994 Edition, Statistics Canada Catalogue 75-507, 65–67.

At the turn of the century, the quest for gender equality in Canada focused on women's demands for the right to vote, which is known as the suffrage movement.[46] Women finally received the right to vote in 1918. However, it was not until the late 1960s and 1970s that women's groups began to put pressure on the government for other forms of equality. Among the most significant events were the appointment of a Royal Commission on the Status of Women in 1967, the formation of a coalition of 170 women's groups in the National Action Committee in 1972, and the creation of the Canadian Advisory Council on the Status of Women in 1973 as a public policy advisory group.

Perhaps the most significant indicator of this changing social structure was the appointment of the Royal Commission on Equality in Employment in 1983 in response to large numbers of women entering the labour force but also identifying other disadvantaged groups including visible minorities, the disabled, and indigenous peoples.[47] Inequality was identified by this body as *systemic discrimination*, meaning that most employment barriers were hidden (usually unintentionally) in rules, procedures, or traditions which encourage or discourage individuals because they are members of a particular group rather than because of their ability to do the job. Instead, the new federal policy was to be that of *employment equity* (less coercive than the quotas of affirmative action) as an action plan to correct discrimination in the workplace. The objective was that employers (beginning with those doing business with the federal government) should work towards a *representative work force* (roughly demographically representative) and demonstrate *reasonable accommodation* (flexibility to accommodate disadvantaged groups, including women).

The quest for gender equality is fraught with controversy because of entrenched values and cultural norms not always amenable to change.[48] The strategies to achieve employment equity and pay equity have also had limited successes and the uneven distribution of domestic labour is also an unresolved issue.[49] Yet public opinion and support for gender equality has increased dramatically since the 1970s, particularly among younger cohorts.[50] There is no denying that significant social structural changes have already occurred to which our institutions and practices are being challenged to adjust.

SOCIAL MOBILITY

The suggestion that class position is not fixed, and that at least some people may experience a change in class position, can only be true when a society possesses a relatively open class system. In contrast, a caste system is found in a society where people are locked into a class position and there is virtually no opportunity to change one's social position while a member of that society. In such a society, status is *ascribed* or assigned. In more open class societies, status is *achieved*; i.e., a status position has been earned through personal efforts. Even in more open societies such as Canada, there is an ascriptiveness to status as a consequence of parental background, age, sex, race, or even ethnic origin. To be born in a working class home does not prevent a person from dreaming of being president of a major corporation and perhaps even eventually attaining that goal. Unfortunately, however, in spite of well-publicized exceptions, the likelihood of that status transformation occurring is not great.

Social mobility is the term used to designate movements or shifts by persons in the stratification system. In a society where the boundaries separating social strata or occupational groups are not permanently hardened, any change in social position produces what is known as social mobility. While mobility may be either upward or downward (i.e., *vertical mobility*), it is most common in our society to speak of upward mobility. If it occurs in one person's lifetime, it is known as *intragenerational mobility*; if it occurs between parent and child, it is known as *intergenerational mobility*. When someone changes occupations or roles that have similar status, we refer to that as *horizontal mobility*.

One of the issues that must be addressed is how much mobility or change in class position actually has occurred in Canadian society. Conflict theorists, in particular, feel the evidence indicates that very little mobility has taken place, and perhaps that the gap between the rich and the poor is becoming more polarized. Before proceeding with that discussion, we will examine the classic argument about the changing Canadian social structure.

Education and Social Mobility

In an industrial society, education is viewed as the primary mechanism for generating social mobility. Regardless of the status of your parents, it is argued, you can, through your own efforts, obtain the educational credentials to become a lawyer, or a nuclear engineer, or anything else you want to be. This view of a stratified society suggests that class position and social mobility are predominantly related to personal achievement. If this is the case, personal initiative should be the only variable quality that determines rank in the stratification system.

It has already been shown that ascribed characteristics, such as sex and ethnicity, serve to moderate tendencies for social mobility. Although education is a factor in social mobility, there are two arguments why achievement may not be considered a simple panacea for improving class or status position. The first argument is rooted in the historical position of education in Canadian society (the macro view); the second argument concerns itself with the home background of the student, and events which transpire in the schools (the micro view).

The Macro View

Based on data gathered in the 1950s, John Porter's *The Vertical Mosaic* stated that Canadians did not experience the kind of upward mobility that they should have in the post-war period. This fact was explained, according to the *mobility deprivation thesis* as the result of a general societal failure in education.[51] The expansion of the urban labour force through industrialization in the post-war period created numerous new occupational opportunities which, argued Porter, could have led to considerable upgrading of the labour force. Post-war Canada, however, possessed a traditional and rather elitist conception of education, and because that conception encouraged advanced education for only a small number of people, social mobility was reduced. The dilemma was further accentuated by perceptions that the United States had better opportunities for advancement, which led to a *brain drain* and *labour drain* of those particularly eager for upward mobility.[52]

The labour force needs that resulted found a rather quick resolution through immigration, noted Porter. When Canada needed skilled and professional people, it was much easier to import them through preferred immigration regulations (a so-called *brain gain*) than to insist on educational reform. Thus Canada was both donor and recipient in what has been labelled the *brain trade*. The emigration of some of the most highly skilled persons, coupled with the additional demands for new skilled and professional persons, should have meant greater opportunities (i.e., upward social mobility) for the population already resident in Canada; but because of large-scale immigration and an outdated elitist model of education, the potential for social mobility was greatly reduced. Porter conservatively estimated that between 1950 and 1960, immigrants filled 50% to 60% of the new, skilled jobs which were the result of the nation's industrial development. At that time, advanced educational opportunity was neither encouraged nor made available to everyone; the social structure, then, remained relatively fixed, producing *mobility deprivation*. There was more movement in and out of the stratification system than there was movement within it. Instead of immigrants entering Canada primarily at the lower social class levels and pushing the resident working class up the social strata, skilled immigrants filled the specialized needs of the workforce because of the lack of preparation for mobility by the resident population.

It is important to note that Porter was not saying that no upward mobility occurred, or that immigrants (particularly skilled immigrants) were detrimental to Canadian society. Even though urbanization was producing a massive shift from manual to white collar occupations (i.e., from farm worker to office worker) in the Canadian labour force, this was not vertical mobility in itself. Obviously some mobility did take place once the necessary skills were acquired; but what disturbed Porter was that immigration was used as a convenient substitute for educational reform, and this substitution retarded both the demand for education and the development of fuller educational participation. In addition, a potentially dynamic social structure remained relatively static because Canada was not a "mobility-oriented society."[53]

Porter analyzed the evidence in the early 1960s just as educational change really began to occur in Canada. Throughout the 1960s and even into the 1970s university attendance increased dramatically, and post-secondary schools of technology were built. Post-secondary enrollment almost tripled by 1970 with close to 20% of the 18–24 age group enrolled at post-secondary institutions. In addition, the rate of increase in the number of undergraduate students was 10–15% annually and graduate enrollment increased sixfold.[54] Therefore, even though skilled and professional immigrants were still given entrance priority, the Canadian labour force was in a much better position to compete than before. In fact, by the middle of the 1970s, the employment concerns of Canadians produced a move to reduce immigration to its barest minimum. Nevertheless, in spite of these changes, and in spite of the fact that other factors besides education affect the extent of mobility, Porter's analysis pointed out the importance of accessibility to advanced education and its relationship to immigration policy as factors influencing the potential for social mobility.[55]

The expansion of educational opportunities was based on the *human capital theory* that a better educated labour force would be a more productive one. Consequently, the emphasis in the ensuing decades has been on improving accessibility to advanced education. It was thought that post-secondary educational institutions in particular should be conveniently located, relatively inexpensive, and that more institutions should be available so that more students could be admitted. Governments poured large sums of money into educational endeavours so as to build human capital which would then have a positive effect on employment and the Gross National Product. Education then was to be the means of equalizing the effects of the existing social structure by creating equality of opportunity so that upward mobility could take place.

Equal opportunity (*equality of opportunity*) suggests that all people have an equal chance to take advantage of opportunities. In reality, by virtue of difference in family background, personal aptitudes, and personal circumstances, some people are more able than others to take advantage of opportunities presented. The absence of *equality of condition* suggests that mobility through equal opportunity will be restricted or modified by other factors.

The Micro View

The analysis of equality of condition has resulted in a clearer picture of the factors that lead specific individuals to take advantage of educational opportunity. One perspective emphasizes the role of schools themselves (particularly junior and senior high schools), in sorting students into program streams. While such sorting is normally perceived to be done on the basis of intellectual capacity and aptitudes, research has found that the most important factor standing behind these performance criteria is family expectations. For example, if the home environment minimizes learning, that environment has a strong negative influence on academic performance. The family also exerts a significant, albeit indirect, influence on program selection in that a person's concept of his or her own ability is related to the socio-economic status of the family. Thus the role of the school in streaming students is strongly associated with family influence.[56]

The results of considerable research by sociologists (including later work by Porter) indicates that the choice of higher education is indeed related to social class.[57] In general, the higher the social class position of the parents, the greater the expectation and eventual outcome that the child will obtain a higher education. But even though lower social status of parents may negatively affect the child's likelihood of attending university, higher education is indeed an important mechanism of upward mobility for some students of lower social class background. To prove the point, foreign-born youth or children of foreign-born parents often view education as the primary tool of upward mobility.

Regardless of these tendencies, it is true that more people are attaining higher levels of education regardless of background and that the educational system can be meritocratic at the same time that it is modified by social class. Education can be the way in which some disadvantaged persons overcome their origin but education (or the lack thereof) is also the way parents transmit their status to their children.[58]

Does Your Parents' Education Matter To You?

About one-half of Canadians age 26–35 report having a higher level of education than their parents. This general rise in level of educational attainment has been going on for some time and improves the level of *intellectual capital* available to the next generation.

Nevertheless, the higher the parents' level of education, the more likely that the child will pursue higher education. Young adults 26–35 are close to three times more likely to earn post-secondary credentials if their parents had a post-secondary education than if their parents had not completed high school.

The socio-economic status of the father's occupation is also associated with their children's higher educational attainment. So it is not just the parents' education that is important but the role parents play in creating *family intellectual capital* through passing on attitudes (self-direction, independence, curiosity) and expectations regarding advanced learning as well as modelling the difference education made in their own self-concept and careers.

In this regard, your future is in the hands of your parents.

Source: Based on Patrice de Broucker and Laval Lavallee, "Does Your Parent's Education Count?", *Canadian Social Trends*, Summer 1991, Statistics Canada Catalogue 11-008XPE, p. 11–15. See also M. Reza Nakhaie and James Curtis, "Effects Of Class Positions Of Parents On Educational Attainment Of Daughters and Sons", *Canadian Review of Sociology and Anthropology* 35(1998)4:483–515.

Evaluating Mobility

In order to evaluate whether real mobility has occurred at all, we need to distinguish between two types of mobility. The first type of mobility is called *circulation mobility* or *exchange mobility*. It is based on individual achievement and suggests that through upgrading of skills and obtaining knowledge, hard work will result in some change in social position from parent to offspring.[59]

The second type of mobility is called *structural mobility*. It is not related to individual efforts but to changes in a society's occupational structure. Macro level factors such as economic depressions or booms, corporate restructuring, technological changes (e.g., computers, robotics), or the entrance of new groups (e.g., women, immigrants) into the labour force create new conditions which affect opportunities. For example, the shift from a rural agricultural population to an urban industrial population in the post-war period led a whole generation to strong perceptions of upward mobility. They exchanged their blue collar agricultural positions with considerable equity but little surplus cash and high indebtedness required for land and machinery for white collar work, regular pay cheques, and suburban living. This massive rural–urban shift is best described as structural mobility. Whether it is necessarily a significant change of social position is debatable.

The availability of a whole new range of white collar jobs, some of which have become increasingly routinized with a high degree of supervision, suggests that class position may have changed little.[60] In fact, the evidence is that while dollar values of income may have increased, there is just as wide a spread or disparity in incomes within the society now as there was forty years ago.[61] The increase in employment that entails menial work (such as various forms of record keeping), supervision (i.e., bureaucratic procedure), and machines (e.g., computers, robotics) reduces the freedom, creativity, and control that is frequently masked by the demand for higher credentials, gleaming office towers, or the white collar nature of the work. This shift from more independent craftsman-like work to routinization and supervision is called *deskilling*.

So on the one hand, the implication is that mobility has occurred in real ways and that Canada is a reasonably open society. The more critical perspective, on the other hand, suggests that most of the new range of jobs may require higher levels of education, but they are increasingly confining and controlled by machines or bureaucratic policy that has its own proletarianizing effects. If the shift away from agriculture from rural to urban was one major structural shift in Canadian society, another significant change is the shift from an industrial to *post-industrial society* in which the service sector predominates. Jobs in agriculture and manufacturing have seen steep declines and the service sector now employs close to three-quarters of the labour force. In conjunction with this transformation has been the rise of what is called *non-standard employment*. This is the shift away from full-time full-year permanent employment to part-time short-term temporary employment. One-third of all jobs are now of this type and most of them are in the service industry with lower wages and fewer benefits.[62] While it is too early to assess the full outcome of this trend, there is some fear that the result will contribute to some forms of downward mobility and create new forms of inequality.

Creese, Guppy, and Meissner have published an important study that evaluates the evidence about mobility in Canada.[63] They found that nearly two-thirds of Canadians have an educational level higher than their parents. Half of this educational mobility reflects individual achievement (circulation or exchange mobility) and half is due to the overall upgrading of the labour force (structural mobility). Mobility for men is more likely to be exchange (i.e., achievement), while for women it is more likely to be structural (i.e., women entering the labour force in greater numbers and doing so in white collar clerical jobs). Gender makes little difference to educational mobility but it does for occupational mobility where women experience less upward mobility from their first to current job than men.

Several concluding points need to be made. First, education can mediate the ascriptive influence of parental values with personal role achievement, but it does not necessarily do so.[64] For middle class people in particular, education is the primary means of maintaining class position in relation to other workers. Second, while there has been a significant reduction in educational inequality, income inequality continues to exist, suggesting that education is no guarantee of other forms of equality.[65] And third, however one interprets the mobility or structural change that has occurred, the evidence in more direct comparisons with other countries is that Canada is no less mobility-oriented than other industrial societies.[66] In fact, Wanner has argued that the association between status origins and class destination is fairly low in Canada, particularly in comparison to the United Kingdom, France, Sweden, and the Netherlands, which suggests a reasonably open society.[67]

SOCIAL POWER

Stratification and inequality imply not only that some people have higher incomes and better education, or have bigger homes and fancier cars, but that with this differential in indicators of social status comes variations in power and control. Because money is a scarce resource, those who have it and use it can, directly or indirectly, control those who do not have it but need it. There is, then, a relational aspect to inequality where groups of people who receive more have advantage over those who have less, and can compete more successfully against them.

Power implies control over the decisions that affect other people. In a democracy, we like to think that power is shared and held by all the people. Yet, when we vote, we are conscious that the choices are already circumscribed for us by groups within the society that control political parties or that have sufficient financial resources to promote particular candidates. Thus, at a minimum, we are aware that power is wielded by a variety of competing groups (e.g., the corporate sector, labour unions, farmers' groups) who vie for public support. This perception of power is known as *pluralism*. Power can also be wielded by *elites*, that is, small minorities who make decisions on behalf of the majority. Elitist power can be formalized through elected or appointed governmental positions of authority, or it can be informal and in some ways invisible, such as through the use of economic power. Clement and Myles refer to this type of power as comprising "unelected economic rulers" who have considerable power affecting society at large.[68]

There are elites in each sector of society (e.g., politics, media, finance), but there has always been a particular fascination with the *economic elite*. The political economy perspective maintains that the nature of economic relations within a society is fundamental to understanding how that society operates, and economic elites naturally wield unusual influence in a capitalist society. Political economy refers to the economic elite as the *capitalist class* because people in it are employers or major investors who own the means of production and employ others to make a profit.

One attempt to explain how Canadian society has developed finds the answer in the actions of the economic elite. In a thesis known as *merchants against industry*, Naylor argued that around the time of Confederation, the Canadian capitalist class chose finance, commerce, and transportation rather than industry as the focus of their investments.[69] The result was a society that had truncated industrial development because the commercial elite profited more significantly from a staples economy and squeezed out industrial capital. Instead, they later mediated the importation of more profitable American branch plants. This thesis placed the Canadian commercial elite squarely in the context of continental capitalism, creating a Canadian dependency on the United States at the same time that they also profited.

A key to Naylor's argument is to understand that the capitalist class can be split into merchant and industrial fractions which are distinct and antagonistic. It was in the best interests of the government-protected banking cartel, for example, to perpetuate a staples economy that inhibited or distorted industrial capital. But in an empirical examination of Naylor's argument, Richardson concluded that the boundaries between these class fractions were not strong.[70] In fact, only 51% of the directorships of banks and insurance companies in the 1920s were held by financiers suggesting that participants in the economic elite were members of both class fractions. Instead of antagonistic class fractions, Richardson suggests there existed considerable capital integration within the elite.

This debate raises fundamental questions about the concentration of power. Is power in Canadian society best understood as a plurality of competing groups and their elites, or is power best understood as concentrated in a single elite? The research of John Porter and Wallace Clement provides an interesting contrast in this discussion.

Elites in Porter

The second half of John Porter's book, *The Vertical Mosaic*, attempts to establish the characteristics of the Canadian elite. Porter is able to identify elites in a variety of sectors of the society, from the economic elite to the media, political, and bureaucratic elite. For example, in studying the economic elite, Porter determined that in the early 1950s there were 985 men holding directorships in 170 dominant corporations, banks, and insurance companies. He noted that it was largely this same group which held most of the common stock (and thus received most of the dividend income), meaning that both ownership and management were concentrated in the hands of a few individuals rather than widely dispersed to many shareholders.

The social homogeneity of this economic elite developed through a number of factors. First, members of this elite recruited internally to serve on each other's boards of directors through what is called *interlocking directorships*. Second, Porter constructed biographical sketches of this elite and discovered that family continuity was a dominant pattern. Third, many members had a university education, and many had attended the same private schools as youngsters. Fourth, persons of British descent were dominant in this group with very few persons of French-Canadian descent or Catholic affiliation included. Fifth, the economic elite socialized among themselves through memberships in private clubs and held prominent board positions in charitable organizations, educational institutions, and trade associations.

The economic elite is clearly the most fundamental segment of the elite, but Porter recognized that other elites also have important decision-making roles. The elite of organized labour had the highest proportion of foreign-born of all elites, the lowest level of education, and tended to come from working class backgrounds. The political elite and the federal bureaucratic elite were very similar in having the highest proportion of native-born, having the highest percentage with university education, and tending to be of British, Protestant, and professional backgrounds. Ontario as a region was overrepresented in this elite. The mass media elite was a smaller group in which ownership was shared among only a few families. The media in French Canada were an exception because they were independent of syndicates and chains. And lastly, Porter identified the intellectual and religious elite—a much less homogeneous group.

For Porter, power was a response to the general social need for order.[71] Elite groups each coordinated and directed their own institutional order and sought an equilibrium between themselves, though this did not mean all elite groups were equally powerful. The emphasis in his analysis was on internal recruitment among elites, cross-memberships between elites, and collegiality between elites as a relatively small group. The plurality of elite dominance is best expressed in a phrase Porter used several times, "the confraternity of power." What Porter argued for, however, was greater mobility into the elite so that it did not become an exclusive domain of power.

Elites in Clement

Wallace Clement, one of Porter's students, sought to bring Porter's 1950s data up-to-date in the 1970s, but with a different emphasis, because his focus was on the corporate or economic elite. As a result of the growth of complex subsidiaries, Clement showed, the number of dominant corporations had been reduced from 170 to 113 since Porter's study.[72] Interlocking directorships were again a dominant feature, and, of the 113 dominant corporations, there were 1848 directorships interconnected, with the Canadian Imperial Bank of Commerce, the Bank of Montreal, the Royal Bank, the Canadian Pacific Railway, and Sun Life most closely interlocked. Significantly, 29% of this total elite of the 113 dominant corporations held 54% of all directorship positions. In sum, Clement found that the concentration of power was tighter and access into the elite had become more difficult.

In a second study published two years later, Clement showed how Canadian and American economic power is inextricably linked.[73] He did this by distinguishing three types of elite: the *indigenous elite* of Canadian-controlled corporations, particularly in transportation, finance, and utilities; the *comprador elite* of native-born directors and management personnel of foreign-controlled corporations operating in Canada, particularly in resources and manufacturing; and the *parasite elite*, largely outside Canada, who control the multinational corporations operating in Canada. Therefore, understanding Canadian economic power is inadequate unless placed within a continental framework.

Clement differs from Porter in giving absolute primacy to the economic elite over all other elites and over society in general. The concentration of elite power occurs via dominant corporations having links with other sectors such as the media, which the economic elite owns and controls and uses to perpetuate its dominant ideology. There are also linkages between the corporate elite and the state, a fact which supports the objectives of profit-making and removes the boundaries between the economic and political sectors through advisory councils, political appointments, and the funding of political parties.[74] In other words, Clement rejects a pluralist notion of power.

How Dominant Is the Corporate Elite?

The question of how dominant the economic elite is within a complex industrial society is not easily resolvable and depends on your point of view. However, continuing research has produced some interesting findings about the corporate elite. The most recent study showed how family ownership groups have grown.[75] More than seventy-six percent of the 170 largest Canadian non-financial corporations are now controlled by 17 dominant enterprises of which 11 are single-owner or family-owned. Names like Reichman, Bronfman, Weston, Thomson, Irving, and Desmarais hold the locus of control and some new upwardly mobile non-British families are also moving into this group. The role of control pyramid structures means that families like the Bronfmans can own parts of hundreds of companies and have controlling interest over all of them.[76] Only 53 of the largest 246 public firms are widely owned by the public and the rest have controlling shareholders, often in family-owned firms.

Other research found that large-scale capital is socially integrated in a densely connected network of directorship interlocks.[77] One study of 250 large Canadian corporations concluded that Canadian firms have more interlocking directorships than American firms do, suggesting a tighter circulation of power.[78] Financial companies, and especially banks, occupy the most central position in the network and, in this way, link foreign-controlled with domestically controlled companies. Commercial capital and industrial capital, therefore, have close ties or are joined so that they are much more independent from external capital than previously thought. An inner circle of closely interlocked capitalists that controls super-blocs of indigenous finance capital makes this possible.[79] Yet the direct links between corporations and the state, while present, were not as strong as expected, with the highest elite involvement on university and hospital boards, and the lowest in federal and provincial bureaucracies.[80] In fact, Ornstein's research demonstrates that there is significant ideological conflict between the capitalist class and the state.[81]

While the existence of an elite is not in doubt, questions are being raised about its composition. Porter, for example, had argued that the elite was a homogeneous British upper class. But Ogmundson's research challenged that view with more recent data by pointing out that this British domination is drawing to a close because of greater openness to the elite countering the old notions of social exclusivity and homogeneity.[82] Nakhaie has countered this conclusion by pointing out that the decline of persons of British origin in the elite is only an absolute numerical decline but is certainly not a decline relative to their proportion of the population.[83] Persons of British descent still have effective control of all categories of the elite in spite of the fact that the political and bureaucratic elite is less exclusive than the economic elite. But even here, employees of British ancestry are overrepresented in the Ontario civil service in positions earning over $100 000. It is agreed though that the relation between ethnic origin and elite position is in flux.[84]

Research, then, has made it clear that corporate ownership is concentrated among a fairly small group of people in Canada.[85] In contrast to those who stress foreign ownership and dependency, the work of Carroll and Niosi indicates that the real issue in inequality is the concentration of economic power within the country.[86] Niosi has shown, for example, that even publicly owned companies are run by members of the capitalist class and their advisors. Thus we can conclude that the power of economic elites in Canadian society is strong. How far that power carries over from the economy to other spheres of life is a matter of considerable debate.

Evaluating Elitism

Some people view elitism as an inevitability. The iron law of oligarchy suggests that there will always be a tendency, in every society, for a small elite to dominate the masses.[87] The reason for this is that people tend to accept passively the flow of power to a few persons at the top. For believers in democracy, however, the long-term perpetuation of elite decision-making weakens the general belief in equality and also reduces public participation in decisions affecting the lives of many people.

On the other hand, some argue that far too much has been made of elite control. A focus on boards of directors of corporations, for example, may miss the fact that persons who serve on boards exercise little formal control. Corporate board meetings are short and infrequent, and the directors are often only advisors. So while real power may be legally vested in the board, the actual control is held by managers, owners, and those who prepare corporate information.[88] In addition, there is the argument that elites are neither monolithic nor completely impenetrable. The maturation of Canadian capitalism may, for example, give rise to the emergence of new elite factions, which may compete against established elites (and each other) rather than form a common class front. Moreover, a distinction has been made between the idea of a *strategic* and a *core elite*, the former made up of those who have achieved key functional roles, the latter of those who have inherited wealth and status. While access to the core elite may remain virtually closed, the strategic elite may be more open to persons of demonstrated competence and skill.[89]

There is also some evidence which might point to the role of the strategic elite in changing the overall ethnic composition of the upper strata of society. For example, while francophones were previously underrepresented in virtually every elite, there has been increasing francophone participation in the federal bureaucratic and political elite, and a stronger French-Canadian economic elite has also emerged.[90]

In concluding this discussion, we should note that although many observers are concerned with "access" to the elite, others find the mere existence of an elite distressing.[91] We will return to this issue at the end of the chapter.

POVERTY

We have already seen in Table 3.1 that the quintile of the Canadian population with the lowest incomes (the bottom 20% of the population) receive only 4.6% of the aggregate Canadian income. But at what income level do we define someone as poor? Does a hierarchy of incomes necessarily mean that those with the lowest income are poor?

To answer this question it is important to distinguish between absolute poverty and relative poverty, for these two measures make use of different assumptions of what constitutes poverty. *Absolute poverty* refers to the income level needed for basic subsistence (i.e., food, clothing, shelter). Anyone not having sufficient income to buy what is essential for survival is considered poor. *Relative poverty*, on the other hand, acknowledges that poverty is dependent on community standards. If, for example, a car is a necessity for transportation to work or school, or for participation in community life, then a person who cannot afford a car is considered poor. Because most other persons in the community use automobiles in their daily life, then owning a car becomes the norm against which others can be measured. Both concepts require value judgements which make the identification of poverty somewhat controversial. For absolute poverty, how is basic subsistence defined and what is the minimum threshold for spending on food, shelter, and clothing? For relative poverty, what is the community standard? Should the minimum be the full community standard? half of it? a third? Clearly, what one person considers an absolute necessity, or typical in a community, another person might consider a luxury or totally optional.

For many years, Statistics Canada has been compiling what they call Low Income Cut-Offs (LICO).[92] Low income is calculated by identifying those who spend more than 56% of their income on the basic necessities of life, and the allowance varies by size of the family

---

RESEARCH CLIP 3.4

Understanding Power in Advanced Capitalist Societies

There are two main expressions of power present in advanced capitalist societies. One is *decision-making* regarding when and where and how much capital is invested in the production process. The other is *authority* (direction or disciplining) of labour. Another way to describe this difference is that one type of power is *strategic* pertaining to a long-term plan and the latter is concerned more with the *tactical* decisions of day-to-day operations. Decision-making and strategic roles are identified with the *capitalist-executive class*, and authority over labour is the responsibility of the *new middle class*.

The new middle class lacks real ownership of the means of production but is given the responsibility of the control and surveillance of labour on behalf of capitalists. In that sense, the new middle class is neither working class or capitalist–executive but is intimately related to both. The old middle class, in contrast, was more independent and individualistic through their own labour (working

for self) but with direct entrepreneurial ownership of their own enterprise. The new middle class is characteristic of large bureaucratic enterprises.

Defined as persons who have *both* decision-making power and labour power over three or more persons, the capitalist–executive class in Canada involves about 6% of the population.* The new middle class of managers (administration, budgets, and personnel) makes up about one-quarter of the labour force. In comparison, the United States has a slightly higher proportion of the capitalist–executive class and new middle class. Finland, in contrast, has a smaller new middle class and larger working class.

---

*Obviously, the size of the capitalist–executive class would be reduced significantly if it were redefined to include only large operations such as those with 10 000 or more employees where power is much greater.

Source: Based on Wallace Clement and John Myles, *Relations of Ruling: Class and Gender in Post-Industrial Societies* (Montreal: McGill-Queens University Press, 1994), Chapter 1.

---

and size of the place of residence. For example, in 1996, the low income cut-off for single persons was $16 061 in cities of over 500 000 and $10 933 in rural areas. Or, for a family of four, the cut-off was $31 862 in large cities and $21 690 in rural areas. Most social policy agencies such as the National Council of Welfare use LICO as the measure of poverty whereas Statistics Canada has claimed that it is not necessarily a measure of poverty but only a means to identify those who are substantially worse off than the average.

Figure 3.2 shows that the incidence of low income varies considerably over time, and the evidence is that such variations are directly related to unemployment rates among working age people.[93] Using LICO, the poverty rate was at about 16% or 2 337 000 million people in 1996. The most important determinant of poverty is family type with two-parent families having the lowest poverty rate, and single-parent families with children under 18 having the highest poverty rate. Poverty rates are higher in large cities and among those with less schooling. Poor education can be both a cause and an effect of poverty. Poverty rates are higher for women than for men.[94] Women however play a key role in keeping families out of poverty as the poverty rates drop among families when wives are working. There are also some regional differences with the highest poverty rates in Quebec and the lowest in Prince Edward Island. Perhaps the most dramatic shift over time has been the significant decline in poverty rates for seniors. In 1980, the poverty rate for the elderly was 19.2% but had dropped to 8.7% by 1996. The role of government, corporate, and personal pension programs was making a big difference for this age group.

It has already been noted that poverty is closely linked to unemployment. In the early 1980s, as Canada shifted from a goods-producing economy to a service economy, and in this decade in response to free trade, large numbers of jobs have been lost, particularly in central Canada.[95] One study done in London, Ontario traces the social psychology of being unemployed from the victim's perspective.[96] This largely invisible minority represents the ultimate condition of powerlessness, and is related to the increasing poverty rates of the 1990s. In addition to this group are the large number of working poor who are indeed part of the work force but who are working either part-time and/or for minimum wage with incomes that keep them in poverty.

Statistics Canada has gone on record noting that income inequality before transfer payments has grown significantly and continues a trend begun in the early 1980s. From 1995 to 1996 alone, the lowest quintile lost $500 in average family income whereas the highest quintile gained $2000 in average family income.[97] This is why the debate about the meaning and measurement of poverty is so important. For example, the richest 20% spend a lower percentage of their income on food and shelter than the poorest 20% and yet the wealthiest eat much better and live in nicer homes. Given the difficulties with establishing poverty lines using the old methods, a new method under testing is the *market basket* approach. The idea is to identify a specific list of goods and services required by all people and to price them in a variety of locations. By adding up the total from this list, a baseline income qualifying as low income can be established. The market basket then would differ from city to city.

The big question is what items should go in the market basket. How many rolls of toilet paper or paper towels? Are allowances made for taxis or just busses? Are first aid supplies included in the shopping list? How about dental checkups, and if so how many? Is a cheaper

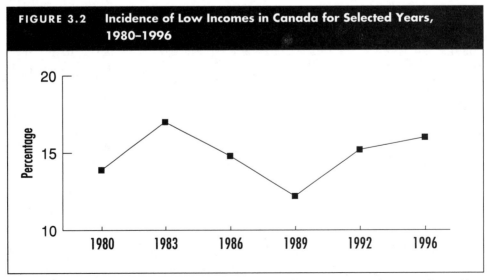

FIGURE 3.2   Incidence of Low Incomes in Canada for Selected Years, 1980–1996

Source: Adapted from "Income Distributions by Size in Canada, 1996," *Statistics Canada*, 1996 Catalogue 13–207, Text Table III.

apartment in a basement with few windows acceptable or is a more expensive apartment on a higher floor a necessity? And what about the need for discretionary income whereby the person can make some additional choices? How much discretionary income is important for buying a magazine, eating out, or taking a vacation for your mental health? These are the kinds of questions that lead to wide swings in the totals of different market baskets. For an excellent discussion of the issues and a feel for the controversy of this issue, compare the work of Christopher Sarlo with that of the National Council of Welfare (NCW).[98] Sarlo emerged with a much lower poverty line with his market basket than others identified by the NCW. He argued that poverty is not a significant problem in Canada and probably only includes about one million people because it includes people like students, or people under-reporting their incomes, and does not take into consideration that people do have access to other forms of assistance in charity programs. The NCW, on the other hand, argues that people have a right to their own dignity, should not be visibly poorer than the rest of society, and should not have to be treated like social pariahs. The fear, from this perspective, is that the market basket approach might lower the poverty lines to the point that the problem of poverty is defined out of existence. This is where ideology comes into play as those who want to minimize the problem clash with those who want to mobilize the government to action in defence of the poor.

In 1996, the federal government made a significant change in the way it allocated funding to provide aid to the poor and provide for the health, education, and assistance needs of Canadians.[99] The previous mechanism, known as the Canada Assistance Plan, required provinces to provide welfare assistance without provincial residency requirements with financing from Ottawa and also cost-shared by the provinces. With the new Canada Health and Social Transfer (CHST), provinces are given more control about how the federal funding is used and federal spending on such assistance is reduced. All of this is taking place in a climate of deficit reduction at both the federal and provincial levels which means that a clear proactive national policy to deal with income inequalities is threatened.

THE STATE AND INEQUALITY

In contrast to the United States where poverty rates are the highest among industrialized countries,[100] Canada has historically been much more active in the use of government programs to reduce inequalities in what is called the *welfare state*. As essentially a post-war phenomenon well established by the 1960s, the welfare state entailed social policies from medical care to old age security to family allowance to provide for human needs which would not be covered by the capitalist mode of production.[101] Rather than just focus on the poor or those who passed income tests, the objective grew to provide for all socio-economic groups, though it was clear that basic needs were most acute for those of low income. A second way in which the state attempted to deal with inequalities was to establish publicly owned businesses called *crown corporations* (e.g., for utilities and telephones, airlines, railroads but also at select times for resource development such as oil with the establishment of Petro-Canada) to provide basic services for a young and sparsely populated country, to stimulate regional economic development, or to build a more diversified economy beyond resource dependence.[102]

A third way in which the state has responded to inequalities (particularly regional inequalities) has been through *equalization grants*. In 1937, the Rowell-Sirois Royal Commission on Dominion–Provincial Relations advocated a more equitable distribution of social-service benefits because of the income and employment inequality that existed at that time. By 1957, the government had established equalization grants which redistributed tax revenues so that regions of Canada with incomes lower than the national average would be able to provide education and health facilities at the same level as regions with higher incomes. Sensing that a more comprehensive program of development was needed, the Department of Regional Economic Expansion was created in 1969, but its successes were limited because of dependence on heavy government tax incentives. As Acheson pointed out, the net effect of these efforts was that underdeveloped areas virtually became "client-states" of the federal government. This was a consequence of their dependence on federal handouts through either grants or transfer payments such as unemployment insurance, or income supplements to raise the standard of living of their residents.[103] Matthews labels this same phenomenon *transfer dependency*.[104]

However the shift to neo-conservatism in the 1990s has threatened the capacity of the state to respond to inequalities. Themes such as the privatization of public companies and the down-sizing of the public sector has changed the role which the state has played in a shift away from dependence on the public sector as a way of responding to societal needs. Most importantly, fiscal cutbacks and tax reductions eliminate the ability of the state to respond the way it had. In combination with the aging of the population and the shrinking of the labour force relative to the growing aging population, Li refers to this as the *fiscal crisis of the state* because of how social programs are threatened.[105] Universal medical care still remains a Canadian distinctive but is under significant duress. In general, the focus of social programs is now primarily on the poor, and even here severe cutbacks are being experienced. But it has also been shown that the effects of government cutbacks have a gender bias and that women have been particularly negatively affected through layoffs, the decline of public sector employment, and the availability of government services.[106]

How successful is the state in reducing inequality? It is clear that income inequality in Canadian society has continued to grow even though government transfer programs have provided minimal supports for the very poor.[107] But should we expect the state to perform this function, and will it really be successful in mitigating inequality? The answers to these questions depend on your concept of the state and who controls it.

The *institutional approach* views the state as an independent body meant to serve as the arbiter between different groups and opposing interests in a society. The focus in this approach is on constitutions, laws, policies, and rights enshrined in government documents and operationalized in government structures. The *instrumental approach* suggests that the state is intimately linked to capitalist interests.[108] In its strongest form, instrumentalism contends that the state is dominated by business interests. The focus, then, is on the imposition of capitalist requirements on state policies. The *structuralist approach* maintains that the state is more or less structurally independent, but that it embodies and supports the assumptions of the capitalist society, as expressed in the phrase "relative autonomy."[109] The latter two approaches attempt to explain how the state operates more clearly in terms of socio-economic forces rather than just policy evaluation.

The question of how autonomous or independent the state is from capitalist interests is extremely important. There is no question that the state underwrites the capitalist economy through the provision of labour power via immigration, education, and health care policies. It also provides loans, depreciation allowances, and direct and indirect subsidies (through various forms of write-offs and employment incentives).[110] Governments also support labour flexibility for profit-making by providing a "safety net" of social programs for citizens when corporations lay them off. Monopoly capitalism, political economy points out, thus benefits as the state pays for labour costs (e.g., education, medical care, provisions for the unemployed or laid off, labour relocation) through the taxpayer while at the same time profits are retained by the private sector.[111] It has been argued, more attention has been given to investment and policing than to

The Quicksand Effect

Since the early 1980s, the policy of countries that are members of the Organization For Economic Co-operation and Development (OECD), which includes Canada, has been to promote economic growth through monetary restraint (low inflation) and fiscal retrenchment (lower state expenditures) as well as globalization of production and distribution. Much to the alarm of these countries, these policies have produced increasing income polarization, high unemployment, and the exclusion of social groups from stabilized living. Thus the economic growth has been somewhat like building on quicksand because at the very time that people need more support due to the new flexibilities demanded in the market, that support has been taken away.

One of the key things contributing to the cohesion of societies is the role which the state plays in providing social protection (e.g., the law) and services (e.g.,

medical care, education) which ensures a sense of personal and collective security but also provides a reason for the resident to be committed to the society in which they live. Perhaps the most basic thing a society can give each member is the sense of worth and sense of place that comes from providing each person with employment and adequate income. A competitive, globalized, market economy has contributed to a significant precariousness in this regard for segments of society which all OECD countries are now recognizing more clearly.

To Ponder:

Do you agree that reductions in the role of the state could have the ultimate effect of reducing residents' commitment to the state? Is this another reason why Canada is becoming so precarious as a society?

Source: Organization For Economic Co-operation and Development, *Societal Cohesion and the Globalising Economy*. Paris: 1997.

welfare.[112] These issues are endemic to any capitalist society, but it is clear that the Canadian state plays a direct and indirect role in the economy to ensure the well-being of its citizens, but does so in a way that is particularly supportive of the interests of the capitalist class.

On the other hand, the state does maintain some distance from capitalist interests. Indeed, without that distance, political action by others would be futile. Public accountability and public pressure groups create an interactive effect that must also be considered. The state itself has its own interests. The fact that 16–21% of the labour force (depending on how it is computed) work in the public sector, and the fact that public bureaucracies have their own agendas suggest that economic power is far from absolute.[113] One study of political and business elites demonstrated that state elites have more contact with the business elite than any other elite group, but that these contacts have little effect on the policy positions of business leaders.[114] This suggests that business may have more of an impact on government than the reverse, in spite of their distance from each other.

To naively expect the state always to be an instrument of the people is idealistic. In contrast, to view the state as only an instrument of capitalist interests suggests despair and futility. To put it more realistically, the state does support inequality but at the same time it attempts to modify some of the harshness of this inequality. How we respond to this situation is the subject of our last section.

RESPONSES TO INEQUALITY

The use of the term "inequality" suggests that we all agree that equality is the normative or moral condition. The fact is, however, that Canada remains a stratified society and there is no ideological consensus on whether that inequality is necessary or unnecessary or, indeed, on the meaning of "equality" itself. (To believe in equality at the ballot boxes, for example, is certainly not the same as to believe in equality in economic matters.) At the same time the reality of individual differences must be integrated with our conceptions of what Canadian society should or could be.

As each of us encounters social reality, we employ interpretive lenses that help us to understand what we see. These lenses can be called *ideology*, or the complex of values, assumptions, and beliefs that helps us "interpret" the social phenomena we observe. Ideology also supplies a "selectivity" which allows one person to perceive one aspect of a phenomenon and another person to see something different. Above all, ideology provides the interpretive apparatus that helps us "evaluate" and judge social reality. It is not unexpected, then, that each of us uses different lenses according to our different experiences, our family background, our class interests, and the values we personally cherish. This is to say that inequality, which has been established in this chapter as objective reality, will be perceived, interpreted, and evaluated from many different perspectives. While there is considerable individual variation in ideological perspective, ideologies tend to cluster in several categories.

In an erudite presentation of ideologies in Canada, Marchak argues that there are two fundamental ideological continuums.[115] The *individual–collectivist continuum* ranges from extreme individualism (the absolute freedom of the individual with few, if any, constraints or conformity pressures) to extreme collectivism (the precedence of the social good and conformity to society's unity and well-being), with many intermediate points in between. The *egalitarianism–elitism continuum* ranges from its elitist extreme (complete power to those who rule) to extreme egalitarianism (absolute equality of condition and opportunity), also with many points in between.

Without dealing with the extreme positions, which have small but sometimes vocal followings, three dominant ideologies in Canada can be identified. By laying one continuum horizontally and the other vertically so that they intersect one another, it is possible to combine elements from both continuums. When egalitarianism and collectivism are combined, the result is an ideological position known as *socialism*. Socialism advocates the unity of society amidst conditions of full equality, therefore condemning any practices that exploit some people to the benefit of others. The combination of elitism and collectivism produces the ideology known as *conservatism*. Conservatives also advocate the unity of society but where everyone has an assigned place in the social hierarchy. It is the government's role in this ideology to preserve the hierarchy and maintain order. The third ideology intersects individualism with elitism in what is known as *liberalism*. In liberalism, society is not so much a unity as it is a collection of individuals whose rights and freedoms must be protected. The role of government is to ensure that there is sufficient equity in the structure of society to allow individuals to achieve their own objectives.

Socialism is not a dominant force in Canadian society except in its social democratic format which accepts the basic values of liberalism, but accentuates the need for greater equality and some government ownership of strategic industries and resources. On the other hand, conservatism in the last half century has also been affected by liberal ideals of individualism. According to Marchak, the "daily life of Canadians is based on liberal premises" (p. 24). Since Marchak penned these thoughts, there has been a marked shift toward conservatism in Canadian society—even to the point that social democratic provincial governments have lost their unique ideological distinctiveness. The divestment of public ownership, the challenge to medicare, and general fiscal stringency through cutbacks in the public sector have diverted more interest from the issue of inequality than at any time in recent history.

The search for a just society is unending because there are different conceptions of what is just. For this reason, we can see responses to inequality as a matter of ideological conflict. However, ideological conflict is more than differences of opinion. It is a matter of analyzing how these ideological positions are reflective of class, regional, ethnic, or gender interests, and how they prevent some people from realizing their potential. This analysis requires careful scrutiny rather than sloppy generalizations or stereotypes. But by conducting such an analysis, we can uncover important dynamics that tell us a lot more about Canadian society.

FURTHER EXPLORATION

1. Why is the issue of inequality controversial? Choose one form of inequality and explain the forces at work in sustaining and disrupting this form of inequality.

2. Which dimension of inequality is most problematic for you? What suggestions do you have for reducing it? Why are some forms of inequality more acceptable than other forms of inequality?

3. Look for evidence in the print media of the shift to the right and the movement away from attention to the issue of inequality. What are the advantages and disadvantages of this shift and how are people affected?

SELECTED READINGS

Armstrong, Pat and Hugh Armstrong. *The Double Ghetto: Canadian Women and Their Segregated Work.* 3rd ed. Toronto: McClelland and Stewart, 1994.

Brodie, Janine M., *Women and Canadian Public Policy* (Toronto: Harcourt Brace, 1996).

Curtis, James, Edward Grabb and Neil Guppy, eds. *Social Inequality in Canada: Patterns, Problems, Policies.* 3rd ed. Scarborough: Prentice-Hall, 1999.

Hamilton, Roberta, *Gendering the Vertical Mosaic* (Toronto: Copp Clark, 1996).

Li, Peter S., *The Making of Post-War Canada* (Toronto: Oxford, 1996).

Nakhaie, M. Reza (ed.), *Debates on Social Inequality: Class, Gender, and Ethnicity in Canada* (Toronto: Harcourt Brace, 1999).

Satzewich, Vic (ed.), *Racism and Social Inequality in Canada* (Toronto: Thompson, 1998).

Statistics Canada. *Women in the Labour Force*, 1994 ed. Catalogue 75-507; and *Perspectives on Labour and Income*, Catalogue 75-001; *Women in Canada: A Statistical Report*, Third Edition 1995, 89–503E.

ENDNOTES

1   The difficulty people have in placing themselves within a class or the tendency for people to see themselves as middle class is documented by John Goyder and Peter Pineo, "Social Class Self-identification," in James E. Curtis and William G. Scott, eds., *Social Stratification in Canada*, 2nd ed. (Scarborough: Prentice-Hall, 1979), 434.

2   Benard Blishen, W. Carroll, and C. Moore, "The 1981 Socio-economic Index for Occupations in Canada," *Canadian Review of Sociology and Anthropology* 24(1987): 465–88.

3   For a review of these approaches and their critics, see Edward G. Grabb, *Theories of Social Inequality: Classical and Contemporary Perspectives* (Toronto: Holt Rinehart and Winston, 1990).

4   For examples of work in this tradition, see Wallace Clement, T*he Challenge of Class Analysis* (Ottawa: Carleton University Press, 1988); and Henry Veltmeyer, *The Canadian Class Structure* (Toronto: Garamond, 1986).

5   Michael Ornstein, "Social Class and Economic Inequality," in James Curtis and Lorne Tepperman, eds., *Understanding Canadian Society* (Toronto: McGraw-Hill Ryerson, 1988), 185–221.

6   Wallace Clement, "Comparative Class Analysis: Locating Canada in a North American Context," *Canadian Review of Sociology and Anthropology*, 27(1990): 462–86.

7   For an application of class analysis and political economy to Canadian society, see Wallace Clement, *The Challenge of Class Analysis* (Ottawa: Carleton University Press, 1988). See also Patricia Marchak, "Canadian Political Economy," *Canadian Review of Sociology and Anthropology* 22(1985): 673–709; Special Issue on Comparative Political Economy, *Canadian Review of Sociology and Anthropology* 26(1989), No. 1; Wallace Clement and Daniel Drache, eds., *The New Practical Guide to Political Economy* (Toronto: Lorimer, 1985); Wallace Clement and Glen Williams, *The New Canadian Political Economy* (Montreal: McGill-Queens University Press, 1989). See also the journal *Studies in Political Economy*.

8   For an excellent analysis of Canadian society from a political economy perspective, see Peter S. Li, *The Making of Post-War Canada* (Toronto: Oxford, 1996). For a more specialized analysis, see Julie White, *Sisters and Solidarity: Women and Unions in Canada* (Toronto: Thompson, 1993).

9   S.H. Milner and H. Milner, *The Decolonization of Quebec* (Toronto: McClelland and Stewart, 1973), chap. 3.

10 Jacques Dofny and Marcel Rioux, "Social Class in French Canada," in Marcel Rioux and Yves Martin, eds., *French-Canadian Society*, vol. I (Toronto: McClelland and Stewart, 1971), 307–18.

11 See Anthony Richmond, *Post-War Immigrants in Canada* (Toronto: University of Toronto Press, 1970), 3–26 for a brief sketch on immigration policy.

12 See, for example, Monica Boyd, "Status Attainment in Canada: Findings of the Canadian Mobility Study," *Canadian Review of Sociology and Anthropology* 18(1981): 657–73.

13 Wsevolod W. Isajiw, Aysan Sev'er, Leo Driedger, "Ethnic Identity and Social Mobility: A Test of the Drawback Model," *Canadian Journal of Sociology* 18(1993): 177–96; Edward N. Herberg, "The Ethno-Racial Socio-economic Hierarchy in Canada: Theory and Analysis of the New Vertical Mosaic," *International Journal of Comparative Sociology* 31(1990): 206–21.

14 Jason Z. Lian and David Ralph Matthews, "Does The Vertical Mosaic Still Exist? Ethnicity And Income In Canada," *Canadian Review of Sociology and Anthropology* 35(1998)4:461–481.

15 Richard A. Wanner, "Expansion And Ascription: Trends In Educational Opportunity In Canada 1920–1994," *Canadian Review of Sociology and Anthropology* 36(1999)3:409–442.

16 Hugh Lautard and Neil Guppy, "Revisiting The Vertical Mosaic: Occupational Stratification Among Canadian Ethnic Groups," in Peter S. Li (ed.), *Race and Ethnic Relations in Canada*, Second Edition (Toronto: Oxford University Press, 1999), 219–252.

17 Carol Agocs and Monica Boyd, "The Canadian Ethnic Mosaic Recast for the 1990's," in James Curtis, Edward Grabb, and Neil Guppy, eds., *Social Inequality in Canada: Patterns, Problems, Policies*, 2nd ed. (Scarborough: Prentice Hall, 1993), 332. For the "new" vertical mosaic, see p. 337.

18 J.A. Geschwender and N. Guppy, "Ethnicity, Educational Attainment And Earned Income Among Canadian Born Men And Women," *Canadian Ethnic Studies* 27(1995)1:67–84; Lian and Matthews, "Does The Vertical Mosaic Still Exist?".

19 Richard A. Wanner, "Prejudice, Profit Or Productivity: Explaining Returns To Human Capital Among Male Immigrants To Canada", *Canadian Ethnic Studies* 30(1998)3:6–23.

20 Peter S. Li, "The Market Value And Social Value Of Race", in Vic Satzewich (ed.), *Racism and Social Inequality in Canada* (Toronto: Thompson, 1998), 115–130.

21 Feng Hou and T.R. Balakrishnan, "The Integration of Visible Minorities In Contemporary Canadian Society," *Canadian Journal of Sociology* 21(1996)3:307–326.

22 Peter S. Li, *Ethnic Inequality in a Class Society* (Toronto: Wall and Thompson, 1988). See also Raymond Breton, Wserolod W. Isajiw, Warren Kalbach, and Jeffrey G. Reitz, *Ethnic Identity and Equality: Varieties of Experiences in a Canadian City* (Toronto: University of Toronto Press, 1990) who argue that the relationship between ethnic persistence and equality can be both an asset and a liability and therefore is highly variable.

23 Mildred A. Schwartz, *Politics and Territory: The Sociology of Regional Persistence in Canada* (Montreal: McGill-Queens University Press, 1974), 336.

24 Robert J. Brym, ed., *Regionalism in Canada* (Toronto: Irwin, 1986), 4–18.

25 This argument is developed in some detail by Carl Cuneo, "A Class Perspective on Regionalism," in Daniel Glenday, Hubert Guidon and Allan Turowetz, eds., *Modernization and the Canadian State* (Toronto: Macmillan, 1978).

26 R. Keith Semple, "Urban Dominance, Foreign Ownership, and Corporate Concentration," in James Curtis et al., *Social Inequality in Canada: Patterns, Problems and Policies* (Scarborough: Prentice Hall, 1988), 343–56; and Benjamin Higgins, *The Rise and Fall of Montreal* (Moncton: Canadian Institute for Research on Regional Development, 1986).

27 Neil Swan and John Serjak, "Analysing Regional Disparities," in James Curtis, Edward Grabb and Neil Guppy, *Social Inequality in Canada*, 2nd ed., 430–48.

28 For a presentation of the metropolis-hinterland thesis, see Arthur Davis, "Canadian Society and History as Hinterland and Metropolis," in Richard J. Ossenberg, ed., *Canadian Society: Pluralism, Change and Conflict* (Scarborough: Prentice-Hall, 1971), 6–32.

29 For one account of the agrarian reaction, see John A. Irving, *The Social Credit Movement in Alberta* (Toronto: University of Toronto Press, 1959). Pierre Vallieres' book is entitled *White Niggers of America* (Toronto: McClelland and Stewart, 1971).

30 For an example of this kind of regional class analysis, see Peter Sinclair, "Class Structure and Populist Protest: The Case of Western Canada," *Canadian Journal of Sociology* 1(1975): 1–17.

31 Ralph Matthews, "Class Interests and the Role of the State in the Development of Canada's East Coast Fishery," *Canadian Issues: Journal of the Association for Canadian Studies* 3(1980): 115–24.

32 Bonnie J. Fox, "The Feminist Challenge," in Robert J. Brym, *From Culture to Power*, chap. 5.

33 E.D. Nelson and Barrie W. Robinson, *Gender in Canada* (Scarborough: Prentice Hall Allyn and Bacon, 1999), Chapter 1.

34 Liviana Calzavara, "Trends in the Employment Opportunities of Women in Canada, 1930–1980," in *Research Studies of the Commission on Equality in Employment*, 517; and Statistics Canada Catalogue #93-110 and #75-507.

35 *Women in the Labour Force*, 1994 Edition, Statistics Canada 75-507, Tables 2.8 and 4.4.

36 Ann DuVy, Nancy Mandell, and Norene Pupo, *Few Choices: Women, Work and Family* (Toronto: Garamond, 1989), 18.

37 Pat Armstrong and Hugh Armstrong, *The Double Ghetto: Canadian Women and Their Segregated Work* (Toronto: McClelland and Stewart, 1994), 9.

38 Vijay Agnew, *Resisting Discrimination: Women In Asia, Africa, and the Caribbean and the Women's Movement in Canada* (Toronto: University Of Toronto Press, 1996)

39 For a good review of the approaches discussed here, see Eileen Saunders, "Theoretical Approaches To The Study Of Women", in Curtis, Grabb, and Guppy, *Social Inequality in Canada*, Third Edition, 168–185.

40 DuVy, Mandell, and Pupo, *Few Choices: Women, Work and Family*, 46.

41 Margrit Eichler, "The Connection Between Paid and Unpaid Labour and its Implications for Creating Equality for Women," in *Research Studies of the Commission on Equality in Employment*, 539–45. Cf. also Ann Duffy and Norene Pupo, *The Part-time Paradox: Connecting Gender, Work and Family* (Toronto: McClelland and Stewart, 1992).

42 Carl J. Cuneo, "Have Women Become more Proletarianized than Men?" *Canadian Review of Sociology and Anthropology* 22(1985): 465–95 and William K. Carroll, "Which Women are more Proletarianized? Gender, Class and Occupation in Canada," *Canadian Review of Sociology and Anthropology* 24(1987): 571–85.

43 Paul Phillips and Erin Phillips, *Women and Work: Inequality in the Labour Market*, rev. ed. (Toronto: Lorimer, 1993); Pat Armstrong and Hugh Armstrong, *The Double Ghetto*, rev. ed. (Toronto: McClelland and Stewart, 1984); Meg Luxton and Harriet Rosenberg, *Through the Kitchen Window: The Politics of Home and Family* (Toronto: Garamond, 1986); Carl Cuneo, *Pay Equity: The Labour/Feminist Challenge* (Toronto: Oxford, 1990); and Jane Jenson, Elisabeth Hagen, and Ceillaigh Reddy, eds., *Feminization of the Labour Force: Paradoxes and Promises* (New York: Oxford, 1988).

44 Meg Luxton, Harriet Rosenberg, and Sedef Arat-Koc, eds., *Through the Kitchen Window: The Politics of Home and Family* (Toronto: Garamond, 1990); Kevin McQuillan and Marilyn Belle, "Who Does What? Gender And The Division Of Labour In Canadian Households", in Curtis, Grabb, and Guppy, *Social Inequality in Canada*, Third Edition, 186–198.

45 Roberta Hamilton, *Gendering the Vertical Mosaic* (Toronto: Copp Clark, 1996).

46 S.J. Wilson, *Women, the Family and the Economy*, 3rd ed. (Toronto: McGraw-Hill Ryerson, 1991). See also Sandra Burt, Lorraine Code, and Lindsay Dorney, eds., *Changing Patterns: Women in Canada*, 2nd ed. (Toronto: McClelland and Stewart, 1993).

47 *The Report of the Royal Commission on Equality in Employment* was published in 1984 and the Employment Equity Act was passed in 1986. The results of the research reports done by the Commission was published in 1985 as Research Studies Of The Commission On Equality In Employment.

48 For good discussions of gender relations and gender socialization, see Marlene Mackie, *Gender Relations in Canada: Further Explorations* (Toronto: Butterworths, 1991) and *Constructing Men and Women: Gender Socialization* (Toronto: Holt Rinehart and Winston, 1987).

49 Gillian Creese and Brenda Beagan, "Gender At Work: Seeking Solutions For Women's Equality", in Curtis, Grabb, and Guppy, *Social Inequality in Canada*, Third Edition, 199–211. See also Janine Brodie, *Women and Canadian Public Policy* (Toronto: Harcourt Brace, 1996) and Caroline Andrew and Sanda Rodgers (eds.), *Women and the Canadian State* (Montreal: McGill-Queens University Press, 1997)

50 Joanna Everitt, "Public Opinion And Social Movements: The Women's Movement and the Gender Gap in Canada", *Canadian Journal of Political Science* 31(1998)4:743–765.

51 John Porter, *The Vertical Mosaic* (Toronto: University of Toronto Press, 1965), 38–59. For a good review of the legacy of *The Vertical Mosaic*, see Rick Helmes-Hayes and James Curtis (eds.), *The Vertical Mosaic Revisited* (Toronto: University of Toronto Press, 1998).

52 For an excellent discussion of the nature and significance of the brain drain, see Walter Adams, ed., *The Brain Drain* (Toronto: Macmillan Co. of Canada, 1968); also K.V. Pankhurst, "Migration between Canada and the United States" in *The Annals of the American Academy of Political and Social Science* 367(1966): 53–62.

53 For an assessment of John Porter's analysis of class, mobility, education, and power in Canadian society, see a special issue (No. 5) of the *Canadian Review of Sociology and Anthropology* 18(1981) in memory of John Porter.

54 Economic Council of Canada, Seventh Annual Review, 1970, 56–61; and Max Van Zur-Mehlen, "The Ph.D. Dilemma in Canada," in Sylvia Ostry, ed., *Canadian Higher Education in the Seventies* (Ottawa: Economic Council of Canada, 1972), 79.

55 Michael D. Ornstein argues that the extent of mobility must be related to features of the labour market such as employment opportunities or the hiring and promotion policies of corporations. "The Occupational Mobility of Men in Ontario," *Canadian Review of Sociology and Anthropology* 18(1981): 183–215. See

also Harvey Rich, "The Vertical Mosaic Reconsidered," *Journal of Canadian Studies* 11(1976): 14–31, who argues that Porter described an archaic rather than contemporary view of Canadian society.

56 Sid Gilbert and Hugh A. McRoberts, "Academic Stratification and Education Plans: A Reassessment," *Canadian Review of Sociology and Anthropology* 14(1977): 34–47.

57 John Porter, Marion Porter, and Benard R. Blishen, *Stations and Callings: Making it Through the School System* (Toronto: Methuen, 1982), 311–15; and Neil Guppy and Bruce Arai, "Who Benefits from Higher Education? Differences by Sex, Social Class, and Ethnic Background," in Curtis, Grabb, and Guppy, eds., *Social Inequality in Canada*, 214–32.

58 Monica Boyd, "Status Attainment in Canada: Findings of the Canadian Mobility Study," *Canadian Review of Sociology and Anthropology* 18(1981): 670.

59 Monica Boyd et al., *Ascription and Achievement: Studies in Mobility and Status Attainment in Canada* (Ottawa: Carleton University Press, 1985), 517–23. For an interesting historical study of the role of achievement in the growth of the Canadian middle class, see Robert Lanning, *The National Album: Collective Biography and the Formation of the Canadian Middle Class* (Ottawa: Carleton University Press, 1996).

60 Harry Braverman, *Labour and Monopoly Capital: The Degradation of Work in the Twentieth Century* (New York: Monthly Review, 1974).

61 Alfred A. Hunter, *Class Tells*, 2nd ed., 63.

62 Graham S. Lowe, "Labour Markets, Inequality, and The Future Of Work", in Curtis, Grabb and Guppy, eds., *Social Inequality in Canada*, 113–27. See also Harvey Krahn and Graham Lowe, Work, *Industry and Canadian Society*, 3rd ed. (Toronto: Nelson, 1998).

63 Gillian Creese, Neil Guppy and Martin Meissner, "Ups and Downs on the Ladder of Success: Social Mobility in Canada," Statistics Canada Catalogue 11-612E, 1991.

64 Edward B. Harvey and Ivan Charmer, "Social Mobility and Occupational Attainments of University Graduates," *Canadian Review of Sociology and Anthropology* 12(1975): 134–49; John C. Goyder and James E. Curtis, "Occupational Mobility in Canada over Four Generations," *Canadian Review of Sociology and Anthropology* 14(1977): 303–19. For a good review of the recent evidence relating stratification to accessibility, see Paul Anisef and Norman Okihiro, *Losers & Winners: The Pursuit of Equality and Social Justice in Higher Education* (Toronto: Butterworths, 1982).

65 Alfred A. Hunter, *Class Tells*, 83–84.

66 Michael Ornstein, "The Occupational Mobility of Men in Ontario," *Canadian Review of Sociology and Anthropology* 18(1981): 193–215. See also Robert Brym, *From Culture to Power,* 93–95.

67 Richard A. Wanner, "Patterns and Trends in Occupational Mobility," in Curtis, Grabb and Guppy, eds., *Social Inequality in Canada*, 174. See also Edward N. Herberg, Op. Cit. who argues that a contest model of mobility is more appropriate to Canada than an ascriptive model.

68 Wallace Clement and John Myles, *Relations of Ruling* (Montreal: McGill-Queens University Press, 1994), p. 4.

69 Tom Naylor, "The Rise and Fall of the Third Commercial Empire of the St. Lawrence," in Gary Teeple, ed., *Capitalism and the National Question in Canada* (Toronto: University of Toronto Press, 1972), 1–41.

70 R.J. Richardson, "Merchants Against Industry: An Empirical Study of the Debate," *Canadian Journal of Sociology* 7(1982): 279–95.

71 John Porter, *The Vertical Mosaic*, chap. 7.

72 Wallace Clement, *The Canadian Corporate Elite: An Analysis of Economic Power* (Toronto: McClelland and Stewart, 1975).

73 Wallace Clement, *Continental Corporate Power* (Toronto: McClelland and Stewart, 1977), chaps. 6–8.

74 See also Dennis Olsen, *The State Elite* (Toronto: McClelland and Stewart, 1980).

75 R. Jack Richardson, "Economic Concentration and Social Power in Contemporary Canada," in James Curtis and Lorne Tepperman, eds., *Images of Canada: The Sociological Tradition* (Scarborough: Prentice-Hall, 1990), 341–50.

76 The conclusion of this study was that countries in which billionaire heirs' wealth is large relative to GDP in contrast to self-made wealth billionaire wealth grew more slowly economically because less was spent on innovation and their preferential access to capital helped preserve less competitive firms. Randall Morck, David A. Strangeland, and Bernard Young note that free trade might change this traditional pattern in Canada. "Inherited Wealth, Corporate Control And Economic Growth: The Canadian Disease?" (University Of Alberta, Institute For Financial Research, Working Paper 4–98, 1998).

77 William K. Carroll, John Fox, and Michael D. Ornstein, "The Network of Directorate Links Among the Largest Canadian Firms," *Canadian Review of Sociology and Anthropology* 19(1982): 44–69.

78 Michael D. Ornstein, "The Boards and Executives of the Largest Canadian Corporations: Size, Composition, Interlocks," *Canadian Journal of Sociology* 1(1976): 411–37 and "The Social Organization of the Canadian Capitalist Class in Comparative Perspective," *Canadian Review of Sociology and Anthropology* 26(1989): 151–77.

79 See the work of William K. Carroll, Corporate Power and Canadian Capitalism (Vancouver: University of British Columbia Press, 1986); and "The Individual, Class and Corporate Power in Canada", *Canadian Journal of Sociology* 9(1984): 245–68.

80 John Fox and Michael Ornstein, "The Canadian State and Corporate Elites in the Post-War Period," *Canadian Review of Sociology and Anthropology* 23(1986): 481–506.

81 Michael Ornstein, "Canadian Capital and the Canadian State: Ideology in an Era of Crisis", in Robert J. Brym, ed., *The Structure of the Canadian Capitalist Class* (Toronto: Garamond, 1985).

82 R. Ogmundson, "Perspectives on the Class and Ethnic Origins of Canadian Elites: A Methodological Critique of the Porter/Clement/Olsen Tradition," *Canadian Journal of Sociology* 15(1990): 165–77 and R. Ogmundson and J. McLaughlin, "Trends in the Ethnic Origins of Canadian Elites; The Decline of the Brits?" *Canadian Review of Sociology and Anthropology* 29(1992): 227–42.

83 M. Reza Nakhaie, "Vertical Mosaic Among The Elites: The New Imagery Revisited", *Canadian Review of Sociology and Anthropology* 34(1997)1:1–24. M. Reza Nakhaie, "Ethnic Inequality: Well-Paid Employees Of The Ontario Public Bureaucracy", *Canadian Ethnic Studies* 30(1998)1:119–139.

84 M. Reza Nakhaie, "Ownership And Management Position Of Canadian Ethnic Groups in 1973 and 1989", *Canadian Journal of Sociology* 20(1995)2:167–192.

85 Andreas Antoniou and Robin Rowley, "The Ownership Structure of the Largest Canadian Corporations, 1979," *Canadian Journal of Sociology* 11(1986): 253–68; and Julia S. O'Connor, "Ownership, Class, And Public Policy", in Curtis, Grabb, and Guppy, *Social Inequality in Canada,* Third Edition, 35–47.

86 Jorge Niosi, Canadian Capitalism: A Study of Power in the Canadian Business Establishment (Toronto: James Lorimer, 1981); and William K. Carroll, "Dependency, Imperialism, and the Capitalist Class in Canada," in Brym, *The Structure of the Canadian Capitalist Class*, 45.

87 Robert Michels, *Political Parties: A Sociological Study of the Oligarchical Tendencies of Modern Democracy* (New York: Free Press, 1966).

88 See for example, D.W. Dimick and V.V. Murray, "Career and Personal Characteristics of the Managerial Technostructure in Canadian Business," *Canadian Review of Sociology and Anthropology* 15(1978): 372–84; and Terence H. White, "Boards of Directors: Control and Decision-Making in Canadian Corporations," *Canadian Review of Sociology and Anthropology* 16(1979): 77–95.

89 Merrijoy Kelner, "Ethnic Penetration into Toronto's Elite Structure," *Canadian Review of Sociology and Anthropology* 7(1970): 128–37.

90 See Jorge Niosi, *Canadian Capitalism: A Study of Power in the Canadian Business Establishment* (Toronto: James Lorimer, 1981). For a discussion of the issue of francophone participation in the federal bureaucracy, Cf. Christopher Beattie, Jacques Desy, and Stephen Longstaff, *Bureaucratic Careers: Anglophones and Francophones in the Canadian Public Service* (Ottawa: Information Canada, 1972); and Christopher Beattie, *Minority Men in a Majority Setting* (Toronto: McClelland and Stewart, 1975).

91 For a discussion of the ideological use to which elite analysis may be applied, see Harvey Rich, "John Porter's Sociology and Liberal Democracy," *Canadian Journal of Sociology* 17(1992): 193–98.

92 See Statistics Canada, Catalogue 13-207.

93 National Council Of Welfare, Poverty Profile 1996 (Ottawa, 1998); David. P. Ross and E. Richard Shillington and Clarence Lochhead, *The Canadian Fact Book on Poverty 1994* (Ottawa: Canadian Council on Social Development, 1994); Sandra Harder, *Poverty in Canada* (Library Of Parliament Research Branch 88–14E, 1996); and *The New Face of Poverty* (Economic Council Of Canada, 1992).

94 This is understood as the feminization of poverty. For a discussion of women and poverty, see Morley Gunderson, Leon Muszynski, and Jennifer Keck, *Women and Labour Market Poverty* (Ottawa: Canadian Advisory Council on The Status of Women, 1990).

95 Garnett Picot and Ted Wannell, "Job Loss and Labour Market Adjustment in the Canadian Economy," The Labour Force 1987: 85–135 (Statistics Canada); and David Sobel and Susan Meurer, *Working at Inglis: The Life and Death of a Canadian Factory* (Toronto: James Lorimer, 1994).

96 Patrick Burman, *Killing Time, Losing Ground: Experiences of Unemployment* (Toronto: Wall And Thompson, 1988).

97 Statistics Canada, Catalogue 13-207, *Income Distributions By Size*, 1996.

98 Christopher Sarlo, Poverty in Canada (Vancouver: Fraser Institute, 1992), and National Council Of Welfare, *A New Poverty: Yes, No, Or Maybe?* (Ottawa, 1998–99)

99 Therese Jennissen, "Implications For Women: The Canadian Health And Social Transfer", in Raymond B. Blake, Penny E. Bryden, J. Frank Strain, eds., *The Welfare State in Canada: Past, Present, and Future* (Toronto: Irwin, 1997)

100 Poverty rates among non-elderly families for the following countries are: United States 18.7%, Canada 15.7%, Australia 15.4%, France 8.9%, Germany 8.5%, Belgium 5.4%, Netherlands 4.7%. Ross, Shillington, Lochhead, *The Canadian Factbook on Poverty 1994*, 111.

101 See Gary Teeple, "The Decline Of The Canadian Welfare State: Policies And Implications Of Retrenchment", in B. Singh Bolaria (ed.), *Social Issues and Contradictions in Canadian Society*, 3rd Edition (Toronto: Harcourt Brace, 2000), 434–468; and Blake, Bryden, and Strain (eds.), *The Welfare State in Canada.*

102 G. Bruce Doern and Richard W. Phidd, *Canadian Public Policy: Ideas, Structure and Process* (Toronto: Methuen, 1983), chap. 1, and Allan Tupper and G. Bruce Doern, eds., *Public Corporations and Public Policy in Canada* (Montreal: Institute for Research on Public Policy, 1981), chap. 1.

103 T.W. Acheson, "The Maritimes and 'Empire Canada'," in David J. Bercuson, ed., *Canada and the Burden of Unity* (Toronto: Macmillan, 1977), 103.

104 Ralph Matthews, *The Creation of Regional Dependency* (Toronto: University of Toronto Press, 1983), 69–76.

105 Peter S. Li, *The Making of Post-War Canadian Society* (Toronto: Oxford, 1996), 91.

106 Patricia M. Evans and Gerda R. Wekerle (eds.), *Women and the Canadian Welfare State: Challenges and Change* (Toronto: University Of Toronto Press, 1997); and Janine M. Brodie, *Politics on the Margins: Restructuring and the Canadian Women's Movement* (Halifax: Fernwood, 1995).

107 Keith G. Banting, "The Welfare State and Inequality in the 1980s," *Canadian Review of Sociology and Anthropology* 24(1987): 309–38.

108 Ralph Miliband, *The State in Capitalist Society* (London: Weidenfeld and Nicolson, 1969).

109 Nicos Poulantzas, *Political Power and Social Classes* (London: Verso, 1975).

110 Gregory Albo and Jane Jenson, "A Contested Concept: The Relative Autonomy of the State," in Clement and Williams, *The New Canadian Political Economy*, 180.

111 Peter S. Li, *The Making of Post-War Canadian Society*, Chapter 5.

112 Cf. Leo Panitch, ed., *The Canadian State: Political Economy and Political Power* (Toronto: University of Toronto Press, 1977), 18–19.

113 John Calvert, "Government Policy and Economic Crisis," in James Curtis et al., *Social Inequality in Canada*, 423.

114 A. Paul Williams, "Access and Accommodation in the Canadian Welfare State: The Political Significance of Contacts Between State, Labour, and Business Leaders," *Canadian Review of Sociology and Anthropology* 26(1989): 217–39.

115 Much of the following discussion is based on M. Patricia Marchak, *Ideological Perspectives on Canada*, 3rd ed. (Toronto: McGraw-Hill Ryerson, 1988). It is interesting to read of Marchak's own ideological pilgrimage in the book's introduction, from reformist liberalism to neo-Marxism, to a contemporary search for a better theoretical perspective.

WEBLINKS

www.ccsd.ca

The Canadian Council on Social Development provides data and discussion papers on the various dimensions of poverty in Canada.

www.hc-sc.gc.ca/seniors-aines/

Health Canada's Division of Aging and Seniors provides access to research, educational activities, and policy issues related to aging in Canada.

www.cfc-efc.ca/menu/eng013.htm

The Child and Family Canada Web site provides access to a number of papers dealing with issues related to poverty in Canada.

www.cmec.ca/

Council of Ministers of Education (Canada) is the national voice for education in Canada. The site includes reports about education in Canada and around the world.

www.swc-cfc.gc.ca

The Status of Women Canada (SWC) is a federal organization committed to promoting gender equality and the full participation of women in every aspect of daily life.

THE ISSUE OF REGIONALISM

The economic history of Canada has been dominated by the discrepancy between the centre and the margin of western civilization. Energy has been directed toward the exploitation of staple products and the tendency has been cumulative.

—Harold A. Innis, acclaimed University of Toronto political economist, early leader of the social science community, and originator of the staples thesis, in his The Fur Trade in Canada *(1930:385).*

It should not be surprising in a country as large as Canada that regions should be important. Because segments of the society are separated by huge distances in space, regions develop quite naturally. But vast territory in itself is not a sufficient explanation for why regions develop because we know that even in relatively small countries like Switzerland, coherent regions have emerged (see Chapter Six). Regions then must be understood as the product of people in interaction, that is, how people sort themselves out in space, how they create their own culture, and how this interaction rooted in local conditions helps to differentiate themselves from other people from other regions. It is not just physical features (e.g., mountains, rivers) which divide up space but the activity of people creating their own communities. This is why it makes a difference whether you live in Grand Falls, Newfoundland; Trois Rivières, Quebec; Regina, Saskatchewan; or Victoria, British Columbia. It is because people who share a territory interact with each other and share a local history, climate, and economy that they produce their own traditions, social structure, and culture. In short, *regions are social constructions* because people both respond to the elements of their surroundings and initiate actions to transform them and thereby create their own local communities.[1]

Chapter One presented some of the problems of defining a region, and the reader may want to review that material. In that chapter, our concern was to show the demographic differences between areas in Canada. Chapter Three demonstrated the existence of regional inequality using several key indicators. The data presented in these chapters showed descriptive differences with little explanation about what they meant, why they existed, or their consequences. So now we turn our attention to the dynamics of regionalism, its causes and consequences, and try to understand why it is such an important factor in Canadian society. The chapter concludes with an illustrative discussion of three Canadian regions: the West, the Atlantic region, and the North.

REGIONALISM AS A SOCIAL FACTOR

The concept of region implies the idea of space and, therefore, is always related to geography. Typically, we look for areas with similar topographical features and note how these areas are distinguished from one another by mountains, bodies of water, or changes in foliage. Regions can then be demarcated by types and amounts of precipitation, variations in temperature, soil conditions, and plant life.

But, if geography is a critical basis for identifying a region, the nature of soil conditions and variations in temperature, for example, have a major role to play in the attractiveness of that space as a place to live, and the economic ability of that space to support a population. Thus, if the first dimension of regionalism is *geographic*, the second dimension is *economic*; i.e., what do people do to earn a living? The rocky soil of much of the Atlantic region does not allow the grain farming typical of the Prairies. Similarly, the landlocked Prairies do not support the fishing and marine industries common to the Atlantic area. The importance and economic value of what people do to earn a living shapes the nature and quality of their lives, and gives a region a distinct identity. Social institutions (e.g., grain growers or fish cooperatives, manufacturing unions) which grow up around these economic activities help to produce a regional culture, a similar view of the world, a folk culture of customs and traditions, a common history, linguistic idioms, and, consequently, a personal attachment to an area and group identity.

While homogeneous regions may exist in theory, or reflect images propagated by the media, modern societies are far too complex to establish simple regional distinctions. People outside central Canada usually think of Ontario as the industrial heartland of the nation, and yet, Ontario also possesses a strong mixed farming sector. Similarly, the stereotype of the Prairies as a wheat farming region ignores the fact that Prairie people are now overwhelmingly an urban people. The point is that changes within these regions, as a consequence of urbanization and other socio-technical changes, have blurred the simple distinctions that may have once existed between the regions. Nevertheless, it is still possible to say that the dominant oil and gas industries of Alberta and Saskatchewan, for example, give those provinces a significantly different cast from the strong manufacturing sector of Ontario and

Quebec. Similarly, the mining, lumbering, and shipping industries of British Columbia clearly distinguish that region from the Prairies, and help to explain why the Prairies and British Columbia resist being lumped together into one homogeneous Western region. Regions are seldom easily distinguished, but differences in the economic components of a region do combine with other factors (e.g., a sense of history or ethnic composition) to assist in the creation of regional cultures.

It is not without significance that the first modern sociologists to take up the study of regionalism were prompted in their investigations by the negative comparisons made in distinguishing their region from other regions in the national whole. Sociologists Howard Odum and Rupert Vance at the University of North Carolina noted how the American South in the 1920s and 1930s had not participated in the industrialization characteristic of the North.[2] Their study of the regional South led them to seek both a material and cultural renaissance of the South because of the comparative disadvantage with the North. Even though industrial expansion in the American South over the last few decades has removed some of the economic differences, it has been argued that Southerners still possess a strong regional identity and regional culture.[3] What makes the study of regions significant then, from this perspective, is that it suggests place of residence may be an important means by which to analyze a society because of the comparisons that are made between regions.

Does region of residence help us to explain behaviour or help us to understand the dynamics of a national society? There is considerable debate on this issue because some social scientists believe social class, occupation, or ethnicity to be more powerful determinants of behaviour.[4] Region is thought to be only a container which in itself does not explain anything. And yet why do we continually refer to region as an important variable in understanding Canadian society? The answer is to be found in the fact that people who share a territory create their own localized society. This regional society may have all kinds of external links and the boundaries may be imprecise. Regions also interact with each other and through this interrelationship become aware of their distinguishing characteristics. Normally, however, regions are not actors but their constituents are, and it is always intriguing to see how residents are mobilized for action using territory as the basis for unity. This is where region and regionalism comes together.

Region then is the result of people who share a territory creating their own society with its own unique culture and social structure. The dimensions and characteristics of that region can be catalogued using a wide variety of indicators from per capita income to unemployment rates and occupational structure to ethnic origins and community and institutional components. From these traits, a population sharing a territory create their own *regional society*. *Regionalism*, on the other hand, is the politicization of these local traits into a consciousness of kind or regional identity. It is the mobilization of key elements of regional culture (e.g., dominant occupational groups, significant natural resources, aspects of the economy) and attempting to translate them into a dominant worldview with which residents of a region encounter other regions.[5] The important idea here is that the contents of this regional ideology or interpretive apparatus may change over time, and it may rise and wane depending on circumstances. So although *region* itself is just a descriptive category, it becomes dynamic when it is transformed into a relationship between regions, thereby provoking the emergence of regionalism. So, for example, if one region of a country has a strong manufacturing sector and another region has virtually no manufacturing, that fact reflects a relationship between the two regions that must be explored and explained. But furthermore, that fact potentially develops strong feelings or perceptions between people among (external) and within (internal) regions. This interregional defence of territorial interests is the stuff of regionalism. Region then is by definition a passive concept whereas regionalism is always dynamic and volatile.

Our study of regionalism then must attempt to understand the constitutive elements of a region as well as keeping an eye on how regional traits contribute to a way of under-

Differing Perspectives

Structural Functionalism

The structural functionalist perspective understands regions as part of the unique tapestry of Canadian society. Regions have different histories, cultures, economies, and different populations and these differences are not problematic as much as reflective of how they each contribute differently to Canadian society as a whole. In that sense, regional differences are natural results of different locations and opportunities. Some regions will play more dominant roles because they are more central or they have more people whereas other regions may have less industry or a shrinking employment base due to their hinterland location. When disparities exist, the society as a system will develop ways to provide support for less prosperous regions in order to retain the status quo and keep the society intact.

Conflict

The conflict perspective emphasizes how regions are created particularly by differential access to economic resources. When one region becomes more dominant, it does so at the expense of other regions. The tendency towards the concentration and centralization of regional power occurs in a variety of ways but is most reflective of the capitalist system which conceives of the whole country as its market and enhances profit by centralizing its operations making some regions hinterlands for the products of economically dominant regions. Regional elites may attempt to challenge dominant elites in other regions, and in doing so may seek to enlist grass-roots regional support which may produce regional movements. Regional feeling develops as a result of both collective resistance to regional disparities and perceptions of regional superiority, as well as use of political power by elites to create regional confrontations. Regions are therefore the end result of power struggles in either overt or covert forms.

Symbolic Interactionism

The symbolic interactionist perspective begins with how people sharing a regional territory create meaning and develop a sense of community. The emphasis is on how people construct regional traditions, institutions, and other symbols of regional sentiment that are unique and not necessarily shared with people in other regions. The way persons come to understand themselves in terms of their regional identity can be compared with the way they view people in other regions. The focus is on the things that give local people a unique identity because of different locale and shared experiences. Region then is something that is lived and part of daily life which in a real sense becomes part of who a person is as an individual and provides a view or perspective on the world outside.

standing the world or at least other regions within their own national society. Before engaging in case studies of regionalism in Canada, it is important to examine explanations for why regionalism persists as a societal issue.

WHAT CAUSES REGIONALISM?

The *dynamic approach* to regionalism views regions as not just different territories with different names and characteristics but as units that must be understood in relation to one another. By analyzing how regions relate to one another within a country, we understand more clearly how power is distributed throughout that society. Regional characteristics can serve merely as benign descriptors unless people within the various regions become aware of the meaning of their regional differences. What transforms these regional characteristics into a more politicized form of regional awareness which is the essence of regionalism? Five explanations can be identified.

1. Uneven Development

One of the most dramatic causes of regionalism in Canada has been the unevenness of economic development in different parts of the society. For example, the original industrial strength of the Maritime region was displaced by greater industrial centralization in central Canada, and the Atlantic provinces consequently went into a decline from which they have never recovered.[6] Conversely, Ontario and Quebec developed an industrial strength that gained new momentum in the post–World War II era; 75% of the leading Canadian corporations and 85% of the major financial institutions established their head offices in Toronto or Montreal.[7] Using the protective tariff to guarantee a Canadian market for their products, there was little need to develop industries elsewhere, and the rest of Canada became a market hinterland to central Canadian industries. Freight rate squabbles and animosity regarding mortgages held by central Canadian financial institutions frequently became symbolic of hinterland resistance to regional dominance.

While Ontario and Quebec have been the centres of economic development, it is clear that the focus of this activity were the metropolitan galaxies of Toronto and Montreal. Both cities spawned an elaborate suburban system and drew supporting cities into their orbit. For example, while Toronto and Hamilton were once distinct cities separated by considerable green space, they are now linked in a megalopolis with little intervening green space. This is a consequence of the growth of new interstitial cities such as Burlington, Oakville, and Mississauga.

From a national point of view, what is significant is that disproportionate economic and population growth took place within these two metropolitan areas. Vancouver, as a Pacific port city with a coastal climate, experienced some growth, but the foci of economic development in Canada clearly centred on Toronto and Montreal. Analysts use the term *primate city* to describe a situation where a country has one or two surpassingly large cities which dominate the rest of the country, and whose development has been at such a pace that significant socio-economic and even cultural differences emerge between these cities and their supporting regions, and the rest of the nation. The overdevelopment of these metropolitan areas in comparison to the underdevelopment of other urban centres in other regions, has become an important aspect of the dominance of central Canada over other regions. The employment opportunities in the industrial regions have meant that persons seeking work or career advancement are forced to leave the hinterland regions and move to Ontario or Quebec.

REAL PEOPLE 4	Call Centres: A New Form of Regional Economic Development

Moncton, New Brunswick

Bill (to cousin Joe, formerly from the province and who now lives in Peterborough, Ontario, who he talks to on the phone two or three times a year): "You wouldn't believe what they are saying about this province where you grew up. Yup, they are calling it the "Call Centre Capital of North America." Sounds pretty important doesn't it? That's something new we have around here. We never thought that the day would come when people in this province would work for the big fancy corporations. We were more used to agriculture and small businesses. Now it's Fedex, Xerox, Royal Bank, and UPS plus airlines and car rental companies and hotels, and lots more. The paper the other day said there were over 80 call centres in New Brunswick now employing close to 9000 people.

Joe: I never knew what a call centre was until last year when I called to make a reservation with a hotel chain. I commented about the weather and the representative said she was not in my city or even in Ontario but in St. John's, N.B. Now every time I make a reservation for anything, I ask where they are answering the phone at. You never know, it might be someone I know or whose parents I grew up with if they are answering in New Brunswick.

Bill: Ya, you know those 800 numbers. I guess they handle calls from all over North America. It is really great. It provides lots of jobs in clean offices. Better than industries that pollute the environment or unpredictable resources.

Joe: I wonder what kind of jobs these are? I mean it is good that the unemployed and especially the young have a chance at jobs in the province so that they don't have to go elsewhere like I did. But I hope these jobs really use the skills of your people and give them some opportunity for advancement."

Note: New Brunswick has developed an explicit strategy to attract call centres which are customer contact facilities that deal largely with incoming telephone inquiries from all over Canada and often the United States, and sometimes the world. This strategy attempts to address an unemployment rate in the 11% range and promises corporations a skilled and knowledgeable work force to deal with customers in one central location. In some ways, call centres have the appearance of a high technology assembly line implying many low-paying jobs. Yet the government argues that these are indeed good jobs with a pay rate above the average salary in New Brunswick.

This movement contributes to further population imbalances. Chapter Three demonstrated how important socio-economic indicators such as income, education, and unemployment reveal the existence of significant disparities based on region.

To emphasize that regional identities are the result of inter-regional relationships, Clement has argued that the overdevelopment of one region can only take place at the expense of the underdevelopment of other regions.[8] The assumption is that national societies with closed boundaries force a power struggle between regional units in which some regions win and others lose. One study of import–export trade ratios with Ontario demonstrated that, whereas Quebec's ratio with Ontario was quite close (4:5), Alberta's (1:8) and Saskatchewan's (1:15) were unbalanced and Prince Edward Island (2:47) and Newfoundland (3:1000), were even more unbalanced in favour of Ontario.[9]

The dominance of central Canada does not mean that all other regions are equal. On the contrary, because some regions have raw materials that are in higher demand or resources the industrial centre needs, they have a more favourable exchange ratio than regions with less to exchange. Yet it is precisely this exchange of finished goods for raw materials that ensures the continued dominance of the industrial regions. It is for this reason that the West, and particularly Alberta, attempted to use their resources as a basis for industrial development in order to participate in the employment and technological growth that could result. It is also for this reason that Newfoundland attempted to use the development of its own offshore oil as an employment opportunity for Newfoundlanders first, rather than for any other Canadians who might apply. All of these developments, and others which are likely to follow, symbolize efforts to rearrange the old imbalances which have been such a major part of regional inequalities.

Uneven development causes regionalism in that it creates economic winners and losers in a spatial system. It is for this reason that some have defined *regionalism as the result of inequality.*[10] Whether regionalism would go away if there were equality is certainly debatable but there is a strong sense that regionalism is more easily mobilized in the presence of inequality. Defence of territorial advantage is a major issue and attempts to seek redress from territorial disadvantage often successfully mobilize regional feeling.

2. State Policy

Development imbalances do not just happen. They are the result of human action which our next three points demonstrate. Here the emphasis is on state action.

The policies of the Canadian state which promote economic growth normally are designed to direct growth to specific places or to have indirect effects on specific places. By altering its policies, such as on energy (e.g., the National Energy Policy of 1980), the state negatively affected oil-producing regions at the same time that it also positively impacted oil-consuming regions. Even though it was called the National Energy Policy and was presumably in the "national interest," there was a variable regional impact to this policy. It is seldom that government policies are spatially neutral for they may affect some regions more than others, or what is helpful to one region may be harmful to another. Even apparently neutral policies pertaining to things like the environment or minimum wage have differential effects on regions.

Brodie has argued that this regionalizing impact of state policies was evident in *three national policies* which the government developed at different points in its history.[11] The first was the National Policy of 1879 which tried to build a transcontinental economy to the West (see the discussion later in this chapter). The protective tariff was applied at all borders but with the eventual effect that Central Canadian industries flourished, the Maritimes became deindustrialized, and the West was limited to providing primary products as an exporting hinterland. Canada was tied together with this policy but with significantly different regional impacts.

The second state policy was the post-depression World War II shift in policy to encourage more American direct investment in Canada to strengthen the economy. This was the era of the American branch plant subsidiary which especially benefitted Ontario and which led to efforts to redistribute some of Central Canada's economic advantage to other regions through regional development grants and equalization grants to maintain social welfare policies but which only sustained regional hegemony. Clear regional disparities emerged from this policy.

The third national policy began in the late 1980s with free trade that supported policies that eliminated a protected economy in favour of global competition, hemispheric integration, a reduced role of the state, increased privatization, and market-driven values. Again, some regions were better able to take advantage of integration into the global economy than others, and other regions were not only hurt by their inability to do so, but were further disadvantaged by the lack of federal transfer payments to support their services infrastructure. As one illustration of that changed mode of thinking, it has been argued that the federal state was the cause of the disparities between rich and poor regions because it provided transfer payments that encouraged people to stay where they were rather than to migrate to regions where the economy was stronger.[12] In all of these instances, it is asserted that it has been state policies that have exacerbated regionalism.

In fairness, however, it must be pointed out that the state has also taken action to attempt to reduce regional disparities as a tenet of national unity. In post-war Canada, the government established a range of agencies of which the most well-known was the Department of Regional Economic Expansion (DREE) in 1968, followed by others such as Western Diversification (WD) and Atlantic Canada Opportunities Agency (ACOA). While there may have been some limited successes, regional disparities remain.[13]

3. Elite Control and Capital Flows

The next related cause of regionalism linked to human action is capitalist decision making by elites. As we will see, these elites work closely with political elites to create state policy. In Chapter Three, it was noted that the research of Porter and Clement demonstrated that the economic elite of Canada was primarily resident in Ontario and Quebec. The corporate power that developed in these two central Canadian provinces meant that weaker corporations in other parts of Canada were either bought out to reduce competition or were subject to price wars which were usually won by central Canadian corporations.[14] Such *consolidation* meant that capital, control, and power became regionally concentrated and centralized. But by focusing on elite control, it becomes clear that it is not so much geopolitical units such as Ontario or Quebec that maintain a regional dominance over the rest of Canada; rather, such dominance is the result of activities of the *capitalist class*, which resides primarily in the two primate cities of Toronto and Montreal and even goes beyond to external capital markets and foreign centres of capital control.[15] The desire of the economic elite to expand markets and maintain production efficiency is driven by the desire to maximize profits, an objective that often has regional effects. Building a plant in a region where the unemployment rate is high and labour is cheap, and where tax incentives are provided, will happen only so long as this decision fits corporate objectives. Plant shutdowns and failure to show a profit leaves little room for concern about regional disparities.

Because of their power and interrelatedness with other elites, the economic elite is able to lobby for federal and provincial policies that support its interests. For example, a protective tariff is essentially an economic mechanism that would not exist without legislative decree. Therefore, a proposed tariff that would support a central Canadian industry requires that the capitalist class demonstrate to the political elite why such legislation is in the national interest, and not just their personal interest. Labour unions and their elite, and the voting public in central Canada, are then drawn in to support such a policy, because it protects both the jobs and the capital of supporting services and industries. The problem is that capital investment and control are regionally concentrated rather than dispersed, and hinterland regions seldom share directly in the benefits of such national policies. Instead, the centralization of capital and political control is more likely to lead to discussions in these outlying regions about the cost of Confederation. Such discussions in the past often centred around the higher price of manufactured goods charged by protected, monopolistic industries located far from their captive markets.

The traditional strength of the capitalist class in Ontario and Quebec does not mean that there is no economic elite in other regions. In fact, each region has its own local elite who may benefit from the regionalization of Canadian society as agents for the central elite. In some situations, the local elite may even try to challenge the capitalist class in other regions. While regionalism can provide a range of populist symbols that are appealing to regional residents, it has also been argued that regionalism can be an ideology that disguises the process of capitalist concentration on the periphery.[16] The regional capitalist class may benefit but they may also be vocal advocates to national political elites of regional policies such as equalization grants to reduce the effect of regional disparities.

Attempts by regional elites to marshall the powers of the region through the political apparatus of a province have been called *province building*.[17] The goal of province building is to use the legislative power of the province to provide tax incentives, grants, or policy challenges aimed at other regions that will assist in providing a more favourable environment for capital formation and economic development in a particular region. Regions then may compete against each other, as happened in 1980 when Alberta unsuccessfully attempted to wrest some economic activity away from Ontario and Quebec. Clearly, then, within a national state, regional units struggle against each other for development, and it is the economic and political elite in each region who are frequently at the centre of the heightened competition and struggle between regions. Because federal elections are usually won or lost in Ontario and Quebec (where the most parliamentary seats are), the elite which dominate this region are the elite which have inordinate control of national policy.

If the dominance of central Canada is supported by a symmetry between this regional elite and the federal elite, then effective challenges to this regional dominance require an alternate legislative vehicle. Thus, capitalist classes in the regions that seek expansion will form alliances with their local provincial governments to challenge the dominance of the national-central Canadian bourgeoisie. For this reason, regionalism has become equated with provincialism because the local economic and political elite use the province to challenge federal control, and to promote local development. Federal–provincial hostilities and confrontations reflect the interests of the regional elite, and long-standing popular sentiment may even be manipulated in order to create regional solidarity.[18] Some politicians have successfully won provincial elections precisely through accentuating regional–national cleavages.

In short, regionalism is intimately related to internal power, and struggles for power, within a national society. Elites internal to a region and elites external to a region play a significant role in charting the nature of regional economies and regional relationships.

4. Political Structures

There is another way in which human action contributes to regionalism and that is in the creation and operation of the political system. The principle of *"representation by population"* provides for greater political representation for areas with a larger population.[19] Consequently, population imbalances within the nation (e.g., almost two-thirds of the population live in Ontario and Quebec) create an awesome concentration of power. The votes of persons in regions other than Ontario and Quebec are seldom vital to the outcome of an election. When elections are essentially decided in those two provinces, residents of other regions feel disenfranchised. If those in Quebec and Ontario cast their vote with the party that is elected, there is the feeling that the government will cater to the majority in central Canada. When residents in less populous areas elect a Member of Parliament whose party forms the opposition, they realize that their representative has no input into the formulation of the ruling party's policy. In either case, many regions feel the federal government has little sympathy or obligation to address their needs.[20]

Furthermore, the strong *party discipline* required by the parliamentary system gives little opportunity for the expression of regional interests.[21] When this is combined with perceptions that the major national parties are controlled by central Canadian interests, a sense of futility emerges in the hinterland regions. Occasionally, this sense of futility erupts into anger, and a "protest party" (or a "third party") with a strong regional basis may emerge on the national scene to challenge the major parties. These protest parties have been particularly successful in the West, where their ideologies have contained a strong anti-central Canadian sentiment. There is, however, as yet no federal vehicle (such as a regionally apportioned Senate) to enable regions to encounter one another on an equal footing.

Political structures also sustain regionalism through the actions and rhetoric of provincial governments. Provincial boundaries provide opportunities for territorially-based discussions in relation to other territorial units. Interest groups within each territory can use the provincial government as the vehicle to strike out at interest groups in other regions. Provincial political parties may fight elections on a platform of defending regional interests in the face of competing regional interests or seek regional solidarity in the face of external threats. Governments then confront other governments as large and powerful institutions, each with their own civil service personnel, each concerned about survival, and each struggling to establish or retain jurisdictional competence over their territory. Cairns has called this form of regionalism *governmentalized societies*.[22] The relationship between inter-governmental conflict and elite control becomes clearer as peripheral political and economic elites become frustrated with their hinterland position. Through a policy of economic provincialism, priority is given to development within a particular region.[23] An example of this policy would be Newfoundland's argument in 1981 that, in any jobs created by an offshore oil boom, Newfoundlanders rather than any other Canadians should have employment priority. Regional confrontations are produced by the attempts of hinterland regions to challenge the status quo. Thus, the more regions seek equality through industrial development, the more they struggle and compete over scarce commodities, and this struggle strengthens the regional conflict.[24] It is for these reasons that regionalism is, at least partially, politically propagated.

5. North–South Linkages

Another explanation of regionalism is based on Canada's intimate relationship with the United States. Natural alliances and mutual interests are viewed as emerging from geographical proximity of Canadian and American regions. Stevenson has argued that regionalism in Canada must be seen in its continental context, as Confederation and the National Policy of 1879 sought to obliterate the north–south cross-border regional relationships that had existed long before 1867.[25] He noted that some opponents of Confederation in the Maritimes based their opposition on the fact that they felt closer attachments to the New

England states, and feared the dominance of central Canada. Similarly, some people in the southwest peninsula of Ontario felt that they had very strong ties with residents of New York and Michigan.

If these north–south linkages were displaced by Confederation, Stevenson demonstrates that they have been revived as a consequence of the decline of European ties, and by the shift of economic power and people away from the American Northeast and central Canada, to the West and (in the case of the US) to the South. Neighbouring provinces and states have begun to look to each other in an effort to find solutions to mutual problems (e.g., energy, the environment) through cooperation. For example, the New England Governors and Eastern Canadian Premiers (known as NEG/ECP Conference) meet regularly and form agreements on important issues.[26] In the West, a new form of binationalism has formed in the Pacific Northwest linking Alaska, the Territories, British Columbia, Alberta, Montana, Idaho, Washington, and Oregon in what is known as Cascadia or Pacific Northwest Economic Region (PNWER). Each Canadian region then develops its own pattern of interrelationships with an allied American region based on economic development, travel, and even cable TV and professional sports. Energy agreements (e.g., the Columbia River Treaty, Quebec–New York power grid), industrial development (e.g., the automobile industry that links Ontario and Michigan), religious ties (e.g., Mormons of Utah and Alberta), and sports (e.g., hockey and baseball divisions) are all based on north–south links, and each can detract from, or compete with, national ties.

In this context, one way to understand regions that traverse borders is that they are *natural economic zones* that create their own sense of community with their own political agendas. The political will of the region may be presented to the host nation(s) as a challenge to other regional interests or, in a globalized world, they may try to avoid the state altogether. Free trade has the potential of lowering border barriers and accentuating regionalist trends across the American border to a greater extent than has been experienced so far.[27]

Regionalism has also been exacerbated by the proximity and accessibility of regionalized corporate activity in the United States that carries over into specific regions of Canada. For example, many American subsidiaries in British Columbia have headquarters in California, Alberta subsidiaries are tied to American southwestern multinationals, corporations based in Michigan, Illinois, or New York have been more likely to choose Ontario as the location for their Canadian activity, and Quebec business activity is more likely linked to Massachusetts, New York, or New Jersey. The fact that the traditional centre of industrial strength in the United States has been the Northeast meant that Ontario and Quebec were more likely to benefit from their proximity than other regions, a fact that also contributed to uneven economic development.[28]

It is not so much that American investment caused regionalism as that it sustained regional imbalances that already existed.[29] Regions with a manufacturing industry competed strongly to retain their leadership, and were successful in attracting American industries. Regions with little manufacturing, but a strong resource base, also attracted American capital—but only for the extraction of resources. Thus, US investment in Canada retained regional patterns already established and, furthermore, brought Canadian regions into closer contact with similar American regions. If it is manufacturing that drew together Toronto, Cleveland, and Detroit, it is energy that joins Calgary, Denver, and Dallas.

Because this foreign investment is so important to the regional economy, the host region will be far more sympathetic to foreign investment than other regions might be. Ontarians may ridicule the American multinational oil companies in Alberta, but Westerners are quick to point out that it is American firms that play a huge role in providing employment for thousands of Ontarians in the manufacture of vehicles and appliances. Thus, north–south linkages help accentuate regional disparities and hostilities.

The Region/Class Debate

No explanation for the persistence of regionalism can rest on a single factor. Regionalism is a complex phenomenon and we have only sketched the more dominant structural conditions which have the potential to change a region from a unit of analysis to an element of social structure. But regionalism is produced by human responses to these underlying conditions. Being a wheat farmer in Saskatchewan may be little more than a typical occupation in that region until that farmer begins to compare the position of farmers in that region with other regions, compares the position of farmers with other occupation groups in other regions, attempts to ascertain the impact (or lack thereof) on farmers of federal economic policy, or seeks an explanation for spiralling costs for purchased goods and services that jeopardize their agrarian operation. It is thus the interpretation farmers give to their position in society at large and as a dominant group in that region of Canada which creates regionalism. Again, regional differences are benign unless they are interpreted and articulated as a factor in interregional relations. If people in an area where agriculture dominates feel that the interests of other regions are given priority within the society as a whole, then the interests of farmers will be translated into a regional issue in opposition to the interests of other regions.

The above example illustrates a major debate in regional analysis. Do people really possess a regional identity which guides and directs their actions or is the regional identity only a mask for class interests? Could it be that farmers in Ontario, Nova Scotia, and Saskatchewan have far more in common than all the people who live on the Prairies and form a geographic region? The region/class debate then focuses on whether geography is an appropriate unit for analysis or whether social class is a more basic structural condition. If we take the regional approach, Prairie farmers are opposed to central Canadian industry (with the emphasis on location). If we take the class approach, Prairie farmers as small independent producers are opposed to large Canadian and multinational corporate capitalists located in central Canada (with the emphasis on position in the capitalist system).

Analysts taking the class position tend to devalue the significance of regions on the grounds that what passes for regionalism is primarily an expression of class struggle.[30] Regionalism is regarded as a consequence rather than a cause because class is considered the prior and more important condition. It is not the Prairies versus central Canada but the interests of small entrepreneurs versus the interests of the capitalist class that is at issue. The class position is a penetrating perspective because it forces us to look beyond regions as homogeneous geographic units to the divisions that may exist both within regions and between regions of competing economic interests. From this perspective, regionalism is more likely to be understood as an ideology that masks real class interests.

On the other side are those analysts who continue to view region as an important unit of analysis. This perspective points to the existence of regional cultures and regional identities that may even have stronger explanatory power than status, class, or ethnicity.[31] Sharing a common political and economic environment may give people an interpretive apparatus for what is happening in their society both because of their commitment to a region with which they identify as a place different from other regions in the society, and because their region is a meaningful place to them personally.

The region/class debate is not easily resolved except to say that both perspectives make valid points. Class analysts stress the material basis of regionalism and, though they may argue that they are not advocating an economically determinist position, they make little effort to discuss the cultural side of regional life. The region analysts, on the other hand, may borrow freely from class analysis to stress the impact of dependency and capital control, but also include other factors related to history or a collective consciousness within a region which helps build a regional culture.

Regional Culture

The region/class debate provides an appropriate caution that regions, just like countries as a whole, are divided by class and other interest groups. Therefore, to speak of a regional culture as though it were an undifferentiated amorphous mass in geographical space can mask important class-based realities or even sub-regional differences. However, where regions are separated by thousands of kilometres as they are in Canada, with different histories, economies, and settlement patterns, it is possible to speak of the existence of regionalized cultures, though the distinctiveness of these cultures may not be as sharp or unique as some might expect.[32]

A *culture* refers to the complex of beliefs, morals, customs, laws, and habits which people share as a consequence of their group experiences. Culture also includes material aspects such as art, technology, and objects which represent a people's expression of their struggle with their physical and socio-economic environment.

As each region's population tries to adapt to its own topographical and climatic features, and responds to its own economic challenges, it produces its own unique matrix of traits. Such traits are reflected in its literature, folklore, self-understanding, and perception of itself in relation to other regions of Canada. The media frequently picks up symbols of regional character (e.g., pictures of the idyllic fishing village of Peggy's Cove, the skyscrapers of Toronto in the shadow of the CN Tower, the Prairie grain elevator surrounded by flat land and open skies) which help perpetuate regional images. Institutions, traditions, and social movements develop within this regional context often with features that are distinguishable from other regions. What makes culture regional is its contrast with the whole, or with other units of the whole. Although there are many influences which contribute to the reduction of regional cultures and the promulgation of a national or continental culture (e.g., television, urbanization, federal efforts to promote national identities), the history, population composition, and political economy of the region provide the cultural matrix that allows regional distinctions and identities to occur.

If regional cultural differences exist, then these differences should be reflected in the attitudes of individuals. For this reason, virtually every national study of the opinions, attitudes, and behaviour of Canadians breaks down the responses by region in order to identify regional differences which frequently exist. We know, for example, that there are regional differences in church attendance rates, attitudes towards gun control, acceptance of multiculturalism, perceptions of the federal government, and identification with region. Of course, differences across regions do not necessarily mean that location of residence is a more powerful explanatory variable than other variables such as occupation, education, or gender, but it does suggest region may be an element in differences in attitudes and behaviour.

The most typical products of regional cultures in Canada are the attitudes that produce stereotypical evaluations of other regions. Devaluing other regional cultures on the basis of the presumed superiority of one's own regional culture is an attitude known as *ethno-centrism*; but the negative attitude, or feeling of distance and detachment that is the consequence of unbalanced interregional interaction, is know as *alienation*. Some regions maintain cultural or economic superiority to others, at the same time as inhabitants of other regions feel dominated or exploited. Regional attachments are then paralleled by perceptions and attitudes about other regions with whom relationships are usually unequal. It is the nature of this inequality that usually heightens the regionalization of attitudes.

There is some question about whether regional identities and attitudes are necessarily exclusive from, or in direct competition with, national identities and attitudes (i.e., might it be possible for national and regional loyalties to coexist?).[33] One of the key questions that often is asked to measure this is whether people identify themselves in terms of their region or province first or whether they identify themselves as Canadian first.[34] While there is some variation in responses, Ontarians are the most likely to see themselves as Canadian first. Quebecers and Newfoundlanders are least likely to see themselves as Canadian first. Maritimers and Westerners are somewhere in between depending on current issues and debates.

There is a danger in assuming that national and regional identities are exclusive, or that both identities are equally important, or that regional identities are always less important than national ones. In reality, identities may vary with the issue, the person, and may vary over time depending on circumstances. Nevertheless, differences in identity and culture are not adequate explanations for regionalism in themselves. Perhaps at its deepest level, regional identity is intimately tied to the economy of the region. But without a consciousness-raising about the meaning and interpretation of regional differences within the context of the wider society, regionalism does not exist. For that reason, we must move beyond the structural conditions to the human responses to the conditions encountered to understand why regionalism exists.

Our discussion can now shift to illustrations of how these factors have operated in specific regional situations. Three regions have been selected for a closer analysis. The Prairies and the New West will provide the first case study; then, we will turn to the Atlantic region and, finally, to the North. All three areas have had relatively high visibility and recognition as peripheral regions to central Canada. They make a significant comparative study, however, because their geographic and economic contexts support different social worlds.

The Case of Quebec

Before we move on to our specific regional analysis however, we should note that no discussion of regionalism in Canada would be complete without a rather lengthy analysis of Quebec. In fact, it could reasonably be argued that the salience of regionalism in the society as a whole is at least partially a consequence of the regional solidarity of Quebec. This solidarity is based upon a linguistic and ethnic commonality grounded in a historical group perception. This commonality, in combination with territorial dominance and political control in the province, has led some francophone Quebecers to argue that Quebec is *not just a region* of Canada, but a *distinguishable nation*. As long as Quebec remains a part of Canadian society, its socio-cultural attributes make it perhaps the most distinctive region of all. Most Quebecers share a language and an ethnic heritage quite different from those of most other Canadians.

Since the act of Confederation, Quebec has been rather successful in negotiating special considerations with the federal government that accommodate its own cultural needs. This fact has not gone unnoticed by other regions in Canada who have periodically demanded special concessions for their own regional aspirations. In this way, the example of Quebec has been instrumental in heightening regional desires for more localized control and more equitable economic policies, and in using the province as the bargaining mechanism to obtain desired ends. Thus, from at least one perspective, Quebec has helped contribute to the regionalization of Canadian society. Other regions may lack an ethnic basis for their regional community, but the large economic gap between their region and central Canada has accentuated their regional grievances.

A more detailed discussion of Quebec will be left for the next chapter even though many of the same regional dynamics discussed here apply. The importance of Quebec as a significant region in Canada, however, needs to be acknowledged at the outset, and the decision not to discuss it in detail at this point in no way should be construed as underestimating Quebec's critical position as a powerful and distinctive region of Canada.

REGION STUDY I: THE PRAIRIE WEST AND THE NEW WEST

No one who has driven from Winnipeg to Calgary can forget the wide open spaces marked only by grain elevators jutting up into the sky to remind one that indeed, far up ahead, another town is situated. Bounded by the tundra of the territories to the north, the Prairies are intimately tied to the Great Plains of the Dakotas and Kansas to the south, where grain farming remains a staple crop. It is in this geographic area that a regional culture has emerged, reflecting a people's social and economic adaptation to a particular environment.

Separated from central Canada by the Canadian Shield, the West had no natural ties with the East. Similarly, the Rockies prevented a natural continuity with the coastal communities of British Columbia to the west. If the space between Vancouver and Toronto was to be claimed and held as Canadian territory, then deliberate steps would have to be taken to integrate the Prairie region and, thereby, prevent British Columbia from being totally isolated. The program established by the federal government to accomplish these objectives was known as *the National Policy*.[35] The policy had three main features: the settlement of the Prairie region through encouragement of immigration and use of the Homestead Act, which provided land for settlement at an extremely low price; the establishment of an east–west transportation system, the Canadian Pacific Railroad, to link Vancouver with Toronto and thereby facilitate the movement of persons and goods needed by the Prairie community and reverse the more natural north–south ties; and the legislation of a protective tariff to ensure a market for central Canadian manufactured goods. In this way, the National Policy succeeded in settling, claiming, and integrating the Prairie region into the Canadian fabric.

The society that grew up in this regional territory was an extension of central Canada, yet also separated from it. The burgeoning and aspiring industrial economy of the "centre" was easily distinguished from the single industry agricultural economy of the Prairies, and a metropolis–hinterland relationship developed. While it is clear that both regions needed each other, the tariff, by inhibiting the purchase of cheap machinery or goods produced in the United States, created a regional resentment that led Prairie people to view their interregional Canadian relationship as one of exploitation. Almost from the beginning, then, a regional attitude of alienation developed among persons resident on the Prairies.[36] That attitude was the consequence of a political economy of dependency.

Regional discontent became widespread because it touched everyone. Mortgages were held by central Canadian banks; appliances, farm implements, and automobiles were manufactured in the "East"; canned goods came from Ontario. Virtually everything was imported into the region, and the region had little to exchange except grain, which was primarily sold on international, rather than national, markets. The instability of international prices for this grain was even more problematic due to uncertainties in crop productions, insect infestations, and drought. The unbalanced import–export situation made Prairie residents realize that they had become captive to national policies. This realization was heightened during the Depression, as frustrated and economically beleaguered Prairie farmers struggled to pay their central Canadian creditors.

The "J-curve theory" suggests that social unrest is most likely to occur when rising expectations are frustrated, and conditions become worse rather than better.[37] The new settlers on the Prairies were prepared for hard work because, ultimately, they expected prosperity; but these expectations were frustrated by climatic, market, and general economic conditions over which they had little control—control was exercised by a dominant central Canada. The Prairies then produced a series of reform movements such as the Non-Partisan League, United Farmers of Alberta, Social Credit, and the Co-operative Commonwealth Federation, which were based to a large extent on the hostilities felt towards central Canada and monopoly capital.[38]

Western alienation, then, has a unique history based on agrarianism in the Prairie provinces. Sometimes it was expressed in the perception of a regional conspiracy against the West. Most frequently, however, alienation focuses on elite control from central Canada, whether it be that of large corporations, banks, or political parties. Gibbins speaks of this attitude as a *regional ideology* because it is a socially shared set of beliefs with a recognized history and constituency, all based on estrangement from the Canadian heartland.[39]

The Prairies were the last large area to be settled in Canada in which land was still available for agriculture, with most of this settlement occurring from 1870 to 1920. The source of immigration, and pattern of settlement, helped make the Prairies unique. For one thing, the federal government encouraged large numbers of Europeans to settle in the West. Many of these settlers came directly from Europe and organized their relocation in a bloc settlement. Other immigrants came as individuals from Ontario, the United States, or England, and settled next to people with whom they had little in common. The result was that the Prairies became an interesting, multi-ethnic, agricultural community without parallel in rural Canada.[40] For this reason, many Prairie residents were later offended by the proposed federal policy on bilingualism and biculturalism.

Transition from the "Old West" to the "New West"

The Depression years were difficult, as the newly settled population struggled to survive, but the post-war experience totally changed the face of the Prairie population, as agriculture went through a significant consolidation. From 1941 to 1966, the number of farms on the Prairies fell by one-third, the average farm increased in size by 80%, farm land was used more intensively (cow herds increased by 72%), and the number of farmers and farm labourers decreased substantially.[41] People moved to Prairie cities, and then frequently to Toronto or Vancouver for the employment available in these booming cities. Thus the changes that took place between the 1940s and 1960s meant that it was no longer possible to speak of the people of the Prairies as primarily an agrarian population.

As the agrarian population became overwhelmed by an urban population, the economy of the region shifted from agriculture to service, retailing, administration, and a small amount of manufacturing.[42] Perhaps most significant was the discovery of oil at Leduc in 1948, which inaugurated the modern era of energy production in Alberta. The discovery of oil and gas at various locations in Alberta led to the development of an active petroleum industry, with strong linkages to American capital and corporate expertise. Thus, the north–south ties, which were natural with agriculture, were supplemented by energy relationships. Calgary became the administrative centre for this development and, due to the fact that the provincial government was considered the owner of these resources, the province demonstrated a new-found prosperity from the rents and royalties accruing from energy development. For this and a variety of other reasons, Alberta developed an economic edge over the other Prairie provinces.

The discovery of gas in British Columbia, and both conventional oil and heavy oil discoveries in Saskatchewan, has contributed to a "New West." Whereas wheat farming had created a commonality between the three Prairie provinces of Manitoba, Saskatchewan, and Alberta in the early years, these later years have seen the energy-producing provinces of British Columbia, Alberta, and Saskatchewan develop a commonality. But, just as grains were a staple extracted from Prairie soil and shipped and processed elsewhere, so energy became a staple extracted in the West and marketed in the industrial centres of Canada and the United States. In either case, the raw material was taken out of the region and the West essentially remained a hinterland. This unchanged condition did not go unnoticed as perceptions of dependency and truncated regional development amidst potential prosperity evoked lingering alienation.[43]

As energy became an even more valuable commodity through the 1970s (as OPEC countries threatened the industrial countries with cutbacks and price increases), it became increasingly clear that the supply and price of energy could give the Western region enormous advantages. Instead of being a resource-rich hinterland from where the staple was to be transported to industrial markets elsewhere, governments in possession and control of such resources

Is the Prairie Region One Region or Two?

A *strong staple* is a resource with high demand and limited supply thereby yielding greater revenue (e.g., oil). A *weak staple* is a resource with lower demand and greater availability thereby yielding smaller revenues (e.g., wheat).

While agriculture is a common staple activity throughout the Prairies, the three Prairie provinces can be divided into the western part (Alberta and western Saskatchewan) where a strong staple (oil) is present and most of Saskatchewan and southern Manitoba where a weak staple (wheat) predominates.

Initially, the Prairie region was focused on Winnipeg, the "Gateway to the West" as the centre of commerce, industry, and transportation. Manitoba's former role is now totally eroded except in manufacturing where its output exceeds the other three provinces. Not only has the wheat economy declined there but Manitoba has had little participation in the new strong staple. Manitoba, as the eastern terminus for wheat exports, is no longer as pivotal as it once was as Churchill and Thunder Bay are now shipping only a fraction of the wheat that is exported out of the region.

Source: Based on Paul Phillips, "The Canadian Prairies—One Economic Region or Two?" in James McCrorie and Martha C. MacDonald, eds., *The Constitutional Future of the Prairie and Atlantic Regions of Canada* (Regina: CPRC, 1992), 37–49.

sought to use them as the basis for greater regional development. Furthermore, income from energy provided provincial governments with a significant economic advantage which threatened to change the whole balance of power in Canadian society.[44] Some of the proceeds from these oil revenues were placed in the Alberta Heritage Trust Fund, for example, which made the Alberta government a major creditor and investor within Canada; but, more than that, it was thought that this money could be a means of fostering regional economic development.

The item most symbolic of the hinterland position of the West through the years has been "discriminatory" freight rates, frequently referred to as the "Crow rates." As a consequence of the Crow's Nest Pass Agreement of 1897, the federal government approved the movement of grain by railroad at rates below cost in order to assist farmers to get their product to market.[45] The fact that this low rate only applied to grain, however, discouraged the shipment of other products processed in the West. Furthermore, a higher rate prevailed for shipping manufactured goods into the West, and Westerners were constrained to buy these products as a consequence of the protective tariff. While the Crow rate was beneficial to farmers in one way, it created higher prices for durable goods. As the population in the West became less agrarian and more urban, the new urban middle class Westerner tended to favour the abolition of the Crow rate because industrial development in the West would provide new opportunities for employment and upward mobility. The tensions and disagreements produced by the elimination of the Crow rate in 1995 reflected the concern among Westerners that they maintain their solid agricultural base while participating in new prospects for economic development.

It was the expanding middle and upper classes of urban professionals, entrepreneurs, and provincial civil servants, particularly in Alberta, that began to look to the province to help diversify and strengthen the local economy.[46] Simultaneously with the rise of a new regional bourgeoisie, small Canadian energy companies emerged in the West to take advantage of the boom. The availability of jobs in the West, combined with an industrial slowdown in Ontario and Quebec, resulted in heavy shifts of population to the West in the late 1970s and early 1980s. These events had a widespread societal significance because they indicated a potential dramatic alteration of the traditional metropolis–hinterland relationship. The regional elite and the ascendant regional middle class formed a coalition that sought to use the provincial government as the vehicle to protect and advance regional interests.

A Western separatist movement burst on the scene in the early 1980s as a direct consequence of the new expectations by Westerners for regional economic development.[47] The February election of 1980 was decided in the "East" before many Westerners even voted, and this, coupled with the fact that only two members of the governing party (Liberals) were elected in the entire West, reawakened the old sense of disenfranchisement among Westerners. The federal–provincial confrontations over energy revenues, and particularly the National Energy Policy, which removed the energy dynamic from the West in the "national" interest, suggested to Westerners that federal assertiveness in the face of Western aspirations was really another expression of central Canadian control.

In any event, important forces had been set in motion that might have contributed to a change in traditional central Canadian–Western relationships. Yet the principle enunciated earlier—that the growth of one region usually must take place at the expense of another—helps to explain why there was resistance to any significant shift in regional relationships. In fact, while Toronto and southern Ontario were booming in the mid-1980s, the West (and particularly Alberta) was in a significant recession.[48] For this reason, support for free trade has been generally strong in the West as the region's inability to diversify within Canada has encouraged the search for participation in a larger continental market. To the extent that the diversification of the economy away from the staples industries remains an issue, the West is likely to engender continuing regional conflict.

The economic and demographic expansion of British Columbia and Alberta through the 1980s and 1990s distinguishes the urban West from the more agrarian West. Whereas Manitoba and Saskatchewan have had little new growth in population, the cities of Vancouver, Calgary, and Edmonton have not only attracted population but have also served as growth poles for new employment primarily in the service industry. Lower costs and taxation favourable to business have been used by the Alberta government in particular to promote what it calls the "Alberta Advantage" as a means of attracting economic opportunities to the province. Interestingly enough, Ontario has fought back with its own lowered tax rates to prevent the erosion of their traditional dominant position.

RESEARCH CLIP 4.1   **The Western Roots of the Reform Party**

The Reform Party was formed in 1987 and, while it aims to be a national party, its roots are clearly in the West, and its successes to date have primarily been in the West. In the federal election of 1993, Reform won 52 seats but 46 of these were in British Columbia and Alberta with five elected in Saskatchewan and Manitoba. Reform did even better in the 1997 election winning 60 seats with 49 seats in Alberta and Saskatchewan and 11 in Manitoba and Saskatchewan.

It is noteworthy that in the 1993 election, another regionalist party, the Bloc Québécois with representatives only from Quebec, was the Official Opposition in Parliament. In the 1997 election, Reform won more seats while the BQ lost some seats and Reform began the Official Opposition. These strong political expressions of regionalism speak volumes about the regionalization of Canadian society.

With the failure of the Meech Lake agreement and distrust of the distinct society idea, fears of the economic crisis caused by public debt, as well as the crisis of the continuing viability of the Canadian state, those who felt most marginalized and dislocated within Canadian society were far-Westerners who felt that they had lost status and lacked power in defining what Canada should become. These largely Anglo-European Protestants were farmers and people of rural background, persons in technical and professional fields, and small business owners who challenged the premises of collapsing welfare state liberalism rooted in central Canada with their new vision of Canada based on neoconservative principles. These ideas were then combined with populist ideas of power to the people, anti-big government, and greater accountability of elected officials.

Thus, whatever the Reform Party might become, and whatever the Reform Party resists being (it does not contest provincial elections—only federal elections), its roots are very much in the West and it is the product of a specific regional context. Paradoxically, in its own way, the West is playing a key role in reshaping Canadian society from the margins.

Source: See Trevor Harrison, *Of Passionate Intensity: Right Wing Populism and the Reform Party of Canada* (Toronto: University of Toronto Press, 1995).

However, perhaps it is the inability of Canada to resolve the aspirations of Quebec for recognition as, among other things, a distinct society that has contributed to a new expression of Western regional alienation. Provoked by anger that Quebec (again as a Central Canadian province) controls the national agenda in which Ontario (the other Central Canadian province) is driven by compromise, the West has birthed a distinct regional vision for a reformulated Canadian society.[49] Based on the notion of political equality (not to be confused with economic equality), the Reform Party has taken a position against the accommodation of special interest groups (such as Quebec) in calling for "One Canada" in a single national community, and is best known for its call for a Triple E Senate (elected, equal, effective) which would serve as a countervailing force to Central Canadian dominance in Parliament. The slogan "The West Wants In!" articulates the Western desire for redress from perceptions that the status quo marginalizes them.

REGION STUDY II: THE ATLANTIC REGION

In our examination of the West, we have seen how agriculture and energy have provided the stimuli for regional identities and established socio-economic structures and traditions. Shifting focus to the eastern end of the country, we note that fishing serves here as the backbone of regional identity. As Prairie residents are "people of the land," Atlantic residents are "people of the sea." The ocean has inspired shipbuilding and overseas transportation, which have facilitated regular contact with international trading partners. The ocean, too, has offered seafood as part of the regular diet, and mist and fog as part of the climate.

The relationship of this region to the sea has led to its designation as the "Maritimes." It is significant to note, however, that just as British Columbia has a somewhat different history and settlement experience from the Prairies in the west, so Newfoundland at the eastern extremity of Canada possesses its own unique identity and heritage quite apart from the provinces of Nova Scotia, New Brunswick, and Prince Edward Island. While the body of water (Cabot Strait) separating Newfoundland from these provinces symbolizes significant distinctions in geography, culture, and politics, it is possible nevertheless to speak of this cluster of provinces as one Atlantic region, for there is much in their socio-economic condition they hold in common.

The fishing village image of the region is unfortunate in one respect, because it is based on a worn stereotype. In the first place, a declining proportion of the population is engaged in commercial fishing; the majority of the population is urban. Second, the image is essentially pre-industrial in nature, and implies that the region has never embraced the process of industrialization. In point of fact, the region did have a thriving industrial base at one time and then lost it through a process of interregional transfer.

The long stretches of Atlantic coastline characteristic of the region have meant close contact with ocean-going vessels. This contact has resulted in regular interaction with Europe (particularly Britain) and the New England states. Early settlers came from Britain and France (Acadiens). Later, with the arrival of the Loyalists from the United States, the period from 1815 to 1860 became known as a time of considerable prosperity: the shipping industry grew rapidly, the merchant marine expanded to rank fourth in the world, and banks and insurance companies were established to finance and protect the capitalist expansion. Rawlyk and Brown refer to the eve of Confederation as the "Golden Age" in Atlantic Canada, when the prospects for an industrial future were bright indeed.[50] The Atlantic region was not oriented towards the interior of the continent, but to trading links with the eastern US seaboard and Britain. Nova Scotia, in particular, developed industries around iron, steel, textiles (including cotton mills), rope factories, glass works, and sugar refineries.

The prospect of participating in Confederation was met with mixed feelings.[51] On the one hand, there was the "beachhead" possibility of the Atlantic region serving as the key trading centre between the interior provinces and Europe. There were also potential markets for local products in the Canadian interior. On the other hand, there was a legacy of fear surrounding central Canadian ambitions and politics. The breakdown of reciprocity negotiations with the US, however, and the failure of railway development (the Intercolonial Railway was not completed until after Confederation), together with a sense of the inevitable, led to provincial decisions to join Confederation at the time of its formation in 1867 (except Newfoundland which joined much later, in 1949).

Some regret has always remained in the region. Nova Scotia, in particular, spawned an anti-Confederate movement in the 1860s and secession was considered in the 1880s.[52] Perhaps most notable was the post–World War I Maritime Rights Movement, which was essentially a regional protest against the inequities of Confederation. What were the long-term effects of Confederation for the region?

Perhaps the most dominant feature of post-Confederation years was that the anticipated industrial expansion of the region never materialized and, in fact, recession took place. One reason for this decline was a decline in the overseas staples trade (e.g., fish and lumber), but a second problem was that the region was unable to compete with industries in central Canada. While the Intercolonial Railway initially provided access to Western markets for Maritime industries, a change in the freight rate structure (which had originally made it cheaper to ship goods to the West than to the East) took away the advantage from Maritime industries and these industries were never able to recover.[53] Third, the lack of both capital and markets forced many Maritime industries to sell out to central Canadian interests. This fostered a continual process of *consolidation* and *centralization* of industry in central Canada.[54] Fourth, federal policy became preoccupied with the problems of the West, and this put the Atlantic region in competition for federal attention. The addition of the Western provinces to Confederation meant that the strength of the Maritime provinces in political decision making was diminished considerably.

The end result of this process was the industrial decline of the Maritimes. The Maritime Rights Movement (1919–1927) was a protest against the declining status of the region, which was an effect of the growing dominance of central Canadian metropoles and the rise of Western competition.[55] The growing weakness of one region was clearly related to the increasing strength of another region, as the National Policy produced net benefits to central Canada at the expense of other regions, such as the Prairies.[56] The Prairies, however, had no industry, while Maritime industries had, at one time, thrived. As the Maritimes grew weaker, therefore, a process of *deindustrialization* occurred. Symbolic of this reversal was the significant emigration of population between 1900 and 1930. Most of these people went to the industrial centres of New England.[57] A pattern of regional exploitation was established whereby central Canada marketed its consumer goods in the Maritimes but, in turn, did little to provide a strong economic base for the region. The Maritimes then reverted to exporting staples such as coal, potatoes, wood and wood products, apples, and fish, and returned to a position of economic dependency on central Canadian metropoles.

Conrad speaks of the ongoing struggle between Ottawa and the Atlantic provinces in the mid-1950s to mid-1960s as the *Atlantic revolution*.[58] A new class of middle class professionals and bureaucrats within the region responded to post-war economic decline, on the one hand,

Comparing the Prairie Region and Atlantic Region

Similarities:

- High dependence on primary industries, whether fishing, lumbering, agriculture, or natural resources
- Staple products exported from region in raw or semi-processed state
- Dependence on industrial heartland for finished goods, finance, and commercial direction
- Perceptions of hinterland status sustained by design and supported by federal policies. Regional sense of political and economic powerlessness

Differences:

- Greater ethnic heterogeneity in the West and sense of openness as a more recent frontier. Greater ethnic homogeneity in Atlantic region and lengthier settlement history
- Successful history of third parties in West that have thrived on protest ideology. Greater political conservatism in Atlantic region
- A mix of resources which are both strong and weak staples, an entrepreneurial spirit, and larger cities give the Prairies a stronger economic dynamic. Atlantic agriculture less important, shipping and fishing historically important but less important now, offshore oil potential.

Source: Based on Thérèse Arsenau, "The Prairies and Atlantic Canada: Constitutional Common Ground," in J. McCrorie and M.L. McDonald, eds., *The Constitutional Future of the Prairie and Atlantic Regions of Canada* (Regina: CPRC, 1992), 326–30.

and the demand for expansion of state services on the other hand. Their negotiations with Ottawa for a more meaningful federalism won recognition of principles of *equalization* and *regional development assistance* that remain in place as institutionalized themes in Canadian society, but which perpetuate *dependency*. It has also been argued that the collapse of the regional economy produced a concentration of regional capital in the hands of several key families (e.g., McCain, Sobey, Irving) who monopolized and expanded their regional control of trade.[59] For example, potato farmers in New Brunswick were transformed from independent businesses to agribusinesses dominated by one company that told them what to plant and how much to plant. In any case, staples remained the backbone of the economy and little new development occurred.

Newfoundland's relationship to Canadian society is particularly interesting because of that territory's relatively late entrance into Confederation and the circumstances under which it occurred. The initial settlements on the eastern shores of the island were based on a fishing economy with markets in Britain and also more distant places such as Spain and Brazil.[60] Newfoundland obtained responsible government in 1855 and actually entered into treaties and agreements with other countries in subsequent years. However, the volatility of foreign markets in combination with over-expansion in earlier years led to a financial crisis in 1931 (many other governments faced similar situations, it should be noted, without the same result) out of which came the replacement of responsible government by a commission government under British sponsorship.[61] Newfoundland's strategic location as a military base and stopover for trans-Atlantic flights during World War II, and in the years thereafter, led to significant prosperity which helped prepare the way for the consideration of union with Canada.

The decision to join Canada was far from unanimous as many resented the loss of independence and questioned the "engineering" of the referendum.[62] In fact, two referendums were held with the final result in 1948 showing 52.3% in favour of joining Confederation. Clearly many were apprehensive about losing their earlier independence and questioned the nature of the benefits they would receive. If Newfoundland experienced no significant improvement in its economic conditions as a result of its union with Canada, dependency and underdevelopment would remain. This is precisely what has occurred in a process known as *transfer dependency* whereby "Uncle Ottawa" (directly and indirectly through federal subsidies to the provincial government) has been responsible for a majority of the spending in the province.[63] A high birth rate (the highest in Canada for much of the post-war period), a declining fishery, and a resettlement program[64] aimed at providing better services (e.g., schools, water systems) to a population previously dispersed, all contributed to a more urban population but with little increase in employment opportunity. What new industries were established, such as mining and pulp and paper, were still staple-based and subject to enormous fluctuations in demand. In sum, Newfoundland's quality of life improved in many ways but the economic indicators of lower per capita income, high unemployment and underemployment, and lack of industrialization demonstrate that dependency and underdevelopment are substantial and perpetual.

It is clear from the discussion above that the Atlantic region has not fared well within Canadian society, at least in terms of economic indicators.[65] Rawlyk refers to the feelings engendered as "a paranoid style of regionalism," sustained by a conspiracy theory focused on central Canada.[66] In an attempt to reconcile economic disparities, the federal approach has been to use transfer payments, or equalization grants (unemployment insurance and grants for hospitals, roads, and universities) to ensure a higher standard of living for the region. In the early 1990s, federal transfer payments made up 37–40% of Atlantic provincial revenues, and government employment made up a higher share of the regional workforce than elsewhere.[67] Some incentives have also been provided to private enterprise (e.g., Bricklin, Michelin Tire) and the Atlantic Canada Opportunities Agency (ACOA) was established, but these efforts have been marginally successful at best.[68] Most significant to other centres of economic growth in Canada, the Atlantic region has provided a large reverse labour pool of short-term and long-term migrants to other regions where labour is needed.[69]

In attempting to change this peripheral condition, it was not surprising that the prospects of offshore oil, particularly for Nova Scotia and Newfoundland, were considered new opportunities for regional development.[70] Three problems arose from these expectations. In the first place, offshore oil was under federal jurisdiction so there was no chance for provincial governments to obtain the same level of economic benefits from whatever production occurred as the Western provinces experienced without a confrontation with the federal government. Premier Peckford of Newfoundland engaged in a particularly protracted battle with the federal government over this issue, sometimes presented as a hinterland revolt. Second, conflicts developed between the traditional industry—fishing, and the new industry—oil. Oil can be characterized as a strong staple because it is in higher demand in world markets and is tied to large capital and corporate conglomerates, whereas fish is a weak staple because of less demand and less organization of its commodity sector.[71] Whenever the two are copresent, oil tends to dominate the fishery to the point that the fishery will be disturbed or restructured, and fishing cultures and communities will be eroded or transformed. Third, oil is still only another staple, perhaps of higher demand, but also subject to depletion and exportability in its raw form with little benefit to the region.

RESEARCH CLIP 4.2   Coasts Under Stress: The Fishery Crisis

July 1992 is a very important date in Canadian life. It is the date that the cod fishery in Atlantic Canada was closed by the federal government due to depleted stocks, with the consequence that 40 000 people were put out of work and the survival of dozens of communities was thrown into question. Due to sheer overfishing, especially owing to the capacities of large factory freezer trawlers and longliners and technological innovations such as fish sounders to assist in locating fish, the biomass, and particularly the reproductive portion, had declined greatly since the early sixties. Because their work was largely seasonal in nature, fishers and fish factory workers had never had large incomes to begin with and various adjustment techniques through an informal economy (e.g., building your own home with the help of neighbours and kin) were part of the community sustenance pattern.

While the impact of this closure affected all of the Atlantic provinces, there is no doubt that Newfoundland experienced the greatest harm as around 28 000 persons (about 70% of the total) lost their primary means of income. The government instituted a special program known as TAGS (The Atlantic Groundfish Strategy) to provide income support and job retraining opportunities to cushion the blow. About 72% of those affected had not completed high school and 40% had less than a grade nine level of education, a situation that had great implications for finding alternative employment. In the end, TAGS was criticized because it merely supported people financially (about 79% of recipients in Newfoundland were heavily dependent on TAGS payments) rather than actually putting them back to work. The problem of the remote location of many of these outport communities combined with the age and lack of education of those most affected reduced the options for new forms of employment and made job retraining less appropriate.

What has been the effect of the closure of the cod fishery besides unemployment? Of course, there have been ripple effects throughout the community as, for example, the viability of restaurants and schools have been threatened. The latter in particular has occurred as the out-migration of young people and people in child-bearing years who leave for opportunities elsewhere has meant that communities consist of a higher proportion of older people and a shrinking tax base to sustain community institutions. Persons affected also reported feeling like second-class citizens often experiencing little empathy from persons living in urban centres. On the other hand, in spite of the trauma, the evidence was overwhelming that the kinship and friendship network in these communities was very strong and heightened the capacity to absorb the shock. Children did not exhibit maladaptive behaviour and parents did not exhibit lower self-esteem, mental distress, or weakened social supports that were typical of unemployment in other places. Attachment to the community and involvement in its activities remained strong.

There is an increasing realization that despite the continuance of some forms of fishing such as crab and lobster, that whenever the cod fishery is reopened there will be a severe reduction in the employment opportunities which will greatly affect the existence of outport communities. The closure of the Catalina processing plant on the north coast which once employed 1100 persons is a good example of what happens to a community and region when its economic backbone is removed. The long term implications of this tragedy for Newfoundland society in terms of rural–urban migration and out-migration from the province provide a counterpoint to the new opportunities created by off-shore oil but threaten the existence of communities that have been in existence for hundreds of years.

While the consequences have so far been not as severe, the depletion of salmon stocks on the Pacific coast in the 1990s is also threatening communities there.

Source: Rosemary E. Ommer, "Sustainability of Communities of Fish and Fishers in Canada", *Breakfasts on the Hill*, 1998, hssfc.ca; John C. Kennedy, "At the Crossroads: Newfoundland and Labrador Communities in a Changing International Context", *Canadian Review of Sociology and Anthropology* 34(3)1997:297–317; HRDC Canada, *The Atlantic Groundfish Strategy: Post-TAGS Review Report* (1998); Dianne Newell and Rosemary E. Ommer (eds.), *Fishing Places, Fishing People: Traditions and Issues in Canadian Small-Scale Fisheries* (Toronto: University Of Toronto Press, 1999). For a good analysis of the social organization of the Newfoundland inshore fishery, see David Ralph Matthews, *Controlling Common Property: Regulating Canada's East Coast Fishery* (Toronto: University Of Toronto Press, 1993).

Energy has recently begun to be a factor in the economies of some Atlantic provinces primarily through off-shore fields, and has served as a catalyst for discussions in the region about using energy as a lever to reduce dependency. While we await an assessment of this development, it is clear that the goal is to use oil and gas as a means to reduce unemployment, underemployment, and out-migration.[72] In Newfoundland with the vast Hibernia field, the objective was also that of controlled development by the province rather than by the federal government or corporations coming into the province with their own agendas. The challenge of oil was to use it to benefit the people of the region.

In many ways, the crisis in the fishery and the restructuring which it entails are symptomatic of what is transpiring throughout the Atlantic region as corporatism is restructuring all forms of primary production.[73] When forests come to be perceived as pulp plantations, the effect on small woodlot operators is great, creating a clash of interests that affects not only the economy but the social structure of the region. If government has provided the mechanisms (e.g., transfer payments) to ensure the stability of the region in the past, it is unclear how the radical downsizing of the state and its revenue streams, and the emphasis on market forces will now affect a region in change.[74] The potential independence of Quebec would also be a threat in territorially separating the Atlantic region from the rest of Canada on which it has fiscal dependence. For this reason, Atlantic residents have been strong supporters of confederation in spite of the disadvantages it brings, and much like the West have been frustrated by exclusion from the full benefits of union and national participation.[75]

REGION STUDY III: THE NORTH

For many Canadians who live in the southern extremities of the country, the North may simply refer to the upper regions of their provinces where rugged adventure (e.g., fishing and hunting) or relaxation takes place as a get-away from urban life. These northern areas within existing provinces have much in common with the area north of 60° latitude that does not have provincial status.[76] However, for our immediate purposes, "the North" will refer to that territory north of 60° latitude occupied by the Yukon, Northwest Territories, and now Nunavut. Images of this area are of tundra, permafrost, short summer nights, ice, and snow.

The Middle North

The Middle North is a vast sub-Arctic belt in the northern part of existing provinces that is sparsely populated, economically unstable, and populated primarily by Aboriginal people. All provinces except the Maritimes have such a "provincial north" and, in most cases, this territory makes up more than 50% of the province (e.g., Quebec 81%, Newfoundland and Manitoba 74%, Ontario 65%). In being attached to a province, these regions, while similar, have very little sense of a common identity and are overwhelmed by the power of their southern regions. In that sense, these northern regions are internal colonies of the southern population. In territorial size, the provincial norths comprise over a third of Canada's land mass.

Southern Canadian governments and corporations pay little attention to this region unless it has natural resources of value to industrial Canada or global industrial needs. Indians and Métis frequently live in isolated settlements until their lives are disrupted by resource development. Gold, coal, oil sands, uranium, forestry, and hydroelectric power are the primary engines of economic growth in the region. Perhaps the most well-known development that had a major effect on indigenous peoples was the James Bay hydroelectric project in northern Quebec that flooded much of the land important to local Native culture. Natives receive little benefit from these developments as raw materials are shipped to markets external to the area.

Source: Based on Ken Coates and William Morrison, *The Forgotten North* (Toronto: James Lorimer, 1992). See also Ken Coates and William R. Morrison (eds.), *The Historiography of the Provincial Norths* (Thunder Bay: Centre For Northern Studies, Lakehead University, 1996).

Since 1961, the population of the Northwest Territories and Nunavut has more than doubled (68 000), and the Yukon population has almost doubled (32 000). The population of Canada's smallest province, Prince Edward Island, is one and one-half times the combined populations of the Territories and Nunavut, even though these two territories are more than 6000 times bigger in land space. While many of the conditions of life are similar in all three territories, one striking difference is that the Yukon has three-quarters of its population in one city—Whitehorse. Yellowknife, a smaller city than Whitehorse, is the major city in the Northwest Territories and contains about 20% of the territory's people. Both cities have a significant population of civil servants, but beyond the confines of these cities, and particularly in the Northwest Territories and Nunavut, the population is considerably dispersed.

Another significant contrast between the two territories is that the Northwest Territories has a much higher proportion of Native peoples. In the Yukon, Native people are a minority (about 20%) whereas in the Northwest Territories, Native groups are a majority composed of Indian or Dene, Inuit, and mixed-blood Métis. The Inuit form a clear majority in what is known as the eastern Arctic (Nunavut). In the north (but particularly the Yukon), the non-Native population has grown especially rapidly due to in-migration of a transient rotating workforce from the south with different objectives, a pattern that tends to overwhelm the Native population in a variety of ways.[77]

The sparse population and remote location of the North have meant that the region traditionally has been of minor importance to the Canadian economy. Even after the area was claimed as part of Canada, the government maintained a laissez-faire approach to the development of the region, leaving the major initiatives to the fur traders (The Hudson's Bay Company) and the church (Anglican and Roman Catholic).[78] The vast area and the relatively inhospitable climate meant that both the traditional economy (fishing, hunting, and trapping) and the small settlements of semi-nomadic people were far removed from direct southern Canadian influences.

Southern Canadians have been attracted repeatedly to the North by resources which, though difficult to obtain, offered the promise of quick wealth. Early examples of the activity surrounding this attraction can be observed in the Yukon Gold Rush of 1898 and, later, the mining boom around Yellowknife in the 1930s. As well as gold, there was oil, and considerable activity was generated by the discovery of oil at Norman Wells in 1921, on the north slopes of Alaska in 1968, as well as by the more recent exploration at several land points throughout the Territories and offshore in the Beaufort Sea. Other mineral developments which have attracted interest because of their industrial uses are tungsten, silver, lead, and copper.[79]

Much of this resource-based activity has occurred in "boom or bust" cycles typical of a staples economy. What has produced these fluctuations? In the first place, these economic developments have taken place with southern capital put forward by large southern corporations

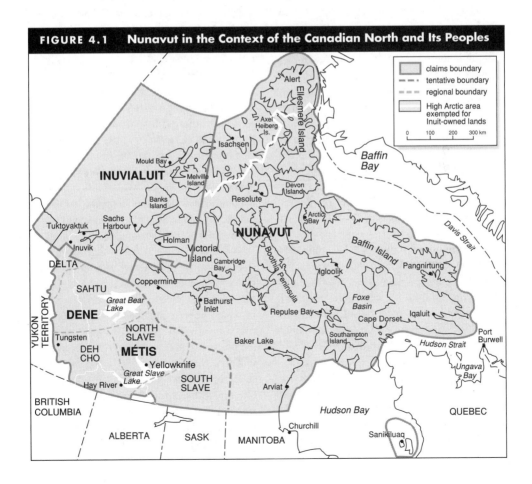

FIGURE 4.1 Nunavut in the Context of the Canadian North and Its Peoples

Nunavut: A New Regional Territory, a Distinct Society, a Sense of Nationhood

A new Territorial government was created on April 1, 1999, when the old Northwest Territories was divided into east and west with the eastern two-thirds forming Nunavut as the third territorial government. The remaining Northwest Territories in the western Arctic is in the process of its own constitutional discussions.

Nunavut (meaning "Our Land") is a huge geographical area north of the tree line and is the largest political jurisdiction in Canada. Composing one-fifth of the Canadian landmass at 2 242 000 square kilometres, Nunavut is larger than Mexico, or larger than France, Germany, Great Britain and Italy combined. Yet its population of 27 000 could almost fit in a typical NHL hockey arena. Residents live in 31 communities, half of which are north of the Arctic Circle and most of which have between 500 and 1500 people. There are no highways in this vast region and the area is linked by air travel and sophisticated communication technology.

In contrast to the western Arctic, the eastern Arctic has little resource development. Both areas, however, have high unemployment.

The most striking demographic difference between the eastern and western Arctic is that Nunavut is more ethnically homogeneous. Eighty percent of Nunavut is Inuit and Inuktitut is the mother tongue of 74% of the residents (About 20% speak neither French nor English). Radio broadcasts are available in Inuktitut, there are bilingual signs, a trilingual telephone book and a bilingual newspaper (Nunatsiaq News). In many ways then, the people of Nunavut are a *distinct society.*

The decision to establish Nunavut was made by a plebiscite in 1992 after an agreement was reached between federal and territorial leaders. An important part of the agreement was the settling of land claims which gives the Inuit subsurface rights over part of the territory, financial compensation, and participation in the control and management of Crown lands. The establishment of Nunavut then is, in essence, a form of self-government for Inuit.

The remaining area of the Northwest Territories is much more pluralistic. The northwest area is the home of the Inuvialuit and the southwest region contains five Dene and Métis bands—the Delta (Gwich'in), the Deh Cho, the Sahtu, the North Slave, and the South Slave. With the exception of the Inuvialuit, most of this population lives south of the tree line, which essentially is the area south of a line from Churchill to Inuvik.

"Nunavut's most important meaning is that it is a government which reflects the life and life styles, and language, of the people who live along the coasts and by the caribou hunting grounds of our homeland. It is not a government which is trying to make our people act or look or speak like someone down south. It is a government for a largely Inuit community, and in which people can speak, write, work, make important decisions and govern themselves in Inuktitut. . . . What Nunavut will do is make sure that in Canada with its several provinces and territories, there is one government that is always speaking for the Inuit and making sure that Canada as a country has a large and important Inuit character as part of its national identity."

In some ways, then, Nunavut is similar to Quebec in that a distinct people with a clear ethnic background and a common language share a territory in which they have considerable control. The paradox is that Nunavut is both a distinct region of Canada at the same time that it is a distinct society or nation in the political-ethnic sense.

Source: Excerpts from the Nunavut Constitutional Forum published in Information North (Arctic Institute of North America) 19(1993): 7 and "Nunavut" ("Our Land") by Mark O. Dickerson and Karen M. McCullough in the same issue. See also Mark O. Dickerson, *Whose North? Political Change, Political Development, and Self-Government in the Northwest Territories* (Vancouver: UBC Press, 1992); Donald Purich, *The Inuit and Their Land: The Story of Nunavut* (Toronto: James Lorimer, 1992); Cameron W. Stout, "Nunavut: Canada's Newest Territory In 1999", *Canadian Social Trends*, no. 44, 1997:13–18, and Nunavut Implementation Commission, Nunavut: Changing The Map Of Canada, 1999.

employing a transient southern work force who moved into the North only for the duration of a project. In the second place, resource extraction has depended on external markets, where gains or slippage in price could either accelerate, or entirely close down, the extraction process. Problems of transportation, accessibility, and high labour costs meant that high retail prices were necessary to maintain operations. Conversely, drops in the prices of resources led to the abandonment of expensive extraction procedures. Thirdly, Native workers, usually hired for temporary or seasonal terms, were poorly integrated into the operation. Not only did the wage economy change expectations among Native workers, but it also began to bring into conflict socio-economic elements within the structure of the traditional Native economy. At the very least, the flurry of activity in the boom phase contrasted greatly with the bleakness of shut-down, and this contributed to instability in Native society. Finally, because most of the wages and profits were taken out of the region, the resource activity had little lasting impact on the development of the region—a classic condition of colonialism and underdevelopment.

Prattis and Chartrand applied this internal colonial model to the Inuit in the North and found that there was indeed a disproportionate exclusion of Inuit from the labour force and a systematic underrepresentation of Inuit in the positions of highest rank.[80] In that sense there was a *cultural division of labour*. But it was through a strong sense of cultural identity (e.g., strong retention of their indigenous language Inuktitut) that efforts were being made to reshape the material conditions of their lives in the region.

In any case, what development took place in the North was clearly related to the industrial needs of southern Canada in the post–World War II era. It should be noted also that the North represented a strategic political territory for defence in the Cold War between the United States and the Soviet Union.[81] The establishment of a series of radar lines such as the Dew Line and Pine Tree Chain Line, as well as the construction of the Alaska Highway and recent demonstrations of arctic sovereignty—all spoke of the increasing frequency of southern intrusions into a previously unimportant territory. In sum, the needs of regions and countries external to the North contributed to the area's increasing importance within Canadian society. This developmental pressure is clearly changing the fact of the North— both environmentally and socially.

No other region of Canada is tied as directly to federal controls as the North, even though there is a legislative assembly and the people elect representatives to the federal parliament.[82] Lacking status as provinces, all natural resources in the territories (and the resultant royalties) have been under the control of Ottawa. The federal government appoints a Commissioner for each territory. In the case of the Northwest Territories, the Commissioner lived in Ottawa until

1967, at which point white civil servants were transferred to Yellowknife to administer the territory. In addition, the federal government exerts political control through the Department of Indian Affairs and Northern Development (DIAND), serves as a major employer, and is also the primary source of funds for health and welfare. Because nurses and teachers, as well as wildlife and resource officers, are all hired by the government, the number of civil servants in the North is three times the national average.[83] Additionally, transfer payments, in the form of welfare and unemployment assistance, illustrate further dependency on federal funds and institutions.

Amidst this colonial reality, a political awareness has begun to emerge among indigenous peoples, reflecting a desire for more direct control and power over the affairs of the North. Abele has traced the evolution of this changed consciousness by distinguishing three phases in Native–non-Native relations in the North.[84] In the first phase, the Native people maintained their traditional lifestyle but were needed by non-Natives (e.g., traders, police, missionaries) for survival assistance in the harsh environment. In the second phase after World War II, the skills of the Native people were in less demand and non-Natives excluded them from the economy and polity which was being developed. The third phase began in the late 1960s when the Native people began to demand participation in the shaping of their own region. Perhaps no single event was more symbolic of the new mood articulated by Native northerners (and belatedly shared by an increasing number of non-Native residents as well) than the ideas and ideals expressed in the Mackenzie Valley Pipeline hearings (Berger Report) held in communities all over the North in the mid-70s.[85] Southern Canada was being served notice that the North could no longer be considered a passive hinterland in which the environmental and social costs of intrusive development would be ignored. So the first way in which political awareness began to develop was through a reaction to forms of economic development in which the people of the North would participate only marginally and likely also become victims.[86]

Second, the response to external intrusion and control produced new organizations of Native people to negotiate with outside groups such as corporations and, in particular, the federal government. Groups such as the Indian Brotherhood of the Northwest Territories, the Métis and Non-Status Indian Association of the Northwest Territories, the Council of Yukon Indians, the Inuit Tapirisat, the Federation of Natives North of Sixty, the Committee for Original Peoples' Entitlement, and the Tungavik Federation of Nunavut were organized in the early 1970s and have effectively represented the positions of Native people in negotiation with southern Canadians.

The third expression of this new awareness can be focused on the issue of land claims and the desire for self-government. When the Dene Declaration was signed at Fort Simpson in 1975, outsiders only heard the bold assertion of the Dene claiming to be a nation. The meaning of nationhood was essentially self-determination, for they wanted to be able to control what was happening to their own society rather than being victimized by the actions of others. Real control in this instance did not mean necessarily blocking all development, but the control of what developments did occur and the pace at which they took place, and the minimizing of the negative impacts. So whereas in the mid-70s the pipeline faced large-scale rejection,[87] by the late 80s, Native groups were ready to assess new investment in their region.

Self-government, then, means the exertion of more localized and less bureaucratic federal control in matters ranging from the delivery of health and social services to education, resource ownership, and local taxation.[88] Land claims go far beyond land control or cash compensations to include the ability of a Native group to retain the viability of their community. For this reason, land claim agreements and self-government have been intertwined. Several claims have already been settled and others have been agreed to in principle.

There still remains the need to resolve many issues. One issue is that the federal government has no obligation to deal with the North as it does other provinces as illustrated in both the negotiations on the Constitution and the Meech Lake Accord in the 1980s.[89] Another matter deals with the need to prepare Native people to be full participants in whatever development does occur, through job training and the reconciliation of hunting and gathering (the traditional economy) with wage labour (the industrial economy) to sustain Native culture.[90] The fact that 75% of the communities with more than 50 inhabitants do not have a consistent economic base only accentuates the dilemma.[91] Nevertheless, much like the people in provinces in the Western and Atlantic regions, Northerners have increasingly come to the conclusion that decisions about resources should benefit their own region first, rather than so obviously treat the region as a hinterland with needs secondary to those of southern metropoles.[92] It is in this sense that resources, regionalism, and underdevelopment contribute to a complex saga that evokes comparisons with those regions of Canada discussed above.

REGIONALISM REVISITED

While the history and economy of each of these regions is quite different, and the conditions of social life are quite varied, there are some aspects which denote a common existence. First, prosperity in each region depends greatly on staple extraction and resource development, whether it be grain, coal, fish, fur, oil, or minerals. Second, these primary industries are export-oriented, and little if any secondary industry has developed in the hinterland region. Third, the existence of qualitative differences between these regions fails to mask the fact that they support the industrial heartland of Canada. Fourth, each region has its own list of grievances focusing on control from outside the region. Fifth, a new class of regional elites and middle class boosters are seeking greater regional control over development and change within each area. It should not be surprising if regional conflict over the distribution and redistribution of opportunity and control should continue to exist.

In using the term *hinterland* to describe areas as diverse as the North, the Atlantic region, and the West, it is important to note that there are vast differences within each region. Urban areas are vastly different from remote rural areas just as northern Ontario may be vastly different from southern Ontario. Furthermore, modern technology and consumerization has reduced many of the differences that might have existed thirty years ago, and there are many ways in which life in these regions is identical to life in core regions. In addition, to speak of Vancouver, Halifax, Calgary, Fredericton as hinterlands is absurd unless it is understood in the context of intra-societal relations.

Regionalism, as the politicized articulation of concerns expressed in a territory, will have different manifestations depending on the location, the issue, and the economy. Some forms of regionalism will be short-lived, some will be sustained by enduring cleavages, while others will be deliberately created.[93] Historically, most of the regionalist movements have been based on protest. *Protest regionalism* is a socio-political reaction triggered by erosion of position, and is aimed at either reversal of the decline or protection against further decline.[94] Such slippage involved both the Maritime Rights Movement and the United Farmers Movement in the West. More recently, regionalist activity has been oriented towards new opportunities for growth. *Entrepreneurial* or *expansionist regionalism* describes the actions that result from the desire to generate or take advantage of new opportunities to benefit a region and its inhabitants. It is not surprising that the high demand for energy has made oil and gas the basis for new hopes and expectations of regional growth and development.

As noted in Chapter Three, the federal government is keenly aware of the issues presented by regionalism. Bickerton has argued that the state has three strategy options when attempting to reconcile such divergent structural conditions.[95] One option is *inaction* in the hope that market mechanisms will produce their own self-correction. Another option is a welfare state strategy of *subsidized protection* (e.g., income supplements) to artificially reduce disparities. A third option is *administrative recommodification* whereby labour is made more saleable through training or mobility subsidies and industries are rationalized or modernized to be more competitive. The Canadian state has used all of these strategies jointly or at different times. One of the key debates is whether government involvement cushions and supports adaptive processes or whether it interferes or even retards adaptation and change.[96] It is for this reason that regionalism goes far beyond interesting cultural differences and strikes at the heart of structural disparities within Canadian society.

FURTHER EXPLORATION

1. Discuss regional stereotypes thought to be representative of your region. Explain why they exist, and assess their accuracy.

2. Are the regional categories discussed in this chapter too large? What sub-regional units exist within these regions? Are they important?

3. Are regional disparities inevitable? Do "have" regions have responsibilities to "have not" regions when we are all part of the same society? How do you feel about regions that are more or less prosperous than yours?

SELECTED READINGS

Brym, Robert J., ed. *Regionalism in Canada.* Toronto: Irwin, 1988.

Coffey, William J., and Mario Polèse, eds. *Still Living Together: Recent Trends and Future Directions in Canadian Regional Development.* Montreal: Institute for Research on Public Policy, 1987.

Gibbins, Roger and Sonia Arrison. *Western Visions: Perspectives on the West in Canada.* Peterborough: Broadview, 1995.

Matthews, Ralph. *The Creation of Regional Dependency.* Toronto: University of Toronto Press, 1983.

McRoberts, Kenneth. *Beyond Quebec: Taking Stock of Canada.* Montreal: McGill-Queens University Press, 1995.

McCrorie, James N., and Margaret L. McDonald, eds. *The Constitutional Future of the Prairie and Atlantic Regions of Canada.* Regina: Canadian Plains Research Centre, 1992.

ENDNOTES

1   Harry H. Hiller, "Region As A Social Construction", in Keith Archer and Lisa Young (eds.), *Regionalism and Party Politics in Canada* (Toronto: Oxford University Press, 2000).

2   Odum and his colleagues devote specific attention to economic factors such as regional differences in income, occupation, and other indicators of standard of living. John Shelton Reed, "Sociology and Regional Studies in the United States," *Ethnic and Racial Studies* 3(1980): 40–51.

3   John Shelton Reed, *One South: An Ethnic Approach to Regional Culture* (Baton Rouge: LSU Press, 1981).

4   Ralph Matthews, "Understanding Regionalism as Effect and Cause," in Dennis Forcese and Stephen Richer, eds., *Social Issues: Sociological Views of Canada*, 2nd ed. (Scarborough: Prentice-Hall, 1988), 77–79.

5   This statement is consistent with Matthew's view that regions are not natural but created. Ralph Matthews, *The Creation of Regional Dependency* (Toronto: University of Toronto Press, 1983).

6   T.W. Acheson, "The Maritimes and Empire Canada," in David J. Bercuson, ed., *Canada and the Burden of Unity* (Toronto: Macmillan, 1977), 87–114.

7   Carl Cuneo, "A Class Perspective on Regionalism," in Daniel Glenday, Hubert Guindon, and Allan Turowetz, eds., *Modernization and the Canadian State* (Toronto: Macmillan, 1978), 188.

8   Wallace Clement, "A Political Economy of Regionalism in Canada," in Glenday, Guidon, and Turowetz, *Modernization and the Canadian State*, 100.

9   Kenneth Campbell, "Regional Disparity and Interregional Exchange Imbalance," in Glenday, Guidon, and Turowertz, *Modernization and the Canadian State*, 120. For other evidence of regional disparities, see D.F.G. Sitwell and N.R.M. Seifried, *The Regional Structure of the Canadian Economy* (Toronto: Methuen, 1984); and F.J. Anderson, *Regional Economic Analysis: A Canadian Perspective* (Toronto: HBJ Holt, 1988).

10 Janine Brodie, "The New Political Economy Of Regions", in Wallace Clement (ed.), *Understanding Canada: Building on the New Canadian Political Economy* (Montreal: McGill-Queens, 1997), 242.

11 Janine Brodie, "The New Political Economy Of Regions", in Wallace Clement (ed.), *Understanding Canada: Building on the New Canadian Political Economy* (Montreal: McGill-Queens, 1997), 240–261.

12 The study also argued that while economic disparities have lessened between regions since the Second World War, that they are still higher than among US border states. The assumption is that migration is the answer to these regional disparities. Serge Coulombe, report released by the C.D. Howe Institute, Calgary Herald, March 10, 1999.

13 For a good review of all of these policies and an attempt to calculate levels of disparity, see Donald J. Savoie, *Regional Economic Development: Canada's Search for Solutions*, Second Edition (Toronto: University of Toronto Press, 1992).

14 This explains why the argument that a region lacks development because it lacks entrepreneurs must be qualified by the power of greater corporate strength. For a discussion of this point, cf. Matthews, *The Creation of Regional Dependency* (Toronto: University of Toronto Press, 1983), 46–47.

15 Carl J. Cuneo, "The Class Dimensions of Regionalism," in Lorne Tepperman and James Curtis, eds., *Readings in Sociology: An Introduction* (Toronto: McGraw-Hill Ryerson, 1988), 671–81.

16 James P. Bickerton, *Nova Scotia, Ottawa, and the Politics of Regional Development* (Toronto: University of Toronto Press, 1990), 326–27.

17 Cf. Larry Pratt, "The State and Province-Building: Alberta's Development Strategy," in Leo Panitch, *The Canadian State: Political Economy and Political Power* (Toronto: University of Toronto Press, 1977), 133–62.

18 This is essentially the point of Roger Gibbins, who argued that regionalism might be a much more salient idea to provincial elites than to their electorates. *Regionalism: Territorial Politics in Canada and the United States* (Toronto: Butterworths, 1982), 176.

19 R. Kent Weaver has shown how plurality elections in single member districts has exaggerated regional differences. "Political Institutions And Conflict Management In Canada," *Annals of the American Academy of Political and Social Science*, 538(1995):54–68.

20 Donald J. Savoie, *Governing from the Centre: The Concentration of Power in Canadian Politics* (Toronto: University Of Toronto Press, 1999).

21 For discussions of the political basis of regionalism, cf. Roger Gibbins, *Regionalism: Territorial Politics in Canada and the United States*.

22 Alan C. Cairns, "The Governments and Societies of Canadian Federalism," *Canadian Journal of Political Science* 10(1977): 707.

23 Larry Pratt, "The State and Province Building: Alberta's Development Strategy," 157.

24 Richard Simeon and Donald E. Blake, "Regional Preferences: Citizens' Views on Public Policy," in Elkins and Simeon, *Small Worlds: Provinces and Parties in Canadian Political Life*, 101–102.

25 Garth Stevenson, "Canadian Regionalism in Continental Perspective," *Journal of Canadian Studies* 15(1980): 16–28.

26 Martin Lubin, "The Routinization Of Cross-Border Interactions: An Overview Of NEC/CCP Structures And Activities", in Douglas M. Brown and Earl H. Fry (eds.), *States and Provinces in the International Economy* (Berkeley: Institute of Governmental Studies Press, University Of California, 1993); and Paul Schell and John Hamer, "Cascadia: The New Binationalism Of Western Canada and the U.S. Pacific Northwest", in Robert L. Earle and John D. Wirth (eds.), *Identities in North America* (Stanford: Stanford University Press, 1995), 140–156.

27 Kenichi Ohmae develops this idea perhaps to the point of overstatement in referring to this new phenomenon as "region states." "The Rise Of The Region State", *Foreign Affairs* 72(2)1993:78–87.

28 Cf. Bell and Tepperman, *The Roots of Disunity: A Look at Canadian Political Culture*, 146.

29 Bernard Bonin and Roger Verreault, "The Multinational Firm and Regional Development," in William J. CoVey and Mario Polès, eds., *Still Living Together* (Montreal: Institute for Research on Public Policy, 1987), 159–202.

30 See, for example, Wallace Clement, *The Challenge of Class Analysis* (Ottawa: Carleton University Press, 1988), chap. 9.

31 Ralph Matthews and J. Campbell Davis, "The Comparative Influence of Region, Status, Class and Ethnicity on Canadian Attitudes and Values," 90–122, and Douglas House, "The Mouse That Roars: New Directions in Canadian Political Economy—The Case of Newfoundland," 162–96, in Robert Brym, ed., *Regionalism in Canada* (Toronto: Irwin, 1986).

32 Richard Simeon and David J. Elkins suggest that unique historical and sociological factors may be important contextual elements that create cultural differences between provinces. "Provincial Political Cultures in Canada," in D.J. Elkins and Richard Simeon, eds., *Small Worlds: Provinces and Parties in Canadian Political Life* (Toronto: Methuen, 1980). Ralph Matthews argued that regionalism is the sum product of economic, social organizational, and political factors. "The Significance and Explanation of Regional Divisions in Canada: Toward a Canadian Sociology," *Journal of Canadian Studies* 15(1980): 51.

33 Simeon and Blake, *Regional Preferences: Citizens' Views of Public Policy*, 100.

34 See, for example, Roger Gibbins and Sonia Arrison, *Western Visions: Perspectives on the West in Canada* (Peterborough: Broadview, 1995), 59–69. For an older account, see David Elkins, "The Sense of Place," in David J. Elkins and Richard Simeon, eds., *Small Worlds: Provinces and Parties in Canadian Political Life* (Toronto: Metheun, 1980), 21–23.

35 For an excellent summary discussion of the National Policy and its implications in one volume, see the *Journal of Canadian Studies* 14:3(1979).

36 George F.G. Stanley, "The Western Canadian Mystique," in David P. Gagan, ed., *Prairie Perspectives* (Toronto: Holt, Rinehart and Winston, 1970), 6–27.

37 James C. Davies, "Toward a Theory of Revolution," *American Sociological Review* 27(1962): 5–19.

38 J.F. Conway makes an interesting argument that these movements were essentially a class challenge for reform of the capitalist system by the agrarian petit-bourgeoisie. The fact that the Progressives also reached into Ontario illustrates that this protest had more of a social class, rather than regional basis, he suggests. "The Prairie Populist Resistance to the National Policy: Some Reconsiderations," *Journal of Canadian Studies* 14:3(1979): 77–91. For an excellent review of the problems of the West in Confederation, see also his *The West: The History of a Region in Confederation* (Toronto: James Lorimer, 1983). Some of the key book-length studies on these movements include W.L. Morton, *The Progressive Party in Canada* (Toronto: University of Toronto Press, 1957); S.M. Lipset, *Agrarian Socialism: The Co-operative Commonwealth*

Federation in Saskatchewan (New York: Doubleday, 1968); C.B. Macpherson, *Democracy in Alberta: Social Credit and the Party System* (Toronto: University of Toronto Press, 1953); John A. Irving, *The Social Credit Movement in Alberta* (Toronto: University of Toronto Press, 1959).

39 Roger Gibbins, *Prairie Politics and Society: Regionalism in Decline* (Toronto: Butterworths, 1980), 167–69.

40 Howard Palmer, ed., *The Settlement of the West* (Calgary: The University of Calgary, 1977) as well as the books of C.A. Dawson. For an account of the social organization and evolution of the Prairie community system, see Carle C. Zimmerman and Garry W. Moneo, *The Prairie Community System* (Agricultural Economics Research Council of Canada, 1970).

41 John Stahl, "Prairie Agriculture: A Prognosis," in David P. Gagan, ed., *Prairie Perspectives*, 66.

42 Gibbins argues that the breakdown of the dominance of the rural agricultural economy has reduced the distinctiveness of the region and brought it into increasing competition with other urban industrial areas of Canada. *Prairie Politics and Society: Regionalism in Decline.*

43 Cf., for example, John Barr and Owen Anderson, eds., *The Unfinished Revolt* (Toronto: McClelland and Stewart, 1971).

44 For an assessment of the actual possibility of such a shift in power, see a symposium entitled "Power Shift West: Myth Or Reality?" in *Canadian Journal of Sociology* 6:(1981): 165–83.

45 For an assessment of the freight rates issue, cf. David Harvey, *Christmas Turkey or Prairie Vulture? An Economic Analysis of the Crow's Nest Pass Grain Rates* (Montreal: Institute Of Research for Public Policy, 1980); and Howard Darling, *The Politics of Freight Rates* (Toronto: McClelland and Stewart, 1980).

46 John Richards and Larry Pratt, *Prairie Capitalism: Power and Influence in the New West* (Toronto: McClelland and Stewart, 1979).

47 Larry Pratt and Garth Stevenson, eds., *Western Separatism: The Myths, Realities and Dangers* (Edmonton: Hurtig, 1981).

48 Andrew Nikiforuk, Sheila Pratt, and Donald Wanagas, eds., *Running on Empty: Alberta after the Boom* (Edmonton: Newest, 1987).

49 Gibbins and Arrison, *Western Visions: Perspectives on the West in Canada.*

50 G.A. Rawlyk and Doug Brown, "The Historical Framework of the Maritimes and Confederation," in G.A. Rawlyk, *The Atlantic Provinces and the Problems of Confederation* (St. John's: Breakwater, 1979), 4

51 E.R. Forbes and D.A. Muise (eds.), *The Atlantic Provinces in Confederation* (Toronto: University Of Toronto Press, 1993).

52 Colin D. Howell, "Nova Scotia's Protest Tradition and the Search for a Meaningful Federalism," in David J. Bercuson, ed., *Canada and the Burden of Unity* (Toronto: Macmillan, 1977), 169–91.

53 Ernest R. Forbes, "Misguided Symmetry: The Destruction of Regional Transportation Policy for the Maritimes," in David J. Bercuson, ed., *Canada and the Burden of Unity* (Toronto: Macmillan, 1977), 60–86. It should be pointed out that as a response to the recommendations of the Duncan Commission, the Maritime Freight Rates Act was passed by the Federal Government in 1927 to restore some of the previous freight advantages to the region, but these rates lacked the previous flexibility and failed to have the desired result.

54 T.W. Acheson, "The Maritimes and Empire Canada," in David J. Bercuson, ed., *Canada and the Burden of Unity*, 93; and E.R. Forbes, *Challenging the Regional Stereotype: Essays on the 20th Century Maritimes* (Fredericton: Acadiensis Press, 1989), 200–216, who argues that the way Canada was constitutionally set-up created a tightly integrated union of central urban dominance that hurt Atlantic Canada and that the region was not to blame for the effect.

55 Ernest R. Forbes, *The Maritime Rights Movement, 1919–1927: A Study in Canadian Regionalism* (Montreal: McGill-Queen's University Press, 1979).

56 Ernest R. Forbes explores aspects of the common hinterland condition of the Maritimes and the Prairies and discusses the factors that have prevented them from forming a coalition as allies. "Never the Twain Did Meet. Prairie-Maritime Relations 1910–1927," *Canadian Historical Review* 59(1978): 19–37. For an analysis of the growth and decline of Maritime industry, see T.W. Acheson, David Frank, and James D. Frost, *Industrialization and Underdevelopment in the Maritimes*, 1880–1930 (Toronto: Garamond Press, 1985).

57 Rawlyk and Brown estimate that 300 000 people left the region during this period with three-quarters migrating to the United States. "This Historical Frame-work of the Maritimes and Confederation," in Rawlyk, *The Atlantic Provinces and the Problems of Confederation*, 33.

58 Canada," in James N. McCrorie and Margaret L. MacDonald, eds., *The Constitutional Future of the Prairie and Atlantic Regions of Canada* (Regina: CPRC, 1992), 18–36.

59 Gary Burrill and Ian McKay, eds., *People, Resources and Power: Critical Perspectives on Underdevelopment and Primary Industries in the Atlantic Region* (Fredericton: Gorsebrook Research Institute, 1987).

60 Cf. G.A. Rawlyk, "The Historical Framework of Newfoundland and Confederation," in *The Atlantic Provinces and the Problems of Confederation*, 48–81; and James Hiller and Peter Neary, *Newfoundland in the Nineteenth and Twentieth Centuries: Essays in Interpretation* (Toronto: University of Toronto Press, 1980).

61 S.J.R. Noel, *Politics in Newfoundland* (Toronto: University of Toronto Press, 1971).

62 Peter Neary, "Newfoundland's Union with Canada, 1949: Conspiracy or Choice?" in P.A. Buckner and David Frank, eds., *Atlantic Canada after Confederation* (Fredericton: Acadiensis Press, 1985). For an interesting contemporary interpretation expressing sadness at this decision, see Bryn Walsh, *More Than a Poor Majority: The Story of Newfoundland's Confederation with Canada* (St. John's: Breakwater, 1985).

63 Matthews, *The Creation of Regional Dependency*, 57.

64 In 1961, there were 815 communities of less than 300 inhabitants in Newfoundland and this was reduced to 545 communities in 1971. Ralph Matthews discusses the resettlement program, its objectives, and consequences in *The Creation of Regional Dependency*, Chapter 9. For an interesting study of small communities that resisted resettlement, see his *There's No Better Place Than Here: Social Change in Three Newfoundland Communities* (Toronto: Peter Martin, 1976).

65 For an interesting lay expression of the frustrations of Maritime underdevelopment, cf. Paul MacEwan, *Confederation and the Maritimes* (Windsor, N.S.: Lancelot Press, 1976). David Alexander also suggests that Atlantic Canada could have a stronger role in Confederation in his *Atlantic Canada and Confederation* (Toronto: University of Toronto Press, 1983).

66 George Rawlyk, "The Maritimes and the Canadian Community" in Mason Wade, *Regionalism in the Canadian Community 1867–1967* (Toronto: University of Toronto Press, 1969), 102.

67 Robert Finbow, "Atlantic Canada: Forgotten Periphery In An Endangered Confederation", in Kenneth McRoberts (ed.), *Beyond Quebec: Taking Stock of Canada* (Montreal: McGill-Queens, 1995), 61–80.

68 The ACOA 1998 Five Year Report to Parliament 1993–1998 claims that over the duration of the program that Atlantic unemployment has dropped by 2.8%. See also Donald J. Savoie, *Rethinking Canada's Regional Development Policy: An Atlantic Perspective* (The Canadian Institute For Research On Regional Development, 1997) for a critique that points out that even though money is poured into the region, nothing much happens because of the Canadian reluctance to make structural changes.

69 Robert J. Brym and R. James Sacouman argue that the capitalist system itself through competition, concentration, and the desire for cheap labour and raw materials has produced underdevelopment in Atlantic Canada. The disparity in the region between large external capitalists and producers at

subsistence and wage labour levels (e.g., miners and fishermen) results in capital drain, a subsistence economy, and chronic unemployment. Underdevelopment and Social Movements in Atlantic Canada (Toronto: New Hogtown Press, 1979). For an emphasis on the effect on the region's primary producers, see Gary Burrill and Ian McKay, eds., *People, Resources and Power* (Fredericton: Acadiensis Press, 1987).

70 For an overview of the relation between dependency and oil as a mechanism for greater independence in Newfoundland, see Harry H. Hiller, "Dependence and Independence: Emergent Nationalism in Newfoundland," *Ethnic and Racial Studies* 19(1987): 257–75.

71 The distinction between strong and weak staples is made by J.D. House in "Fish is Fish and Oil is Oil: The Case for North Sea Comparisons to Atlantic Canada," in his *Fish vs. Oil: Resources and Rural Development in North Atlantic Societies* (St. John's: Institute for Social and Economic Research, 1986), 133–37.

72 J.D. House, *The Challenge of Oil* (St. John's: Institute for Social and Economic Research, 1985). See also the report of the Royal Commission on Employment and Unemployment of which House was chair, entitled *Building on Our Strengths* (1986).

73 Bryant Fairley, Colin Leys, and James Sacouman, eds., *Restructuring and Resistance: Perspectives from Atlantic Canada* (Toronto: Garamond, 1990).

74 Donald J. Savoie and Ralph Winter (ed.), *The Maritime Provinces: Looking to the Future* (Moncton: Canadian Institute For Research On Regional Development, 1993).

75 For this reason, Finbow has said that the region is destined to be someone's periphery whether Central Canada, the United States or whomever. "Atlantic Canada: Forgotten Periphery In An Endangered Confederation?" 77. Forbes has argued that what Atlantic regions want more than anything is to be full participants in an equitable federation. "The 1980's" in Forbes and Muise (eds.), *The Atlantic Provinces in Confederation*, 515.

76 Duncan Knowler points out that the North is not an undifferentiated territory but can be divided into regions which include the northern parts of provinces. He identifies 21 remote regions. "Basic Industry in Remote Canadian Regions," *The Northern Review* 2(1988): 44–66.

77 Kenneth Coates and Judith Powell, *The Modern North: People, Politics and the Rejection of Colonialism* (Toronto: James Lorimer, 1989), 16–19.

78 K.J. Rea, *The Political Economy of the Canadian North* (Toronto: University of Toronto Press, 1968), 345ff.

79 For a good discussion of the role of minerals in the economy of the North, see Rea, *The Political Economy of the Canadian North*, chap. 4.

80 J. Ian Prattis and Jean-Phillippe Chartrand, "The Cultural Division of Labour in the Canadian North: A Statistical Study of the Inuit," *Canadian Review of Sociology and Anthropology* 27(1990): 49–73.

81 E.J. Dosman, ed., *The Arctic in Question* (Toronto: Oxford University Press, 1976); John Honderich, *Arctic Imperative: Is Canada Losing the North?* (Toronto: University of Toronto Press, 1987); and Shelagh D. Grant, *Sovereignty or Security? Government Policy in the Canadian North 1936–1950* (Vancouver: University of British Columbia Press, 1988).

82 Mark O. Dickerson, *Whose North? Political Change, Political Development, and Self Government in the Northwest Territories* (Vancouver: UBC Press, 1992).

83 Gurston Dacks, *A Choice of Futures: Politics in the Canadian North* (Toronto: Methuen, 1981), 18.

84 Frances Abele, *Gathering Strength* (Calgary: Arctic Institute Of North America, 1989), vii-viii.

85 Thomas R. Berger, *Northern Frontier; Northern Homeland: The Report of the Mackenzie Valley Pipeline Inquiry, Volumes One and Two* (Ottawa: Minister Of Supply And Services, 1977)

86 Robert Page, *Northern Development: The Canadian Dilemma* (Toronto: McClelland and Stewart, 1986).

87   For some opinions on the impact of pipelines on the north, cf. Donald Peacock, *People, Peregrines, and Arctic Pipelines* (Vancouver: J.J. Douglas, 1977); Earle Gray, *Super Pipe: The Arctic Pipeline* (Toronto: GriVin House, 1979); and James Woodford, *The Violated Vision: The Rape of Canada's North* (Toronto: McClelland and Stewart, 1972).

88   Department of Indian and Northern Affairs Canada, Information Sheet No. 3, September 1987. See also Gurston Dacks, ed., *Devolution and Constitutional Development in the Canadian North* (Ottawa: Carleton University Press, 1990).

89   Coates and Powell, *The Modern North*, 76–80.

90   Abele, *Gathering Strength*, and Kenneth Coates, "On the Outside in Their Homeland: Native People and the Evolution of the Yukon Economy," *The Northern Review* 1(1988): 73–89.

91   Louis-Edmond Hamelin, *Canadian Nordicity* (Montreal: Harvest House, 1979), 220. See also Colin Alexander, *Angry Society* (Yellowknife: Yellowknife Publishing Co., 1976) for the views of a Euro-Canadian Northerner who rejects the concept of no development but prefers it to take place under the auspice of Northerners.

92   Some issues are whether Northerners should be given priority in hiring or training for employment and whether full-time positions should be restricted to Northerners. For a good discussion of all the issues related to Northern control of development, see Robert F. Keith, *Northern Development and Technology Assessment System* (Ottawa: Science Council of Canada Background Study 34, 1976).

93   Peter McCormick, "Regionalism in Canada: Disentangling the Threads," *Journal of Canadian Studies* 24(1989): 19.

94   The distinction between protest regionalism and expansionist regionalism is made by Raymond Breton, "Regionalism In Canada" in David M. Cameron, ed., *Regionalism and Supranationalism* (Montreal: Institute for Research on Public Policy, 1981), 64–67.

95   James Bickerton, *Nova Scotia, Ottawa, and the Politics of Regional Development*, 313–15.

96   Fred Wien, "Regional Inequality: Explanations and Policy Issues," in James Curtis, Edward Grabb, and Neil Guppy, eds., *Social Inequality in Canada: Patterns, Problems, Policies*, 2nd ed. (Scarborough: Prentice-Hall, 1993), 463; And Peter R. Sinclair, "Underdevelopment and Regional Inequality," in B. Singh Bolaria, ed., *Social Issues and Contradictions in Canadian Society* (Toronto: Harcourt Brace, 1995), 396–98.

WEBLINKS

www.nunavut.com

The information gateway to Canada's newest territory, Nunavut!

www.reform.ca

Founded in western Canada, this is the home page of Canada's official opposition, the Reform Party.

www.acoa.ca

The Atlantic Canada Opportunities Agency (ACOA) is a federal government agency set up to improve the economy of Atlantic Canadian communities through the successful development of business and job opportunities.

THE ISSUE
OF ETHNICITY

The process of becoming Canadian in outlook has gone far in the Canadian-born children of immigrants. It will go on to completion in their children, or at least their children's children.... At the same time community conflicts and institutional disturbances tend to retard it [assimilation] and render doubtful the seeming advantages of a sudden precipitation of new peoples into a great variety of contacts with those who differ so widely from themselves. It is for this reason that assimilation ... is such a disturbing matter for all concerned.

—Carl A. Dawson, the first sociologist in Canada,
and the founder of the only Department of Sociology in
Canada for many years (at McGill University), in his
classic Pioneering in the Prairie Provinces:
The Social Side of the Settlement Process *(1940), 38.*

Perhaps the most dominant feature of the "New" World as opposed to the "Old" World, as seen through European eyes, was the vast amount of sparsely settled territory in the New World. It is this basic fact of a relatively small population in an enormous area, compared to the crowded Old World, in combination with the expansionist ambitions of European powers, that predestined ethnicity to be a salient issue in the building of Canadian society. First it was the contact of European cultures with Native peoples, then the intermingling of European peoples with each other in the new land, and now more recently, immigration from new densely populated source areas such as Asia and South America. Even after years of residence in Canada, people are still asked about their ethnic origin in the census, and the government policy of multiculturalism ostensibly encourages members of the society to remember, rediscover, or retain their ethnic origins. Clearly, ethnicity has been, and continues to be, a significant feature of Canadian society!

Ethnicity is an amalgam of objective factors relating to place of birth, citizenship, mother tongue, and customs and traditions which are transmitted through a person's heritage and characterize that individual.[1] In the Canadian experience, ethnicity is frequently rooted in reference to another nation-state, which provides a "foreign" dimension to the concept. But ethnicity does not only involve objective traits such as language and customs; it also involves a subjective element pertaining to how people view themselves, i.e., their ethnic identity. There is a difference, then, not only in whether a person speaks Italian or English, or whether that person is a citizen of Canada or Italy, but also whether the person embraces an identity as Italian, Italian-Canadian, Canadian, or even Canadien. Each alternative tells us something important about that person in relation to others in the wider society.

The diversity of contemporary responses people give to questions about the objective and subjective facts of their background makes the analysis of ethnicity both a dynamic and an essential undertaking for the understanding of Canadian society.

ETHNIC ORIGIN AND ETHNIC IDENTITY

It was established in Chapter One that immigration from numerous sources has been an important component of growth in Canadian society. For this reason, the decennial census has always asked questions that would indicate ethnic backgrounds of the population through a category known as *ethnic origin*. For the 1981 census, ethnic origin was broadened from paternal ancestry to include the ethnic or cultural group to which the respondent or respondent's ancestors belonged on first coming to this continent. Note that the respondent can choose what best represents his or her ethnic origin (whether it is technically correct may be another matter), and that it is assumed that the respondent's ethnicity is something other than Canadian—at least until the 1991 census. By 1996, a "Canadian" origin had replaced "foreign" origins for 18.7% of the total population, most likely among those who formerly would have declared themselves of British and French descent.[2] Also, for the first time in 1981, respondents could state that they were of multiple origins (though this was not requested), if they chose to do so. As a result of these changes, the data gathered in 1981 and especially 1986 (when respondents were explicitly requested to specify as many ethnic origins as applicable) differs from the data gathered prior to those years (see "A Note on Ethnic Origin" in Chapter One).

Figure 5.1 indicates that just under two thirds of the population claim that they are of single ethnic origin and just over one third claim that they are of multiple ethnic origin. Again, remember that this is a self report and a respondent might claim one ethnic origin when two or more might in fact be technically correct. In that sense, the response might also be a good indicator about a person's *ethnic identity* and not just ethnic origin. For example, someone who claims that their ethnic origin is "Canadian" might be deliberately ignoring their ethnic heritage either because it reaches too far back or because they "feel" Canadian. Or someone who claims to be German might be ignoring the fact that their ancestors spoke German as a language but actually immigrated from Poland or Austria. So responses to questions of ethnic origin are really open to divergent interpretations.

However, as noted above, the majority of the population claim to have a single ethnic origin. Of that group, Figure 5.1 reveals that the largest single group are the 29.1% who claim that their ethnic origin is Canadian. About 70% select other ethnic categories; 17.9% are British and 14.7 % are French. Of the 20.4% who are European, Southern Europeans are the largest group followed by western Europeans. These figures might seem surprising because the British, French, and western Europeans were formerly the largest component of the Canadian population. But since this is the group that has been here the longest, one could expect that they would be the ones most likely to have switched their ethnic identity to Canadian. Indeed about 34% of those claiming multiple origins include "Canadian" in their origin, and most of them also combine it with British Isles and French ethnic origins. The end result, however, is that the well-known French–English duality has been transformed from an ethnic duality to a language duality (i.e., French and English as languages) where many now see themselves as Canadian in ethnic terms. The other significant feature of the change over time is that there is now a substantial third force representing a diversity of other groups which moderates the former strength of the two dominant groups. In fact, of the largest groups in the "third force," persons of Chinese, South Asian, and Italian origin were much more likely to claim to be of single origin whereas persons from western Europe and the British Isles were more likely to claim to be of multiple origin. The more recently that members of an ethnic group settled in Canada, the less likely they were to report multiple origins.

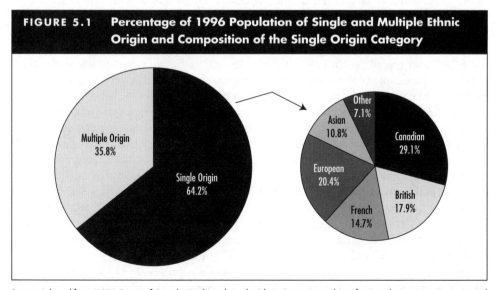

FIGURE 5.1 **Percentage of 1996 Population of Single and Multiple Ethnic Origin and Composition of the Single Origin Category**

Multiple Origin 35.8%

Single Origin 64.2%

Other 7.1%

Asian 10.8%

European 20.4%

French 14.7%

British 17.9%

Canadian 29.1%

Source: Adapted from "1996 Census of Canada, Total Population by Ethnic Categories and Sex, for Canada, Provinces, Territories and Census Metropolitan Areas," Catalogue No. 93F0026XBD96002.

What is clear is that census data need to be interpreted carefully, for ethnic origin by itself does not indicate the degree of attachment a person may feel towards his or her ethnic group. Ethnic background or ancestry does not tell us much about the saliency of ethnicity in a society. One study explicitly measuring ethnic identity found that persons preferring an ethnic identity other than Canadian were more likely to be first or second generation residents in Canada, or living in a geographic territory with a high concentration of persons from the same ethnic background, or to have married within their ethnic group, or to have learned a language other than English as a child.[3]

So perhaps it is appropriate to ask whether ethnicity might not be exaggerated as an issue in Canadian society. Is it a fleeting phenomenon that will disappear in succeeding generations as more persons, regardless of ethnic descent, are born in Canada? Indeed, has ethnicity already become irrelevant to the majority of Canadians? Or, to put the question differently, why is ethnicity given such importance in any discussion of Canadian society? Has the policy of multiculturalism fooled us into thinking that ethnicity is more important than it really is?

FACTORS SUSTAINING THE IMPORTANCE OF ETHNICITY

There are a number of reasons why ethnicity is far more important in Canadian society than may be readily apparent from the statistical data. The six reasons described in this section combine elements of history, government policy, intergroup struggles, and the social psychology of group belonging.

1. The Legacy of Early European Settlement

The initial settlement of the Atlantic region and the St. Lawrence lowlands by the French was challenged first by the Treaty of Utrecht in 1713 and then by the Conquest in 1759 on the Plains of Abraham. In both cases, an established and vigorous community of French settlers was taken under direct control by the British. By the time of Confederation it had become clear that while Canada was composed of two founding groups (the French and the English), the English had the upper hand in determining the structure of the new society.

John Porter coined the term *charter group* to refer to the ethnic group that first settles a previously unoccupied territory and that then controls which other groups can come in.[4] While it is true that Porter's definition ignored the existence of Native peoples already resident in the territory, the idea that a charter group is itself a foreign people who merely happen to be the first of a diverse stream of immigrants to enter the country makes the concept a useful one. It must be remembered however, that French and British charter groups were not of equal strength: the British were the higher charter group and the French the lower. Ultimate control of the immigration process favoured the British because the political apparatus was in their hands. One effect of this power role was to enforce among Native groups, as well as ethnic groups permitted entry from other nations, an awareness of subordinate status and power. Thus, beginning in the colonial era, a power relationship emerged not only between the two charter groups, but between these and all other groups. These ethnic power relationships continue to have an effect on Canadian society.

Several features of Canadian society flow from this legacy. First, the organizational framework of the new society was based on British institutions and traditions—a fact other ethnic groups would not always appreciate. Second, the British allowed francophones to retain some control over events in Quebec, and this is why Confederation is sometimes viewed as a pact between these two founding groups. Clearly the French and English have developed different interpretations of this ethnic power relationship, but it is this very relationship which is at the root of the famed duality of Canadian society. This fact was to become an important justification for the linguistic arguments that Canada ought to have two official languages. In general, the relationship gave the French more or less equal status, and, above all, elevated that group above other ethnic groups. While the implications of these perceptions are still not clear in the minds of many Canadians, the evolution of the French–English duality issue, and the struggle to arrive at a common understanding of that duality, help maintain ethnicity as an important issue in Canadian society.

A third consequence of this duality is that the divisiveness and conflicting loyalties between the two charter groups sets a pattern for other ethnic groups who seek to retain their own ethnic loyalties. Since the British and French were in conflict themselves, the society had a greater built-in tolerance for the perpetuation of ethnic identities.

2. Territoriality

In Chapter One it was argued that territoriality is necessary to establish a sense of society. When an ethnic group is concentrated in a particular area, that group is more likely to maintain its identity as a subgroup of the national society. If members of all ethnic groups were evenly dispersed throughout the country, ethnicity would not be so important; but because this is not the case, ethnicity remains a critical variable in Canada.[5]

Perhaps the most important factor sustaining ethnicity as a critical variable in Canadian society is not immigration but the regional concentration of francophones in the province of Quebec. Quebec francophones have increasingly used the political structure of the province as a vehicle to sustain their ethnic identity in a manner almost impossible without a sense of territoriality. This geographic factor has two consequences. In the first place, the majority–minority relationship between English and French in Canada as a whole is reversed in the province of Quebec. Anglophones in Quebec who view themselves as part of the Canadian linguistic majority find themselves threatened as a declining linguistic minority in that province. Because their concept of territoriality extends to the country as a whole, anglophones in Quebec expected protection by the federal government and found it increasingly difficult to exert power within Quebec. In sum, actions by the Quebec government have raised the issue of minority rights within Quebec, sparking national debate about the principles which guide Canadian society.

Second, the vigour with which Quebec is able to make its ethnic claims has inspired francophone communities in other parts of Canada (e.g., St. Boniface, Manitoba, or northern New Brunswick) to assert their ethnic/linguistic claims. Thus, the territorial concentration of the French community in Quebec, in conjunction with the political actions the government of Quebec has taken, have helped to ensure that ethnicity is a vital factor within the society. It could also be argued that the federal government's response to this territorial fact helped produce the policy of bilingualism.

Furthermore, other ethnic groups have also responded to these territorial precedents by agitating for greater recognition in their territories. For example, Ukrainians in Manitoba and northern Saskatchewan and Alberta have been somewhat successful in obtaining language support in the school system there. Francophones in northern New Brunswick were able to obtain their government's support for full bilingualism in that province (a position rejected by all other provinces). Inuit in the Nunavut Territory have some school instruction in their native tongue and experience broadcasting in their own language.

Another form of territorial concentration of significance has been the ethnic segregation found in urban areas.[6] Generally speaking, the larger the urban area, the higher the segregation, with Western and Northern Europeans the least segregated, Eastern Europeans somewhat segregated, and Southern Europeans and Asians most segregated.[7] When residential segregation is not typical, other mechanisms, such as ethnic associations, keep ethnicity repeatedly before urban residents. Most large Canadian cities have ethnic enclaves in which ethnic retailing and leisure opportunities also play a prominent role, of which "Chinatowns" are probably the most widely recognized.[8] Given the fact that urban areas are almost exclusively the reception centres for new immigrants, any further immigration will continue to heighten the visibility of ethnicity in these locations, and serve as a reminder that ethnic differences are an important feature of the society.

3. Immigration Policy

A third reason for the continuing significance of ethnicity in Canada can be found in the waves of immigration which have been so characteristic of the society. At the time of Confederation, there was a 2:1 ratio of British to French in the total population, and these two ethnic groups made up 90% of the population. Other ethnic groups were small and usually consisted of other Northern Europeans. In the succeeding years (particularly in the last decade of the nineteenth century when the policies of Clifford Sifton, Minister of the Interior, were in force), the desire to populate the West and fill labour needs led to the immigration of large numbers of other Europeans including Ukrainians, Germans, and Scandinavians. This immigration lasted until the onset of the Depression. After World War II, immigration from Europe began again, though it was not until the 1960s that large numbers came from Southern Europe (particularly Italy and Portugal). The migration source in the 1970s shifted again, and encompassed peoples from the West Indies and Asia, and in the 1980s included Central and South America.

Figure 5.2 compares the source countries of immigration to Canada for two five-year periods, 1956–1960 and 1993–98. The British Isles and Europe were the dominant source regions during the first period, almost to the exclusion of other areas. Immigration in the second period was distributed more widely on a global basis, though especially Asian, but also African, and South/Central American immigration became much more pronounced. This largely non-Caucasian immigration has been called the *fifth force* (following the British, French, European, and indigenous peoples).[9] It has produced new issues about integration into Canadian society when religion, cultural practices, race, and social structure differ from more familiar patterns (e.g., the debate over whether Sikh RCMP officers could wear turbans).

Immigration to Canada was not random, but rather expressed government policy about the suitability of the migrating group. In essence, this meant that immigration was particularly encouraged from Great Britain, with some preference also given to other Northern European countries.[10] Other European groups were encouraged to settle less preferable land in the northwest, or to fill blue collar industrial needs. In this way, the British charter group maintained its control over the development of the society. More importantly, however, these repeated waves of immigration reinvigorated ethnic groups already resident in Canada, and reminded residents of their own ethnicity.

In 1967, a point system was introduced as a way of evaluating the merits of a potential immigrant. This system reduced the *source discrimination* of previous immigration policy.[11] This, in conjunction with the new Immigration Act in 1978, encouraged more migration by non-Europeans, who were less likely to be Caucasian. Perceptions of responsibilities for the economic and political refugees of Third World countries and the desire for cheap labour on the one hand, or capital investment by immigrant entrepreneurs on the other hand, have raised controversies that are at the heart of the question of what ethnic groups are preferred in a multicultural society.[12] Residents of the society have not only been reminded of their own ethnicity,

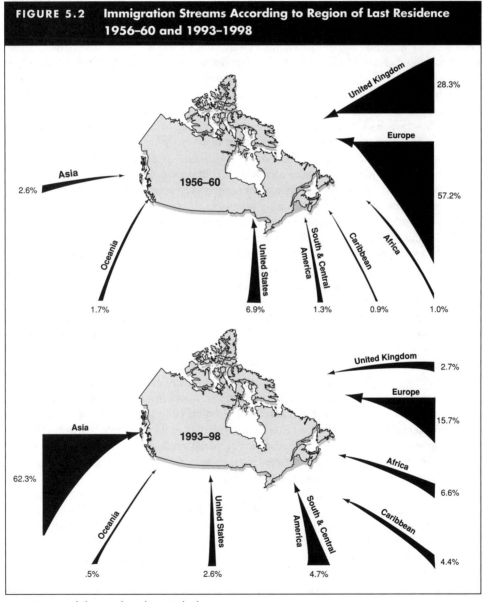

FIGURE 5.2   Immigration Streams According to Region of Last Residence 1956–60 and 1993–1998

Notes: Oceania includes Australia and New Zealand

Source: Statistics Canada Catalogue 91–527.

but of differences between themselves and the new immigrants. In other words, the proportion of immigrants in the population has remained roughly the same (about 16%) since 1951,[13] but repeated waves of immigration have made the matter of ethnicity a livelier issue in Canada than it would be in a society where immigration had ceased or was minimal.

4. In-Group Solidarity

There are two ways of describing ethnic identity. When a person possesses knowledge of or pride in their ethnic origin, we refer to this as *symbolic ethnic identity*. But when a person displays outward expressions of their ethnicity such as the ability to speak a heritage language, belonging to an ethnic organization, or choosing their friends or marriage partners from within an ethnic group, this is referred to as *behavioural ethnic identity*.[14] Ethnic identity is more easily consolidated when ethnicity is translated into participation in an ethnic organization. In an unfamiliar social world, the individual can find in the minority group an alternate society with norms, customs, and values which are more congenial.

The importance of ethnic organizations in sustaining ethnic loyalties varies with the ethnic group. Raymond Breton coined the term *institutional completeness* to refer to the degree to which ethnic communities provide a structure of organizations which provide most of the services required by their members.[15] Ethnic periodicals, welfare organizations, medical care, retail outlets, religious institutions, and even sport clubs provide a wide range of the services needed by the ethnic group member.[16] According to Breton, the more institutionally complete an ethnic group is (i.e., the more services available to the ethnic group member within the ethnic group), the greater the likelihood that social interaction with the rest of the society will be limited. Breton found that relatively high institutional completeness was registered by Greek, German, Hungarian, Italian, Lithuanian, Polish, and Ukrainian groups, while low institutional completeness was indicated by Austrian, Belgian, Spanish, and Swedish ethnic groups.

The greater the difference between the ethnic group and the predominant culture in an area, the greater the likelihood that the ethnic group will be more institutionally complete. The concept of *social distance* indicates that cultural differences can serve to distinguish ethnic groups even when different groups are living in close physical proximity. A British immigrant is not nearly as socially distant from the dominant culture in Anglo-Canada as an Italian or an Asian Indian; hence the ethnic group is of less importance to the Briton.

Group solidarity or cohesiveness is related to a number of factors, which include social distance and institutional completeness, but are related to other variables as well. The size of a group in a given location and the tendency to marry within the ethnic group (endogamy) are also important. Perhaps most significant is the retention of the ethnic language which most clearly distinguishes the group member from the outsider.[17]

Numerous studies have demonstrated that many ethnic groups have developed mechanisms to tie their own people together. We have seen that the English elite developed institutions and mechanisms to maintain its own ethnic superiority. As we shall see, the French have been very successful in ensuring their own relative institutional completeness. The Italians in Toronto have grocery stores, newspapers, television shows, churches, social clubs, and social/medical assistance groups, all of which provide solidarity for Italians who are the second largest ethnic group in Toronto.[18] The Jewish community in Canada has likewise established its own institutions (to a large extent centred around the synagogue), to provide assistance to new

| RESEARCH CLIP 5.1 | **Ethnic/Racial Residential Enclaves** |

What causes people in racial/ethnic groups to live in similar residential areas? Is it economic and status issues or is it something else?

Eric Fong studied the residential housing patterns of twenty Canadian cities and made comparisons with American cities. In the United States, median household income seems to be the dominant factor in home ownership as supply and demand controls the housing market. Income then determined what you could afford and where you would live. In contrast, in Canada, there seems to be more of a commitment supported by government to socially mixed housing, subsidized housing, rent-geared-to-income, rent controls, and coop housing which mediates housing market forces.

Instead of the *social status hypothesis*, the *social capital hypothesis* seems more relevant to Canada. The amount of social capital is measured by the proportion of immigrants in the group and the proportion of group members not knowing either official language. Immigrants who do not know either official language rely on the social capital of ties with fellow ethnic/racial group members for adjusting to the wider society. Dependence on this social capital is particularly high for East Europeans, South Asians, and East/Southeast Asians. New immigrants have strong incentives to live in close proximity because of their limited language skills and limited experience in the new country. This pattern seems to follow among both groups that are relatively disadvantaged such as blacks and Southern Europeans as well as East and Southeast Asians who are better positioned. Social capital seems to be a more important explanation for residential clustering than social or economic status.

Source: Eric Fong, "Residential Proximity With The Charter Groups In Canada," *Canadian Studies in Population* 24(2)1997:103–123.

immigrants and to support Jews and Jewish causes in other countries. These institutions also serve to sustain Jewish identities in Canada.[19] The Greek community in Montreal has approximately sixty organizations which serve a variety of needs among people of this ethnic background.[20] Pakistani Muslims, who previously formed an "incipient" community, have now been able—as a consequence of the infusion of immigrants in recent years—to provide a wide range of structures to accommodate their kinfolk.[21]

To some extent, these ethnic associations may be transitional ties which help immigrants to adjust to their host society. Ethnic organizations may even go into decline if there is no fresh wave of immigration and as the first generation of immigrants ages (e.g., Hungarians).[22] In-group solidarity will, however, remain important for some people because of intense ethnic loyalties, or because of a perceived social distance between themselves and the dominant ethnic groups in their area. Ethnic organizations, moreover, can contribute to the *politicization of ethnicity*; i.e., the articulation of ethnic group interests to the wider society. Thus, we are made aware of ethnic concerns and differences through organizations which have as their mandate the advancement of ethnic interests.

5. Visible Minorities

The concept of ethnicity has been used throughout this chapter in a manner which implies that ethnicity includes race. Race and ethnicity are clearly not the same thing, though they may be related. A *racial group* is physically identifiable, and an *ethnic group* is culturally identifiable. It is possible to be of the same race but be culturally different (e.g., Caucasians may be either British or French), just as it is possible to be of the same culture but racially different (e.g., Americans may be either white or black). Racial differences frequently set in motion a complex of cultural differences because of the visibility of race. People who are of the same race, but of different ethnic backgrounds may have to work harder to sustain their cultural differences when they live together in the same society. In this discussion, ethnicity includes race, and will refer to any group whose culture sets them apart. But it is important to understand that race itself is a significant factor in Canada where Caucasians have been the dominant group.[23] In this context, non-Caucasian groups are referred to as visible minorities.

Race is a highly visible distinction among persons. It is something that no amount of cultural adaptation can completely eradicate. Colour of skin identifies people to each other, and leads to the development of stereotypes or generalizations about persons of different skin colour. Both *prejudice* as an attitude and *discrimination* as behaviour resulting from that attitude may occur when people associate race with cultural attributes or behavioural traits with which they are unfamiliar, and to which they feel superior. Indeed, many non-European origin groups, most of whom are not Caucasian, have experienced problems with social acceptance and job discrimination in Canada.[24]

Non-white immigration to Canada was initially related to the importation (after 1834) of blacks as slaves or escaped slaves from the United States to Ontario and Nova Scotia.[25] On the West Coast, Chinese were brought into British Columbia to work on the Canadian Pacific Railway through the 1880s, and some Japanese and East Indians also came to Canada during that period. Each of these Asian groups encountered a generally hostile reaction from most members of the host Caucasian society. A head tax of $10 was imposed on Chinese immigrants in 1884, and gradually raised to $500 by 1904.[26] A Chinese exclusion law was passed in 1923 banning poor Chinese immigrants and it was not repealed until 1947. Chinese were sometimes denied the right to vote and were excluded from certain occupations thereby restricting opportunities to the running of laundries and restaurants. Japanese immigrants faced many of the same restrictions but were tolerated because they too provided cheap labour.[27] After the Japanese attack on Pearl Harbor during World War II, Japanese people in Canada were interned in remote camps and many lost all they had. Through the years, federal policy has always been basically racist and non-white immigration was discouraged. It was not until after World War II, and even later when the point system was established as the basis for immigrant selection, that the more obvious forms of *institutional discrimination* were reduced.

Institutional racism refers to social practices that are systematic and legal and that are rationalized by beliefs in the superiority or preferability of one group over another.[28] The right to exclude certain groups because of their physical characteristics, to deny them the vote, to relegate them to low paid work or a differential pay scale have all been part of Canada's past. But even if the legal mechanisms that support such racism are removed, discrimination can still exist. In fact, if the old discrimination was based on skin colour and appearance, the new discrimination attempts to apply universalistic standards by denying the relevance of race so that racism exists more covertly.[29] Henry and others have proposed the term *democratic racism* to refer to the coexistence of two competing sets of values: democratic principles of justice and equality versus negative attitudes and behaviours about minority groups and the differential treatment of these groups.[30] Thus, values of fairness and openness do not always match up with actual behaviour, and as the number of immigrants from non-traditional source countries increases, these persons find themselves at a competitive disadvantage because of their race.[31]

It could be argued that significant improvements have occurred in inter-group relations over the past forty years. And yet, racial controversy in both its cultural and economic dimensions (see Chapter Three on ethnic stratification) has taken on new importance. Tolerance and appreciation may represent ideals, but many have difficulty putting them into practice. While Nova Scotia blacks and British Columbia Chinese and Japanese have a long history in Canada,[32] they have more recently been joined by immigrants from the West Indies, Haiti, Vietnam, Hong Kong, Taiwan, China, India and many other countries. Each of these immigrants brings with him or her a cultural and racial identity. For example, blacks from Haiti bring with them their French language, while blacks from the West Indies typically use English, and their culture reflects their many years of British cultural influence. Rather than finding cohesion with others of their racial group, these visible minorities each maintain important cultural/ethnic differences. The Employment Equity Act defines *visible minorities* as all persons who are non-Caucasian in race or non-white in colour, but excludes aboriginal peoples whom we will discuss later in the chapter.

Thus, visible minorities, and Caucasian responses to them, also contribute to the centrality of ethnicity as an issue in Canadian society. Visible minorities represent about 11.2% (3.2 million persons) of the Canadian population—up considerably from 6.3% a mere ten years ago and largely the result of immigration. Figure 5.3 indicates that the Chinese are the

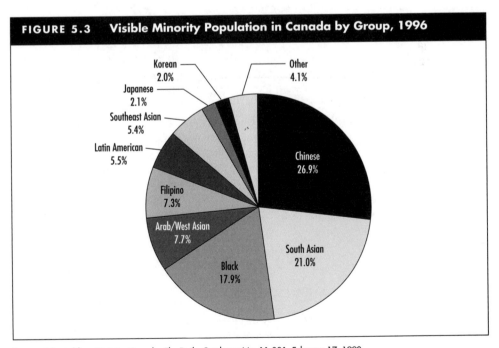

FIGURE 5.3   Visible Minority Population in Canada by Group, 1996

Korean 2.0%
Other 4.1%
Japanese 2.1%
Southeast Asian 5.4%
Latin American 5.5%
Filipino 7.3%
Arab/West Asian 7.7%
Black 17.9%
Chinese 26.9%
South Asian 21.0%

Source: Adapted from Statistics Canada, *The Daily*, Catalogue No. 11-001, February 17, 1998.

largest group in this category followed by South Asians, blacks (these three groups together make up about 7.5% of the Canadian population), and then a wide variety of other groups. Current world demographic pressures imply that one hundred years from now, Canadian society will have a very different ethnic and racial character than it does now—just as it has been transformed over the last one hundred years.

6. Unresolved Aboriginal Issues

As the original peoples in the Canadian territory were swept aside by European settlement, it was expected that domination and assimilation would eventually remove "the Indian problem." But if French Canadians have defied all odds and retained their language and culture on an anglophone continent, it is much more significant that Native groups, lacking similar institutional supports, have embarked on a rediscovery of their own group identity. The assimilationist objectives of Euro-Canadians in relation to Aboriginal peoples has been both a failure and an international embarrassment. High unemployment, low incomes, and poor housing among Natives in combination with anger, alienation, and even self-destructive behaviour have intensified aboriginality as a public issue in Canadian society.[33]

As a response to dependency and domination, Native groups have attempted to secure more direct control over their destiny and to reverse the downward spiral of cultural confusion. The rise of Aboriginal leadership to confront established elites and oppressive conditions has occurred simultaneously with the rise of a new collective consciousness among Aboriginals, which has led to a new level of negotiations between Natives and the state to redefine their place within Canadian society. Rejecting the notion of being considered just another ethnic group just as French Canadians have done, Aboriginals perceive themselves as the original peoples and founding nations of this territory.

Native people are now in a process of decolonialization. As people who have been dehumanized by colonization, they (as post-colonialists) are attempting to reverse the negative effects they have experienced. The shift in position from quiescent subordination to more activist negotiation as "nations within"[34] intensifies ethnic relations as a significant issue within Canadian society. We will return to this topic in more detail later in the chapter.

The six factors discussed above are not meant to be exhaustive, but are meant to demonstrate why ethnicity has been, and will continue to be, a vital issue in Canadian society for some time to come. While the structure and substance of ethnic diversity has changed over time, and while new generations of children born in Canada develop different feelings and expressions regarding their ethnic background, the continuation of immigration in conjunction with government policies encouraging the maintenance of ethnic traditions and identities has supported ethnicity as an important underlying variable in the population. At the very least, the continuing negotiation with Canada's first peoples, and among the French and English charter groups, politicizes ethnicity as a major factor in Canadian society and reminds others of their own ethnic differences.

THE MOST DOMINANT FORMS OF GROUP CONFLICT

The presence of persons with a wide variety of ethnic backgrounds in Canadian society is of greater importance if ethnicity is a significant basis for group formation among members of the society. Furthermore, the mere presence of minority groups does not in itself mean that

Differing Perspectives

Structural Functionalism

Race and ethnicity accentuate the fact that society is an interesting kaleidoscope of diverse groups that must be "managed" or accommodated to ensure its effective functioning. Rather than emphasizing how race and ethnicity is divisive, efforts must be made to help racial and ethnic groups feel more comfortable within Canadian society (e.g., the policy of multiculturalism) and/or to explore how barriers can be broken down between these groups (e.g., adaptation programs in language training, skills development, or entrepreneurship programs). When minorities organize themselves to counter their positions of marginality, efforts need to be made to accommodate their concerns so that society can be stabilized. Recent arrivals into the country should expect to start at the bottom and through their own efforts work their way to the position they deserve. If it does not happen in their life-time, at least some persons from the next generation should benefit from an open society.

Conflict

Dominant groups use racial and ethnic differences as ways to sustain their own position of power and privilege. Members of some groups may be more accepted over time if they are able to acculturate to the dominant group but other groups almost seem to be permanently disadvantaged. Even when new immigrants enter Canadian society, some enter with more privileges than others who, in contrast, experience various forms of discrimination because of their place of origin or skin colour. Visible minorities in particular may constantly struggle with prejudice and are unable to find full acceptance into the society. Partially as a defence mechanism and to provide mutual support, racial and ethnic groups may form solidarities to challenge the status quo. In any case, racial and ethnic differences often serve as mobilizing factors in the face of differentials in power that sustain division in society.

Symbolic Interactionism

Race and ethnicity are an essential part of the personal identity of all people— whether they are aware of it or not. Each individual learns of their identity in racial or ethnic terms through a process of negotiation and interaction with others in their society. In some people, it becomes very public through identification with customs, language, and other aspects of culture, and in other persons, it is highly privatized and hidden. The question of how personal identities are related to familial groups and reference groups, and then how these identities are related to the dominant group in society and its attempt to create a society-wide collective identity tells us a lot about how subgroups are related to and interact with the national society.

ethnic conflict will result. A minority group may accept its subordinate status quite passively unless it is sparked by two factors: a feeling of deprivation and a sense of group awareness.

Relative deprivation is the disadvantage a group feels when comparing its own status or opportunities with those of another group. For example, when the French began to compare their status with that of the English, especially in the 1960s, they began to resent their subordinate status, and conflict became more explicit. *Group awareness* is the consciousness of kind or unity which is felt by persons who share similar characteristics. For example, when Canadian Native people who were for many years just a loose aggregation of people in dispersed bands, began to develop a sense of group awareness in relation to the more dominant group, a collective sense of power ensued. So as an ethnic group becomes more conscious of itself as a group that is comparatively disadvantaged, and then takes the next step to transform that situation, ethnic group conflict becomes more likely.

The two most visible unresolved ethnic group conflicts in Canadian society are the French–English conflict and the Aboriginal–nonAboriginal conflict. These concerns dominate the public agenda in this country, and we will now discuss each in turn.

QUEBEC AND FRENCH–ENGLISH RELATIONS

A phrase that is typically used to describe Canadian society is that of "two solitudes" or "two nations warring within one bosom." The reality of two ethnic groups with different ideas about the shape of Canadian coexistence has been maintained to a large extent through considerable territorial segregation. Nowhere is this clearer than in the comparison of the two provinces in Canada with the largest populations: Ontario and Quebec. In Ontario, persons of British ethnic origin are the largest single ethnic group, and persons of French descent are a small minority. Quebec on the other hand, has a population which is overwhelmingly of French descent, and an equally small minority of English descent. Ironically, each province has close to the same percentage of the other province's majority group as a minority (5–6%). Quebec is also 86% Catholic whereas Ontario is only 35% Catholic. When it comes to the language most frequently used at home, 85% use English and 3% use French in Ontario, but in Quebec 83% use French and 11% use English. These figures illustrate why these two neighbouring provinces represent such different conceptions of society. Evidence presented in Chapter One suggests that these differences also extend to Quebec's uniqueness in relation to other provinces.

The Evolution of Quebec Society

In contrast to many of the early settlements in the United States, the early French settlements were not populated by dissenters, but by people who wanted to retain ties to France through church, state, and commerce. Thus, the key persons in these settlements were initially administrators, missionaries, traders, and explorers. Monière has argued that, even after the conquest of the French by the British in 1759, there was a vitality to the francophone community that was only suppressed by the defeat of the Patriots in the 1837–38 Rebellion.[35] This rebellion was the first movement for independence among francophones in Quebec.

What did the British conquest imply for Quebec society? First of all, it caused resentments and antagonisms towards the British that were sometimes submerged, but never obliterated. This event and all that it came to symbolize, has been referred to as a *primordial event* because it made an indelible mark on the French-Canadian people, and produced a minority complex which they have struggled to overcome.[36] The second effect of the conquest was the *social decapitation* of Quebec. The previous French leadership, which returned to France, was replaced by British leadership, particularly in political administration and in mercantile commercialism. Thus, a pattern of anglophone control was established which also produced resentment. The third effect is based on *"the beacon of light"* theme (i.e., the mission to preserve French language and culture on the continent), in which the French community insulated itself against alien British influence by organizing the agricultural *habitant* family around the small-town parish. Parish priests emerged as the leaders of this society, buttressing a French identity by promoting both Catholicism and the French language in the midst of anglophone identification with Protestantism and the English language. The ideology that emerged from this blend of church and state, the primacy of agriculture and the rejection of industrialization, and the belief in the moral mission of French Canadians in North America, is known as *ultramontanism.*

The British were content not to interfere with French culture because British ambitions for Canada revolved primarily around economic development. In exchange for their subordination to British political and economic control, the French were allowed control over their own culture, which focused at that time on parish and school life. The Quebec Act of 1774 restored French civil law, and placed education under the control of the Catholic church. The will to survive as a French cultural entity led to *agrarian isolationism* which was reflected by defensive and conservative Quebec governments. Led by doctrinally conservative priests (many of whom had fled France in disagreement with the liberalizing effects of the French Revolution), and supported by an extremely high fertility rate, the French-Canadian community succeeded in preserving its cohesiveness and strength.[37] In fact, the community grew to the point of overpopulation and this caused great numbers of francophones to migrate to the New England states as employment from industrialization became available there.[38]

Anglophone dominance went largely unquestioned as long as Quebec remained rural and agrarian. By the middle decades of the twentieth century, however, significant changes had occurred. These included greater urbanization, and the growth of an emergent industrial complex centred around textiles. Cheap hydroelectric power and capitalist demands for natural resources contributed to a significant movement away from agriculture as the material basis of the population. Accompanying these changes was a decline in the birth rate, and a desire for education oriented towards active participation in the technological society. In sum, increasing urbanization, secularization (i.e., in the cities, the church was no longer the centre of community life), and industrialization, brought the French community in more direct contact with the anglophone elite and capitalist structures.[39] This contact became the source of a sense of group awareness, and a sense of relative deprivation among francophone Quebecers.

The defeat of the provincial Union Nationale party in 1960 by the Liberals is usually viewed as symbolic of a changing world view in Quebec. This change became known as the *Quiet Revolution.* Underlying the Quiet Revolution was urbanization and industrialization, which had two class-related effects. The first was the growth of a working class of industrial workers who developed critical views of anglophone capitalist exploitation.[40] The second was the growth of a new middle class of white collar workers in the public sector (and to some extent also in the private sector), who saw their ambitions for upward social mobility blocked by anglophone dominance and control.[41] Learning English, and discarding French accents, were typically viewed as necessary for success in the anglophone system, though such changes could not alter the fact that anglophones were both the owners of capital, and the real decision-makers in Quebec. As a result of this entrenched anglophone dominance, francophone Quebecers sought changes in French–English relations, as well as a restructuring of traditional Quebec society.

The first thrust of the Quiet Revolution was devoted to *rattrapage* ("catching up"), in order to bring Quebec into the stream of modern Western economic development. The cre-

Quebec: The Velocity of Demographic Social Change

Not only are the socio-political changes which have occurred in Quebec fascinating, but the demographic shifts within the province also tell a significant story with enormous implications for the future.

The research of Caldwell and Fournier has shown that the 1960s were a significant turning point for Quebec—in fact, a global record for rapid population change in the industrialized world from a high to a low birth rate. In the late 1950s, Quebec still had one of the highest fertility rates among industrialized societies. But, by the 1980s, the fertility rate had dropped to the bottom, close to the Scandinavian countries. In 1954, the birth rate was 31.0 per thousand, but by 1984, it had dropped to 13.4 per thousand. The birth rate required for replacement was passed (on the way down) in 1970 and, though there was some increase due to births to baby boomers (known as the baby boom echo), the birth rate declined further. Furthermore, after 1986, the older age structure of the female population reduced the possibility of increased births.

The second trend of note is the decline in nuptiality. Caldwell and Fournier predict that Quebec is close to a scenario where only half of the population marries, and of that half, between a quarter and a half divorce, further depressing the fertility rate. The third trend is the aging of the population as the result of the low fertility rate. By the year 2001, almost half of the Quebec population could be over 50 years of age.

What has exacerbated these trends even further is the single most important factor that has contributed to the decline of Quebec's growth rate—that is, negative net migration. First, there was a heavy outflow of Quebec residents to other parts of Canada during the '60s and '70s. While some of these out-migrants were francophone, the vast majority were anglophone. This outflow reached its peak in the 1976–81 time period of Parti Québécois rule. Second, the flow of in-migrants from other parts of Canada, as well as international migration, had reduced considerably. By the 1980s, French speaking immigrants from Haiti and Vietnam provided the largest group of new residents (though these numbers were not large). In any case, by the '80s, Quebec had become a much more stable francophone society, but with the new demographic problem of shrinking population growth.

Caldwell and Fournier's research points out that Quebec is not unique in possessing a declining growth rate, but that the velocity and extremes of the change have been so rapid that it has enormous consequences for the future viability of Quebec. Not only has Quebec lost its one-third proportion of the Canadian population, but the researchers also project restricted economic expansion and blocked opportunities within Quebec if there is no growth. While strengthening the boundaries of the francophone linguistic community has enhanced cultural survival, the province cannot ignore the dramatic changes in values and social behaviour that will determine how the society will survive.

Source: Gary Caldwell and Daniel Fournier, "The Quebec Question: A Matter of Population," *Canadian Journal of Sociology* 12(1987): 16–41.

ation of a provincial Ministry of Education in 1964 replaced church control of education with a new emphasis on technological and industrial skills such as engineering and accounting. One result of this change was that university enrollments grew at an unprecedented rate. As a means of fostering economic development in Quebec, francophone-owned enterprises such as the steel corporation SIDBEC, were given financial aid. In addition, as an effort to provide employment opportunities within a francophone milieu of an important Quebec resource, Quebec Hydro was nationalized in 1962. These were some of the means used by the government of Quebec not only to encourage Quebec participation in industrial development, but also to strengthen francophone control over Quebec's destiny. These measures were adopted in the hope that Québécois might become *maître chez nous* ("masters in our own house"). Just as the existing structure of society had excluded francophones from control (a structural theory of exclusion), so Québécois now sought to challenge the English establishment, to remove the barriers that restricted their own opportunities, and to create a new structure of society using the apparatus of the provincial state in which their control was clear.[42]

Many of the processes identified with the Quiet Revolution actually began before 1960 and continued on into the 1970s. But in 1970, an event occurred that shattered the stillness of the so-called "quiet" revolution. On October 16, Prime Minister Trudeau invoked the War Measures Act in response to the kidnapping of Quebec Cabinet Minister Pierre Laporte and British High Commissioner James Cross by the terrorist Front de Libération du Québec (FLQ). This event, known as the *October Crisis,* was symbolic of the escalation of the need for change in Quebec and demonstrated the depth of nationalist feeling at the extreme. 1970 was also the year of the much-publicized nine Brinks truck cavalcade from Montreal to Toronto representing anglo fear of Quebec nationalism. It was also the year in which the avowedly separatist Parti Québécois made political advances by taking about a third of the votes in the provincial election.

During the 1970s, the process of *l'épanouissement* ("flowering") of Quebec continued with a heavy reliance on the government of Quebec as a mechanism of change.[43] During this decade, measures were taken which not only affected the economy, but also the culture in which the language issue dominated. Ironically, immigration had made Quebec much more ethnically pluralist than it had been before, and this was particularly so as the declining birth rate made immigration more important. By 1971, only 10.8% of immigrant children were attending French schools.[44] Similarly, the drawing of Quebec more tightly into the North American economy threatened the distinctiveness of the Quebec community. The French language, then, became the mechanism for integrating the people of Quebec regardless of background, and reinforced the boundaries of Quebec. Whereas once French was the language of a particular ethnic group, now French was to become the language of the people of Quebec (regardless of ethnic descent).

When the separatist Parti Québécois was elected in 1976, it made strong decisions but its approach to sovereignty was one of *gradualism* (étapisme). Bill 101, the Charter of the French Language in Quebec, was passed in 1977, but the increasing use of French as a requirement had been building support for some time. French was not to be just the language of the shop floor but was to be used by management in all communications throughout both the public and private sectors. To prove their compliance, businesses were to obtain a *francization certificate*. Immigrant children were to be educated in French. The status of French was to be elevated by ensuring that French lexicons would be available for all situations from computer usage to automobile repair manuals. Flying in the face of the Canadian government's official policy of bilingualism, the government of Quebec made French the official language of Quebec. Whether all of these regulations were enforceable or not may be another matter but Quebec did take on a clearly French public character.

Quebec government activity also became more pro-active in other areas. Quebec immigration officers were placed in federal foreign immigration offices to encourage immigration into Quebec that would be compatible with the province's cultural goals. The province also began to participate in the francophone commonwealth of nations. A Department of Cultural Affairs was created to strengthen Quebec culture in spite of anglo-Americanization. All of this activity had the effect of strengthening the French character of the province of Quebec, a process that was symbolized by the identity transformation of its residents from "French Canadians" to "Québécois."[45]

With a goal of *sovereignty association* (meaning political independence accompanied by economic association including a common currency with the rest of Canada), the Quebec government issued in 1979 its White Paper entitled *Quebec–Canada: A New Deal.*[46] This document prepared the way for the promised referendum concerning Quebec independence. Held on May 20, 1980 with 85.6% voter turnout, the referendum was defeated, though with 40% in favour of independence. The precise meaning of sovereignty association was sufficiently ambiguous, and the supporters of this objective sufficiently numerous, that many interpretations could be given to the results.[47] It is significant that the separatist position of the Parti Québécois was rejected in the referendum in 1980 but the party advocating independence was re-elected in 1981. However, when the Parti Québécois was replaced by the Liberals in 1985, the new government continued many of the Québécois nationalist themes, though without the threat of independence until the Meech Lake issue heated up in 1990. In any case, it was widely believed that the independence movement was far from dead.

In sum, since 1960, the Quebec state has abandoned its traditional position of defensive nationalism, adopting instead a philosophy of advocacy and intervention on behalf of its constituent French majority. The provincial government became a means of collective advancement, and frequently its policies were a challenge to the federal government. Refusal to sign the new federal constitution (1982) symbolized Quebec's fusion of historical and contemporary group consciousness.[48]

Herein lies the dilemma for Quebec society within Canadian society. The federal policy of two official languages (bilingualism) was in large measure an attempt to appease Quebec in particular and francophones throughout Canada in general. By redesigning Canada to more clearly include francophones, it was hoped that the two founding partners of Confederation might accept each other in a new way, and the historical anglophone dominance of francophones would be forgotten. However, instead of embracing bilingualism, the mood in Quebec has been one of support for increasing unilingualism, which challenges federal policy.

The failure of Quebec to sign the new Constitution in 1982 was precisely over the ability of Quebec to control its own future as a society. Given the embarrassment of having a Constitution not ratified by the province containing one-quarter of Canada's people, Prime Minister Mulroney sought and obtained Quebec's support, as well as the other provinces, for what is known as the Meech Lake Accord on April 30, 1987.[49] The thrust of the accord was the decentralization of more power and authority to provincial governments, such as in matters of immigration or the selection of Senate members. Perhaps the most significant feature of the agreement for Quebec, however, but also controversial for some of the other provinces, was the recognition of Quebec as a "distinct" society. This phrase implied that, in significant ways, Quebec was different from the rest of Canada, though it was unclear what implications this recognition had for the rest of Canada or Quebec.[50] What some viewed

The Royal Commission on Bilingualism and Biculturalism

The social changes occurring in Quebec in the1960s challenged previously existing ideas of anglo-dominance that subjected francophones to inferior positions in the work world, assumed English unilingualism in federal government institutions, and expected the disappearance of the French language and culture. Instead, an awakening of the defence of French traditions was occurring and the spectre of Quebec separatism was being raised. The federal government was sensitive to these changes and appointed a Royal Commission to explore the concept of Canada as a bilingual and bicultural society.

The Report of the RCBB fundamentally restructured Canadian culture. One of the key results was the Official Languages Act passed in 1969 which made both French and English official languages in Canada. It was this Act which attempted to give both languages equal status whether on product labels, on airline flight announcements, or in the federal civil service.

The Commission distinguished between *individual bilingualism* (command of both languages) and *institutional* or *state bilingualism* (where principal public and private institutions provide services in both languages) and opted for the latter. At the same time, education in both English and French was to be available throughout the country. Language training was especially to be available in the federal civil service so that both groups would have opportunity for management positions and the Canadian public could be served in both official languages.

The notion of the equality of both languages to make Canada "an equal partnership between the two founding races" generated controversy that is still often debated. But perhaps the most unexpected outcome was the response of people who were neither French nor English in what has been labelled the "third force" of persons of other ethnic origins. This plurality of ethnic groups, particularly in the West, also sought recognition and acceptance and led to the deletion of "biculturalism" (to "bilingualism within a multicultural framework") and eventually the policy of multiculturalism.

Further Reading

The multi-volume Report of the Commission is a valuable, if cumbersome, piece to read. A one-volume abridged edition by Hugh R. Innis, *Bilingualism and Biculturalism* (Toronto: McClelland and Stewart, 1973) presents the highlights of the original report.

as a tacit recognition of what already existed anyway, others viewed as special status for Quebec that threatened Canadian unity, while still others viewed such an acknowledgement as merely another step towards Quebec independence. For these reasons, the "distinct society" clause in the Meech Lake agreement became a critical issue for all Canadians.

The *Meech Lake Accord* was initially an agreement made by the ten provincial premiers with the federal government in 1987 after protracted bargaining behind closed doors. Each premier was then to obtain the ratification of their respective provincial legislatures within three years. The problem was that during that interim period, some provinces changed governments and new leadership did not necessarily feel bound by the commitment to the original agreement. This was particularly the case with Manitoba and Newfoundland where the strongest opposition to the accord was expressed. Despite feverish last minute negotiations, Newfoundland failed even to put the accord to a vote, and Manitoba was unable to put the accord to a vote due to the lack of unanimous consent for the suspension of normal legislative procedures to consider this issue. As a consequence, the Meech Lake Accord died on June 23, 1990.

The failure of Meech Lake is generally thought to have contributed to another national crisis. Not only was Quebec still not part of the constitutional process but the province claimed that the failure to recognize its unique status was tantamount to rejection by the rest of Canada. Premier Bourassa then announced that Quebec would not return to the bargaining table, would only deal with the federal government rather than the provinces in ongoing matters, and would activate a commission to explore alternatives for the province's future. Ironically, it was also the refusal of the only Native member of the Manitoba legislature, Elijah Harper, to provide unanimous consent that held up the final ratification in that province on the grounds that Native peoples have been totally ignored in the constitu-

The Failures in Renegotiating Canadian Federalism: A Chronology

Perhaps the key item in a renewed Canadian polity has been the search for some way to acknowledge the uniqueness of Quebec as a distinct society. The chronology of the key events are as follows:

Constitution Act 1982

The federal government proceeded to adopt a new Canadian Constitution without the support of Quebec (known in Quebec as "the night of the long knives" in reference to a compromise meeting to which they were not invited).

Meech Lake Accord

Signed in 1987 but failed to win approval of all provinces in 1990

Charlottetown Agreement

Rejected by national referendum held October 26, 1992
Result 55% No – 45% Yes

National Elections in 1993 and 1997

The consequences of the failure to resolve Quebec's place within Canadian society were the formation of the sovereigntist Bloc Québécois, which elected members to the Canadian Parliament in 1993 (ironically becoming the official opposition party), and the election of the Parti Québécois to govern the province of Quebec in 1994 with a clear agenda of sovereignty. In the West, the Reform Party which wanted to block Quebec's claim for special status arose in the 1993 election and became the official opposition in 1997, trading places with the Bloc Québécois. These two elections clearly divided the country along regional lines. The Liberals primarily won the election because it took most of the seats in Ontario, Canada's most populous province.

tional process and that they too were a distinct society. Thus, instead of serving as a mechanism of unity, Meech Lake fostered discord and new uncertainty.

Another attempt to bring Quebec in under acceptable constitutional arrangements was made in 1992 in what is known as the *Charlottetown Accord.*[51] The agreement had many of the same features as Meech Lake, and in particular acknowledged that Quebec was a distinct society, guaranteed Quebec 25% of the seats in the House of Commons, and accepted the principle of *asymmetrical federalism* (in other words, that Quebec was a special case and not just the same as other provinces). Yet in the months between the agreement and the national referendum held to ratify it on October 26, 1992, support unravelled through challenges from former Prime Minister Trudeau, the Reform Party, and even as the result of Prime Minister Mulroney's own declining popularity. Even in Quebec support faltered. The uncertainty of the meaning and consequences of the distinct society idea, whether among francophones (it does not go far enough) or among anglophones (it goes too far) clearly played a major role in undermining the agreement. In the end, the referendum was defeated 55% "No" to 45% "Yes." Opposition was strongest in the West and in Quebec and support was strongest in the Atlantic provinces except for Nova Scotia (51% No). Ontario accepted the agreement but only barely, with a 51% margin. In any case, a clear place for Quebec within Canadian society remains unfinished business.

Amidst frustration at the inability to achieve a reconciliation, a feeling emerged among some francophones, and even some anglophones, that the time for compromise and negotiation was over and that it was time for Quebec to decide once and for all.[52] The 1995 Quebec referendum provided that opportunity and yet its exceedingly close vote resolved nothing. In fact, support for sovereignty increased by ten percentage points over the first referendum in 1980, and another referendum in the near future appears likely. Perhaps the key idea which led to a significant increase in "Yes" support in the final days was the shift in the campaign strategy from "sovereignty" to the idea of "sovereignty partnership" which emphasized the negotiation and retention of links with Canada if the referendum passed.[53] The Canadian government, however, did take the issue of the legality of Quebec unilaterally declaring independence to the Supreme Court, and in 1998 it ruled that if a "clear" referendum question produced a "clear" result that independence could not take place unilaterally but must require negotiation by both sides in good faith. Thus negotiation and change continue to be elusive ideals in the effort to preserve the Canadian entity.[54]

Understanding Quebec Nationalism

In many developing societies, modernization has meant the blurring of cultural distinctions as the impact of foreign influence led to massive changes within the traditional society. Somewhat paradoxically, Quebec has experienced both social changes and economic development at the same time that cultural distinctions have been sharpened. Instead of yielding to the pressures of anglo-conformity, Quebec has accentuated its cultural uniqueness. What underlying forces made this development possible? How can we understand this surge of nationalist spirit? While this is a very complex matter which resists simple explanations, five interpretations can be offered.

The most obvious explanation is the *historical resistance to colonialism*, which was heightened by the more direct contact with anglophones resulting from industrialization and urbanization. Industrialization only accentuated the issue of anglophone (whether Canadian or American) control, and provoked a collective spirit of resistance to that control, most strongly expressed in the desire for complete independence from that control. While this explanation does

The 1995 Referendum: A National Crisis

October 30, 1995

"Do you agree that Quebec should become sovereign after having made a formal offer to Canada for a new economic and political partnership, within the scope of the Bill respecting the future of Quebec and of the agreement signed on June 12, 1995?"

Results: No   50.6%
                Yes   49.4%
Turnout: 94% of 4.8 million eligible voters
Spoiled ballots: 86 000 (more than the margin of difference between the two sides)

The Campaign in National Context

This referendum in the province of Quebec precipitated the greatest crisis in Canadian history as the possibility of an independent Quebec and a fractured Canada was driven home to many Canadians who had previously conceived of Quebec nationalism as a minority dream. As the momentum shifted in the last two weeks of the campaign under the leadership of the charismatic Lucien Bouchard, many Canadians began to panic and a great outpouring of emotion supporting a united Canada was expressed. On the Friday before the referendum, a rally in Montreal attracted 100 000 people from all over the country pleading with Quebecers to stay in Canada. Throughout the weekend, rallies were held in other parts of Canada, prayer vigils were organized, telephone companies offered free phone calls to Quebec, airlines lowered their fares to Montreal, and children wrote letters imploring Quebec to keep Canada united.

The campaign prompted the most fervent and spontaneous expression of Canadian nationalism in history.

The Meaning of the Results

Questions have been raised about the variant meanings of the term "sovereignty" and "partnership," and the complexity of the referendum question. Polls indicated that some Quebecers expected that a sovereign Quebec would still remain part of Canada and continue to send representatives to Ottawa. The meaning of a "Yes" vote is therefore open to debate. Was it primarily an expression of ethnic pride, a mandate for a strong negotiating position, or a clear declaration of independence?

The Internal Division of Quebec Society

While 90% of anglophones and allophones (persons of non-English/non-French mother tongue) voted "No," francophones themselves were divided on the issue, even though approximately 60% voted "Yes." Many rural areas were especially supportive of the "Yes" side, while in Montreal both the francophone east end and anglophone/allophone west end supported the "No" side. The "Yes" side was also not as strong in Quebec City as expected, though it did have the majority. The intensity of feeling on both sides within the province, compounded by linguistic/ethnic and rural/urban divisions, demonstrates further the uncertainties about the future.

Just days prior to the referendum, the Cree and Inuit of northern Quebec held their own referendums on Quebec sovereignty as a way of declaring their own position, which was that of near-unanimous opposition. Aboriginals threatened to withdraw their territory (added to the province's borders in 1898) in the event of independence, which would have meant the loss of natural resources and the gigantic James Bay hydroelectric project. This was the beginning of the idea of *partitionism* expressed by some anglophone/allophone groups as well, in which they argued that their region had the right to stay in Canada and reject the secession decision.

Outside Quebec, the federal government shifted from Plan A which sought reconciliation as a means to maintain unity to Plan B which sought to specify the precise terms (including legality and costs) on which Canada would allow separation to occur (a type of "tough love" scenario). The Canadian government also immediately passed a resolution (not the same as a Constitutional amendment) recognizing Quebec as a distinct society as a gesture of appeasement.

not explain who led the resistance, the implication is that only when anglophones and francophones came into *competition* with each other through urbanization (as opposed to their previous position of isolationism) did reaction to colonialism became more heated.[55]

The second and third explanations suggest that the new spirit developed because specific social groups sought to destroy the double class structure in Quebec—the francophone world on the one hand, and the anglophone world on the other hand. One explanation points to the role of the *francophone bourgeoisie* whose economic interests were well served by the ideology of the Quiet Revolution and sovereignty association. A stronger state which protected francophones from alien influences meant the strengthening of the francophone business class in Quebec, and the new spirit was congenial because it challenged the competing Canadian bourgeoisie.[56] Gagnon and Montcalm have argued that francophone entrepreneurs have risen to new prominence in Quebec because of that province's growing economic peripheralization in the continental economy which still has not been reversed.[57] In any case, it is widely recognized that the francophone business class have been the clear winners of the Quiet Revolution.

Quebec nationalism was not only in the interests of the francophone elite, but also in the interests of the new middle class of young, university educated, and upwardly mobile persons who were angered by obstacles to mobility within Quebec. Thus, the *rise of the new middle class* provides a third explanation for the new Quebec spirit.[58] Confident of their own abilities, and frustrated by the blockages and control encountered in anglophone corporations, these francophones found government, government corporations, and government agencies to be growth industries in the economic development of Quebec. During the 1960s, the number of civil servants mushroomed from 32 000 to 70 000.[59] Here they could not only find employment but also exert policy control. Thus, the new middle class strongly supported and participated in provincial state intervention. Indeed, research has shown that, among Quebecers embracing the new identity as "Québécois," those preferring this to the old French-Canadian label were likely to be younger and possess higher levels of education.[60] As part of this middle class, it has been pointed out that "intellectuals" (e.g., scientists, scholars, teachers) play a role in the transmission of new ways of thinking about Quebec through their writing and their verbal presentations.[61]

The fourth and fifth explanations suggest that Quebec underwent social change that may have been too rapid. The swiftness of social change, including the destruction of the old order, produced uncertainties about making the transition to the new order. Some people sought to reassert traditional values, while others had new ideas about the direction in which things should move. Rather than deal with internal disagreement, one solution to confusion was to *direct internal aggression against outsiders*.[62] The need to unite against external threats provided the basis for much collective action which would not have been possible in other circumstances. Fifth, the changes within Quebec also reflected an *intense desire to forge a new identity*.[63] The movement for greater self-determination was meaningful to Quebecers who sought a new image, a new self-concept, and a new and more modern collective identity. Coleman notes that the replacement of the old values with North American materialist values in Quebec produced an identity crisis and sense of loss which was translated into an active search for a distinctive culture.[64] Finding their new image in the designation "Québécois," many strove to replace the old identity by uniting ethnicity and polity in an assertion of nationalist sentiment.

Evaluating Forty Years of Change

There is no question that Quebec has indeed undergone massive change and that its provincial government has taken significant steps to change the province since 1960. We are now in a position where we can begin to evaluate these initiatives in terms of their results.[65]

The Changing Québécois Identity and Support for Independence

In 1970, 44% of the Quebec population identified themselves as French-Canadian and 34% as Canadian. Only 21% thought of themselves as Québécois. This was about 10 years after the Quiet Revolution had begun.

By 1990, the percentage identifying themselves as French-Canadian had dropped from 44% to 28% and the percentage viewing themselves as Canadian had dropped even more significantly from 34% to 9%. In contrast, the relatively new and more nationalist identification as Québécois had increased from 21% to 59%.

Furthermore, support for Quebec independence in the 1960s was usually less than 10% though it increased through the 1970s to a peak of 24% in 1980. After the loss of the referendum in 1980, support for independence decreased to 15% in 1985 but then showed spectacular growth from 1989 to 1992 in the 40% range with a high of 56% in 1990 after Meech Lake died.

Increased support for independence seems to be linked with the maintenance of economic and political ties to Canada. But increased support for independence has also reduced the class and age-specific support (young, educated professionals) which had characterized earlier separatist feeling.

Support for sovereignty must be seen as a positive assertion of a collective identity rather than merely as a sense of injustice within the federal system.

Source: Maurice Pinard, "The Quebec Independence Movement: A Dramatic Reemergence," *Working Papers In Social Behaviour*, McGill University, 1992, and Andre Blais and Richard Nadeau, "To Be or Not To Be Sovereignist: Quebecker's Perennial Dilemma," *Canadian Public Policy* 18(1992): 89–103.

The most obvious area of change is in language. French has clearly become the language of Quebec. Many anglophones have left Quebec and those who have stayed cannot ignore the French environment around them. While there are exceptions, French is the language of the workplace and of the schools (except for anglophones educated in Quebec). This is not to imply that English is absent. Indeed, the opposite is true as, for example, 30% of the time spent watching television is spent watching English programming.[66] However, the linguistic hierarchy or economic inequality between English and French in Quebec that formally existed has been considerably reduced if not reversed. For example, 32% of Montreal's highest paid workers were unilingual anglophones in 1961, but this number was reduced to 7.8% in 1985.[67] One-half to two-thirds of all Montreal's anglophones are now bilingual. Marc Levine's interesting book entitled *The Reconquest of Montreal* has traced how Montreal as an English city with many French inhabitants has been transformed into a French city with English as a second language, and he has shown how this issue revolved around the language of schooling.[68] Montreal has always been the primary meeting ground between French and English but French language and culture have now become pivotal rather than subordinate.

Montreal's place within Canadian society has also changed. Whereas it was once paired with Toronto as the centre of commerce for all of Canada, Toronto has become the hub on the east–west axis as well as the access point for American capital and to American markets. Montreal, symbolic of Quebec's feelings in general, is much more oriented to the United States than to Toronto and English-Canada.[69] Ironically, Montreal's linkages to the northeastern states, and the decline of that region in relation to economic growth towards the West has contributed to the economic weakening of Quebec. In other words, the continentalization of the Canadian economy elevated Toronto in importance and has contributed to the economic marginalization of Montreal and Quebec.[70] Consequently the rivalry between Ontario and Quebec is not just based on ethnic differences but demonstrates economic disparities (e.g., compare Quebec's higher unemployment rates). Gagnon and Montcalm have argued that this growing economic peripheralization of Quebec in the continental economy was not caused by the emergence of Quebec nationalism but even preceded it. In fact, they argue that the use of the state as a technique of intervention was an attempt to take control of an economy that had already begun to decline.

It is also useful to examine what effect state interventionism has had on the Quebec economy. Again it is clear that there have been important shifts in ownership to francophone control in sectors such as food and beverage, printing and publishing, metal fabrication, and mineral products. Small- and medium-sized businesses are increasingly controlled by francophones. Quebec crown corporations are still important to the economy and play a key role as symbols of national pride. There are major pools of francophone capital in Quebec such as Groupe Desjardins and Caisse de dépot and there are major companies such as Provigo, Bombardier, and Power Corporation that even reach beyond Quebec's borders in commercial activity. This is not to ignore the American or English-Canadian economic presence but to state that Québécois have made major strides in controlling their own economy.

Virtually all analysts agree that by the mid-1980s, there began a move away from state capitalism and state intervention in the economy to free market principles. The public sector middle class that had embraced the Quiet Revolution now feels increasingly squeezed by neoconservative principles and downsizing. As Quebec becomes more entrepreneurial and captivated by free market principles, the provincial economy becomes more international, and in this sense, free trade also contributes to a *de-Canadianization* (i.e., a move away from dependency on Canadian markets). Thus, the old economic ties that bound Quebec into the Canadian economy are slowly being weakened, though clearly not severed.

Indicators of Quebec as a Distinct Society

1. Over 80% of the population have French as a mother tongue and continue to use it as a home language. Language then is a symbolic marker of a distinct collectivity.

2. The term "Québécois" reflects an intimate relationship between culture and personal identity (who I am and how I relate to others).

3. It is the only province in Canada that has had a government elected several times with the explicit platform of removing Quebec from the existing Canadian federation.

4. Quebec has had many distinct institutions such as a dual confessional public school system and the caisses populaires (alternatives to national banks) and CEGEPS (public colleges).

5. Quebec understands itself as distinct as a totality (not just the random sum of its parts) which initially included primarily francophone Quebecers but now attempts to include all residents of the province.

6. Quebec has a distinct sense of history and nationhood that began before the Conquest and is reflected in the phrase "Je me souviens" ("I remember") printed on automobile licence plates.

7. The provincial state has been empowered with the role of intervening and regulating the society to promote the collective identity.

Further Reading: Marcel Fournier, Michael Rosenberg, and Deena White (eds.), *Quebec Society: Critical Issues* (Scarborough: Prentice-Hall, 1997), particularly the Introduction and the Chapter 4 by Greg Neilsen, "Culture and the Politics of Being Québécois: Identity and Communication."

Language and Group Survival

Nationalist feeling in Quebec is primarily energized by the conviction that francophone cultural survival is a critical issue.[71] The maintenance of linguistic distinctiveness, moreover, has become pivotal to cultural survival. Immigration provided one threat to francophones, because most immigrants learned English and became part of the anglophone majority, thus upsetting the earlier balance of power both in the country as a whole and in Quebec. Bill 101, the Charter of the French Language, made French the official language of the province of Quebec in 1977. The goal was to ensure that the children of immigrants were educated in French as well as that French would be the language of business.[72] There were elaborate regulations to ensure that all of this happened. In response to a challenge to the Supreme Court over the legality of this exclusivity in a bilingual country, Quebec Premier Bourassa introduced Bill 178 which invoked the *"notwithstanding clause"* of the Charter of Rights to override the decision and ensure the universal presence of French in the province. The *indoor-outdoor solution* was to require only French signage outside stores but to allow some English signage inside.

Francophones Outside Quebec

Francophones outside Quebec, with some exceptions, were dispersed throughout anglophone communities, and found it difficult, therefore, to maintain their mother tongue. Because francophone migrants to English-Canada were concerned more with adaptation and adjustment to their new environment than with cultural survival, they became *invisible minorities*.[73]

Furthermore, over the generations, children of francophones found it virtually impossible to maintain their mother tongue and became *francogènes* (people who do not speak French but have some degree of attachment to the French culture of their ancestry). The French language was much more likely to survive where residential segregation supported a reasonable amount of institutional completeness, and, above all, schooling in French.[74] Areas such

RESEARCH CLIP 5.2	How Do Francophones Survive in Anglophone Canada?

The conventional wisdom has been that French-speaking persons face enormous assimilationist pressures in anglophone regions of Canada. In fact, it is assumed that francophone survival is well-nigh impossible in the long term. Yet francophone communities do exist. One study of 85 francophone adults in the city of Calgary (where 10 000 francophones reside almost invisibly) produced some striking results.

Francophones in Calgary were not a homogeneous ethnic group but were persons of diverse backgrounds and origins. They traced their heritage not only to Quebec but to Europe, North Africa, and South Asia. They possessed a wide range of values, beliefs, and practices and certainly were not territorially concentrated. Despite their ethnic differences, what they shared was a mother tongue (French) or a mutual commitment to retain French capability.

Most of the francophones were bilingual but made a deliberate choice to use French for their own enjoyment, or to develop or maintain linguistic competence, or in order to help sustain the francophone community. Since their work world and service activities were normally in English, the use of French became associated with leisure. The study found that leisure as unobligated activity that was part of daily living (not just recreation)

meant that French could be deliberately spoken at home to children or at social gatherings, or could be expressed by reading French or buying French greeting cards, or by patronizing commercial enterprises where French was available (e.g., stores, professional services, restaurants).

The key contribution of the study was the identification of what is called a francophonie in the city of Calgary. A *francophonie* is a loose network of French-speaking persons in a community that has a set of organizations and interpersonal ties but that has no territorial boundaries. It is a symbolic community that serves as a reference group for francophones who choose to retain their language skills and which provides the resources to do so. The francophonie consists of persons who deliberately pursue a lifestyle that makes the maintenance and transmission of French possible. But it is not just the existence of formal organizations (e.g., a French-language church and school) that is important to the francophonie but the informal interactions outside work or school that sustain the community in a minimally coalescing fashion.

Source: Robert A. Stebbins, *The Franco-Calgarians: French Language, Leisure, and Linguistic Lifestyle in an Anglophone City* (Toronto: University of Toronto Press, 1994). See also Rene Guindon and Pierre Poulin, *Francophones In Canada: A Community Of Interests* (Heritage Canada, 1996).

as St. Boniface, Manitoba, and rural areas adjacent to the Quebec borders in New Brunswick (the only officially bilingual province in Canada) and Ontario, continue to contain French-speaking communities. More recently, we have learned that francophone minorities can demonstrate vitality without a territorial basis in what is called *L'espace francophone* (francophone spaces) in niches such as schools, churches and community organizations.[75] Generally, however, the greater the distance from Quebec, the greater the extent of language loss.[76]

Anglophones in Quebec

The issue of language and group survival had, as its initial focus, the survival of francophones outside Quebec. More recently, however, Bill 101 and Bill 178 have raised the question of the survival of anglophones inside Quebec. When French became the official language of Quebec and English lost its official status, the anglophone community felt its own existence threatened. The initial militant reaction of anglophones exacerbated the antagonism already felt by francophones towards anglophones, and seemed to strengthen Quebec nationalist objectives.[77] Bill 101, in particular, employed language as an economic and political tool in such a way as to *transform ethnic nationalism into territorial nationalism.*[78] In other words, the unifying element of the entire population was now to be the common French language regardless of other differences. The heightening of the Québécois identity placed all Quebec anglophones in a dilemma which accentuated their minority group status.

The massive concentration of Quebec anglophones (75%) in the metropolitan Montreal area, and in some rural settlements in the Eastern Townships and Ottawa Valley, in conjunction with the fact that only one in three of these anglophones were likely to be bilingual, suggested that the anglophone population maintained its identity through close ties with English North America; e.g., Ontario and New York.[79] Quebec anglophones have in recent years felt overwhelmed by the strength of the changes happening around them and have been severely weakened by large-scale out-migration. Increasingly, anglophone minorities have been subject to the same pressures as francophone minorities in the rest of Canada.[80]

Bilingualism

The federal policy of *bilingualism* was meant to reaffirm to francophones, located in Quebec and elsewhere, that they were not second-class citizens.[81] As a founding partner of Confederation, francophones were to possess the same rights and privileges as anglophones. The policy declared the federal government's commitment to make its services accessible to both anglophones and francophones throughout Canada. The new nationalist spirit in Quebec spilled over to francophone groups elsewhere in Canada so that they became bolder in demanding their rights to bilingualism (particularly in education). At the same time, however, the tightening of the boundaries of nation and state (as expressed in the new identification of the Québécois), created distance between francophones inside and francophones outside Quebec. In the end, as Guindon expresses it, the policy of bilingualism became politically irrelevant to Quebec and a political irritation to anglophones outside Quebec.[82] Many anglophones became defensive about their own language, and viewed bilingualism as a threat. Others found it difficult to accept a policy of federal bilingualism so long as the government of Quebec established a converse policy of French unilingualism in that province.

The emerging pattern of French–English relations seems to support the idea, proposed by Richard Joy, that two languages of unequal strength cannot coexist in intimate contact.

Calling this the bilingual belt thesis, Joy points out that linguistic segregation in Canada is proceeding in such a way that linguistic minorities are disappearing.[83] Just as French is being overwhelmed as a living language outside Quebec, so English is being overwhelmed by the strength of French in Quebec. Bill 101, for example, is just another in a series of developments that have made anglophones less comfortable in Quebec. The bilingual belt, where French and English coexist, can only be found, according to Joy, in a narrow strip along the Quebec border. This area includes the Eastern Townships of Quebec, the Ottawa Valley, Northern Ontario, and the City of Montreal. The effect of Bill 101, moreover, may actually have been to shrink this bilingual belt, for since Joy's initial study, the evidence is that the majority linguistic group in every region is growing while linguistic minorities are shrinking. As a result, duality is being replaced by linguistic polarization.[84] In sum, in spite of the existence of linguistic minorities, Canada seems to have moved towards territorial unilingualism with bilingual federal institutions at the core.[85]

The type of bilingualism described above suggests that each language has its own territory of operation for which unity and common ground is found in federal institutions (*institutional bilingualism*). Yet the ideal implied in both the work of the Royal Commission on Bilingualism and Biculturalism and the actions of the federal government since that time is that individual Canadians ought to know both languages (*individual bilingualism*). As we noted in Chapter One, francophones are more likely to be bilingual. In fact, 40.8% of francophones are bilingual whereas only 8.8% of anglophones and 11.2% of allophones are bilingual.[86] About two-thirds of all anglophones in Quebec are bilingual whereas only about one-third of francophones in Quebec are bilingual. But in the rest of Canada (outside Quebec), over 80% of francophones are bilingual while less than 7% of anglophones are bilingual.

Since programs to teach adults the "other" language are not highly successful, second language education has been promoted quite strongly for children through the school system. About 7% of Canadian children participate in French immersion with a high of about 18% in New Brunswick, 14% in Prince Edward Island, 10% in Manitoba, 7% in Ontario, and rates in the Western provinces and Newfoundland under the national average at around 5%.[87]

Somewhat less demanding are the French second language programs that are available for second language education at about 80% of the public schools outside Quebec. In 1981, 17.7% of teenagers (ages 15–19) across Canada considered themselves bilingual, and that number increased to 24.4% in 1996. These bilingual rates were highest in New Brunswick (49%) and Quebec (42%) but were between 10–20% in most of the rest of the country.[88] Interestingly, second language French education is stronger at the elementary level than it is at the secondary level where it falls off dramatically. While familiarization with the "other" official language is noteworthy, it is likely that many are picking up only a rudimentary knowledge of the language as children, which is not to be interpreted as functional or working bilingualism.[89] The extent to which knowledge of the country's "other" second language is necessary for functioning within the society will clearly be a matter of continuing debate.

Developments in Quebec since 1960 have clearly affected the nature of Canadian society, and have restructured French–English relations. These relationships coexist in dynamic tension. Many aspects have yet to be resolved. In recent years, however, another restructuring of ethnic relations has occurred among Canada's Aboriginal peoples, and it is this restructuring upon which we now focus our attention. In both cases, there are longstanding unresolved issues and a case to be made for a historically validated, unique, or special position within Canadian society.

ABORIGINAL–NONABORIGINAL RELATIONS

Who Are the Indigenous People?

At the time Europeans arrived in Canada, there were fifty-five separate nations sharing the territory (see Figure 5.4).[90] Native contact with Europeans first came through dealings with explorers, traders, and trappers, who needed the assistance of Native peoples in the new land. The increasing immigration of Europeans adopting agriculture as a livelihood, however, posed problems to the Native way of life due to differences in attitude towards land ownership, commercial use of plants, and domestication of animals. With their superior technology (such as railroads) and sheer numbers, white people used either brute force, or the threat of force, in addition to the treaty process to remove Native people from the path of European settlement. In this way, the Euro-Canadian domination of Native peoples in Canada began.[91]

Denied self-government, removed from most of their land and livelihood, and partially transformed by European culture, Aboriginal peoples took on the character of a classic colonized minority.[92] Not only was their own social structure significantly eroded, but their place

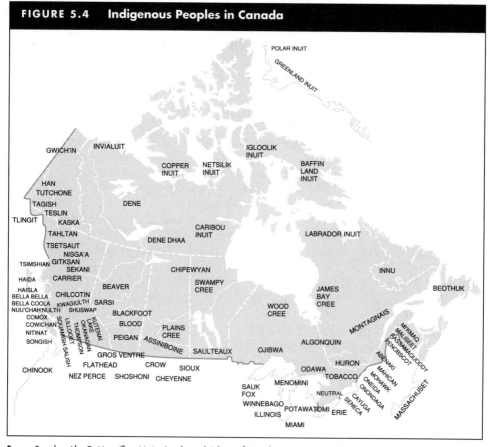

FIGURE 5.4   Indigenous Peoples in Canada

Source: Based on Alan D. Macmillan, *Native Peoples and Cultures of Canada*, Vancouver, Douglas & McIntyre, 1988; John Price, *Indians of Canada: Cultural Dynamics*, Scarborough, Ont., Prentice-Hall, 1979.

within Canadian society caused them to become perpetually disadvantaged. With the somewhat contradictory objectives of "protecting" and "civilizing" Aboriginals, the end result was the marginalization of Native people whereby their own societal structures were dismantled at the same time that their participation in the dominant society was restricted.[93]

The *Indian Act* of 1876 made Native people, in essence, wards of the federal government, placing them on tracts of land called reserves. More importantly, the Act defined explicitly who would be given the *legal status of "Indian."* This definition divided first nations into those with treaty status as opposed to other types of status such as *non-status Indian* and *Métis*. Until recently, persons were considered status Indians (and therefore entitled to receive whatever benefits were forthcoming from that status) only if their fathers were considered Indians, regardless of their mothers' status.[94] The marriage, or informal sexual association, of large numbers of whites with Indian women resulted in offspring that formed a marginal group of Aboriginal people. It was not until 1985 that the Indian Act was amended through Bill C-31 in accordance with the Charter of Rights to eliminate sexual discrimination. Many who had lost their Indian status then began to apply for reinstatement as legal Indians, and by 1996, about 104 000 persons (about one-fifth of all registered Indians) had their Indian status reinstated.[95] As long as government definitions of who was an Indian were based on an arbitrary legal interpretation rather than utilizing social, cultural, or self-definitions, the Native community was divided by invidious distinctions.

There are many ways of counting Aboriginal people and the numbers vary depending on the criteria used. For example, as we have seen, the Department of Indian Affairs has a stricter definition because of its legal implications. This method of counting yields slightly over half a million Indians in Canada (see box below). However, a broader definition includes persons who self-declare their *ancestry* as Aboriginal and/or who are of partial Aboriginal origin. The ancestry question in the 1996 census revealed that about 1.1 mil-

---

Registered (Status) Indians in Canada

- It is estimated that there were approximately 250 000 Natives in what is now Canada in the 1600s. Due to epidemics, poor health, and combat, this number was reduced to about 102 000 by 1867.

- There are approximately 573 000 registered Indians in Canada today. In 1961, there were only 192 000 registered Indians. This dramatic increase is due to changes in the Indian Act in 1985 as well as a high birth rate.

- About 60% of status Indians live on reserves and about 40% live off reserves. Though some of these reserves are near urban centres, most registered Indians live in more remote locations or at some distance from urban centres.

- There are approximately 2284 reserves across Canada; they vary considerably in size.

- The basic political structures among Indians are called bands. There are over 600 bands in Canada with an average size of around 500 persons.

While the birth rates and death rates among Indians are higher than among non-Indians, the gap seems to be narrowing.

Source: Based on James S. Frideres, *Native Peoples in Canada*, 5th ed. (Scarborough: Prentice-Hall, 1998), Chap. 5.

lion persons (3.9% of the Canadian population) reported Aboriginal ancestry, over half of which were of mixed ancestry. However, an *identity* question was also added to determine whether respondents explicitly considered themselves either North American Indian, Métis, or Inuit. Using this counting method, about 0.8 million (2.8% of the total population) are Aboriginal. Just under 70% of the Aboriginal population are North American Indian, 26% are Métis, and 5% are Inuit. This tighter definition of Aboriginal is the one we will use.

Figure 5.5 shows that the Aboriginal population is distributed rather evenly across the provinces from Ontario westward with each province having 14–17% of all Aboriginals in Canada. Quebec has about half of that number with most of the other provinces and territories having a low proportionate share of the Aboriginal population. On the other hand, when

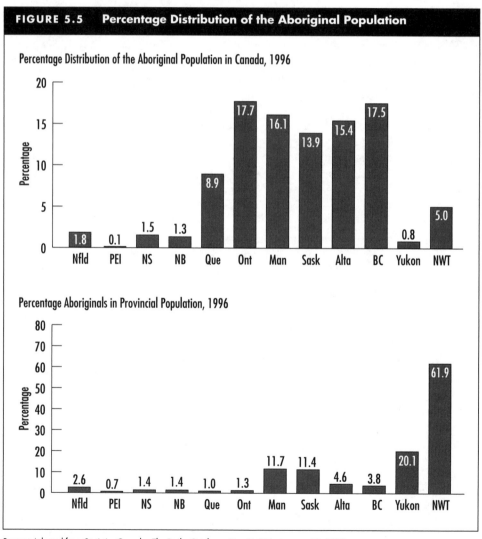

FIGURE 5.5   Percentage Distribution of the Aboriginal Population

Percentage Distribution of the Aboriginal Population in Canada, 1996

Percentage Aboriginals in Provincial Population, 1996

Source: Adapted from Statistics Canada, *The Daily,* Catalogue No. 11-001, January 13, 1998.

Aboriginals are considered as a percentage of the provincial populations, the Northwest Territories is over 60% Aboriginal, the Yukon 20%, and the population of Manitoba and Saskatchewan are 11–12% Aboriginal. When considering the three Aboriginal groups, North American Indian and Métis show similar patterns to what has just been presented. It is only Inuit who are specifically concentrated in Nunavut, with a significant presence also in Quebec and Newfoundland.

Persons with partial Indian ancestry are called *Métis*—though the term was formerly used to describe only children of French–Indian unions. Again, as a result of the Charter of Rights, Métis are taking on the character of a distinct group, particularly those who live in (or came from) Métis settlements (such as in Northern Alberta). The 1996 census lists somewhat more than 210 000 Métis in Canada, most of whom reside in the northern parts of the four western provinces. Traditionally, they were Catholic and French-speaking.[96] There is now also a significant mixed blood community that is urban, dispersed elsewhere in the country, and of more varied descent.

When the Métis realized that western lands were being transferred from the jurisdiction of fur trading companies to the Canadian government, with no recognition of their rights, they formed a provisional government which attempted to negotiate a new accord with Canada. In 1885, the Métis, led by Louis Riel, staged a rebellion. The rebellion ended with the defeat of the Métis, and Riel was found guilty of treason and hanged.[97] Most Métis today subsist on marginal farmland with high levels of dependency and unemployment. The history of their mistreatment has recently inspired renewed protests for the redress of Métis grievances.

The smallest group of distinct Native people are the *Inuit*. There are about 41 000 Inuit in Canada. In spite of their small numbers, the Inuit population is not dying out.[98] A birth rate twice as high as the Canadian population as a whole and substantial decreases in infant mortality have produced a growth rate substantially above the Canadian growth rate. Most of the Inuit are found in small communities of 600–800 people such as Pangnirtung, Igloolik, Baker Lake, and Tuktoyaktuk. (See Chapter 4 for other discussions on the Métis and Inuit).

If the Inuit as a people are thriving, their culture and economy are not surviving nearly as well. About two-thirds of Inuit have Inuktitut as their mother tongue, and about half (55%) of children under 15 speak Inuktitut at home.[99] On the one hand, this indicates that a substantial proportion of Inuit still retain their mother tongue, and, the more remote the community, the more likely this is the case. Consequently, Inuktitut remains a significant medium of communication particularly in the eastern Arctic.[100] On the other hand, more than two-thirds of the Inuit now know English, and the trend is towards greater use of English, especially among the young as they are exposed to southern-style education. As the traditional economy has become more marginal, and resettlement within communities (rather than living in nomadic groups) has increased exposure to southern culture (e.g., magazines, television), the Inuit are struggling to maintain their identity. The creation of Nunavut as a new Territory largely controlled by the Inuit will play a key part in strengthening group consciousness and in the retention of the traditional language.

These four groups (both status and non-status Indians, Métis, and Inuit) constitute the indigenous people of Canada. Together with other Aboriginal peoples living within nation-states throughout the globe, they form what has been called the fourth world.[101] However, a more contemporary term is *indigenous peoples* and, and as it relates to Indians, the appropriate term is *First Nations*.

The State and First Nations

From the point of view of the state, the primary objective of federal policy was to remove Aboriginals as impediments to economic and political development. The spread of capitalist agriculture required that Indian people be separated from their land and their land be transformed into private property.[102] The treaties then were a way in which Europeans could consolidate their control while receiving the cooperation of Indian people. So while the reserve represented protection, it also presented a European opportunity to wean Natives from their past life and prepare them for eventual assimilation. Federal policies through the years have been built on these assumptions but without the consent or participation of Native people. Symbolic of this position was the Indian Act of 1876, frequently described as "a total institution" because it paternalistically attempted to structure all aspects of Indian life. Even with good intentions, federal policy was essentially controlling and disempowering. The existence of racist attitudes and stereotypes only intensified the marginalization. In sum, the traditional society was in shambles but there was nothing to replace it since Euro-Canadian culture was alien and repressive to most Aboriginals. Not only was segregation and guardianship with the goal of absorption not working, but it was increasingly being resisted.

The government's first solution was to attempt to terminate Native special status by repealing the Indian Act, abolishing the Department of Indian Affairs and Northern Development (DIAND), and eliminating reserves. This was known as the *White Paper* of 1969 and it was met with strong opposition on the grounds that this would have been the ultimate assimilation technique. Natives, according to this policy, would have had no special status at all. In light of the objections, the White Paper was withdrawn and since then, federal policy has moved in the direction of supporting greater Aboriginal control to put them into a position of having more control over their own destiny.

In 1966, the Hawthorn Report advanced the concept of "citizens plus" whereby it would be acknowledged that Natives are citizens like everyone else but that they have special historic rights as well.[103] This idea was a sharp contrast from earlier practices where it was acknowledged that Aboriginals held special rights at the same time that they had been denied other basic rights (e.g., the earlier denial of the right to vote or the inability to obtain loans because reserve property was not acceptable as collateral). However, a major step forward, and indicative of the changed mood on the federal scene, was the *constitutional recognition* given to Aboriginal and treaty rights in the Constitution Act, 1982. This was also an important document because it acknowledged Métis as a distinct Aboriginal people for the first time. Another major advance was the Penner Committee Report in 1983 which recommended that Indian government be a distinct order of government within Canadian federalism, and that the structure and form of this government should be determined by Native people themselves.

Therefore, in an effort to transform the role of the federal government as their caretakers,[104] Native people and political leaders have increasingly turned to the concept of self-determination as a more respectful approach.[105] *Self-determination* means that Aboriginals must have some type of *political mechanism* at their disposal which allows them to be accountable to their own people and to make decisions on matters that affect them. In order to be effective, it requires a *specific division of powers* between the levels of government and Aboriginal government. It requires Aboriginal *control over group membership, fiscal policy, and land*.[106] The settlement of *land claims* has become the central issue for many Native people because it establishes the basis whereby their community can move away from a dependent position and foster economic development. Land claims, then, go beyond lump sum payments from the government to issues of social policy and service delivery (e.g., health care), establishing a more effective justice system (e.g., policing and sentencing), and mechanisms to strengthen economic development.

The land claims issue is frequently controversial because demand for natural resources makes Native land desireable for capitalist expansion in which governments are caught between corporate and native interests. Capitalist growth also means that Native territory is indirectly threatened. For example, the James Bay Project and several other hydroelectric projects proposed by provincial governments in the northern part of their provinces, as well as the Mackenzie Valley Pipeline, have enormous disturbing effects on Native cultures and economies.[107]

In many ways, the White Paper helped to crystallize Aboriginal solidarity for the first time. It was the catalyst for a response known as the *Red Paper* in 1970 led by Harold Cardinal of the Indian Association of Alberta. While Aboriginal groups were scattered all over Canada in small numbers with no unifying mechanism, perceptions of external threat helped to build a sense of *pan-Indianism*, which emphasized commonalities of the Native experience rather than traditional differences.[108] Furthermore, the need for a common voice in addressing the federal government as an interest group became essential, and political activity increased. National lobbying organizations include the Assembly of First Nations, the Native Council of Canada, the Métis National Council, and the Inuit Tapirisat of Canada. Other organizations exist at the provincial level, such as the Union of Ontario Indians and the Indian Association of Alberta. Realizing the value of having Natives represent themselves and their own interests, the federal government agreed to provide funding for these organizations in 1970, to ensure that Native leadership had adequate opportunity to defend and advocate their point of view. However, there are numerous disagreements about strategies and objectives among Native people which sometimes leads to splits or defections from these organizations.

The political lobbying that is usually necessary to obtain government action on matters of self-government, economic development, land claims settlement, and self-determination kept Native issues high on the national agenda after 1982 until the Quebec constitutional crisis took a higher priority. There was a clear sense that Native issues were no longer to be viewed as "their" problem but were a responsibility of all Canadians.[109] But one of the greatest insults Aboriginals experienced in the contemporary era in Canada was to be virtually

Revising the Dualistic Conception of Canadian Society

"The distinct society perpetuates a myth. Canada was not born when the English and French cultures joined. It was born when the treaties were signed with the First Nations. We allowed people from Europe to come here and settle peacefully."
Georges Erasmus 1990

"We are the founding nations of Canada and we will not allow the lie of two founding nations (English and French) to continue."
Ovide Mercredi 1991

Source: *Maclean's*, July 2, 1990 and *Globe and Mail*, August 27, 1991. Cited in Augie Fleras and Jean Leonard Elliott, *The Nations Within* (Toronto, Oxford, 1992), 23 and 69.

left out of the Meech Lake Accord. As we have seen, it was a Native Member of Parliament from Manitoba (Elijah Harper) who played a key role in its defeat. However, the Charlottetown Accord had much greater input from Aboriginals and accepted the right of Native self-government. Even though the agreement was defeated in 1992, the Royal Commission on Aboriginal Peoples had already been established in 1991 in direct response to the Oka Crisis of 1990.

OKA: A Major Turning Point

Just as the violent action by the FLQ in Quebec produced the October Crisis in 1970, which attracted national and international attention to a cause which desperately needed resolution for Québécois, so the Oka crisis in 1990 represented both a protest of Aboriginal subjugation and a positive affirmation of Aboriginal sovereignty.

Oka is a small village 40 kilometres west of Montreal. Since March of 1990 Mohawk warriors had been protesting the extension of a municipal golf course on land which they considered to be their own. There is no reserve at Oka but there is land held by the federal government. Originally used as a mission by the Sulpician religious order, as granted by the King of France in 1717, the land had been occupied by the Mohawks and a subject of ownership dispute for a long time. What was at issue was who owned this land (did European settlement predate Mohawk settlement?) and what its precise boundaries were.

On July 11, 1990, the Sureté du Québec raided the four-month-old blockade of a road to this disputed land established by the Mohawks of Kanesetake, and in the ensuing confusion an officer was killed. At a nearby bridge (Mercier Bridge), which served thousands of suburban commuters to Montreal each day, the Mohawks of Kahnawake established a sympathy blockade. This became the site of considerable public protest and demonstrations. Thousands of Canadian troops were later brought in for what became a 78-day armed standoff. The Mohawks surrendered on September 26 but succeeded in exhibiting the frustration and impatience which Natives across the country felt with the inability to resolve Native issues. Other sympathy blockades by Natives across the country ensued, and the Canadian public and the government realized that new initiatives and negotiations were required. As one effort in that direction, the federal government announced in 1991 the formation of the Royal Commission on Aboriginal Peoples.

Ironically, this form of militant protest also revealed divergent views within the Native community. The Mohawk Warriors who staged the blockade considered themselves traditionalists and rejected the decisions of the Band Council, which they perceived as an adaptation to the Euro-Caucasian world. While the appropriateness of militancy was debatable, the importance of the standoff in consciousness-raising about Native issues was indisputable.

Further Reading: Robert M. Campbell and Leslie A. Pal, *The Real Worlds of Politics*, 2nd ed. (Peterborough: Broadview, 1991), chap. 4. See also Gerald R. Alfred, *Heeding the Voices of Our Ancestors: Kahnawake Mohawk Politics and the Rise of Native Nationalism* (Toronto: Oxford University Press, 1995).

The *Royal Commission on Aboriginal Peoples* accepted the argument that in addition to the Constitution Act, 1982, there was a historic document that enshrined Native special rights. That document was the *Royal Proclamation of 1763* which is now being referred to as the Magna Carta of Aboriginal rights.[110] The British government here agreed to protect Aboriginal peoples and acknowledged that they were nations (hence independent entities) connected to the Crown by treaty and alliance. In addition, Aboriginals were not to be disturbed in their possession of unceded lands. In other words, lands over which no treaties had been signed were to be Native lands. Thus it is argued that land claims and self-government have historic support which somehow was obscured over the years.

There are three major issues which need to be resolved in order to reorganize Aboriginal–nonAboriginal relations.[111] First, are Native rights *created* (i.e., the result of constitutional provisions) or are they *inherent* (i.e., a consequence of their original position as autonomous Aboriginal communities)? Second, are these rights *circumscribed* (i.e., contained within distinct constitutional limits) or are they *uncircumscribed* (i.e., there are no limits and they apply to any area Natives may choose)? Third, are Native rights *subordinate* (dependent on federal or provincial laws) or are they *sovereign* (Natives have full power to legislate within certain spheres)? The Royal Commission opted in support of inherent rights (rather than rights that the federal government in its beneficence decided to grant), circumscribed rights (distinct areas of responsibility that would be controlled by First Nations), and sovereign rights (areas under Native jurisdiction would be fully under their control). It was thought that once these principles were clearly accepted, progress could be made in resolving the meaning and extent of self-government. (Note in the boxed insert on the following page that the Royal Commission speaks of self-government "within the context of Canadian citizenship.")

The precise means whereby self-government can occur is a complex and difficult matter. Ideas either being considered or already being put into practice include such things as separate Aboriginal seats in Parliament and provincial legislatures, tribal justice programs, community municipality control, various economic development programs, and transferring expenditure controls from government agencies to band councils.[112] There are many ways in which Aboriginal peoples are now being empowered through the settlement of land claims, Aboriginal investments and business, a cultural revival, and some new administrative and constitutional power.[113] On the other hand, disempowerment often lingers through systemic discrimination, racism, and internal difficulties. While there is much to be done, it is clear that new efforts are being made to transform an unsatisfactory outcome of previous patterns of relations with First Nations.

National surveys of public opinion give us some indication of attitudes towards Aboriginal people.[114] While there is a low level of knowledge about Aboriginal issues, and a strong reluctance to grant Aboriginals special status, there is, somewhat paradoxically, strong support for Native self-government and the settlement of land claims. In other words, there is substantial acceptance of the idea of Native self-determination. Yet, after about twenty years of measuring public opinion, it appears that support for Aboriginal peoples has softened somewhat and debilitating stereotypes still prevail. The protest strategies that Aboriginal peoples have used may have been effective as a negotiating device but have led to weaker support from the general public often due to the nature of media coverage.[115] Economic conservatism was found to be the most important predictor of respondent attitudes. The evidence suggested that prejudice is more likely to be dormant until it is activated by direct conflict, and native protest has often heightened such conflict. Since settlement of land claims involve financial compensation, and there has in recent years developed an ideological shift to economic conservatism which opposes large government expenditures, the economic underpinnings of this sense of justice may be more elusive. In the interim, selected forms of self-government are being instituted on a limited basis.

THE MEANING OF MULTICULTURALISM

Much of the dynamic of Canadian society has its origin in ethnic differences among the population. As the response to the Royal Commission on Bilingualism and Biculturalism

The Royal Commission on Aboriginal Peoples

The Royal Commission on Aboriginal Peoples was appointed by the federal government in 1991 and presented a five volume report in 1996. While its recommendations are as potentially influential and ground-breaking for Native issues as the Royal Commission on Bilingualism and Biculturalism was for French–English relations, there is little evidence so far that the government intends to implement many of the recommendations, in large measure because they often involve new costs. However, what the Report does do is propose a new relationship between Aboriginals and nonAboriginals, and it is hoped that this new attitude will shape and inform future decision-making. The 470 recommendations are too numerous to deal with all of them here, but a sampling of them are listed.

"If one theme dominates our recommendations, it is that Aboriginal peoples must have room to exercise their autonomy and structure their own solutions. The pattern of debilitating and discriminatory paternalism that has characterized federal policy for the past 150 years must end. Aboriginal people cannot flourish if they are treated like wards, incapable of controlling their own destiny.

We advocate recognition of Aboriginal nations within Canada as political entities through which Aboriginal people can express their distinctive identity within the context of their Canadian citizenship...

At the heart of our recommendations is recognition that Aboriginal peoples are people, that they form collectivities of unique character, and that they have a right of governmental autonomy." (Volume 5, p. 1.)

Recommendations regarding suicide prevention and criminal justice matters were given greatest urgency, but among the ideas proposed were the preparation of a new royal proclamation outlining the principles of Aboriginal–federal government relations, the creation of an Aboriginal Parliament or House of First Peoples (without law-making power but to advise the House of Commons and Senate), the creation of a new federal Department of Aboriginal Relations, the establishment of an Aboriginal Peoples' International University, the creation of an Aboriginal Languages Foundation and Aboriginal Arts Council, the provision of programs for economic development and training, and the improvement of housing and the provision of incentives for home ownership both on and off reserves

Further Information: In addition to the publications of the RCAP, there is also a CD-ROM entitled *For Seven Generations: An Information Legacy of the Royal Commission On Aboriginal Peoples.*

broadened to include residents of Canada who were neither English or French, it became clear that it would no longer be prudent for government policy to ignore the wide range of other ethnic groups represented in the country. Consequently, in 1971, the federal government declared a policy of bilingualism within a multicultural framework, and in 1988, the Multiculturalism Act established the right of Canadians to identify with a cultural heritage. The official status given to ethnic differences has been a subject of considerable debate as to precisely what it signifies and its true purpose.[116]

As a policy promoting tolerance and diversity, multiculturalism was to be the opposite of *assimilation*, for to assimilate is to lose those characteristics which differentiate a group from the culture which surrounds it. In reality, however, instead of cultural retention, the dominant reality has been that of *anglo-conformity*; i.e., that ethnic groups feel pressured to conform to the anglo-majority. While anglo-conformity may have been the objective in Canada in the past, multiculturalism, on the surface at least, was to represent a new approach.

Multiculturalism was also thought to contrast with *amalgamation*, in which each ethnic group contributes something, but loses its identity as the people of a state find a totally new identity. This was the *melting pot* thesis which at one time was thought to contrast Canada with the United States. In contrast to a melting pot, Canada was said to be a pluralist society. *Pluralism* occurs where cultural differences coexist in an atmosphere of mutual toleration. This Clairmont and Wiens have called "The Canadian Way."[117] In a recent study of ethnic relations in Canada and the United States, however, it was discovered that whatever differences in tone may exist between the two countries, the realities of pressures towards conformity are really very similar, and there are similar levels of discrimination in matters such as employment and housing in both countries (see Chapter 6).[118]

Since many of the early immigrants to Canada settled in rural areas of the country, they were able to retain some of their ethnic identity. At the same time, however, it must be recognized that (at least until World War II), there were very strong pressures on ethnic groups to Canadianize, and discrimination towards non–Anglo-Saxons was strong. This process is known as *nativism*, which is opposition towards any new group that poses a threat (real or imagined) to Canadian life as understood by the dominant group.[119] The greater prosperity of the post-war years, however, caused a relaxation of inter-ethnic attitudes. In addition, the backlash against the Bilingualism and Biculturalism Commission by non-charter ethnic groups, and the model of a proud ethnic identity established by francophones in Quebec, both contributed to the recognition of the need to more fully appreciate the role of ethnic cultures in Canadian society as a whole.

The policy of multiculturalism seems to imply that people are encouraged to maintain their own ethnic cultures in Canada. In reality, that scenario is virtually impossible. Not only will these cultures be modified through the process of relocation, but they will also be difficult to sustain at all. With the exception of francophones in Quebec who have their own school system, media supports, and regulations controlling economic and cultural environment, ethnic groups in Canada are bombarded with media influences, school materials, and the work world of anglophone culture. Ethnic cultures experience enormous struggles in maintaining their languages beyond the first generation.[120] Can a complete culture survive without full institutional supports and a language which sustains it? How is it possible to have two official languages and a plurality of cultures all with equal value?

In the first place, not all cultures are of "equal" value except in the ideal sense of equality. In reality, pressures towards either anglo-conformity or franco-conformity are still strong. In the second place, the fostering of certain aspects of culture should not be confused with the preservation of a complete culture. In the third place, it could be that multi-culturalism aims to affect people psychologically by giving them confidence in their own identity, and seeks to create a "respect for others and a willingness to share ideas, attitudes, and assumptions."[121]

The preservation of ethnic folk dances, cuisine, and other art does not equate to preservation of culture. Instead, it has been argued that these cultural fragments give minorities the illusion of preserving their ethnic identity while at the same time ensuring anglo-conformity.[122] The *critical approach to multiculturalism* understands it as a strategy of containment that sustains the hegemony of the dominant cultural group rather than ensuring access and equity for all members of the society. While the *liberal-pluralist view of multiculturalism* stresses tolerance and quaintness ("saris, samosas, and steel-bands"), the critical approach understands multiculturalism as a way to diffuse "resistance, rebellion, and rejection."[123]

The emphasis on multiculturalism as the preservation of select artifacts of culture which have more nostalgic value than importance in everyday behaviour is referred to as *symbolic ethnicity* or *partialized* or *fragmented ethnicity*.[124] While some segments of an individual's life (e.g., occupation) may be de-ethnicized, other aspects (e.g., kinship and friendship) may retain the link to the ethnic heritage at the same time that the person participates fully in the mainstream of Canadian society. It has also been argued that technological culture seems to heighten the need for identity, and later generations may become involved in "ethnic rediscoveries," selecting a few items from their cultural ancestries and maintaining them in their private lives.[125] Weinfeld describes this as *affective ethnicity* because it is a warm but superficial way of giving distinctiveness to individual identity in a society dominated by conformity and convention.[126]

The shift of immigration to new source countries, and especially the immigration of visible minorities, has helped to bring about a shift in multiculturalism policy. The old cultural retention approach has been replaced by a new emphasis on race relations and the elimination of ethnocentrism and discrimination through greater sensitivity and education.[127] Critics, however have argued that multiculturalism represents a type of image-framing by elites that gives the impression of intergroup harmony while denying the problems of race which have been minimized as ethnic differences.[128] In Quebec, the federal policy of multiculturalism is viewed as a threat because its assumption that all cultures are of equal value challenges efforts to strengthen francophone culture in that province. Therefore, the Quebec program is known as *interculturalism* and emphasizes intercultural understanding rather than intercultural equality.[129]

Perhaps the best way to understand multiculturalism is not in terms of programs or policies but in terms of ideology. Multiculturalism is an ideology because it is prescriptive, i.e., it holds out ideals about the way things should be. Because ideologies constantly shift and change, our views of multiculturalism and what it means will also change. When the idea of multiculturalism was first proposed, it was almost a kind of motherhood issue to which no one could object and which made everyone feel good. However, since the late 1980s, the idea of multiculturalism has been subject to unforeseen debate.[130]

In the first place, multiculturalism has been confused with the issue of immigration and questions about the society's absorptive capacity of new immigrants. Second, the persistent threat of Quebec separation in combination with the in-migration of new visible minorities has worn the patience of anglophone nativists who want to get on with building a strong Canadian identity. To them, multiculturalism is "mosaic madness," "visionless coexis-

The Meaning of Ethnicity

Two Cameo Snapshots

One. "I love my open air jeep. I love to feel the wind around me. I have a flag hanging from the rear view mirror and it is the Croatian flag. Me, I was born here. But my parents were born in Croatia. They love Canada but their heart is still in Croatia and I have been brought up with that culture and identity. They identify with Croatian people and cheer for the homeland, and in a way, I am in to it too. We are not Croatian-Canadian but Croatian and Canadian—I think there is a difference."

Two. "I grew up in Vancouver. Our Oma (Grandma) lived with us so the rule of the household was that we speak German when in the house. So I am fluent in German and English. But like many Canadian kids, I also learned some French in school and when I became an adult, I moved to Quebec City to learn more French. I loved that place. And I decided to stay there. I married a guy there and now we have children. I wanted to pass on my native tongue to my children so German is the language of our home. My husband knew no German and spoke primarily French but he has learned some German. So German is the language at home and French is the language at school, and somewhere in between we fit English in. When people hear us talking German in the stores, it is amazing how many people reach out to us."

Question to Consider:

What does this mixture of ethnic identity and language use mean for people who have a single idea of what Canadian society is?

tence," and "an inadequate national dream."[131] Backlash reactions against pluralism can be found in the United States and Europe as well and these reactions can be related to the erosion of older conceptions of their societies. The danger is that rejection of multiculturalism as openness and tolerance can be the product of racism and intolerance, which breed new anxieties and injustices.[132]

It is interesting that in recent years, concurrent with the rise of neoconservatism, the federal government has emphasized the need for self-sufficiency and integration of immigrants rather than the support of their multicultural attributes.[133] In the end, however, debates about multiculturalism represent tacit acknowledgement that Canadian society is changing and that new ways must be found to accommodate all residents in the process of nation building. There is a growing acknowledgement that ethnicity can be remarkably resilient, and a new way to understand multiculturalism has been through the concept of *social incorporation* in which an ethnic group can still retain its identity while being included and part of the wider society.[134] The policy of multiculturalism is at the heart of an internal struggle over control of the symbolic order of Canadian society in which the status of ethnic groups and the perceptions of what Canadian society should be like leads to considerable debate and controversy.[135]

Assessing the Opposition to Multiculturalism

In recent years, the policy of multiculturalism has come under attack on the grounds that it does not encourage immigrants to think of themselves as Canadians, that it exaggerates differences that serve as the basis for antagonism and resentments, and that it alienates people from the mainstream of society rather than promoting integration.

Kymlicka argues that the evidence is exactly the opposite. Immigrants have a high rate of naturalization (i.e., taking out Canadian citizenship) and immigrants from non-traditional source countries have the highest rate of naturalization whereas immigrants from the United Kingdom have the lowest rate of naturalization. In other words, the greater the cultural gap for new immigrants, the more likely they are to declare their allegiance to the Canadian state. Ethnic groups have also participated in existing national political parties rather than creating their own political vehicles. Immigrants are also heavily committed to learning one of the official languages and intermarriage rates outside of each ethnic group is increasing. In comparison to the United States, Canada's ethnic groups demonstrate higher rates of naturalization and political participation, and lower rates of residential segregation. In short, there is little evidence that the policy of multiculturalism promotes ethnic separation.

Another argument that sustains opposition to multiculturalism, according to Kymlicka, is that people fear that there are no limits to the policy, namely that there are no boundaries to our acceptance of cultural differences. But a more important protection, he argues, is that we would not tolerate anything that threatens individual rights and equal opportunity as defined by the Charter of Rights and Freedoms. Furthermore, he notes that the government spends much more on immigrants for things that promote integration (e.g., language training, job training, child education) than it does on aspects of ethnic culture that divide.

So why is it then that anti-multicultural feelings have emerged? Kymlicka feels that it is due to our inability to resolve the longstanding conflicts of the nations within, in particular the Québécois and First Nations. This failure has reduced our confidence in our ability to deal with ethno-cultural relations so immigrants and multiculturalism become the scapegoats for the fears and frustrations that are based on the inability to obtain internal national reconciliation first.

To ponder:

Why do you think some people oppose or fear multiculturalism?

Source: Will Kymlicka, "The Theory And Practice Of Canadian Multiculturalism," *Breakfast on the Hill* 1998, hssfc.ca. See also his *Finding Our Way: Rethinking Ethnocultural Relations in Canada* (Oxford: Oxford University Press, 1998). For an example of a critique of multiculturalism, see Neil Bissoondath, *Selling Illusions: The Cult of Multiculturalism in Canada* (Toronto: Penguin, 1994).

FURTHER EXPLORATION

1. Some groups, such as the Québécois and Native people, have requested "special" status rather than "equal" status. Why have they done so and what are the implications? Are they "distinct societies"?

2. Why do some people want to "shed" their ethnicity while other people eagerly maintain it? Why do people several generations removed from immigration want to rediscover their ethnic background?

3. In Canada, there is frequent reference to "the French problem" or "the Native problem." Instead, why might it be called "the English problem" or "the white problem?"

4. What type of bilingualism predominates in your area? Why is bilingualism a good policy? Why is bilingualism problematic?

SELECTED READINGS

Driedger, Leo, *Multi-Ethnic Canada: Identities and Inequalities.* Toronto: Oxford, 1996.

Fleras, Augie and Jean Leonard Elliott. U*nequal Relations: An Introduction to Race, Ethnic, and Aboriginal Dynamics in Canada*, Second Edition. Scarborough: Prentice-Hall, 1996.

Fournier, Marcel, Michael Rosenberg, and Deena White (eds.), Q*uebec Society: Critical Issues.* Scarborough: Prentice-Hall, 1997.

Frideres, James S. *Aboriginal Peoples in Canada: Contemporary Conflicts*, 5th ed. Scarborough: Prentice Hall, 1998.

James, Carl E., *Seeing Ourselves: Exploring Race, Ethnicity and Culture.* Toronto: Thompson, 1995.

Kalbach, Madeline A. and Warren E. Kalbach (eds), *Perspectives on Ethnicity in Canada* (Toronto: Harcourt Brace, 2000).

Li, Peter S. *Race and Ethnic Relations in Canada*, Second Edition. Toronto: Oxford, 1999.

Ponting, J. Rick (ed.), *First Nations in Canada: Perspectives on Opportunity, Empowerment, and Self-Determination.* Toronto: McGraw-Hill Ryerson, 1997.

ENDNOTES

1   This paragraph alludes to the subjective and objective aspects of ethnicity which, in their complexity, make the concept of ethnicity very difficult to define simply. For a discussion of the issues involved, Cf. Wsevolod W. Isajiw, "Definitions Of Ethnicity," *Ethnicity* 1(1974): 111–24.

2   Ravi Pendakur and Fernando Mata, "Patterns Of Ethnic Identification And The 'Canadian' Response," *Canadian Ethnic Studies* 30(2)1998:125–137.

3   Frances E. Aboud, "Ethnic Self-Identity," in Robert C. Gardner and Rudolf Kalin, eds., *A Canadian Social Psychology of Ethnic Relations* (Toronto: Methuen, 1981), 43–44.

4   John Porter, *The Vertical Mosaic*, 60.

5   Leo Driedger, *The Ethnic Factor: Identity in Diversity* (Toronto: McGraw-Hill Ryerson, 1989), chap. 4.

6   See Edward N. Herberg, *Ethnic Groups in Canada: Adaptations and Transitions* (Scarborough: Nelson, 1989), chap. 6; Leo Driedger, *Multi-Ethnic Canada: Identities and Inequalities* (Toronto: Oxford, 1996), chap. 9. For an interesting account of an urban ethnic community, see Grace Anderson, *Networks of Contact: The Portuguese in Toronto* (Waterloo: Wilfred Laurier University Press, 1974).

7   T.R. Balakrishnan, "Residential Segregation And Canada's Ethnic Groups", in Madeline A. Kalbach and Warren E. Kalbach (eds.), *Perspectives on Ethnicity in Canada* (Toronto: Harcourt Brace, 2000).

8   See for example, Kay J. Anderson, *Vancouver's Chinatown: Racial Discourse in Canada* (Montreal: McGill-Queen's, 1991) and David C. Lai, *Chinatowns: Towns Within Cities in Canada* (Vancouver: UBC Press, 1988).

9   Patricia E. Roy, "The Fifth Force: Multiculturalism And The English Canadian Identity," *Annals of the American Academy of Political and Social Science* 538(1995):199–209.

10 For a good review of the history of Canada's immigration policy, see Elliot L. Tepper, "Immigration Policy And Multiculturalism," in J.W. Berry and J.A. Laponce (eds), *Ethnicity and Culture in Canada: The Research Landscape* (Toronto: University Of Toronto Press, 1994), 95–123. See also Donald A. Avery, *Reluctant Host: Canada's Response to Immigrant Workers 1896–1994* (Toronto: McClelland and Stewart, 1995).

11 Anthony H. Richmond, "Canadian Immigration: Recent Developments and Future Prospects," in Leo Driedger, ed., *The Canadian Ethnic Mosaic*, 105–23; and Alan B. Simmons, "New Wave Immigrants: Origins And Characteristics," in Shiva S. Halli, Frank Trovato, and Leo Driedger, eds., *Ethnic Demography: Canadian Immigrant, Racial and Cultural Variations* (Ottawa: Carleton University Press, 1990), 141–59.

12 Peter S. Li, *The Making of Post-War Canada* (Toronto: Oxford University Press, 1996), Chapter 6.

13 Statistics Canada, 1986 Census Catalogue 93-155. For a review of Canadian immigration policy, particularly since World War II, see Freda Hawkins, *Canada and Immigration: Public Policy and Public Concern*, 2nd ed. (Montreal: McGill-Queens University Press, 1988).

14 Rudolf Kalin and J.W. Berry, "Ethnic and Multicultural Attitudes," in Berry and Laponce, *Ethnicity and Culture in Canada*, 293–321.

15 Raymond Breton, "Institutional Completeness of Ethnic Communities and the Personal Relations of Immigrants," *American Journal of Sociology* 70(1964): 193–205.

16 Tina O. Walter, Barbara Brown, and Edward Grabb, "Ethnic Identity and Sports Participation: A Comparative Analysis of West Indian and Italian Soccer Clubs in Metropolitan Toronto," *Canadian Ethnic Studies* 23(1)1991:85–96; Daphne N. Winland, "The Role of Religious Affiliation In Refugee Resettlement: The Case Of The Hmong," *Canadian Ethnic Studies* 24(1)1992:96–119; and Joanne Van Dijk, "Ethnic Persistence Among Dutch Canadian Catholics And Calvinists," *Canadian Ethnic Studies* 30(2)1998:23–49.

17 Jeffrey G. Reitz, "Language and Ethnic Community Survival," in Rita M. Bienvenue and Jay E. Goldstein, eds., *Ethnicity and Ethnic Relations in Canada*, 2nd ed. (Toronto: Butterworths, 1985), 105–23.

18 Clifford J. Jansen, "Community Organization of Italians in Toronto" in Leo Driedger, ed., *The Canadian Ethnic Mosaic*, 310–26.

19 William Shaffir, "Jewish Immigration to Canada," in Jean Leonard Elliott, ed., *Two Nations, Many Cultures: Ethnic Groups in Canada* (Scarborough: Prentice-Hall, 1979), 280–89.

20 Efie Gavaki, "Urban Villagers: The Greek Community in Montreal," in Jean Leonard Elliott, ed., *Two Nations, Many Cultures: Ethnic Groups in Canada*, 2nd ed. (Scarborough: Prentice Hall, 1983), 123–47.

21 Regula B. Qureshi and Saleem M.M. Qureshi, "Pakistani Canada: The Making of a Muslim Community," in Earle H. Waugh et al., eds., *The Muslim Community in North America* (Edmonton: University of Alberta Press, 1983), 127–48.

22 Steven T. DeZepetnek, "A History of The Hungarian Cultural Society Of Edmonton, 1946–1986", *Canadian Ethnic Studies* 25(2)1993:100–117.

23 The relationship between ethnicity, power, and race is discussed in Veronica Strong-Boag, Sherrill Grace, Avigail Eisenberg, and Joan Anderson (eds.), *Painting the Maple Leaf: Essays on Race, Gender, and the Construction of Canada* (Vancouver: UBC Press, 1998).

24 Vic Satzewich, "The Political Economy of Race and Ethnicity", in Peter S. Li (ed.), *Race and Ethnic Relations in Canada*, Second Edition (Toronto: Oxford University Press, 1999), Chapter 11. See also Vic Satzewich (ed.), *Racism and Social Inequality in Canada* (Toronto: Thompson, 1998) and B. Singh Bolaria and Peter S. Li, *Racial Oppression in Canada*, Second Edition (Toronto: Garamond, 1988).

25 For a short history of non-white immigration into Canada, see Subhas Ramcharan, *Racism: Nonwhites in Canada* (Toronto: Butterworths, 1982), 12–18.

26 For excellent discussions of the evolution of attitudes towards Chinese, see the Special Issue of *Canadian Ethnic Studies* 19(1987) entitled "Coping with Racism: The Chinese Experience in Canada," and Peter S. Li, *The Chinese in Canada*, Second Edition (Toronto: Oxford University Press, 1998).

27 For a review of the Japanese experience in Canada, see Thomas Berger, "The Banished Japanese Canadians," in Leo Driedger, ed., *Ethnic Canada: Identities and Inequalities* (Toronto: Copp Clark Pittman, 1987), 374–94; and Audrey Kobayashi, "The Japanese Canadian Redress Settlement And Its Implications For Race Relations," *Canadian Ethnic Studies* 24(1)1992:1–19.

28 Peter S. Li, *The Chinese in Canada* , 37.

29 E. D. Nelson and Augie Fleras, *Social Problems in Canada* (Scarborough: Prentice-Hall, 1995), 256–58.

30 Frances Henry, Carol Tator, Winston Mattis, and Tim Rees, *The Colour of Democracy: Racism in Canadian Society* (Toronto: Harcourt Brace, 1995).

31 James Stafford has pointed out that in the past immigrants from non-traditional source countries had to have higher education to compensate for their skin colour for admittance but that recent immigrants from these countries have lower levels of education. "The Impact of the New Immigration Policy On Racism In Canada," in Vic Satzewich, ed., *Deconstructing a Nation: Immigration, Multiculturalism, and Racism in 90's Canada* (Halifax: Fernwood, 1992), 69–91.

32 See Donald H. Clairmont and Dennis W. Magill, *Africville: The Life and Death of a Canadian Black Community* (Toronto: McClelland and Stewart, 1974); Frances Henry, *Forgotten Canadians: The Blacks of Nova Scotia* (Don Mills: Longman, 1973); Morris Davis and Joseph F. Krauter, *The Other Canadians: Profiles of Six Minorities* (Toronto: Methuen, 1978); also Peter S. Li and B. Singh Bolaria, eds., *Racial Minorities in Multicultural Canada* (Toronto: Garamond Press, 1983).

33 Pauline Comeau and Aldo Santin, *The First Canadians: A Profile of Canada's Native People Today* (Toronto: James Lorimer, 1990).

34 Augie Fleras and Jean Leonard Elliott, *The Nations Within: Aboriginal-State Relations in Canada, the United States, and New Zealand* (Toronto: Oxford University Press, 1992).

35 Denis Monière, *Ideologies in Quebec: The Historical Development* (Toronto: University of Toronto Press, 1981), 288. See also Francois-Pierre Gingras and Neil Nevitte, "The Evolution of Quebec Nationalism," in Alain G. Gagnon, ed., *Quebec: State and Society* (Toronto: Methuen, 1984), 3–4.

36 The three concepts developed here (primordial event, social decapitation, and beacon of light) can be found in numerous places, but one good reference is Richard Jones, *Community in Crisis: French-Canadian Nationalism in Perspective* (Toronto: McClelland and Stewart, 1972).

37 Kenneth McRoberts and Dale Posgate, *Quebec: Social Change and Political Crisis*, rev. ed. (Toronto: McClelland and Stewart, 1980), 30.

38 For an interesting study of French-Canadian life in the New England states, see Gerard J. Brault, *The French Canadian Heritage in New England* (Montreal: McGill-Queen's University Press, 1986).

39 For a review of the social changes occurring in Quebec and their implications, see Raymond Breton, "The Socio-Political Dynamics of the October Events," in Dale C. Thomson, ed., *Quebec*

Society and Politics: Views from the Inside (Toronto: McClelland and Stewart, 1973), 213–38; and William D. Coleman, *The Independence Movement in Quebec 1945–1980* (Toronto: University of Toronto Press, 1984).

40 Sheilagh Hodgins Milner and Henry Milner, *The Decolonization of Quebec* (Toronto: McClelland and Stewart, 1973), chap. 10.

41 For the classic statement on this phenomenon, see Hubert Guindon, "Social Unrest, Social Class and Quebec's Bureaucratic Revolution," *Queen's Quarterly* 7(1964): 150–62.

42 Raymond Murphy, "Teachers and the Evolving Structural Context of Economic and Political Attitudes in Quebec Society," *Canadian Review of Sociology and Anthropology* 18(1981): 157–82.

43 For a good discussion of the role of the state in the new Quebec, see Henry Milner, *Politics in the New Quebec* (Toronto: McClelland and Stewart, 1978), chap. 3.

44 William D. Coleman, *The Independence Movement in Quebec 1945–1980* (Toronto: University of Toronto Press, 1984), 148.

45 In their study of the use of the designation "Québécois" in Quebec, Donald M. Taylor and Ronald J. Sigal point out that anglophones in that province reject that label and the political and cultural values it signifies. "Defining Québécois: The Role of Ethnic Heritage, Language, and Political Orientation," in Bienvenue and Goldstein, *Ethnicity and Ethnic Relations in Canada*, 125–37.

46 McRoberts and Posgate, Chapter 10 presents a good discussion on the meanings and objectives of sovereignty association and the strategies involved.

47 For one view, see Reginald Whitaker "The Quebec Cauldron: A Recent Account," in Gagnon, *Quebec: State and Society*, 88–91.

48 Stanley B. Ryerson, "Disputed Claims: Quebec/Canada" in Alain G. Gagnon, ed., *Quebec: State and Society*, 59–67.

49 There are numerous discussions on the Meech Lake Accord available. See, for example, Robert M. Campbell and Leslie A. Pal, *The Real Worlds of Canadian Politics* (Peterborough: Broadview Press, 1989), chap. 5; Michael D. Behiels, ed., *The Meech Lake Primer: Conflicting Views of the 1987 Constitutional Accord* (Ottawa: University Of Ottawa Press, 1989); and Bryan Schwartz, *Fathoming Meech Lake* (Winnipeg: University of Manitoba Legal Research Institute, 1987).

50 Raymond Breton points out that Meech Lake recognizes Quebec as a society but only views the rest of Canada as a population. "The Concepts of Distinct Society and Identity in the Meech Lake Accord", in K.E. Swinton and C.J. Rogerson, eds., *Competing Constitutional Visions: The Meech Lake Accord* (Toronto: Carswell, 1988), 3–10.

51 For a good chronological discussion of issues and events of the Charlottetown Accord, see Chapter Three of Robert M. Campbell and Leslie A. Pal, *The Real Worlds of Canadian Politics*, Third Edition (Peterborough: Broadview, 1994). In terms of its implications for the results of the 1993 federal election which resulted in significant societal division, see Chapter 5.

52 John Conway, Debts to Pay, 1–9; Pierre Bourgault, *Now or Never!: Manifesto for an Independent Quebec* (Toronto: Key Porter, 1991); David E. Smith, Peter MacKinnon, John C. Courtney, eds., *After Meech Lake: Lessons for the Future* (Saskatoon: Fifth House, 1991); Patrick Monahan and Ken McRoberts, *The Charlottetown Accord, the Referendum, and the Future of Canada* (Toronto: University of Toronto Press, 1993).

53 Guy Lachapelle, "The 1995 Quebec Referendum: How The Sovereignty Partnership Proposal Turned The Campaign Around," *Quebec Studies* 24(1997):180–196.

54 Kenneth McRoberts and Patrick Monahan (eds.), *The Charlottetown Accord, the Referendum, and the Future of Canada* (Toronto: University of Toronto Press, 1993); John E. Trent, Robert Young, and Guy Lachapelle (eds.), *Quebec-Canada: What is the Path Ahead* (Ottawa: University of Ottawa Press, 1996); Simon Rosenblum and Peter Findlay (eds.), *Debating Canada's Future: Views from the Left* (Toronto: Lorimer, 1991).

55 An exploration of the competition hypothesis in relation to the restructuring of Quebec by francophones and its current manifestations in perceptions of inequality in Quebec is presented in an analysis by Leslie Laczko, *Pluralism and Inequality in Quebec* (Toronto: University Of Toronto Press, 1995).

56 Pierre Fournier, *The Quebec Establishment*, 2nd rev. ed. (Montreal: Black Rose, 1976), 204–5.

57 Alain G. Gagnon and Mary Beth Montcalm, *Quebec: Beyond the Quiet Revolution* (Scarborough: Nelson, 1990).

58 Marc Renaud, "Quebec New Middle Class in Search of Social Hegemony," in Gagnon, ed., *Quebec: State and Society*, 150–95, and Hubert Guindon, *Quebec Society: Tradition, Modernity, and Nationhood* (Toronto: University of Toronto Press, 1988), 27–37.

59 Gagnon and Montcalm, *Quebec: Beyond the Quiet Revolution*, 46.

60 Bernard Blishen, "Perceptions of National Identity," *Canadian Review of Sociology and Anthropology* 15(1978): 129–32.

61 In this regard, a Quebec sociologist , Fernand Dumont, has played a key role in popularizing a new vision of Quebec. He speaks of the pre-1960 period of Quebec as the winter of survival (a hibernation) that now must be discarded as Québécois builds a new society in dialogue with anglo-Canadians but independent from them. See his *Genèse de la société québécoise* (Montreal: Boreal, 1993).

62 Daniel W. Rossides, *Society as a Fundamental Process: An Introduction to Sociology* (Toronto: McGraw-Hill, 1968).

63 Dale Thomson, "Language, Identity, And The Nationalist Impulse: Quebec," A*nnals of the American Academy of Political and Social Science* 538(1995):69–82.

64 Coleman, *The Independence Movement in Quebec*, 131, 181–82.

65 The best single comprehensive source that monitors these changes is Simon Langlois et al, *Recent Social Trends in Quebec 1960–1990* (Montreal: McGill-Queen's University Press, 1992). For a French language assessment in terms of Quebec-Canada relations, see a special issue of Recherches Sociographiques 30(2–3):1998 entitled *Quebec et Canada: Deux References Conflictuelles.*

66 Pierre Fournier, *A Meech Lake Post-Mortem? Is Quebec Sovereignty Inevitable?* (Montreal: McGill-Queen's University Press, 1991), 87. Fournier argues that individual bilingualism will continue in Quebec but with a priority given to French.

67 Guy Lachapelle, Gérald Bernier, Daniel Salée, and Luc Bernier, *The Quebec Democracy: Structures, Processes, and Policies* (Toronto: McGraw Hill Ryerson, 1993), 345.

68 Marc V. Levine, *The Reconquest of Montreal: Language Change and Social Policy in a Bilingual City* (Philadelphia: Temple University Press, 1990).

69 Robert Chodos and Eric Hamovitch have discussed the pro-Americanism of Quebec nationalism and point out how Quebec is thoroughly North American rather than French European. *Quebec and the American Dream* (Toronto: Between the Lines, 1991).

70 Economic continentalization and the shift to free market principles in Quebec is discussed in a number of places. For example, see Alain G. Gagnon and Mary Beth Montcalm, *Quebec: Beyond the Quiet Revolution*; Guy Lachapelle, Gérald Bernier, Daniel Salée, and Luc Bernier, *The Quebec Democracy: Structures, Processes, and Policies*. These authors also discuss the rise of francophone economic power.

71 Robert M. Gill, "Language Policy, Culture And Identity: The Case Of Quebec," in Andre Lapierre, Patricia Smart, and Pierre Savard, *Language, Culture and Values in Canada at the Dawn of the 21st Century* (Ottawa: Carleton University Press, International Council For Canadian Studies, 1996), 99–114.

72 See Fournier, Rosenberg, and White, *Quebec Society: Critical Issues*, Chapter 3 "The Breaking Point: Language in Quebec Society (Christopher McAll), and Chapter 5 "Immigration And Ethnic Relations In Quebec: Pluralism In The Making" (GRES).

73 The concept of invisible ethnic minorities and its application to francophones in Toronto is developed in Thomas R. Maxwell, "The Invisible French: The French in Metropolitan Toronto"; in Elliott, *Two Nations, Many Cultures*, 114–22. The insecurities felt by francophone groups in an English environment are described in Sheila McLeod Arnopoulos, *Voices from French Ontario* (Montreal: McGill-Queen's University Press, 1982). The role of intermarriage in the anglicization of French minorities is discussed in Charles Castonguay, "Intermarriage and Language Shift in Canada, 1971 and 1976," *Canadian Journal of Sociology* 7(1982): 263–77. The concept of francogènes is discussed in Richard J. Joy, *Canada's Official Languages: The Progress of Bilingualism* (Toronto: University of Toronto Press, 1992), p. 63.

74 Robert Stebbins, *The French Enigma: Survival and Development in Canada's Francophone Societies* (forthcoming, 2000). See also Richard Wilbur, *The Rise of French New Brunswick* (Halifax: Formac, 1989).

75 Michael O'Keefe, *Francophone Minorities: Assimilation and Community Vitality* (Heritage Canada, 1998).

76 Ronald Wardhaugh, *Language and Nationhood: The Canadian Experience* (Vancouver: New Star, 1983), 107.

77 Sheila McLeod Annopoulos and Dominique Clift, *The English Fact in Quebec* (Montreal: McGill-Queen's University Press, 1980), 125.

78 Raymond Breton, "The Production and Allocation of Symbolic Resources: An Analysis of the Linguistic and Ethnocultural Fields in Canada," *Canadian Review of Sociology and Anthropology* 21(1984): 123–44.

79 Gary Caldwell and Eric Waddell, *The English of Quebec: From Majority to Minority Status* (Quebec: Institut Québécois De Recherche Sur La Culture, 1982), 27–71.

80 For an interesting comparison of an anglophone community in Quebec and a francophone community in Prince Edward Island in more peripheral locations where each were disadvantaged, see Maurice Beaudin, Rene Boudreau, and George De Benedetti, *The Socio-economic Vitality of Official-Language Communities*, Heritage Canada Catalogue No. CH3-2/2-1996E.

81 For a thorough and readable review of languages and language policies in Canada and its regional variations, see John Edwards (ed.), *Language in Canada* (Cambridge: Cambridge University Press, 1998).

82 Hubert Guindon, "The Modernization of Quebec and the Legitimacy of the Canadian State," *Canadian Review of Sociology and Anthropology* 15(1978): 227–45.

83 Richard Joy, *Languages in Conflict: The Canadian Experience* (Toronto: McClelland and Stewart, 1972).

84 Jean Dumas, Report of the Demographic Situation 1987, Statistics Canada Catalogue 91-209E, 115, and Joy's updated study *Canada's Official Languages: The Progress of Bilingualism*.

85 For a good review of this trend, see Roderic P. Beaujot, "The Decline of Official Language Minorities in Quebec and English Canada," *Canadian Journal of Sociology* 7(1982): 367–89.

86 Statistics Canada, *The Daily*, December 2, 1997.

87 Louise Marmen and Jean-Pierre Corbeil, *Languages In Canada*, 1996 Census, Catalogue #CH3-2-8/1999, Table 4.6.

88 Stacy Churchill, *Official Languages in Canada: Changing the Language Landscape*, Heritage Canada Catalogue CA3-2-7/1998, Table 4.

89 Ronald Wardhaugh, *Language and Nationhood*, 54–55. For a discussion of issues in official language education in schools, see Heritage Canada, *The Canadian Experience in the Teaching of Official Languages*, Catalogue No. S53-33/1996E.

90 Olive Patricia Dickason, *Canada's First Nations: A History of Founding Peoples from Earliest Times* (Toronto: McClelland and Stewart, 1992).

91 Victor Valentine distinguishes between the "accommodation" typical of the pre-Confederation period between Native people and whites, and the "domination" typical of the post-Confederation era. "Native Peoples and Canadian Society: A Profile of Issues and Trends," in R. Breton, J.G. Reitz, and V.F. Valentine, *Cultural Boundaries and the Cohesion of Canada* (Montreal: Institute for Research on Public Policy, 1980), 71–78.

92 Rita M. Bienvenue, "Colonial Status: The Case of Canadian Indians," in Bienvenue and Goldstein, *Ethnicity and Ethnic Relations in Canada*, 2nd ed., 199–214.

93 Harley Dickinson and Terry Wotherspoon, "From Assimilation to Self-Government," in Vic Sazewitch, ed., *Deconstructing a Nation*, 405–21.

94 Sally M. Weaver, "The Status of Indian Women," in Jean L. Elliot, *Two Nations: Many Cultures,* 2nd ed., 56–79.

95 J. Rick Ponting, "The Socio-Demographic Picture," in his *First Nations in Canada: Perspectives on Opportunity, Empowerment, and Self-Determination* (Toronto: McGraw-Hill Ryerson, 1997), 69.

96 D. Bruce Sealey and Antoine S. Lussier, *The Métis: Canada's Forgotten People* (Winnipeg: Pemmican Publications, 1975); and also their *The Other Natives: The-Les Métis* (Winnipeg: Manitoba Métis Federation Press, 1978).

97 G.F.G. Stanley, *The Birth of Western Canada: A History of the Riel Rebellion* (Toronto: University of Toronto Press, 1978).

98   Norbert Robitaille and Robert Choiniere, *An Overview of Demographic and Socio-Economic Conditions of the Inuit in Canada* (Ottawa: Indian and Northern AVairs Canada, 1985).

99 Statistics Canada, *The Daily*, January 13, 1998.

100 Jean-Philippe Chartrand, "Survival and Adaptation of the Inuit Ethnic Identity: The Importance of Inuktitut," in Bruce Alden Cox, ed., *Native People Native Lands* (Ottawa: Carleton University Press, 1988), chap. 18. See also James S. Frideres, *Aboriginal Peoples in Canada*, Chapter 12.

101 George Manuel and Michael Posluns, *The Fourth World: An Indian Reality* (New York: Free Press, 1974).

102 The relationship between Native policy and capitalist requirements is discussed in Terry Wotherspoon and Vic Satzewich, *First Nations: Race, Class, and Gender Relations* (Scarborough: Nelson, 1993).

103 H.B. Hawthorn, *A Survey of Contemporary Indians of Canada* (Ottawa: Indian Affairs Branch, 1966–67).

104 For a good discussion of the transitions which DIAND has made and the problems of a bureaucratic administration, see J. Rick Ponting, "Relations Between Bands and the Department of Indian Affairs: A Case of Internal Colonialism?" in J.R. Ponting, ed., *Arduous Journey: Canadian Indians and Decolonization* (Toronto: McClelland and Stewart, 1986), chap. 3. This issue of how the federal government attempts to "administer" Indian Affairs is also discussed in J. Rick Ponting and Roger Gibbins, *Out of Irrelevance: A Socio-Political Introduction to Indian Affairs in Canada* (Toronto: Butterworths, 1980); and Leroy Little Bear, Menno Boldt, and J. Anthony Long, eds., *Pathways to Self-Determination: Canadian Indians and the Canadian State* (Toronto: University of Toronto Press, 1984). See also Noel Dyck, *What is the Indian 'Problem'? Tutelage and Resistance in Canadian Indian Administration* (St. Johns: Institute of Social and Economic Research, 1991).

105 For a discussion of the issue of Native rights and self-determination, see Donald Purich, *Our Land: Native Rights in Canada* (Toronto: James Lorimer, 1986); Menno Boldt and J. Anthony

Long, eds., *The Quest for Justice: Aboriginal Peoples and Aboriginal Rights* (Toronto: University of Toronto Press, 1985); and Frank Cassidy, ed., *Aboriginal Self-Determination* (Toronto: Institute For Research On Public Policy, 1991).

106 These points are made by Roger Gibbins and J. Rick Ponting, "An Assessment of the Probable Impact of Aboriginal Self-Government in Canada," in Alan Cairns and Cynthia Williams, eds., *The Politics of Gender, Ethnicity and Language in Canada* (Toronto: University of Toronto Press, 1986), 177–78.

107 Bruce Alden Cox, "Changing Perceptions of Industrial Development in the North," in his *Native People Native Lands*, chap. 16.

108 James S. Frideres, *Aboriginal Peoples in Canada*, chap. 8.

109 James B. Waldram, "Canada's 'Indian Problem' And the Indian's 'Canada Problem,'" in Les Samuelson, ed., *Power and Resistance: Critical Thinking about Canadian Social Issues* (Halifax: Fernwood, 1994), 53–70; and David C. Hawkes, ed., *Aboriginal Peoples and Government Responsibility: Exploring Federal and Provincial Roles* (Ottawa: Carleton University Press, 1988).

110 Royal Commission on Aboriginal Peoples, *The Right of Aboriginal Self-Government: a Commentary*. Ottawa, February 13, 1992. For a different approach to the Royal Proclamation of 1763, see Menno Boldt, *Surviving as Indians: The Challenge of Self-Government* (Toronto: University of Toronto Press, 1993), chap. 1.

111 Royal Commission on Aboriginal Peoples, *Partners In Confederation: Aboriginal Peoples, Self-Government, and the Constitution*, Ottawa: 1993.

112 A good source dealing with initiatives in economic development is Royal Commission on Aboriginal Peoples, *Sharing The Harvest: The Road to Self-Reliance*, Ottawa, 1993.

113 The paradoxical notions of empowerment and disempowerment are discussed in J. Rick Ponting, "An Overview Of First Nations' Empowerment And Disempowerment," *First Nations in Canada*, Chapter 5.

114 All of the national opinion surveys are reviewed in J. Rick Ponting and Jerilynn Kiely, "Disempowerment: "Justice, Racism, and Public Opinion", in Ponting, *First Nations in Canada*, 174–185.

115 James S. Frideres found that media coverage of the Royal Commission on Aboriginal Peoples was quite weak and did not raise Aboriginal-non-Aboriginal relations to a higher level of public awareness. However, he argues that the Royal Commission did capture the imagination of Aboriginal peoples as a vital opportunity to bring about change. "The Royal Commission On Aboriginal Peoples: The Route To Self-Government?," *Canadian Journal of Native Studies* 16(20)1996:247–266.

116 For a good overview of the multiculturalism policy, its diverse meanings and political purposes, see Peter Li, "The Multiculturalism Debate," in Peter S. Li (ed.), *Race and Ethnic Relations in Canada*, Second Edition, 148–177.

117 D.H. Clairmont and F.C. Wien, "Race Relations in Canada," in Jay E. Goldstein and Rita Bienvenue, eds., *Ethnicity and Ethnic Relations in Canada* (Toronto: Butterworths, 1980), 313–15.

118 Jeffrey G. Reitz and Raymond Breton, *The Illusion of Difference: Realities of Ethnicity in Canada and the United States* (Toronto: C.D. Howe Institute, 1994).

119 Howard Palmer, *Patterns of Prejudice: A History of Nativism in Alberta* (Toronto: McClelland and Stewart, 1982).

120 Jeffrey G. Reitz, The Survival of Ethnic Groups (Toronto: McGraw-Hill Ryerson, 1980), and Morton Weinfeld, "Ethnic Assimilation and the Retention of Ethnic Cultures," in Berry and Laponce, *Ethnicity and Culture in Canada*, 238–266.

121 Jean Burnet, "Multiculturalism 10 Years Later," in Jean L. Elliott, ed., *Two Nations: Many Cultures*, 2nd ed., 239.

122 David R. Hughes and Evelyn Kallen, *The Anatomy of Racism: Canadian Dimensions* (Montreal: Harvest House, 1974), 190–91.

123 Frances Henry and Carol Tator, "State Policy And Practices As Racialized discourse: Multiculturalism, The Charter, And Employment Equity," In Peter Li, *Race and Ethnic Relations in Canada*, Second Edition, 95–98.

124 Lance W. Roberts and Rodney A. Clifton, "Explaining the Ideology of Canadian Multiculturalism," *Canadian Public Policy* 8(1982): 88–94; and Raymond Breton, "The Structure Of Relationships Between Ethnic Collectivities" in Driedger, ed., *The Canadian Ethnic Mosaic*, 60–61.

125 Wsvolod W. Isajiw, "Olga in Wonderland: Ethnicity in a Technological Society," in Dreidger, ed., *The Canadian Ethnic Mosaic*, 29–39.

126 Morton Weinfeld, "Myth and Reality in the Canadian Mosaic: Avective Ethnicity," in Bienvenue and Goldstein, *Ethnicity and Ethnic Relations in Canada*, 65–86.

127 Laverne Lewycky, "Multiculturalism In The 1990's And Into The 21st Century," in Vic Satzewich, ed., *Deconstructing a Nation: Immigration, Multiculturalism, and Racism in 90's Canada*, 372–75; Yvonne Hebert, "Citizenship Education: Towards a Pedagogy of Social Participation and Identity Formation," Canadian Ethnic Studies 29(2)1997:82–96.

128 Sheila M. Croucher, "Constructing The Image Of Ethnic Harmony In Toronto, Canada: The Politics Of Problem Definition And Non-definition," *Urban Affairs Review* 32(1997):319–347.

129 Danielle Juteau, "The Sociology Of Ethno-National Relations In Quebec," in Vic Satzewich, ed., *Deconstructing a Nation: Immigration, Multiculturalism, and Racism in 90's Canada*, 323–41.

130 For an analysis of criticisms of multiculturalism, see Yasmeen Abu-Laban and Daiva Stasiulis, "Ethnic Pluralism Under Siege: Popular And Partisan Opposition To Multiculturalism," *Canadian Public Policy* 18(1992): 365–86; and Augie Fleras and Jean Leonard Elliott, *Multiculturalism in Canada: The Challenge of Diversity* (Scarborough: Nelson, 1992), 131–44.

131 Reginald W. Bibby, *Mosaic Madness: The Poverty and Potential of Life in Canada* (Toronto: Stoddart, 1990), 104.

132 Vic Satzewich, "Race Relations Or Racism: Unravelling the New Race Discourse In Canada," in Les Samuelson, ed., *Power and Resistance: Critical Thinking about Canadian Social Issues*, 39–51.

133 Yasmeen Abu-Laban, "Welcome/STAY OUT: The Contradiction Of Canadian Integration And Immigration Policies At The Millennium," *Canadian Ethnic Studies* 30(3)1998:190–211. For a critique of the immigration policy that stresses entrance requirements more than adaptive strategies, see Lorne Foster, *Turnstile Immigration: Social Order and Social Justice in Canada* (Toronto: Thompson, 1998).

134 Social incorporation is meant to provide an alternative to assumptions about inevitable assimilation while still allowing for ethnic vitality. Wsevolod W. Isajiw, "On The Concept And Theory Of Social Incorporation," in W.W. Isajiw (ed.), *Multiculturalism in North America and Europe* (Toronto: Canadian Scholars Press, 1997), 79–102.

135 Raymond Breton, "Intergroup Competition In The Symbolic Construction Of Canadian Society," in Peter S. Li, *Race and Ethnic Relations in Canada*, Second Edition, 291–310.

WEBLINKS

www.crr.ca

The Canadian Race Relations Foundation's Web site provides visitors with documentation of racism in Canada as well as links to other relevant sites.

www.magenta.nl

The Crosspoint Anti-Racism home page is one of the Internet's biggest links in the field of human rights, anti-racism, refugees, etc.

www.pch.gc.ca/offlangoff/english/index.html

The Government of Canada has developed this site to inform the public about planned activities and create a discussion venue as part of the Year of la Francophonie (March 1999-2000) to celebrate Canada's French Canadian Heritage.

www.afn.ca

The Assembly of First Nations is a First Nations institution that brings together government leaders to devise common strategies on collective issues, and to present the views of various First Nations in such areas as Aboriginal and treaty rights, environment, economic development, education, housing, health, social services, and land claims.

THE QUESTION
OF UNIQUENESS

In addition to the things which could be done anywhere to add to the knowledge of human societies, what are the features of Canadian life to which the "more-so" principle might apply—those things which are highlighted somewhat in Canadian life, and from which one might learn something more about some aspect of human society than one would elsewhere.

—Everett C. Hughes, an American analyst of social change in Quebec (1940s), suggesting a distinctive thrust for Canadian researchers.

As you read through this book, you may think that Canadian society is surely unique in having so many distinctive features. This perception is particularly likely for people who live in Canada, and who are caught up in the internal struggles of Canada's societal problems, or who are trying to resolve them as if they had never been experienced anywhere before. The object of this chapter is to show that Canada's situation is not as uncommon as we might think, and to allow us to learn more about Canadian society by comparing it with other societies.

Such comparisons are important because, while each society is unique and no two societies are identical, there is a tendency to assume that the society under review has few parallels elsewhere. A comparative analysis helps us to see that there are other societies with similar problems for which different solutions have been found. For those studying Canadian society from the outside, it is also important to see linkages to other societies with which they may be familiar through the media or personal experience. In sum, a comparative focus enables us to place a society in a global context which sharpens our ability to identify differences and similarities. Not only are our horizons broadened, but we are able to understand the dynamics of Canadian society in a new way.

No attempt is made in this chapter to exhaustively detail the many ways in which Canadian society contrasts with other societies. In fact, some of the contrasts will remain implicit or weakly developed because of space limitations. Yet it is possible to identify some of the characteristic features of Canadian society, to look for parallels in other societies, and to outline some of their significance and meaning in that social context.

We have already seen that the nature of Canada's land surface, settlement history, population distribution, and regional differences has produced a society with its own character. We have also noted that variables such as social class, ethnicity, language, religion, and occupation add a dynamic to these formative features. What has been the experience of other societies where similar factors are present? How unique is Canadian society? In this chapter, our comparisons will be developed by focusing on distinctive Canadian features pertaining to demographic distribution, value differences, immigration, ethnic regionalism, and language. While we could examine societies which are strikingly different from Canadian society (e.g., Brazil, India), most of the comparisons will be drawn from societies which have a level of development similar to Canada's, and where comparisons are frequently made. Those societies include the United States, Australia, the United Kingdom, and selected countries in Europe.

DISTINCTIVE CANADIAN FEATURE:
Large land surface and relatively small population.

Comparison: The Global Context

Russia has the largest land surface of any country in the world. Canada is second, though it is only slightly bigger in area than China and the United States, and somewhat bigger still in territorial size than Brazil and Australia, which make up the world's other largest countries (see Table 6.1). Brazil is approximately 85% the size of Canada, and Australia has three-quarters of the land surface of Canada.

Population size, however, tells us a different story. China's population is the largest by far, followed by the population of India. While Canada has one of the largest land surfaces in the world, comparatively, it has a very small population. Industrialized countries such as France, Germany, and the United Kingdom have more than double Canada's total population located in a territory less than five percent of Canada's total land area. Mexico has almost three times Canada's population in a territory only one-fifth as large. Japan has less than four percent of the territory Canada has, but a population almost five times as large. India's territory is one-third the size of Canada's even though it has a population more than 32 times larger.

The best measure of these national differences is expressed in the population density per square kilometre. Canada has the most in common with Australia, where a smaller population and smaller land size yields a density similar to Canada's. The former Soviet Union,

Brazil, and Argentina also have rather low densities in spite of large land surfaces, suggesting that these countries also have significant portions of their territory which are uninhabited due to an inhospitable climate or terrain. It is interesting to note that even though North Korea, Iran, and the Philippines have populations which are virtually the same, their considerably smaller land surfaces result in these countries having a population density which is much higher than Canada's.

Canada is one of few countries with a large land surface and a low population density. In this characteristic, Canada most closely resembles Australia, which has one of the world's larger territories (though smaller than Canada's), and a population about three-fifths the size. China and the United States are close to Canada in total land area, but their population densities are much higher. So the evidence makes it clear that Canada is somewhat distinctive in terms of both its land size and population density.

DISTINCTIVE CANADIAN FEATURE:
Uneven distribution of the population.

Comparison: Australia

Few countries have their population evenly dispersed throughout their territory. Mountains and forests or cities and jobs combine to either repel or attract population. What is particu-

TABLE 6.1	Population Size, Land Area, and Density for Selected Countries, 1997		
Country	Population (000)	Surface Area (km^2)	Density Person/km^2
Canada	27 297	9 970 610	3
Russia	147 022	17 075 400	9
China	1 160 045	9 596 961	128
United States	248 710	9 363 520	28
Brazil	146 825	8 547 403	18
Australia	16 851	7 741 220	2
India	846 302	3 287 590	285
Argentina	32 616	2 780 400	13
Greenland	49	2 175 600	0
Mexico	81 250	1 958 201	49
Iran	55 837	1 633 188	37
Nigeria	88 992	923 768	125
France	56 634	551 500	106
Germany	77 783	356 733	230
United Kingdom	56 352	244 100	241
North Korea	44 609	99 268	459
Philippines	68 617	300 000	240
Japan	125 570	377 829	333

Source: Compiled from *United Nations Demographic Yearbook*, 1997, Table 3, pp. 134–138.

larly unique in Canada's case is that while possessing such a large territory, the relatively small population to begin with is highly concentrated in a single area, the Golden Triangle, with much of the remaining population huddled at the country's southern extremities. Here again, Canada can be compared with Australia.

Figure 6.1 reveals that the population of Australia is unevenly dispersed throughout its territory. Just as Canada has its Golden Triangle of high population concentration in southern Ontario and southern Quebec, so Australia has its own population concentration in the southeast corner, south of a line from Adelaide to Sydney. Approximately two-thirds of the total population of Australia lives in this relatively small geographic area. The remaining population concentrations are found along the east and southwest coasts with only a small scattered population in inland locations.

One of the consequences of this uneven population distribution is that about 60% of the total population of Australia is found in two states, Victoria and New South Wales (compare with Ontario and Quebec whose percentage of Canada's total population is very similar). Victoria and New South Wales are also the two states where the two largest cities

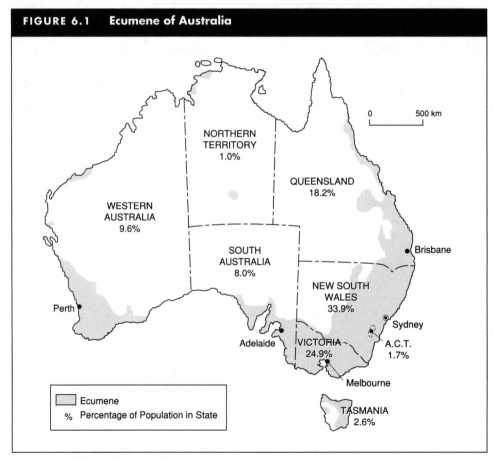

FIGURE 6.1   Ecumene of Australia

Source: Computed from *Yearbook Australia 1998* (Canberra: Australian Bureau of Statistics).

are located, namely Sydney at 3.9 million, and Melbourne at 3.3 million people.[1] The surpassingly large size of these two cities (about 60% of the population of all Australia) in relation to other cities within Australia compares to the position of Toronto and Montreal in Canada. In addition, Brisbane, Perth, and Adelaide, which all have populations around one million residents, make up the other major metropolitan cities of Australia. All of these cities named above are the capital cities for their states, and are the primary destinations for rural–urban and international migrants.

Uneven population distribution means that the dominant states will be those with large urban metropolitan populations while those states with smaller urban centres and with large uninhabited space will have less power. Indeed, political and economic power is concentrated in the southeastern states (meaning New South Wales and Victoria) to the chagrin of Queenslanders (nicknamed "banana benders") and Western Australians (nicknamed "sandgropers").

As a consequence of the vast uninhabited territory separating the southeastern states from the population centres of Western Australia, and in view of the fact that the industrial heartland of Australia is located in the two southeastern states, there has persisted a nagging belief in Western Australia that this imbalance is ultimately responsible for the state's arrested development and hinterland position. Just as Western Canada had its own protest movements in the twenties and thirties, so too did Western Australia.[2] However, in Western Australia, the regional rebellion culminated in a vote in 1933 to secede from Australia. Although the vote was 2:1 in favour of secession, it was never actually carried out. Given continued perceptions about lack of power for the state within Australian federalism, it was not surprising that protest (and even secession) was considered again in the mid-70s when the federal government attempted to centralize its control of natural resources, which Western Australia had in abundance.

In sum, demographic imbalances and geographic factors have combined with other catalysts to provoke a continuing sense of marginality, alienation, and powerlessness in Western Australia. This situation is directly comparable to the role of the Canadian Shield in distancing the industrial heartland of Canada from the West. While the historical details are somewhat different, the structure and dynamics of regional relations within Australian society are very similar. Population imbalances may not be the cause, but they intensify regional conflicts within the society.

Canada has no parallel to the ACT (Australian Capital Territory), which includes the urban centre of Canberra as a small territory similar to the District of Columbia which contains the city of Washington in the United States. On the other hand, the lower level of metropolitan urbanization in Tasmania (Table 6.2) is somewhat like that of the Atlantic provinces in Canada with less employment diversity and opportunity. The weakly populated Northern Territory (one percent of the total population) also has some parallels with the Northwest Territories in Canada with large numbers of Aboriginal peoples and large tracts of uninhabitable land (with the exception that the climate is reversed—hot desert in Australia and cold tundra in Canada).

Canada has a problem with poor soil or poor growing conditions which result from the cold climate in much but not all of its territory. The problem in Australia is that of aridity in some locations, and a tropical rainy climate in other areas. Consequently, just as most of the population of Canada is located at the southern extremities of the country where the climate is more moderate, so the population of Australia clusters along the more temperate south and east coasts. In any event, large portions of the land in both countries are virtually uninhabited. These vast hinterlands, however, have been valued for their resources which are exported to urban centres, or to other countries. As a result, the economies of these regions are drawn into the vagaries of market and price instabilities. Many of the metropolis–hinterland relationships which are developing in Australia are similar to those relationships experienced in Canada.[3]

By way of further contrast, it is interesting to note that with perhaps the exception of the Native or Aboriginal population, the higher level of economic development in Canada and Australia produces much less of a cleavage between rural and urban peoples than is found in a country like Brazil.[4] In that country there is a great disparity between the more modern affluent sector, and the majority of poor people who are primarily rural (though some are also urban poor as well). The technology gap between the traditional society and the more modern sector produces deeper cleavages in Brazil because large portions of the population are excluded from participation in economic growth.

As we will see later, there are other reasons to compare Australia with Canada but the uneven distribution of the population over a large territory that is relatively uninhabited provides many points of similarity between the two societies.

DISTINCTIVE CANADIAN FEATURE: The continued consolidation of central Canadian dominance (especially Ontario).

Comparison: The United States

We have already seen how the southeast of Australia plays an urban economic dominant role in that country much like the Golden Triangle in Canada. Now we will look to the United States for an illustration of how an original dominance of the northeast has been changed in recent years to significant regional dispersal throughout the country

The European settlement of North America meant that the natural internal movement of population on the continent would be from east to west. By the end of World War II, a pattern was clearly established which resulted in the largest population concentrations being located in the Northeastern states, and extending up into Ontario and Quebec. As the centre of industrialization, the New England states had attracted both immigrants and internal migrants to their growing cities. Other industrial cities in the North such as Detroit, Cleveland, and Chicago attracted white rural populations, who had been pushed off the land by the mechanization of agriculture, and Southern black people, who began to seek employment opportunities in Northern cities. With the exception of black migration from the South, Toronto and Montreal experienced the same kind of growth from rural–urban population shifts.

While the dynamics of industrial growth meant that internal migration was clearly in the direction of the northern cities in the United States, the gradual movement of population to the West Coast (cities such as Seattle, San Francisco, and Los Angeles) was also occurring. The geographic centre of the population had been steadily moving westward from Maryland in 1790, to Indiana by 1900, to Illinois in 1960, and still further westward past St. Louis, Missouri by 1990.[5] Most of this shift was due to an internal redistribution of the population, rather than an influx of new residents. By the 1970s, it became clear that the Northeastern region was losing its growth dynamic; its share of the national population declined from 26% in 1950 to 19% by 1997. Even the Midwest declined from 29% in 1960 to 23% in 1997. On the other hand, the Western region had increased its share of the population from 13% to 22%, and the South grew from 31% to 35% over the same period.[6]

With the exception of New York, which always experiences large numerical increases because of its large population, the highest population increases were in the states of California, Texas, and Florida. Essentially the population seemed to be moving from areas of high density such as the Northeast (315 persons per square mile), to areas of low density such as the West (31 persons per square mile).

A similar long-term movement to the West has also been occurring in Canada, particularly in British Columbia, and more recently again to Alberta. It might be argued that Canadians have also been caught up in the general continental population shift to the American South and Southwest, whether as temporary or semi-permanent migrants. What makes Canada different, however, is that the redistribution of population within the country has not as yet had any significant effect on the redistribution of power. One exception to this statement might be the shift away from the earlier industrialization of the Atlantic region to central Canada, noted in Chapter Four. However, southern Ontario in particular,

California: "The Promised Land"

The California of the last two decades is markedly different from the California of the 1960s when most of the migration was from the US Midwest and to an extent from the Eastern seaboard. Now California has become the nation's port of entry for global immigration.

The immigration flows into the United States in the twenty-four year period from 1971 to 1995 have exceeded the 18 million immigrants admitted in the great migration from 1900–1924. Whereas Europe was the dominant source area in the earlier period, Asia and Latin America now produce over 80% of all immigrants and include many illegal migrants.

California grew primarily through internal migration until the last two decades. More than 30 countries each have sent 10 000 immigrants or more to California in the last decade alone. California receives three times as many immigrants as New York, the next largest destination. More than one-fifth of all foreign-born residents in the whole United States live in California. The Latin American originating population make up over half of all foreign born in the state. It is expected that the population of non-Hispanic whites in the state will be a minority around the turn of the century. This change has been relatively sudden; in 1960, California was 90% non-Hispanic white.

Immigrants move to big cities where there are existing immigrant communities. Over 40% of all immigrants to California settle in Los Angeles with another 20% in the Bay area. About one-third of the California population speak a language other than English at home. About one quarter of students in school have limited English proficiency.

This very different ethnic and racial mix raises major questions about assimilation and whether California is a mirror for major changes to be faced by the United States as a whole. While some celebrate this diversity, others fear a balkanization of society into enclaves due to inequalities and social tensions.

Source: William A.V. Clark, *The California Cauldron* (New York: Guilford Press, 1998). See also A. Portes and R. Rumbaut, *Immigrant America: A Portrait* (Berkeley: University Of California Press, 1996).

with an already substantial population at the beginning of the decade, was the single most important growth point in Canada in the 1980s. So Canada has been unlike the United States in that the movement away from the "old" centres of industrial strength has not occurred, instead, growth has intensified in those locations.

One explanation treats the redistribution of population in the United States as a symptom of the redistribution of economic and political power in that country.[7] It is argued that the Southern Rim (that area south of a line drawn from the Carolinas to California) challenged the Eastern economic establishment through agribusiness, defence production, advanced technology, oil and gas production, real estate, construction, tourism, and leisure. Consequently, many cities experienced remarkable growth. The population of Houston, for example, increased from a paltry 385 000 residents in 1945 to 2.7 million in 1980, and this story was repeated in many other Southern Rim cities such as Ft. Lauderdale, Austin, and Phoenix. Instead of relying on secondary industries in manufacturing such as are found in the Northeast, Southern Rim communities encouraged tertiary, service industries (such as electronics) and quaternary, leisure-oriented industries. These initiatives provided new employment opportunities in the Southern Rim, and reduced the economic strength of the Northeast. Some have argued that this power shift has been exaggerated, in spite of the developments in the American South.[8] The truth, though, is that the South has penetrated the political and economic mainstream in a manner which has changed the nature of regional relationships.

In spite of the slow redistribution of the population westward in Canada, there is little evidence that any significant power shift is occurring. The rapid growth of Edmonton and Calgary in the 1970s actually reversed itself in the early 1980s, as their growth was tied directly to the exploitation of oil and gas. The efforts at greater industrial diversification in Alberta (e.g., the establishment of an electronics industry) had only marginal success in the 1980s but had increasing success in the 1990s. Similarly in British Columbia, a coastal climate and transportation base has increased Vancouver's importance and industrial viability, but most of this growth has occurred in the lower mainland with modest growth in interior cities such as Kelowna or Penticton. In sum, if there have been some important shifts of both population and technology away from (or in competition with) the Northeast in the United States, there seems little evidence that any substantial shift of power has occurred in Canada. In fact, southern Ontario in particular appears to have consolidated its position as the centre of economic power.

If the United States has experienced a redistribution of its economic activity to new urban nodes, Canada has had only limited success in doing so. With the comparative decline of Montreal,[9] Toronto and southern Ontario have become even more of a population magnet.

DISTINCTIVE CANADIAN FEATURE: In spite of sharing a continent with the United States, Canadians struggle to explain how and why they are different.

Comparison: The United States

Canada shares with the United States the experience of being a colonial outpost of European empires. Louis Hartz has proposed a *fragment theory* which suggests that these new societies were founded as fragments of European culture and ideology.[10] In his view, contemporary differences between societies in the New World can be traced at least partially to the sponsoring society. While many European societies each contained divergent ideologies such as conservatism, liberalism, or socialism, the societies of the New World tended to be constructed on only one aspect or fragment of the European political culture. Therefore, Hartz argued, the society of New France (French Canada) was established as a fragment of conservative feudal French society while English-America was a much more liberal bourgeois fragment of England.

On one hand, this kind of analysis implies that English Canada and the United States should be very similar. McRae has argued that the conservative French fragment became entrenched with the British conquest in 1759, when the entrepreneurial spirit was removed from Quebec and the Catholic church took over as the guardian of traditional values and social life.[11] On the other hand, the American War of Independence in 1776 also demonstrated the failure of the liberal English fragment to claim the entire continent. At the same time, however, neither Quebec nor what is now English Canada supported the American rebellion, and this rejection of the independence movement reasserted Old World loyalties and ideologies in Canada, which established the basis for essential differences between Canadian and American society.

Perhaps the most significant factor in the rejection of independence by the northern part of the continent was the migration of the Loyalists from the United States to Canada. These Loyalists were persons who wanted to retain British ties. It is estimated that between 30 000 and 60 000 Loyalists arrived in Canada around the time of the American rebellion, and

---

REAL PEOPLE 6

Canadian-American Differences

Banff, Alberta. A summer tourist.

"Hey, these Canadian Rockies are cool. I'm from Colorado and I thought Rockies were Rockies, but the jagged peaks they have up here make the Rockies so much more impressive.

Can't figure it out though. Enjoyed the scenery on the drive up here and Canada seems just like the States, you know, the people, McDonalds and all that. The only thing that bugs me is that they were trying to make me change my money—you know that coloured paper you have up here. I went into one store today and one owner said he just wouldn't take my US money. He said he was proud to be Canadian and that I should get my money changed. Obviously he does not know how business works 'cause he was throwing away a sale.

Then he told me that he had been visiting in San Diego and they sure did not take Canadian money. They even gave him a hard time with Canadian dollar travellers cheques. So he vowed that he would never take US money in Canada. But you know, we're just up here for a few days so it hardly pays to go through all that hassle.

I like Canada because it is just like the United States. But it is also different and I can't say what it is or why. Maybe it's just the different money. I don't know."

Question To Consider: Why are people surprised that Canada and the United States are so similar and yet perplexed because they are different?

prior to this Canada had only about 15 000 anglophone residents in all.[12] Consequently, it becomes clear that in many ways, English Canada emerged as a direct consequence of the American Revolution.

Bell and Tepperman have argued that the irony of the Loyalists' position was that, while they rejected American republicanism, they remained deeply affected by their American experience. *Loyalists* were "anti-American Yankees," creating a "myth" about being British, and embracing a "peculiar form of coat-tails imperialism."[13] Caught between the societal worlds of the United States and Britain, Canada took up the struggle of both retaining British traditions and creating national distinctiveness in a North American environment. The context in which this took place, however, is critical. The American Revolution, and later the War of 1812 in which British forces blocked attempts by American invading forces to end British colonial rule on the continent, both served as *formative events* to delineate basic differences between the two societies.

If the United States was born of revolution, then Canada was born of *counter-revolution*. Revolution had meant breaking ties with the mother country, as the United States did with Britain; counter-revolution meant retaining those ties. The effect of these differences between the two societies has been illustrated in two major ways: settlement of the frontiers, and the formation of basic values.

The *frontier comparisons* have been made by S.D. Clark.[14] Clark felt that both societies had the common experience of settling a series of frontiers in the pursuit of staples. While there may have been similarities in the characteristic features of rugged individualism and nontraditional behaviour, the Canadian frontiers were different in that they were more stable and less disorganized because of the order created by traditional and organized authority. This traditional authority included a military police force (e.g., Northwest Mounted Police), a privileged upper class, large commercial organization (e.g., The Hudson's Bay Company), and representatives of the church (e.g., Anglican and Catholic), who provided greater social stability as outposts of empire controls. The heroes of American frontier settlement, on the other hand, were individualists who encountered the vagaries of disorder because the symbols of law and order did not precede settlement. People like Davey Crockett and Daniel Boone, and the appointed or elected sheriff, are not part of Canadian history, because the institutions of empire were established in advance of settlement and created different traditions and expectations. Therefore, Canadian frontiers reflected empire controls rather than independence and experimentation, and these controls provided a very different foundation for Canadian society.

The argument about differences in basic *values* has been made by S.M. Lipset who concluded that Canada's counter-revolutionary tradition has made that society much more conservative and traditional than American society.[15] His thesis contrasts the two societies using four dichotomous variables indicating that Canada is more elitist, ascriptive, particularist, and collectivity-oriented, whereas the United States is more egalitarian, achievement-oriented, universalist, and self-oriented. The ideology of the United States is replete with egalitarian themes where free enterprise, individualism, and upward mobility through personal achievement, reign supreme. In comparison, Lipset argued, Canada has tended to follow the British pattern of values based on an aristocratic background of privilege, and a more hardened class structure.

What evidence did Lipset use to build his case? He noted that in Canada there was less equality of opportunity through the educational system, and he gathered evidence to suggest that lower levels of educational attainment were good indicators of reduced opportunity in

RESEARCH CLIP 6.1	**Values: Comparing Canadians with Americans and Europeans**

- Canadians show less pride in country than Americans but both groups are considerably higher than Europeans on this dimension. The source of this national pride for Americans develops from scientific achievements and belief in their political system whereas for Canadians, national pride emerges from the health and welfare system.
- The image of Canadians being conformist is not accurate as the evidence is that in the twelve advanced industrial countries considered, Canadians were among the most protest-oriented in their willingness to participate in demonstrations, petitions, and new movements.
- Support for free market and meritocratic principles (e.g., the work ethic) is higher in both Canada and the United States than in Europe.
- Indicators of personal religiosity such as church attendance or the importance of God in one's life are in general much higher in the United States.
- On indicators of moral permissiveness (homosexuality, divorce, euthanasia), Canadians are significantly more permissive than Americans, and the changes that occurred on these dimensions from 1981–1990 were much more rapid in Canada than in the United States.

- **Conclusion:** In some ways, Canadians and Americans hold values that are unique (North American exceptionalsim) in comparison to Europeans, and in other ways Canadians and Americans are clearly different from each other.

Note: Conclusions for this study were based on surveys in 1981 and 1990 in 12 advanced industrial countries in Europe and North America.

Source: Neil Nevitte, *The Decline of Deference.* Peterborough, Broadview Press, 1996.

Canada. He noted that greater acceptance of government participation in the economy indicated that Canada was more collectivist than the United States, where individualist free enterprise ideas were staunchly defended. Government involvement in broadcasting and transportation, for example, and the traditional strength of the Roman Catholic and Anglican church in Canada were viewed as part of a general pattern to reinforce traditional community values and to suppress excesses of individualism. Lipset also noted the greater respect for law and order in Canada, as evidenced by a lower ratio of policemen and lawyers to population, and indicated that Canada possessed a more stable traditional order. In contrast, higher crime and divorce rates in the United States indicated less respect for traditional order.

Lipset's thesis has generated considerable controversy and debate.[16] In the first place, Lipset depended on data from the 1950s, and Canada has undergone considerable changes since that time, particularly in education, and in the growth of divorce and crime rates. Secondly, it is questionable whether any of the data he used really identify dominant societal values. For example, a case can be made that Canada is more (rather than less) egalitarian than the United States. Inequalities between races, and greater gaps between wealthy and poor Americans serve to support this case. In fact, the British working class heritage in Canada puts greater value on equality of living standards and income than on competitive achievement. Third, Canada has produced numerous reform movements which have brought about innovations in medical care, creative third-party politics, and institutional change. Social democratic ideas, such as these listed above, have been tolerated to a much greater extent in Canada than in the United States.

Lipset's Revision

Given recent developments such as free trade (which has linked the economies of the two countries more clearly) and the Charter of Rights and its emphasis on individual rights (which conceivably makes Canada more like the United States), Lipset has recently returned to the question of what distinguishes the two societies. He sees convergence and change on a variety of dimensions in both societies.[17] For example, the United States has become much more involved in state supported welfare (collectivism), and affirmative action programs have recognized the existence of disadvantaged groups within American society (group orientation, ascription). On the Canadian side, access to higher education has improved (achievement-orientation) and crime has increased (individualism).

Yet Lipset argues that the *historical events* (i.e., acceptance or rejection of the American Revolution) upon which the two societies were founded have established *values* and predispositions which continue their effect because they established basic *organizing principles* for the society. So even though Canada and the United States resemble each other more than any other society resembles either of them, value differences exist, but like trains on parallel railway tracks, they are a long way from where they started but they are still separated. Lipset concludes that Canada is more class-aware, elitist, law abiding, statist, and group-oriented whereas the United States "tends" in the opposite direction as a result of its primary emphasis on individualism. The fact that the United States has one of the weakest welfare support networks in the industrialized world; effectively has no socialist or social democratic party; has a relatively small percentage of its labour force in labour unions; and that judges and sheriffs are popularly elected, are examples of pieces of evidence he weaves together to prove his point.

Lipset's "interpretive essay" is intriguing and provocative. He has clearly made an effort to incorporate the changes which have taken place in both Canada and the United States since the 1950s. In some ways, the subtle air of American superiority or "exceptionalism" (his more recent term) is not quite as obvious because it is no longer possible to speak of Canada as a less developed nation. Yet the explanations for why these differences exist are less clear. Can everything be blamed on a single formative event without reduction to absurdity? Can values be specified for an entire nation as though all people embraced them, and are these values perhaps not ideals more than descriptions of reality? What structural explanations can be proposed for why these differences exist?

Lipset concludes by observing that whereas Canada once distinguished itself from American society with a right-wing critique (the US is too "vulgar," "materialistic," "individualist"), such differentiation now comes from the left (Canada as "less elitist," "more egalitarian," more "anti-imperialist").[18] Yet we have already seen that recent developments pertaining to globalization suggest that Canadians may increasingly be less concerned about this kind of differentiation. Value differences that may have existed in the past may not continue to exist. In fact, Nevitte's study concluded that since the 1980s, there has been an extraordinary shift in values in Canada in the same direction as values are shifting in other industrialized countries.[19] The sustained prosperity that these countries are experiencing has led to new post-materialist values in which deference to authority and confidence in

RESEARCH CLIP 6.2

Comparing the American "Melting Pot" with the Canadian "Mosaic"

The dominant metaphors used about ethnic diversity in the United States and Canada suggest that Canada is more tolerant of diversity whereas the United States works towards assimilation and erasing ethnic differences. Are these metaphors accurate descriptions of reality or are they myths?

This question is important because multiculturalism is official federal policy in Canada whereas in the United States, no such policy exists. Furthermore, the proportion of foreign-born in the population is twice as large in Canada as in the United States in spite of the fact that immigration into both societies has been heavy. In the United States, the dominant issue has been the incorporation of racial minorities and particularly blacks into the mainstream of society whereas in contrast, in Canada, the dominant issue has been the accommodation of anglophones and francophones.

What is the evidence of societal differences?

1. There is insufficient evidence that Canada is a society that values and encourages cultural diversity more than the United States, and certainly insufficient evidence that is strong enough to justify the differences implied by the metaphors. For example, only 20% of Americans think of the United States as a melting pot, and in reality more Americans (47%) cherish the ideal of cultural retention than Canadians (34%).

2. The multiculturalism discourse in Canada implies a higher degree of tolerance of diversity in Canada whereas in reality in both Canada and the United States, attitudes towards immigration suggests both a tolerance for diversity *and* a bias towards assimilation.

3. In the United States, assimilation is viewed as a dominant ideology against which the assertion of minority cultures is viewed as an individualist anti-establishment position. Such individualism is more highly valued in American ideology. In Canada, support for cultural retention is an establishment idea most highly favoured among those of the British origin group but highly opposed by the largest minority group (the French) who see multiculturalism as a threat to their own group's position.

4. There is no evidence of less discrimination in Canada and indeed blatant racism has been marginalized in both countries. But racial minorities are a larger proportion of the American population where incomes are considerably less.

5. While the evidence is that interest in ethnicity changes by the third generation so that it no longer is a dominant factor in shaping behaviour, the fact that Canada has a higher proportion of first- and second-generation immigrants than the United States increases the visibility of ethnicity in Canada at this time.

Source: Jeffrey G. Reitz and Raymond Breton, *The Illusion of Difference: Realities of Ethnicity in Canada and the United States* (Toronto: C.D. Howe Institute, 1994).

government and other institutions is waning. Not only does Canada not just follow the United States in this value shift, it is even leading the way. And certainly the adoption of more free market principles and the decline of government intervention in this time span has reduced barriers that formerly helped to sustain value differences.[20]

For most Canadians, such comparisons with the United States are part of everyday life, as residents attempt to grapple with the obvious similarities, yet remarkable (and subtle) differences between the two societies. While the counter-revolutionary thesis is helpful in articulating these differences, it is clear that explaining differences in values is exceedingly complex and resists simple generalizations. It is also difficult to specify how shifts in economic values are related to changing social and political values, and then to determine whether the type of value convergence that may be occurring actually does inevitably erase other national differences.

DISTINCTIVE CANADIAN FEATURE: For an immigrant society in a sparsely settled territory, in-migration and relations with Native groups are significant issues.

Comparison: Australia

Canada and Australia were both originally British colonies, and both countries have remained members of the British Commonwealth. Just as Canada as a nation came into being by an Act of the British Parliament in 1867, so Australia was created by the Commonwealth of Australia Constitution Act, passed somewhat later in 1900. This British sponsorship has affected many aspects of Australian life, just as it has affected many aspects of life in Canada. In Australia however, the most basic feature stems from the primary settlement and exclusive control of Australia by persons from the British Isles.

The British did not have to compete with other European powers or settlers for control of Australia, as they had to do in Canada with the French. In Australia there was also no legacy of armed rebellion from British influences such as occurred in the United States, and which had such a considerable impact on Canadian society. What all three countries had in common was a dispersed Native population, whose culture and constituents were deeply affected by invading colonists hoping to start a new life in the New World.[21] The population of approximately 300 000 Aborigines in Australia was severely reduced as the result of the treatment accorded them by British settlers.

White settlement began in Australia in 1788 through the British military presence, and the shipment to Australia of unwanted British convicts. Sheer distance from Europe, and the popularity of North America as an immigration destination reduced the attractiveness of Australia for European immigrants. The first major intake of free settlers was associated with the gold rush in the middle of the nineteenth century, and around one million persons entered Australia between 1852 and 1861. Between 1850 and 1900, 40% of the total population growth was due to immigration from Great Britain and Ireland. Some migration also took place from Northern Europe, but by the Second World War, Australia was still 90% British.[22] Non-Europeans had been excluded by the *Immigration Restriction Act* in 1901, and immigrant acceptability was related to perceptions of how easily an immigrant group could be assimilated into Australian society. Consequently, this much more explicit immigration policy ensured even greater ethnic uniformity in Australia than there was in North America.

The population of Australia during the Second World War was about six million people. In the next 30 years, an extremely rapid pace of growth increased the population by eight million.[23] Much of this growth was due to a high rate of immigration actively promoted by the government through travel assistance packages, particularly to British and European migrants who agreed to stay in Australia for a minimum of two years. Another source of the growth was the admission of European refugees through the sponsorship of the International Refugee Organization. The goal of migrant intake of about 1% per year during this period was established in response to a minor industrial revolution which occurred in the major cities of Australia, and which created a large demand for labour. World War II had also demonstrated that the sparse population of the country provided little security in the face of a possible foreign invasion, and an alarming decline in the birth rate suggested that this problem demanded attention. The phrase "populate or perish" reflected the urgency with which Australia viewed the necessity of immigration in the immediate post-war era. Though this urgency for settlement came somewhat later than it did in Canada, it is interesting to compare Australia's concern for national security with Canada's concern to claim the West from possible American penetration by populating it with immigrants.

Perhaps the most significant thing about the post-war immigration policy was that the search for settlers moved beyond the British Isles to Southern and East European countries.[24] In 1947, 97.9% of the population was born in Australia, the United Kingdom, Ireland, or New Zealand, and Italians were the largest other group at 0.4%. Between 1947 and 1974, only 40% of the large number of new arrivals came from the British Isles, and only 10% came from Northern Europe, primarily from Holland and Germany.[25] Much larger contingencies came from Southern European communities (e.g., Italy, Greece, and Cyprus), and the Eastern European countries (in particular Yugoslavia). Australia (like Canada) has recently seen a new source of immigration from Asian and African countries. So whereas 78% of the settlers in 1925 were British nationals, that number dropped to 13% in 1995. Furthermore, the proportion of overseas-born Australians from the United Kingdom and Ireland dropped from 79% in 1901 to 29% in 1997.[26] Into the 1990s, the proportion of European-born was declining and the proportion of Asian-born was increasing. In 1972, there was virtually no immigration to Australia from Vietnam and Hong Kong, for example. But by 1997, among the six largest source countries for new immigrants were China, Hong Kong, Vietnam and the Philippines. Because of Australia's location and proximity to Asia in the context of regionalizing and globalizing trends, it is expected that the much higher 24% foreign-born in Australia (compared to 16% for Canada) will mean that Asian immigration will play a more prominent role in the future.[27]

The relatively recent infusion of these non-British groups into Australia is important for several reasons. First, while immigrants compose about 24% of the Australian population, the fact that over one-half of them come from non-English speaking countries, and more than one-third still regularly use a language other than English, suggests that they may have a significant cultural influence on the second generation, even though this generation will be born in Australia.[28] In fact, when immigrants and their second generation are combined, they make up about one-third of the total national population.

The second reason this immigration is thought to be significant is that most of these migrants have settled in urban locations where they are able to establish viable ethnic communities (similar to Canada). For example, by the 1970s, 25% of the population of Sydney was foreign-born, and when their Australian-born children were included, they made up

A Referendum in Australia in 1999

In 1999, a referendum was held in Australia over whether the country should remove the Queen as the symbolic head of state and become a republic. While polls show that there is strong support for an Australian head of state, the referendum failed (55% to 45%) probably due to the fact that the proposal involved a President appointed by the Prime Minister and government rather than an elected President. It is expected that the drive to remove the British monarchy from its constitutional position will continue—though not without fierce debate.

While the question of removing the monarchy as symbolic head of the Canadian state arises from time to time, it has not received strong support. Two of the reasons suggested are that the monarchy is an important factor in differentiating Canada from the United States, and that Canada is too preoccupied with resolving other more critical issues such as Quebec and Aboriginal matters.

It is also interesting that a second question appeared in the same Australian referendum that proposed changing the preamble to the constitution to recognize the historical role and place of Aboriginal people. Even though this proposal was largely symbolic and had little substance, it failed 60%–40%. It is clear that Australia struggles with many of the same issues that Canada does.

38% of the population.[29] Whereas the pre–World War II immigration went largely to rural areas, the post-war immigration located in the largest cities, particularly Sydney, Melbourne, and Adelaide. Consequently, Melbourne has the third largest Greek population in the world behind Athens and Salonika. Southern and Eastern Europeans are most likely to be found in the ethnic enclaves in the inner city, whereas migrants from Holland and the British Isles are much less likely to be residentially concentrated. Furthermore, chain migration from these countries usually strengthens these enclaves as immigrants sponsor the migration of friends and relatives from the homeland.

Perhaps the most critical reason immigration remains a significant issue in Australian society is rooted in the sense of nordic superiority expressed by the British-oriented majority, who have also developed a strong sense of Australian nationalism.[30] In this context, foreigners were historically disliked, and assimilation was expected (as indicated by the label attached to immigrants as "New Australians"). When the Good Neighbour movement was established in 1950, its primary purpose was to condition Australians to accept immigration, and to assist immigrants to learn English and to assimilate as quickly as possible.[31] Such a policy was needed because immigrants came to be viewed as people with problems owing to their social and economic disadvantages, and their heightened urban visibility. Inability to speak English in the schools and underemployment were viewed as symptomatic of the immigrant "problem." The growing viability of their ethnic enclaves, however, and their increasing ability to articulate their group needs, eventually changed these immigrant groups into ethnic pressure groups. The *White Australia policy* was changed by the 1970s to a multicultural model similar to Canada's.[32] In a complete reversal of the earlier approach, ethnic pluralism replaced assimilation, which implied a new approach to ethnic relations.

If Canada had not experienced the diversity of origins of immigrants who settled the West, as well as the concentration of persons of French descent in Quebec, it is probable that Canadian society would have been more similar to Australian society. While British traditions were propagated by British settlers as the dominant charter group in both Canada and Australia, they were considerably softened in Canada because of the multi-ethnic nature of the West, and the French–English duality which was at the foundations of Canadian society. In fact the post-war shift to an official multicultural policy in Canada was a direct response to strong demands by francophone Québécois, and strong representations by other European ethnic groups in the West, rather than primarily a new perspective on ethnic tolerance by the British charter group. Since World War II, immigration patterns in Australia and Canada have been rather similar, although the Dutch, Yugoslavs, Maltese, and Greeks have been more prominent in Australia than in Canada. In establishing its own multiculturalism policy, Australia borrowed heavily from the Canadian experience minus the bilingualism issue.

Another significant comparison pertains to the permanence with which immigrants treated their migration to the New Land. In Chapter One it was pointed out that the impact of immigration into Canada had been somewhat counterbalanced until the Second World War by emigration from Canada. Where emigration took place, residence in Canada was usually stepping stone migration to eventual settlement in the United States. Although without a strongly industrialized neighbour, Australia also lost a significant proportion of its population but through *return migration*—usually to the land of origin. In the past, immigrants from the British Isles and Northern Europe have had the highest rates of departure from Australia, usually estimated at about 20%.[33] The two-year residence requirement for assisted immigrants made it difficult to know how many intended to remain in Australia in the first place, and how many viewed their stay only as a foreign travel experience. Return migration also took place in Canada, but it is doubtful whether much stepping stone migration occurred from Australia. Historically, then, population loss through emigration has been a problem common to both societies, but the reasons for these departures have been different.

The Aboriginal population in Australia is of similar proportion to the population of Native people in Canadian society, as each group represents approximately 2–3% of the population. In Canada, Native people are a distinguishable brown-skinned racial group, in much the same way that Aborigines, as a black-skinned people, are distinguishable from the white Euro-Australians. The original white contact led to severe reductions in the Aboriginal population, though recent growth has resulted in an Aboriginal population of about 372 000 with a large portion living in the southern urban areas.[34] The largest Aboriginal populations are in New South Wales and Queensland, but just as Native people form a larger share of the population in the Canadian Northern territories than they do in the other provinces, so the Northern Territory of Australia possesses the highest percentage of Aborigines at 27%.

Indigenous peoples suffered a fate similar to that of North American Indians, and were placed on Aboriginal Protectorates or reserves, though without the same legal foundation as in Canada. There have also been similar difficulties in ascertaining Aboriginal status although Australia has been more willing to accept social and self-definitions in contrast to hereditary ones.[35] The dilemma of desiring to maintain their traditional way of life while being exposed to white economic goals and urban life, has also created considerable poverty and unemployment among Aborigines. In 1967, Aborigines were made a federal rather than state responsibility, and an Office for Aboriginal Affairs was established in Australia. Used primarily as a vehicle for negotiations, a white-inspired National Aboriginal Consultative

Comparing Indigenous Peoples in New Zealand

In all parts of the "New" world, indigenous peoples had to deal with the intrusion of European powers and their settlers. The typical pattern of domination, resistance, paternalism, and attempts at assimilation represented policy for many years. While Canada, Australia, and New Zealand followed similar patterns in that regard, New Zealand exhibits important differences from the others.

The Treaty of Waitanga was signed in 1840 as an agreement between the British Crown and the Maori people to stem the conflicts that might be part of the settlement process. It provided for the chiefs to give up their land in exchange for the Maori right to govern themselves and gave the Maori all the rights of British subjects. As a result, the Maori were recognized as full citizens over 100 years before such rights were extended to Aboriginal peoples in Australia or Canada.

Maori children usually stayed in their own community and were raised by their extended families rather than being sent away to residential schools and separated from their kin as in Canada and Australia. While cultural conflict and tensions periodically emerged, the Aboriginal experience in New Zealand was generally less rigid and less harsh.

Source: Based on Andrew Armitage, *Comparing the Policy of Aboriginal Assimilation: Australia, Canada, and New Zealand* (Vancouver: UBC Press, 1995).

Council sought to unite dispersed local tribes or clans into a single body to coordinate Aboriginal programs, and to act in an advisory capacity to the government.[36] While the granting of self-determination to Aborigines remains particularly controversial in some states, the granting of land rights has proceeded apace, and this has had great implications in the outback regions where mining and other forms of resource extraction take place. Thus, though the contexts are somewhat different, the history and plight of the indigenous peoples in both Australia and Canada appear rather similar.

ETHNIC REGIONALISM: AN INTRODUCTION

It is generally recognized that in Canada, two different conditions have produced regional political movements. One condition is *uneven economic development and disparities,* which cause regional animosities or hostilities between geographic segments of the society. Examples of these movements include the Western agrarian movements and the Maritime Rights movement. The second condition is related to *ethnic solidarity,* of which the most obvious example is in Quebec. In this province, a francophone majority has evolved a national consciousness from its own heritage and traditions, which is quite distinctive from that of English Canada. While it might appear that the economic and ethnic aspects of regionalism are two different matters, the evidence suggests that regionalist ethnic movements are most effective when they have an economic grievance to mobilize their constituents. Put another way, regional movements with economic/political objectives are much more likely to be convincing when they have an ethnic basis. Thus, from the point of view of the country, a regional ethnic group represents a minority, while from the regional point of view, the ethnic group is a majority in their territory that ought to possess its own right to self-determination. It is from the dynamics of this debate between regional and federal objectives that societal conflict emerges.

Because industrialization and modernization are usually thought to negatively affect traditional culture, it has been assumed that ethnic minorities will eventually lose their historic distinctives, and will be drawn into the dominant social system of the majority. If this were true, we would expect Quebecers to have experienced considerable erosion of their linguistic and cultural uniqueness as they are increasingly drawn into the anglo world. Yet, surprisingly, the post-war period has seen a resurgence rather than a decline of ethnic identity in Quebec. What is noteworthy about this fact is that it has many parallels in other countries of the world where regional ethnic majorities have challenged the power and policies of the federal state.[37]

When a population possessing an ethnic difference is a majority in a given territory, a popular regionalist movement is frequently referred to as *a nationalist movement*. When a nationalist movement agitates not to improve its position within the established political

FIGURE 6.2   European Countries with Features Relevant to Canadian Society

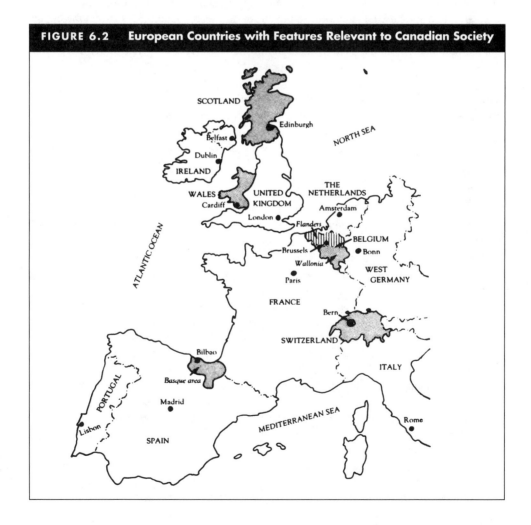

entity (though that may be a goal preferred by some) but to establish its own political entity, it is considered an *independence movement*. One of the moot questions in this kind of change is precisely how much independence is desired because sometimes more regional control (known as *devolution*) from central authority is acceptable.[38] When an ethnic difference exists, as in the case of Quebec, the internal debate is waged over how much separateness from (on the one hand) or cooperation with (on the other hand) the central state should prevail. Needless to say, responses within the territory will vary greatly. In this section, three comparisons will be made to Scotland, Wales, and the Basques of Spain in order to illustrate three different types of regional responses.

In an attempt to explain how and why ethnicity is mobilized by a regional movement, two interpretive perspectives will be proposed: reactive ethnicity and ethnic competition.[39] *Reactive ethnicity* suggests that ethnic solidarity emerges when a disadvantaged group rebels against a dominant authority representing another ethnic group. Ethnicity almost becomes synonymous with class consciousness because inequality intensifies the ethnic consciousness. *Ethnic competition* explains new-found ethnic solidarity by noting that groups formerly separate must now compete for the same occupations, rewards, and resources. In this case, cultural distinctiveness is mobilized to ensure the group obtains its share of the opportunities produced by changed conditions. Rather than treating these perspectives as in conflict with each other, there are elements of both which may be appropriate to our discussion.

DISTINCTIVE CANADIAN FEATURE: Against significant odds, Quebec culture and francophone identity has survived over many years and is now thriving in an unprecedented way in spite of anglophone dominance in Canada. As a result, the reaction against central government control increases the call for more autonomy.

Comparison: Scotland

Scotland is not a separate country but is part of the United Kingdom as a consequence of the Act of Union with England which took place in 1707. Scotland was not conquered by England but agreed to the Union because of the access Scottish industry would have to the British Empire. Many Scots were astounded at this decision at the time but the potential economic benefits were reasonably convincing. As a consequence, when other nation-states were forming in Europe throughout the nineteenth century, there was little expression of Scottish nationalist feeling as the link with England ensured a strong local economy.[40] Scotland then existed as a region within the United Kingdom or Great Britain in which there were no barriers to the movement of people, capital, or goods. Until very recent developments, Scotland did not have its own government and elected representatives to the British parliament where social and economic policies are made and applied to the entire United Kingdom.

In spite of being part of the United Kingdom and experiencing pervasive English influences, certain aspects of Scottish civil society were preserved through social institutions and traditions. For some, the Gaelic language was an important part of Scottish culture, but it is now spoken by less than two percent of the population. Scotland did retain aspects of its own legal system and possessed a distinct religious difference as the established church in England was the Church of England (Anglican) while the Church of Scotland was Presbyterian. In addition, the centuries of past conflict and competition with England had provided a pantheon of folk tales, national heroes, and martyrs which also helped sustain an ethnic identity.

These traditions, including a sense of history and past national greatness, were also taught in the schools. Significantly, while these cultural factors were always present, an articulated and growing sense of ethnic difference intensified only as Scottish people became aware of being marginal to the centre of British power. This awareness of marginality as a region with considerable ethnic homogeneity provided a framework for interpreting economic decline.

After World War I, and again after World War II, unemployment began to grow in Scotland. The more enterprising members of the entrepreneurial class were increasingly enticed to the centres of English finance and industry. In fact, out-migration of Scots to opportunities in England meant a perpetual drain of manpower, brainpower, and even capital. Scottish people became increasingly sensitive to their peripheral status both within the British Isles and in Europe. Scotland had not always had this marginal position, for in the 19th century, it was one of the first parts of Britain to industrialize.[41] However, as the coal, iron, and textile industries went into decline, unemployment began to grow, particularly in the Glasgow industrial region. New investments in new industries, such as electronics, provided some opportunities for more middle class workers, but did not help those who were displaced by the deterioration of the older industries. As a result of these changes, the Scottish economy became more of a branch plant economy largely owned by "outsiders" such as the English, Germans, or Americans, and the sense of external control and marginality increased.[42]

On one hand, it might be said that when economic conditions have been good, there has been little feeling of marginality, and there has been little need to politicize ethnic differences. On the other hand, the distance from the centre of economic and political control in the southeast of England, and the lingering sense of ethnic differences from the English, have led to repeated calls for some decentralization away from London. Scottish complaints about poor treatment and a distant government led to the establishment of a Scottish Office in Edinburgh in 1885 staffed by a government minister with full cabinet status. Yet the lingering animosities remained, and in 1928, the Scots National League and the Scottish Home Rule Association united to form the National Party of Scotland. After several breakaway movements and subsequent mergers, the Scottish National Party (SNP) was founded in 1934. Throughout the 1950s and 1960s the movement began to grow through petitions and electioneering, but only in the 1970s did the SNP begin to see more electoral success, and since 1970 has never polled less than 10% of the popular vote in general elections, reaching as high as 30% in 1974.

If deteriorating economic conditions in Scotland were behind the agitation for greater regional control and Scottish independence from British domination, then it was the discovery of oil in the North Sea off the coast of Scotland that provided the catalyst and new confidence to challenge existing structural arrangements. The SNP put less emphasis on broad cultural issues than on economic grievances, and the oil find instilled an expectation of rising power within the UK, and regionally based leverage against economic decline. At the same time, oil production increased Britain's interest in both maintaining control over its development in Scotland, and responding to apparent public agitation there. After considerable discussion and debate, particularly through the work of a Royal Commission, the British Parliament allowed a referendum to take place in Scotland in 1979 to determine support for self-government, meaning a separate Scottish parliament to effect more local control. The referendum was won by the "yes" side 52% to 48% and yet was lost because the British Parliament had established a 40% rule based on the total population. Only 64% of the population voted, meaning that people who voted "yes" only represented 33% of those eligible to vote. This break from normal voting procedures inspired considerable conflict in itself, and both "yes" and "no" votes were subject to a variety of interpretations. Many considered the results inconclusive and both sides argued that they had won.[43]

Since this first referendum, the issue of self-government and independence continued to be an important concern on the Scottish agenda.[44] Particularly during the years of the Thatcher government, it was thought that the UK had been captured by interests in the southeast of England (the London area) in which they were marginalized.[45] The result was that Scots shifted their voting to parties more sensitive to regional needs (particularly Labour), and which advocated more local control of their society in a process of devolution. Support for some kind of devolution has been widespread in Scotland, and crosses party and social class lines, but the debate focuses on how this idea should be operationalized. The SNP continues to work for outright independence but the Labour government under Tony Blair has also supported greater local autonomy. In 1997, a referendum was held in Scotland that reflected clear support for devolution. Three-quarters (74%) of those voting agreed with the question that there should be a Scottish Parliament (note that this is not the same as independence although there are those who see it as another step in that direction), and a slightly lesser number (64%) agreed that it should have taxing power. Consequently, the first elections were held in 1999 for the Scottish Parliament in which no party received the majority of seats. Even though Labour won the most seats, the SNP was a strong second. The irony of

---

FIGURE 6.3   Responses to Independence Movements in the United Kingdom

Scotland		Wales	
1707	gave up independence in Act of Union	1536	gave up independence in Act of Union
1979	Referendum obtained majority (52% Yes) but defeated on technical rules		Referendum defeated (80% No)
1997	Referendum passed to establish a Scottish Parliament (74%) to give taxation power (64%)		Referendum passed to establish a National Assembly for Wales (50.3%)
1999	Elections for Scottish Parliament		Elections for National Assembly

▼ ▼

Powers	Powers
Can pass laws in areas of responsibility such as education, health care, transportation, culture Can vary taxation by 3%	No taxation or legislative powers Allocate government funds supplied to Wales

course in this result was that Labour was arguing for more independence for Scotland but within the United Kingdom whereas the SNP advocated a more clear-cut independence.

In contrast to those who have argued that Scottish nationalism is primarily a response to Scotland's marginality and dependency within the United Kingdom and global capitalist system, McCrone has argued that Scotland's incorporation into greater Britain was always incomplete because Scotland's elite negotiated some sense of institutional autonomy that has survived.[46] The Church of Scotland was not replaced by the Church of England, higher education has always been far more accessible through university traditions, the legal system has its own distinctive features, Scotland has retained its own national sport teams (e.g., football and rugby), an independent voice in trade unionism has supported home rule, and international capital (not just English capital) has a growing presence in Scotland. All of this has meant that Scotland has expanded its purview beyond the UK and a distinctive civil society has not only been sustained but has also strengthened in recent years. No longer is Scottish nationalism fixated on the past and the myths of old traditions, it is now focused on the present and future, and seeks to carve out a new niche in the changing global system more independent of the central British state.

Scotland serves as a useful comparison to both Quebec as an ethnically distinct society, and to the West and Atlantic regions of Canada with their feelings of geographic distance and economic marginality. It is noteworthy that it is oil in both Canada and Scotland that has helped kindle conflict and arouse regional sentiment. However, neither the West or the Atlantic regions possess an ethnic heritage that can serve as a cohesive factor in external conflict. The comparison with Quebec is significant since in both places, culture and ethnicity have been increasingly marshalled in the political battle for more autonomy. Ethnic survival has been an enduring theme in both places along with a recent demand for greater independence from the central state. The major difference between the two is that Quebec has always had its own provincial parliament which it has increasingly used to promote its local objectives, and which even potentially provides a vehicle for independence; in contrast, Scotland has until recently lacked any localized government. Now that it has its own political vehicle, we can expect even greater nationalist assertiveness. On the other hand, there seems to be considerable evidence that the new nationalism in both places is increasingly less ethnocentric and acknowledges that an internationalizing world requires different hierarchies of identities in which new partnerships rather than restrictive barriers are the dominant themes.

Scotland, like Canada in relation to the United States has less than one-tenth the population of the United Kingdom, implying strong perceptions of dominance. Quebec's position within Canada is somewhat more significant but the end result is the same with both places seeking to alter old dependency relationships with governments in London and Ottawa. Unlike Quebec, Scotland's distinctive language has eroded significantly. McCrone notes how it is remarkable that even though Scotland lost its political identity three hundred years ago, seven out of ten now give priority to their identity as Scottish rather than British. If anything, the identification with regional political structures has increased rather than decreased. In both locations, there is clearly a reaction against a dominant authority acting from outside their territory (reactive ethnicity) at the same time there is a new outward look (rather than the old inward nationalism) that seeks to create new opportunities (ethnic competition) brought by globalism.

DISTINCTIVE CANADIAN FEATURE: As Quebec nationalism has grown, anglophones and allophones have felt less at home in Quebec, and significant out-migration has occurred with the result that there has been less resistance to nationalist sentiment in Quebec.

Comparison: Wales

Wales was an autonomous state until the Act of Union in 1536 incorporated the nation into the English state. As long as the Welsh people remained rural and traditional, British rule, though resisted in some quarters, meant little to Welsh language and culture. With the onset of the industrial revolution in the nineteenth century, however, Wales underwent considerable change. By 1900, the population of Wales had increased fivefold, and by 1911 two-thirds of the population was urban.[47] Urbanization and industrialization, in conjunction with the political integration of Wales into British national parties, and a comparative geographical proximity to the British industrial complex, reduced the sense of marginality in Wales in comparison to Scotland.[48] The fact that Lloyd George, a leader of the Young Wales Movement in the late nineteenth century, became British Prime Minister symbolized this fact.

In spite of having a distinct national language (Welsh), the population of Wales became increasingly anglicized. The immigration of British people into the industrial centres of South Wales reduced the usage of the Welsh language there, and the use of Welsh became restricted to the more rural areas of Northwest Wales. On the other hand, road signs and official documents are in Welsh and English and Welsh language television is available. If Wales, as Hechter has argued, was an internal colony for British capitalist development, it must also be recognized that Wales became a secondary centre of industry (iron and steel), rather than an undeveloped region.[49] For this reason, independence issues of a cultural nature have not had a strong appeal to the working class which has been more concerned about economic issues.

The Welsh nationalist movement, Plaid Cymru, was founded in 1925, but it has had little impact on Welsh politics. Its base has traditionally been in Northwest Wales, and it has taken a gradualist nationalist approach by focusing on cultural matters such as language. While the creation of vital Welsh institutions such as the University of Wales, the Welsh Department of Education, and the Church of Wales, had the potential of supporting language as a source of ethnic differentiation, the absence of a Welsh middle class unintegrated into British structures has removed one of the common foundations of a nationalist movement.

A referendum was held in Wales in 1979, similar to the one held in Scotland, on whether to establish a Welsh national assembly. Amidst economic insecurities, the proposal was defeated by a 4 to 1 margin. Advance polls had indicated that a majority of persons of Welsh descent had wanted a Welsh parliament; however, the large number of non-Welsh residents who had migrated to Wales overwhelmed the Welsh nationalists in the vote. Indicators are that the English-speaking Welsh voters (i.e., residents of Wales who could not speak Welsh) were fearful that the nationalists would insist on Welsh being spoken in an independent Wales, and that this would put them at a distinct disadvantage.[50] In other words, the English-speaking majority was reluctant to support the nationalists who formed only a 20% linguistic minority.

In Wales, regionalist/nationalist feeling is essentially cultural and not economic, as Wales (particularly Southeast Wales) is economically integrated into the British economy. If 90% of the residents of Scotland are born Scots and conscious of their Scottish identity, the same cannot be said of Wales where an influx of persons from England has taken place.[51]

Cultural regionalism/nationalism has then been restricted to a minority of the population found in the rural northern areas. This example illustrates how residents of a former nation-state (Wales) can hold a dual identity (i.e., British and Welsh at the same time), almost in a regional rather than nationalist manner. The integration of at least South Wales into the British economy, and the influx of persons from England into Wales, has dissolved the potency of potential nationalist appeals.

In 1997, a second referendum was held in Wales parallel to the referendum in Scotland and consonant with the British Labour government's support of further devolution. The question was similar to the one in Scotland and inquired whether the voter agreed that there should be a Welsh Assembly. With a 50% turnout, 50.3% said "Yes" and the National Assembly for Wales was established in 1999. This was barely enough to support this initiative suggesting both that there was strong nationalist feeling and that there were many others either opposed or apathetic. The major difference between the power of the Scottish Parliament and the Welsh Assembly is that the latter has no legislative or taxation powers and its primary purpose is to allocate government funds spent on Wales. Thus we see that devolution has meant different things to different UK constituencies and no single structure was expected for both regions. The meaning of voting for the Welsh Assembly then had much weaker nationalist implications, and it was harder for opposition to gel against it. In some ways, this constitutional change was primarily a moderate variant of the status quo but with important symbolic significance.

There has been considerable intermingling of English and Welsh people in Wales, and the Welsh economy has been intimately tied to a strong British economy. In contrast, francophones and anglophones in Canada are becoming increasingly territorially separate, particularly as the result of out-migration from Quebec and language assimilation pressures within and outside Quebec. While Quebec's economy has been intimately tied to the Canadian economy, it also has strong linkages to the United States which creates a stronger sense of confidence of economic survival outside of Canada. The UK has shown a willingness to allow different patterns of devolution whereas Canadians are divided over anything that suggests special status for particular regions or social groups.

DISTINCTIVE CANADIAN FEATURE: Quebec has sought more regionalized control and a sense of autonomy but nationalist movements often divide the population and create considerable concern over the economic welfare of the region.

Comparison: The Basque Region of Spain

In the northeast corner of Spain live 1.5 million Basques. The Basques live on approximately three percent of the land surface of the country. The Cantabrian mountains almost serve as a barrier to the rest of Spain, and the coastal location of the most significant Basque population provides more of an international frame of reference, rather than an inward link to Spain. Here shipyards, steel mills, and manufacturing provide the highest average per capita income of any region of Spain which as a country has the highest unemployment rate in the European Union. Spain itself is made up of several linguistic/cultural groups including the Castilians, Galicians, Andalusians, Catalans, and the Basques.

The Basques occupy an area between France and the rest of Spain. For this reason early Spanish monarchies sought the cooperation of the Basques in border defense and, in efforts to maintain their loyalty, agreed to allow the Basque provinces to retain their own legal system, which provided a substantial measure of self-governance. Part of the legacy of these concessions was the concept of *collective nobility*, which automatically granted noble rank to any person of Basque parentage. While this entitlement meant little in actuality, it provided a heritage of uniqueness among these people which later came to serve as part of the rationale for greater autonomy.

Basque uniqueness is also related to language and lineage. The Basque language, Euskera, is unrelated to any Indo-European language and has a character all its own. The Basque people, moreover, have the highest incidence of Rh negative blood factor of any population in the world—a biological reflection of closed social groupings.[52] When these two factors are observed in combination with geographic location and noble status, the perception of Basque character as unique is strong. On the other hand, only one in four Basques uses Euskera and most are fluent in Spanish.

Considerable self-governance was allowed by the Spanish monarchs until the 19th century, when attempts were made by the Spanish government to override local autonomy. The Spanish goal of greater centralization threatened the Basque community, and the Basque nationalist movement began in the 1890s. The Basque language was a primary focus of government attack and, in the period following the Spanish Civil War (1937), it became illegal to use Euskera both in public, and in the media, or to teach it in school. By the late 1960s, Euskera was allowed back in the schools, and the new constitution of 1978 made regional languages co-official with Spanish. But all of this did not occur without considerable agitation and conflict from those in the Basque nationalist movement, who by this time had renamed their land Euzkadi.

The industrial opportunities available in Basque cities meant that in conjunction with a tax system that discouraged agriculture, the Basque population became more urban. These same opportunities also attracted non-Basques to cities like Bilbao. Now only 65% of the population of the Basque provinces is indigenous. This decline is chiefly attributable to 20–25 000 people per year who have migrated into the region since the 1950s.[53] As a consequence of this immigration, the use of Euskera has declined, and traditional Basque family life has been in a state of upheaval. Anxious to maintain their economic position, the Basque bourgeoisie have frequently compromised their ethnicity in order to build economic bridges to other countries, or to other regions of Spain. It was precisely this greater intermingling, however, which threatened the Basque identity among the working class and the middle class. The frustration among some grew so strong that an organization called Basque Homeland and Freedom (ETA) engaged in revolutionary insurgent activities, including kidnapping and assassination. A more moderate Basque Nationalist Party is also active.

The legacy of feelings of persecution by the Spanish government, and a convincing but troubled ethnic identity were further exacerbated by regional grievances of inequality. It was felt that high government taxation was not being reciprocated by either government spending or the availability of services in the Basque region, and that this uneven distribution was the result of Spanish bias against the Basques. Consequently, when the Spanish government offered a referendum to the Basque region in 1979, which proposed greater autonomy in matters of language, taxation, and the judiciary, it was overwhelmingly accepted, although about 50% of the Basque population abstained from the vote.[54] The first elections to the Basque parliament were held in 1980 and Basque nationalists have gained control over all key institutions.

Just as the Basques have argued that they are an ethnic people with a distinct and unique heritage, so have francophone Quebecers asserted that they also have a distinct "people-hood" which has a long history but is firmly rooted in the Conquest. As a result, in both locations, increasing central government control threatens the group. What perhaps makes the Basque region unique, however, is that its own concern for self-determination is also related to having been the richest region in Spain—a position aspiring Basques were particularly zealous to guard- and as we will see began to erode. It is essentially a similar group of aspiring francophones which has been effective in mobilizing Quebec opinion, though Quebec's economic position has not been comparatively as strong.

The industrial strength of the Basque region in the '60s and '70s was a significant magnet for migrants seeking employment from other parts of Spain. In other words, the economic success of the Basque area has in a sense been responsible for its problems. In-migrants dilute the Basque identity of the region and threaten the language. Success also meant that central government tax revenues were likely to be diverted to more needy parts of Spain (of course the question of which area has the most pressing needs is itself controversial). The Basques, then, feared that central government control of policies pertaining to the economy and language could weaken the Basque region both economically and culturally in deference to policies that create a levelling effect for Spain as a whole. Indeed, in the years since obtaining home rule, an economic crisis has occurred in which unemployment has increased and the legitimacy of the Spanish state continues to be under question.[55] The violence involving the ETA has led to several hundred deaths and the ETA receives its support from the most vulnerable parts of the population. The internal battles between the Basques and non-Basques (people with Basque heritage and identity but not supportive of a Basque nation) as well as the actions of the Spanish police seems to be used to justify more concerted action.[56] The election of a right-wing Spanish government in 1996 which was committed to a strong Spanish state renewed the animosities and tensions.

Basques, like the Québécois, want more control over their own territory to preserve the ethnic identity of the region.[57] Yet internal divisions between Basques and non-Basques and a less healthy economy have created tensions and power struggles that are difficult to resolve and create new gulfs between radicals and more moderates. Two points emerge here with relevance to Quebec. One is that concerns for a healthy economy with low unemployment is an important objective in a nationalist movement and its absence can trigger all kinds of new tensions. The second is that nationalist movements can easily become polarized between moderates and radicals when conditions or events deteriorate, and can either weaken the nationalist movement or elevate it to more concerted action. Additionally, it should be pointed out that devolution to more local autonomy in 1980, in conjunction with other issues, has not resolved the matter for all time either.

POLITIES WITH MORE THAN ONE OFFICIAL LANGUAGE: AN INTRODUCTION

If you want to create some controversy in a group of Canadian people, there is no faster way to do it than to bring up the issue of bilingualism. Everyone has an opinion about bilingualism and everyone also has stories or anecdotes to tell from everyday life to justify their position. Whether it is hearing a bilingual version of "O Canada," hearing two sets of pre-flight instructions on an airplane, or seeing a simultaneous translation of a document or instructional sign, bilingualism is an issue many Canadians are still grappling with because it is foreign to the unilingual manner in which most people live their lives.[58]

It is frequently assumed that most countries operate with one dominant universal language. Many Canadians, for example, are aware that the United States has taken in many immigrant peoples utilizing numerous languages, but they note that one language (English) is still used as the primary means of communication. What is perhaps less well-known is that the large influx of Spanish-speaking peoples into the southern United States in recent years has created a real battle in some areas (e.g., California and Florida) over whether two languages (English and Spanish) should be endorsed.[59] The national English-speaking majority has so far successfully argued that unilingualism should be the American norm. The facts of Canadian history and polity, however, are somewhat different, though there is a tendency for people to assume that unilingualism ought to be the normal pattern in Canada as well.

But if unilingualism is the norm in many countries, are there countries where more than one language is officially recognized, or does Canada stand alone on this issue? The existence of informal regional linguistic enclaves is one thing but the formal recognition of more than one language is another. Is it possible for countries to officially recognize the existence of more than one language as a basis for communication within their society as a whole? If so, what has been their experience?

The purpose of this section is to become familiar with two countries where more than one language is officially sanctioned. These countries are Belgium and Switzerland.

DISTINCTIVE CANADIAN FEATURE: The federal policy of bilingualism sought to reorganize Canadian society by declaring that there would be two official languages which would be universally available for government services but also subtly implying that Canadians throughout the country ought to work towards becoming bilingual.

Comparison: Switzerland

Switzerland had its beginnings as a loose alliance of Alpine valley communities banding together to defend themselves against challenges to their independence. The idea of a voluntary federation of political communities led to a constitution in 1848 which established political neutrality, and the idea of one foreign policy, one citizenship, and a customs union. On the other hand, matters of education and culture were left totally in the hands of local jurisdictions called *cantons*.[60] No attempt was to be made to secure national political unity based on descent or language, but rather on local allegiance which was to be paid directly to the canton.

The *principle of cantonal autonomy* is directly related to the ethnic diversity which varies with locality. About 74% of the population of Switzerland speaks German, 20% French, 4% Italian, and less than 1% Romansch.[61] Consequently Switzerland has 23 cantons of which 14 are German, 4 French, 1 Italian, 3 bilingual, and 1 trilingual. Ninety-five percent of German Swiss live in German regions, 86% of French Swiss live in French regions, and 85% of Italians live in Italian regions, indicating considerable cantonal homogeneity.[62] A referendum in 1996 approved semi-official status for Romansch meaning that government services, but not all government documents, would be available in that language

Each canton is entitled to preserve its own language and all immigrants must learn the language used in that canton. Language boundaries are guaranteed and cannot be changed although when conflict emerges, a canton may be split (as happened when the new canton of Jura was established from a part of the canton of Berne).[63] The split was accepted because it separated the French Catholic community (Jura) from the German Protestant one (Berne), and it removed the bases for much internal conflict. The recent interest in adding the teaching of English to school programs has produced considerable debate as a wedge in violating linguistic purity. Each canton writes its laws and documents in its own language and forms its own military units as part of the Swiss army. The primary basis for group identity is thus the canton, not one's ethnic or language group, although language becomes the marker of the canton.. Political decentralization and local autonomy remove the frustrations minorities normally feel in a highly centralized state.

Switzerland is frequently perceived as a model of linguistic harmony for, in spite of the inequality of strength of the linguistic groups represented, the territorial sub-units known as cantons provide the structure to ensure more localized control. However, while this most basic element of organization is critical to understanding Switzerland's success, other supporting factors also come into play.[64] These include:

1. An appreciation of cultural diversity and required second language learning is viewed as a positive feature of Swiss society by its residents. The socialization of children from a young age inculcates these attitudes. This situation is also supported by the fact that the three language groups are dominant in the surrounding European community.

2. A rejection of the concept of minority status in preference to strict equality is embodied in the Constitution. The Constitution gives Switzerland three "official" languages and four "national" languages. The federal civil service is linguistically proportionate. As a result of these federal efforts, linguistic groups tend to overestimate the strength of other language groups (e.g., even though French is technically a minority language, it has high prestige) with the consequence that no group possesses a minority complex. The existing pluralingual cantons serve as bridges between the language groups even though linguistic territoriality extends to within the canton as well. Wherever possible, more-than-proportionate representation is the norm.

3. Cantons are sovereign in linguistic matters, meaning that each canton has the right to protect its own linguistic character against both external forces and in-migrants who are obligated to adjust to cantonal language practices. Federal authorities must deal with each canton in their own language.

4. Language divisions are cross-cut by other divisions such as political affiliation, religion, social class, and rural-urban differences, making it hard to mobilize one language group against the other. For example, approximately one-half of all French are Catholic and one-half are Protestant. Language is only one of many divisions in the society which are decentralized through cantonal control.

5. Economic disparities between cantons are small. In fact, disparities within cantons are greater than those between cantons. Wherever disparities have occurred, programs for regional economic development become part of federal policy. Appeasement of all disadvantaged groups through fiscal support is a dominant objective of the federal government and political elites.

Canadian federal policy has clearly rejected the idea of *linguistic territoriality*, though demands for acceptance of the "distinct society" idea suggests pressures in that direction. Bilingualism as a national policy has aimed to make both languages available throughout the country and has sought to protect each official language group when it is a minority in a particular region, though it has been less than successful in doing so. Local autonomy and control on language and cultural issues have been shunned in preference to federally initiated policies. Furthermore, economic disparity and competition between regions have added further fuel to the politicization of language groups. In Switzerland, strong cantonal and federal identities and loyalties are considered compatible whereas in Canada, and particularly in Quebec, provincial and national loyalties are considered to be in conflict.

Canadian society follows a very different principle of social organization than Swiss society. The federal objective has been to create a more highly integrated society and a centralized policy around the principle of bilingualism rather than encouraging and supporting more regional control in language use. Switzerland provides a significant example of decentralized control and tolerance through the principle of linguistic territoriality which has produced surprising stability.

DISTINCTIVE CANADIAN FEATURE: In an attempt to include francophones more clearly in the fabric of Canadian society, bilingualism became a legislated ideal that ignored the subsequent realities of increasing territorial unilingualism.

Comparison: Belgium

The country of Belgium had its origin in the Belgian Revolution of 1830. The northern half of the country was populated by persons of Dutch origin in an area known as Flanders, and those of French descent populated the southern section of Belgium in an area called Wallonia. At the time of the creation of Belgium, Wallonia was the stronger section, and partly because of the influence exerted from France, French became the official national language of Belgium. French also was the cultured language of the upper class, and therefore became the language of secondary education and upward mobility throughout Belgium.

By the latter half of the nineteenth century, a significant change in the balance of power between these two regions had begun to occur.[65] A higher birth rate in Flanders led to sizeable population increases there, and a Flemish national consciousness had emerged. Challenges were raised to the exclusiveness of the French language because the Flemish desired to use Dutch in the courts, public administration, as well as in the schools. Regional bilingualism was first initiated in Flanders, and, by 1898, Flemish became an official language of the country along with French.

The emergent Flemish consciousness also evoked a Wallonian consciousness.[66] The apparent concessions to the Flemish along with the comparative weakening of the Wallonian position (two-thirds of the total population was now Flemish), made control of the large city of Brussels critical. Flemings who moved to Brussels were becoming bilingual, whereas Wallonians remained unilingual; and yet there were still clear differences between bilingual Flemings and the French-speaking Walloons. The Flemish middle classes preferred language policies which ensured the survival of Dutch, yet they were also aware that urbanization meant greater use of French.

By World War II, Belgium essentially consisted of two unilingual areas: Flanders (Flemish or Dutch) and Wallonia (French). Flemings were conscious of the fact that Brussels was already considerably French, and that this French dominance of the city was increasing. Conflicts became particularly intense as the urban population moved into the predominantly Flemish suburbs, and the battle between the two groups continued. The Constitution adopted in 1970 proposed a solution that would see Belgium have three administrative units: Flanders where Dutch would be used; Wallonia where French would be used; and Brussels where there was to be parity between the two groups with some regional unilingualism in the suburbs.[67] At the federal level, a parity principle was to prevail so that the cabinet would be composed of an equal number from both linguistic groups. The Dutch agreed to parity in the cabinet in exchange for parity in Brussels where they were a minority. The language of instruction in schools was to be the language of the area, although residents of Brussels could make a free choice. Parity was also to be sought in the civil service where the Dutch were under-represented. Two cultural councils were to be established to ensure the cultural survival of both ethnic groups.

Thus, a rather sharply defined linguistic frontier exists across Belgium in an east-west direction, dividing the Flemish dialects and Dutch to the north from the Walloon dialects and French to the south. This language boundary is not co-existent with any political barriers and trade and commerce proceed freely across the two language regions. The French language traditionally had the upper hand, but over the last one hundred years, a renaissance in Flemish socio-political life transformed the old relationship between the two linguistic groups. The result has been decades of conflict and negotiation in which Brussels, as the major Belgian city—a predominantly francophone capital in Flemish territory—has been the centre of inter-group tension. Consequently, inter-group sympathy ratings are much lower in Belgium than in Switzerland.[68]

The Flemings (56%) now outnumber the Walloons (32%). An additional 10% of the population is bilingual and the small remainder is German.[69] Even though the country is linguistically divided, most Belgium residents are Catholic. The regional imbalance continues though the modern industries are now in Flanders and the declining industries are in Wallonia. In 1993, Belgium was officially transformed from a unitary state to a federation of linguistic communities with three self-governing regions (Dutch speaking Flanders, French speaking Wallonia, and bilingual Brussels) each with directly elected assemblies. Only defense, foreign relations, and monetary policy are reserved for the federal government. This has meant that the size of the federal government has been reduced considerably.

If Switzerland has been a model of political stability within a decentralized system, Belgium has experienced much more upheaval and realignment, similar to Canada (though Canada's period of such change has been much shorter). Both Belgium and Canada possessed a uniform central language policy and attempted to impose it on the entire country. But the changing position of the two groups in Belgium has meant a long period of negotiation and transition which eventually led to a policy not so much reorganizing the society linguistically but acknowledging and accepting the regional linguistic differences. In Canada, at least at the federal level, there has been considerable resistance to such a plan in spite of actual realities.

Rather than move to a national policy of bilingualism as Canada has done, Belgium has moved to *territorial unilingualism*, and established mechanisms to institutionalize *parity* and the survival of both groups. Thus the idea of losers and winners in ethnic interaction is considerably muted by parity and territorial unilingualism. The Canadian bilingualism policy also represented an attempt to minimize the idea of losers and winners, although it has been less successful because it has not anticipated the tendencies towards greater territorial unilingualism. The demographic difference in size of the two charter groups has also made the concept of parity less palatable in Canada.

DISTINCTIVE CANADIAN FEATURE: Longstanding barriers between Canada and the United States were at least partially removed by trade agreement which integrates the two societies in a new way but with uncertain consequences for the future.

Comparison: The European Union

The increasing integration of the North American economy through free trade agreements raises questions about the survival of an autonomous and sovereign Canadian society as was discussed in Chapter Two. While the creation of regional trading blocs is currently a global phenomenon, it is unclear whether economic integration necessarily must also result in some form of political, social, or cultural integration.

The changes occurring in Europe through the creation of the European Community (EC) or what is now known as the European Union (EU) provides an interesting counterpoint to the Canadian experience. In many ways, the EU began as an experiment in economic collaboration but has moved more and more towards a type of political integration. Whereas nation-states usually guard their sovereignty, the voluntary sharing of sovereignty as represented by the European Union is unprecedented in modern history—and particularly in consideration of the fact that not long ago many of these countries were bitter enemies.

The first half of the twentieth century was a time of much turmoil for Europe as hostilities between nation-states broke out and world wars resulted in massive destruction. These experiences, followed by the Cold War between the Soviet bloc and Western capitalist democracies, placed European countries into a rebuilding period with a mutual commitment to prevent such continental devastation from ever occurring again.[70] The two industrial powers of Western Europe—Germany and France—who had been at war with each other so often,[71] became the leaders in establishing the European Coal and Steel Community in 1951, which also included Belgium, Italy, Netherlands, and Luxembourg. The idea was to harness coal and steel—the two key ingredients of a strong industrial economy—in the cause of peace and economic collaboration. These six countries broke new ground again in 1957 when the Treaty of Rome was signed, forming the European Economic Community. Over the next years, efforts were made to create a customs union or a common market which would remove internal barriers to trade among the member countries while establishing a common external barrier to other countries.

In 1973, Denmark, Ireland, and the United Kingdom joined the EC followed by Greece in 1981, and Portugal and Spain in 1986 (see Figure 6.4). The apparent economic success of the EC and the dynamic created by new and continuing initiatives in the last couple of decades has meant that every nation in Europe has wrestled with the appropriateness of membership in the EC, but even those within the EC have had second thoughts (e.g., Denmark) or have become ambivalent partners (e.g., United Kingdom). In 1995, Austria, Finland, and Sweden joined but Norway declined. The collapse of the eastern bloc has produced new interest in economic collaboration by countries in Eastern Europe, and even countries such as Turkey have applied for admission. Clearly the size of this economic community is widening but the further question is whether the impact of the community should also be deepening (i.e., to involve matters of politics, culture, and well-being and not just trade).[72]

There are two things that are remarkable about this evolving entity. One is that the EC is indeed moving towards *full economic integration* as represented by the *Maastricht Treaty* in 1992, which created the European Union (EU) to replace the EC. Not only was there to be the free movement of goods and services, but capital and labour could move without restriction anywhere within the entity. Passport controls were removed in 1995 between France, Germany, Spain, Portugal, Belgium, Luxembourg, and the Netherlands. Perhaps the most dramatic step, and certainly the one that most clearly affected people in everyday life was the establishment in 1999 of a new unit of currency called the *euro* which will eventually lead to the abolition of national currencies in 2002. There are also increasing pressures for the EU to protect its worldwide interests by developing its own foreign policy and a Common Foreign and Security Policy is in effect.[73] Thus while the EU is certainly not a superpower in terms of military might, it is certainly a power in terms of economic strength and has developed more and more of the organizational apparatus to make it so.

So far, then, NAFTA is considerably different from the EU. It creates a free trade area rather than a customs union or common market.[74] The emphasis is on trade of goods and services with only limited interest in labour mobility. It does not create new institutions with autonomy or authority over governments. A common currency is not in the immediate plans and was only recently proposed. And yet in the end, the North American experience may not be significantly different. Integration into the hegemon may occur more subtly but nevertheless be no less real. For example, the American dollar may already indirectly serve as the com-

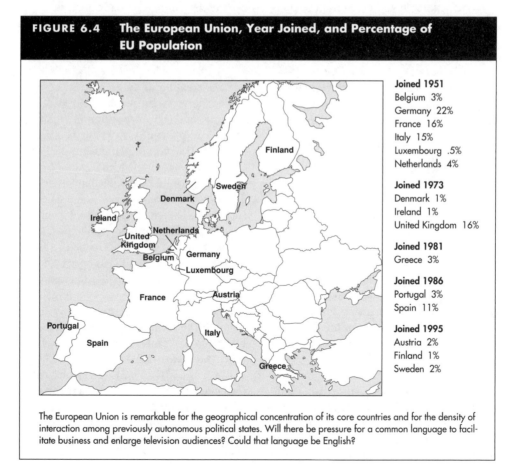

FIGURE 6.4 The European Union, Year Joined, and Percentage of EU Population

Joined 1951
Belgium 3%
Germany 22%
France 16%
Italy 15%
Luxembourg .5%
Netherlands 4%

Joined 1973
Denmark 1%
Ireland 1%
United Kingdom 16%

Joined 1981
Greece 3%

Joined 1986
Portugal 3%
Spain 11%

Joined 1995
Austria 2%
Finland 1%
Sweden 2%

The European Union is remarkable for the geographical concentration of its core countries and for the density of interaction among previously autonomous political states. Will there be pressure for a common language to facilitate business and enlarge television audiences? Could that language be English?

Source: Compiled from *Eurostat, Social Portrait of Europe,* 1998, p. 29.

The Euro: A Currency Revolution

On January 1, 1999, the euro became the new unit of currency for eleven of the fifteen member states of the European Union. EU countries not included in the European Monetary Union were the United Kingdom, Denmark, Sweden, and Greece.

Local currency exchange rates became fixed as of that date and all dealings where hard cash was not required is done in the euro currency. Shops and merchants began to dual price merchandise so that people began to think in euros. Many banks sent their customers statements in both euros and local currency. Where hard cash was required, the local currency was still used. Because participating countries do not share a common tax system or have identical minimum wage laws, there will still be price differentials, but it was expected that there might be consumer pressures towards price harmonization.

On January 1, 2002, Euro notes and coins come into circulation, and wages, for example, will be paid in euro. National currencies will no be longer legal tender. Currencies that have had a long and glorious history such as francs, marks, lira, and guilders will go the way of the dodo bird.

How important is a distinctive currency to national identity? Does it matter that Canada have its own distinctive currency with the emblem of the Queen?

The second remarkable element is that the EU has developed its own *supranational institutions*, including a civil service and policy initiation and implementation body called the European Commission, a directly elected European Parliament (which is assuming more powers such as in budgets and treaties), a powerful Council of Ministers (consisting of cabinet ministers from representative states), a European Council (consisting of heads of state), and a European Court of Justice to administer the legislation of the community. In some important ways, then, the EU is already a type of supranational state.[75] It even has its own tax base through the value added tax (VAT). However, in other ways it is still dependent on the voluntary participation of member states- and some do opt out of some things like the monetary union. As power and authority is given or assumed by the EU and its headquarters in Brussels, the role of the member state changes but not without controversy and concern among some Europeans with strong national identities.

The creation of the EU is still very much in process. Its member states have a "semi-sovereign"[76] position in which some key political powers are still retained. The working languages of the Commission are English and French but all EU publications are printed in the languages of the member states. Some states such as the United Kingdom have maintained a more independent position while others are highly committed to the EU. In general, however, the EU has been a creation of political elites rather than populist action. The lack of systematic accountability to the popular will, through the relative weakness of the European Parliament, has led to what is called *the democratic deficit*[77] of the EU. In that sense, while the EU has created its own internal dynamic, it is still a product of its member nations. But the level of integration already achieved is indeed remarkable with future plans suggesting even more integration.[78]

Is the EU a paradigm for NAFTA? Will integration of the nature experienced in Europe occur in North America? While this is very much a question for the future, it can be stated quite unequivocally that NAFTA has none of the supranational institutions which the EU has created. And while there are no plans to do so, discussion of a monetary union with the United States has already begun. Furthermore, as Figure 6.4 indicates, while there is some disparity in population size and GDP among EU members, it is not of the magnitude present in North America where the United States is a *regional hegemon.*[79] Germany's power is somewhat counterbalanced by France in Europe and there is a plurality of smaller nations in the EU. But in North America, there is an enormous asymmetry between the United States and all other countries including those in Latin America where interest is also expressed in forming new economic arrangements.

mon currency. And just as the EU discovered that a relationship established to facilitate economic flows has cultural effects,[80] so Canada is very aware that matters of economy and culture cannot be separated. When rules and regulations are deliberately changed by governments to facilitate interaction with other societies, this is known as *formal integration* and involves a clear decision to move in that direction[81] When market forces, technology, and communication create more interaction, it is known as *informal integration* because it occurs more spontaneously and without state sanction. It is this dual process of formal integration and informal integration that causes political boundaries to lose their significance and become primarily symbolic with uncertain consequences for the future.

UNIQUENESS RE-EXAMINED

In spite of the brevity with which some of these comparisons have been made, it is clear that many other societies struggle with issues similar to those identified in Canadian society. More lengthy analyses are needed to explain the factors that produce the different effects and that result in alternate solutions.

One idea that stands out from this comparative study is the way in which power is used either to accommodate or to repel minority interests, whether in marginal regions, weakly populated areas, among poorer people, or minority language and cultures. The basic democratic principle of majority rule can legitimate policies that create considerable societal tensions when minorities feel marginalized and powerless and become vocal and strident. While political states may be somewhat reluctant to support the devolution (dispersal) of their powers, decentralization may be a better way to accommodate local interests. When power is shared or dispersed between groups, rather than centrally mandated by a majority, the result is a *consociational* form of society.[82] Canada is not unique in attempting to struggle with regional and ethnic interests and uneven economic development, so it might be expected that much can be learned by examining the experience of other societies.

FURTHER EXPLORATION

1. How can Canada learn from experiences of other societies? Discuss and illustrate with examples.

2. Why do people outside of North America frequently visualize Canadian society and American society as essentially the same? List some of the reasons why this assumption is true or not true and elaborate on them.

3. Compare the current federal policy on bilingualism with the principle of linguistic territoriality. Which is a better solution for Canada?

4. What do you think the consequences of free trade might be? Watch for articles in your newspaper on the European Union and compare with what is unfolding in North America.

SELECTED READINGS

Burridge, Kate, Lois Foster, and Gerry Turcotte (eds.), *Canada-Australia: Towards a Second Century of Partnership.* Ottawa: International Council For Canadian Studies, Carleton University Press, 1997.

Close, Paul. *Citizenship, Europe and Change.* London: Macmillan, 1995.

Isajiw, W. W. (ed.), *Multiculturalism in North America and Europe.* Toronto: Canadian Scholars Press, 1997.

Lipset, S.M. *Continental Divide: The Values and Institutions of the United States and Canada.* New York: Routledge, 1990.

Thomas, David (ed.), *Canada and the United States: Differences that Count.* Peterborough: Broadview, 1993.

ENDNOTES

1   Australia Yearbook 1998 (Canberra: Australian Bureau of Statistics, 1998), 136–139.

2   Further discussions of this material on Western Australia can be found in my "Secession in Western Australia: A Continuing Phenomenon?" *The Australian Quarterly* 59(1987): 222–33; and "Western Separatism in Australia and Canada: The Regional Ideology Thesis," *Australian-Canadian Studies* 5(1987): 39–54.

3   L.S. Bourne and M.I. Logan, "Changing Urbanization Patterns at the Margin: The Examples of Australia and Canada," in Brian J.L. Berry, ed., *Urbanization and Counter-Urbanization* (Beverly Hills: Sage, 1976), 116–18.

4   Elisa Maria Reis and Simon Schwartzman, "Spatial Dislocation and Social Identity in Brazil," *International Social Science Journal* 30(1978): 98–115.

5   Statistical Abstract of The United States, 1998, 118th ed. (Washington D.C.: Bureau of Census, 1998), 27.

6   Statistical Abstract of The United States, 1984, p. 10 and p. 12, and 1998, Table 29.

7   Kirkpatrick Sale, *Power Shift: The Rise of the Southern Rim and its Challenge to the Eastern Establishment* (New York: Random, 1975).

8   Robert B. Cohen, "Multinational Corporations, International Finance, and the Sunbelt," in David C. Perry and Alfred J. Watkins, eds., *The Rise of the Sunbelt Cities* (Beverly Hills, Sage, 1977), 211–26.

9   Benjamin Higgins, *The Rise and Fall of Montreal?* (Moncton: Canadian Institute for Research on Regional Development, 1986).

10 Louis Hartz, ed., *The Founding of New Societies* (New York: Harcourt, Brace and World, 1964), chap. 1. For a critique of Hartz, see Gad Horowitz, "Conservativism, Liberalism, and Socialism in Canada: An Interpretation," *Canadian Journal of Economics and Political Science* 32(1966): 143–50.

11 Kenneth McRae, "The Structure Of Canadian History," in Hartz, *The Founding of New Societies.* See also his "Louis Hartz's Concept of the Fragment Society and its Applications to Canada," Etudes Canadiennes 5(1978): 17–30.

12 David Bell and Lorne Tepperman, *The Roots of Disunity* (Toronto: McClelland and Stewart, 1979), 45.

13 Bell and Tepperman, *The Roots of Disunity*, 76, 79.

14 See in particular "The Social Development of Canada and the American Continental System," Culture 5(1944): 132–43, and "Canada and her Great Neighbor," *Canadian Review of Sociology and Anthropology* 1(1964): 193–201.

15 *Revolution and Counter-Revolution: Change and Persistence in Social Structures,* rev. ed. (Garden City: Doubleday, 1971); and "Canada and The United States: A Comparative View," *Canadian Review of Sociology and Anthropology* 1(1964): 173–85. For a broadening of his comparison to Britain and Australia, see "The Value Patterns of Democracy: A Case Study in Comparative Analysis," *American Sociological Review* 28(1963): 515–31. A recent restatement of Lipset's argument can be found in "Canada and The United States: The Cultural Dimension," in Charles F. Doran and John H. Sigler, eds., *Canada and the United States* (Englewood Cliffs: Prentice Hall, 1985).

16 See, for example, Tom Truman, "A Critique of Seymour M. Lipset's Article," *Canadian Journal of Political Science* 4(1971): 513–25; Irving Louis Horowitz, "The Hemispheric Connection: A Critique and Corrective to the Entrepreneurial Thesis of Development with Special Emphasis on the Canadian Case," *Queen's Quarterly* 80(1973): 336–37; Craig Crawford and James Curtis, "English Canada-American Differences in Value Orientations: Survey Comparisons Bearing on Lipset's Thesis," *Studies in Comparative International Development,* 1979; and Bell and Tepperman *The Roots of Disunity,* 24–32. For a good review of these critiques, see Robert J. Brym, *From Culture to Power: The Sociology of English Canada* (Toronto: Oxford, 1989), 29–32.

17 Seymour Martin Lipset, *Continental Divide: The Values and Institutions of The United States and Canada* (New York: Routledge, 1990). Published first in 1989 by the C.D. Howe Institute and the National Planning Association.

18 S.M. Lipset, *Continental Divide,* chap. 12.

19 Neil Nevitte, *The Decline of Deference* (Peterborough: Broadview, 1996)

20 Gordon Laxer, "Constitutional Crises And Continentalism: Twin Threat's To Canada's Continued Existence," *Canadian Journal of Sociology* 17(2)1992:199–222.

21 Pierre L. Van Den Berghe, "Australia, Canada, and The United States: Ethnic Melting Pots of Plural Societies?" *Australia and New Zealand Journal of Sociology* 19(1983): 238–52.

22 See Charles A. Price, "The Immigrants," in A.F. Davies, S. Encel, and M.J. Berry, eds., *Australian Society: A Sociological Introduction* (Melbourne: Longman Cheshire, 1977), 331–55; and Dennis Laurence Cuddy, *The Yanks are Coming: American Immigration to Australia* (San Francisco: R and E Research Associates, 1977) 4–5. For an explicit analysis comparing the immigration policies of Canada and Australia, see Freda Hawkins, *Critical Years in Immigration: Canada and Australia Compared* (Montreal: McGill-Queen's University Press, 1989).

23 M.L. Kovacs and A.J. Cropley, *Immigrants and Society Alienation and Assimilation* (Sydney: McGraw-Hill, 1975).

24 First Report Of The National Population Inquiry, Population and Australia: A Demographic Analysis and Projection, vol. 1 (Canberra: Government of Australia, 1975), 99.

25 Australian Council on Population and Ethnic Affairs, Multiculturalism for all Australians (Canberra, 1982), 33–34. Statistics in this section are also from Yearbook Australia 1988, 263–64.

26 *Australia Yearbook* 1998, 159 and 170.

27 Christine Inglis, "Globalisation and the Impact of Asian Migration on Australia and Canada", Kate Burridge, Lois Foster, and Gerry Turcotte (eds.), *Canada-Australia: Towards a Second Century of Partnership* (Ottawa: International Council For Canadian Studies, Carleton University Press, 1997), 45–75.

28 *Multiculturalism for all Australians*, 1. The emphasis on second generation effects of immigration is repeatedly found in the Australian literature whereas it is mentioned much less in the Canadian literature. This may reflect the greater concern for assimilation in Australian society.

29 I.H. Burnley, "Geographic-Demographic Perspectives on the Ecology of Ethnic Groups in Australian Cities," in Charles A. Price and Jean I. Martin, eds., *Australian Immigration: A Bibliography and Digest*, Part I (Canberra: Australia National University, 1976), 124–49.

30 *Immigrants and Society: Alienation and Assimilation,* chap. 4

31 Jean I. Martin, *The Migrant Presence: Australian Responses 1947–1977* (Sydney: George Allen and Unwin, 1978).

32 See Malcolm Alexander, "Globalisation And Civil Society: Multiculturalism, Citizenship and Nationalism in Australia and Canada", 125–137, and Lois Foster and Paul Bartrop, "The Roots Of Multiculturalism In Australia and Canada", 267–286 in Burridge, Foster, and Turcotte (ed.), *Canada-Australia: Towards a Second Century of Partnership*; Freda Hawkins, "Multiculturalism in Two Countries: The Canadian and Australian Experience," *Journal of Canadian Studies* 17(1982): 64–80; and Anthony H. Richmond and G. Rao, "Recent Developments in Immigration to Canada and Australia: A Comparative Analysis," *International Journal of Comparative Sociology* 17(1976): 183–205.

33 *The Migrant Presence: Australian Responses 1947–1977*, 30–31; and *Population and Australia: A Demographic Analysis and Projection*, 124. The difficulties in determining intentions of people on arrival and on departure make precise figures a problem to obtain. However, emigration is clearly recognized as a significant matter in Australia.

34 Rita Bienvenue, "Comparative Colonial Systems: The Case of Canadian Indians and Australian Aborigines," *Australian-Canadian Studies* 1(1983): 30–43. Donald Edgar, *Introduction to Australian Society: A Sociological Perspective* (Sydney: Prentice-Hall, 1980), 297. Australia Yearbook 1998, 154.

35 Bradford W. Morse, *Aboriginal Self-government in Australia and Canada* (Kingston: Queen's University Institute of Intergovernmental Relations, 1984).

36 Colin Taz, "Aborigines: Political Options and Strategies," in R.M. Berndt, ed., *Aborigines and Change* (Canberra: Australian Institute of Aboriginal Studies, 1977), 384–401.

37 For brief comparison, see Mary Beth Montcalm, "Quebec Separatism in Comparative Perspective," in Alain G. Gagnon, ed., *Quebec: State and Society* (Toronto: Methuen, 1984), 45–58; and Peter A. Gourevitch, "Quebec Separatism in Comparative Perspective," in Elliot J. Feldman and Neil Nevitte, eds., *The Future of North America* (Cambridge: Center for International Affairs, 1979), 238–52. See also Edward Tiryakian, "Quebec, Wales, and Scotland: Three Nations in Search of a State," *International Journal of Comparative Sociology* 21 (1982): 1–13.

38 Mark O. Rousseau and Raphael Zariski, *Regionalism and Regional Devolution in Comparative Perspective* (New York: Praeger, 1987).

39 For a discussion of these two perspectives, see Charles C. Ragin, "Ethnic Political Mobilization: The Welsh Case," *American Sociological Review* 44(1979): 619–35, and Francois Nielsen, "The Flemish Movement in Belgium After World War II: A Dynamic Analysis," *American Sociological Review* 45(1980): 76–94.

40 Tom Nairn, *The Breakup of Britain* (London: NLB, 1977), 105–106.

41 Jack Brand, "The Rise And Fall Of Scottish Nationalism," in Charles R. Foster, ed., *Nations Without a State* (New York: Praeger, 1980), 33ff.

42　Milton J. Esman, "Scottish Nationalism, North Sea Oil, and the British Response" in M.J. Esman, ed., *Ethnic Conflict in the Western World* (Ithaca: Cornell University Press, 1977), 256–58.

43　John Bochel, David Denver, and Alan Macartney, eds., *The Referendum Experience Scotland 1979* (Aberdeen: Aberdeen University Press, 1981).

44　For example, see the document by Owen Dudley Edwards, ed., *A Claim of Right for Scotland* (Edinburgh: Polygon, 1989).

45　John Foster, "Nationality, Social Change and Class: Transformations of National Identity in Scotland," in David McCrone, Stephen Kendrick, and Pat Straw, *The Making of Scotland: Nation, Culture, and Social Change* (Edinburgh: Edinburgh University Press, 1989), 31–52.

46　Jack Brand takes the view that ethnicity is not as important to the Scottish movement as the attempt to seek redress from economic marginality by a depressed yet hopeful region. But he does show how Scottish folk songs act as a mobilization device among young voters. *The National Movement in Scotland* (London: Routledge and Kegan Paul, 1978). Other approaches that use a world systems or class-based approach include Michael Hechter, *Internal Colonialism* (London: Routledge Kegan and Paul, 1975) and Tom Nairn, *The Breakup of Britain*. For a different emphasis on which much of the following discussion is based, see David McCrone, *Understanding Scotland: The Sociology of a Stateless Nation* (London: Routledge, 1992) and Michael Keating, Nations Against The State (London: Macmillan, 1996).

47　John Osmond, "Wales In The 1980's," in Charles R. Foster, ed., *Nations Without a State*, 45.

48　Ray Corrado, "The Welsh as a Nonstate Nation," in Judy S. Bertelsen, ed., *Nonstate Nations in International Politics* (New York: Praeger, 1977), chap. 6.

49　Tom Nairn, *The Breakup of Britain*, and Michael Hechter, *Internal Colonialism: The Celtic Fringe in British National Development* (Berkeley: University of California Press, 1975).

50　Walker Connor, "The Political Significance Of Ethnonationalism Within Western Europe," in Abdul Said and Luiz R. Simmons, *Ethnicity in an International Context* (New Brunswick, N.J.: Transaction, 1976), 117; and Osmond, 62.

51　H.M. Drucker and Gordon Brown, *The Politics of Nationalism and Devolution* (London: Longmans, 1980).

52　Davydd J. Greenwood, "Continuity In Change: Spanish Basque Ethnicity as a Historical Process," in Milton J. Esman, ed., *Ethnic Conflict in the Western World*, 84–87; and Pedro G. Blasco, "Modern Nationalism in Old Nations as a Consequence of Earlier State Building: The Case Of Basque-Spain," in Wendell Bell and Walter E. Freeman, eds., *Ethnicity and Nation Building: Comparative, International, and Historical Perspectives* (Beverly Hills, Sage, 1974).

53　Robert P. Clark, "Euzkadi: Basque Nationalism in Spain Since the Civil War," in Charles R. Foster, ed., *Nations Without a State*, 77.

54　832 000 voted for regional autonomy and only 47 000 voted against it. International matters, trade, defense, and coinage were still to be federal matters. Clark, Ibid, 75–100.

55　Maria Heighberg, *The Making of the Basque Nation* (Cambridge: Cambridge University Press, 1989), 227–230.

56　Thomas C. Davies, "Patterns Of Identity: Basques And The Basque Nation", *Nationalism and Ethnic Politics* 3(1)1997:61–88.

57　Stanley G. Payne, "Nationalism, Regionalism And Micro-Nationalism In Spain", *Journal of Contemporary History* 26(1991):479–491.

58　Ronald Wardhaugh, *Language and Nationhood: The Canadian Experience*, 26.

59　E. Erlich, "Should English-only be the Law of the Land?" *Business Week*, Nov. 10, 1986, regarding the referendum in California; and "Language War in Florida," *Newsweek,* June 30, 1986. See also William A.V. Clark, *The California Cauldron* (Guilford, 1998).

60 E.K. Francis, *Interethnic Relations* (New York: Elsevier, 1976), 104.

61 Carol Schmid, "Comparative Intergroup Relations And Social Incorporation In Two Multilingual Societies: Canada And Switzerland", in W.W. Isajiw (ed.), *Multiculturalism in North America and Europe* (Toronto: Canadian Scholars Press, 1997), 484.

62 Kenneth D. McRae, *Conflict and Compromise in Multilingual Societies: Switzerland* (Waterloo: Wilfrid Laurier University Press, 1983), 55.

63 Kurt Mayer, "Ethnic Tensions in Switzerland: The Jura Conflict," in Charles R. Foster, ed., *Nations Without a State*, 189–208.

64 These points are found in McRae, Conflict and Compromise in Multilingual Societies: Switzerland. and Schmid, "Comparative Intergroup Relations And Social Incorporation In Two Multilingual Societies: Canada And Switzerland." It is important not to overstress the unity aspect because the 1992 vote on joining the European Union split the two largest linguistic groups as there was strong French support but mostly German opposition which because of their size carried the vote (see Schmid, 484).

65 Jaroslov Krejci and Vitezslav Velimsky, *Ethnic and Political Nations in Europe* (London: Croom Helm, 1981), 103–104.

66 Reginal DeSchryver, "The Belgian Revolution and the Emergence of Belgium's Biculturalism," in Arend Lijphart, eds., *Conflict and Coexistence in Belgium* (Berkeley: Institute of International Studies, 1980), 13–33.

67 Aristide R. Zolberg, "Splitting the Difference: Federalization Without Federalism in Belgium," in Milton J. Esman, ed., *Ethnic Conflict in the Western World*, 103–142.

68 Kenneth D. McRae, *Conflict and Compromise in Multilingual Societies: Belgium* (Waterloo: Wilfrid Laurier University Press, 1986), 109.

69 *The Political Handbook of the World* 1998, 84–88.

70 The peace incentives that stand behind economic cooperation in Europe is a strong theme in all accounts of the EU. For example, see Desmond Dinan, *Ever Closer Union? An Introduction to the European Community.* (Boulder: Lynn Rienner, 1994). A good overview of the issues in European integration is Brigid Laffan, *Integration and Cooperation in Europe*, (New York: Routledge, 1992).

71 James Laxer discusses the historic battleground between France and Germany which he calls a major "fault-line" in Europe from where the strongest desires for cooperation were expressed. *Inventing Europe: The Rise of a New World Power* (Toronto: Lester, 1991), 16.

72 "Widening" and "deepening" are two critical and debatable concepts within the European Union.

73 Christopher Piening, *Global Europe: The European Union in World Affairs* (Boulder: Lynn Rienner, 1997).

74 Edelgard Mahant and Xavier DeVanssay, "The Origins of Customs Unions and Free Trade Areas," 181–210; and Brigitte Lévy, "The European Union and NAFTA: Two Regional Economic Blocs in a Complex Globalized and Interdependent International Economy," 211–33 in *Journal of Economic Integration*, vol. 17, no. 2–3, 1994.

75 Gretchen Macmillan, "Managing Convergence in the European Union," in Donald Barry, ed., *Toward a North American Community? Canada, the United States, and Mexico* (Boulder: Westview, 1995), 229–40.

76 Gretchen M. Macmillan, "The European Community: Is it a Supra-National State in the Making?," in Stephen J. Randall and Roger Gibbins, eds., *Federalism and the New World Order*, (Calgary: University of Calgary Press, 1994), 233.

77 Peter H. Smith, "Decision Rules and Governance," in Peter H. Smith, ed., *The Challenge of Integration: Europe and the Americas*, (New Brunswick, N.J.: Transaction, 1993), 366.

78 There is considerable discussion about whether the European Union means the death of individual European states, much of it disagreeing that it is likely. See, for example, Alan Milward, *The European Rescue of the Nation-State* (London: Routledge, 1992); Michael Mann, "Nation-states In Europe And Other Continents: Diversifying, Developing, Not Dying," *Daedalus* 122(1993), and "Has Globalization Ended The Rise Of The Nation-State?, *Review of International Political Economy* (41997); and David McCrone, *The Sociology of Nationalism* (London: Routledge, 1998), Chapter 9.

79 C.F. Peter H. Smith, Ibid, 377–79.

80 Bruno de Witte, "Cultural Linkages," in William Wallace (ed.), *The Dynamics of European Integration* (London: Pinter, 1990), 192210.

81 William Wallace, "Introduction", in *The Dynamics of European Integration*, 9.

82 The distinction between majoritarian and consociational societies was made by Arend J. Lijphart in his preface to Conflict and Coexistence in Belgium.

WEBLINKS

www.pch.gc.ca/multi/html/english.html

The Web site for the Government of Canada's Secretary of State for Multiculturalism and the Status of Women gives information about its projects, reports, publications, and the federal Multiculturalism Act.

europa.eu.int/euro/html/home5.html?lang=5

Visit this Web site hosted by the European Union to learn more about the Euro, the single currency Europe will use by 2002.

tceplus.com/different.htm

"How Are Canadians Different from Americans?" is an article by Rae Corelli, originally published in *Maclean's* magazine.

www.un.org/Depts/unsd/sd_social.htm

Visit this section of the United Nations Statistics homepage to view demographic and social statistics from around the world.

THE QUESTION
OF IDENTITY

The Canadian social scientist cannot take the existence of this society for granted. There is nothing about the society that can be fully understood except in relation to how the society developed, how its very survival as a society, flanked as it was by the powerful republic to the south, remained problematic...

Canadian nationhood was attained, not by the making of different people into one, or by the strengthening of forces of consensus, but by fostering the differences between people within the nation and thereby securing the differences between Canadian people and American.

—S.D. Clark, the dean of Canadian sociology,
whose career began in the 1930s.

The comparative analysis conducted in the previous chapter is very important in the study of Canadian society because it reveals to us that Canadian society is not the only society that is fraught with internal conflicts and pressures towards change. The imagery of nation-states as harmonious families where all are united towards common objectives seldom exists in reality. It is important to recognize this because many Canadians lose patience with the constant negotiations, debate, and uncertainties that pervade national life—as though Canadian society was some kind of outlier in the world of nation-states.

The enormous amount of energy that is put into seeking some kind of consensus and the resolution of longstanding and new-emerging divisions has made negotiation and its attempted codification in constitutional reform almost a national preoccupation. It is this context which leads to endless use of pessimistic descriptors such as "perpetual crisis," "anguished introspection," "inconclusive attempts at self-definition," "world champions of insecurity," or a country of "ceaseless self-psychoanalysis" when discussing Canada and Canadians. The impact of all this uncertainty is a national neurosis that is reflected in the self-deprecating question "why does a Canadian cross the road?" The chicken may have said it is to get to the other side, but for the Canadian, in the relentless pursuit for acceptable compromise, "it is to get to the middle." So Keith Spicer sums up these feelings by saying "Canada's identity is its identity crisis."[1]

While most people live their lives somewhat removed from any daily sense of threat and leave most of this debate to politicians, most Canadians are indeed aware that Canadian society is in the midst of significant transitions in which the end result is still unclear. The material presented in the earlier chapters attempted to "unpack" the constituent elements of the society into the regional, class, and ethnic cleavages which serve as the basis for social conflict within the society. In many ways, we may have shattered the romantic images of the nationalists or patriots who truly love their country and are only too willing to overlook the trouble spots. Yet there are too many recent events that remind us that societies are fragile negotiated entities always "in the making." People who think of Canadian society in terms of what it was 50 years ago or 20 years ago may be truly disconcerted by the changes they see around them. In this chapter, we will see that not only do the constituent groups within a society change but so do our conceptions of the good society. Indeed, our minds are constantly being expanded to consider new structural forms for Canadian society as a consequence of such things as free trade, Quebec separatism, and Aboriginal self-determination. The focus in this chapter, then, is to examine the search for common ground, and its competing elements, as well as to explore alternative ways of looking at society.-It is this kind of thinking that will be necessary as we face the transitions of the contemporary Canada.

ISSUES IN ASSESSING THE CANADIAN IDENTITY

Analyzing a Societal Identity

It is the commonality of sharing a territory (in spite of its size) and participating in its polity (in spite of its inequities) that makes the country's residents Canadian. To the extent that borders are real, they demarcate territory in which *people transform simple space into places where they live and share relationships with others inhabiting that space*. A societal identity emerges as people engage in this type of *place-making*.[2] Through collective interaction among people who share the symbol "Canadian," a national identity is constructed.

A societal identity is the sum of the sentiments, cultural attributes, and structural arrangements people share which gives them a feeling that they belong together. Individuals and groups *create* and contribute to that identity; but they can also *internalize* the national identity into their personal definition of themselves (though to varying degrees). A societal identity, then, has a *collective* component as well as an *individual* dimension. For this reason, it is possible to speak of the residents of Canada jointly creating and constructing a national society, and individual members accepting that collective identity as something that is personally meaningful.

Flowing from this key idea that national societies are social constructions is a second point that they are not fixed but are *constantly changing* and *in process* due to the existence of *competing visions* represented by *conflicting groups*. Rather than understanding societies as fixed and immutable and resistant to change, it is clear that at least in contemporary Canada, there are constant pressures towards new structures and formulations, and they are difficult and often painful to resolve. Just as the Senate, for example, was created as an arm of government, so there are pressures to change it from an appointed to an elected body, and yet resistance to such change promotes considerable conflict. Acceptance of Quebec as a distinct society is another new idea which reveals the pressure for change but resistance to the idea is also promoting conflict. On the other hand, the policy of bilingualism was at one time a new idea which became policy in spite of resistance. So we do not just accept or internalize things as they are; we seek new and better ways to do things and respond to changes as they occur, thereby modifying the nature of societies.

A third aspect in analyzing a societal identity is the repeated effort to distinguish Canadian society and its interests from other societies. One study found that members of Canadian society became most aware of their national identity through their travels outside the country and through interacting with foreigners.[3] It has been argued that the only time that Canadians wave the flag is when they are on vacation in Europe and do not want to be mistaken for Americans. It could also be argued that state negotiations with other societies make Canadians more aware of their national interests. For example, the turbot dispute with Spain in 1995 and the armed stand-off with fishing vessels in international waters off Newfoundland not only made a public global statement about Canadian concerns about fish conservation but defended the interests of Atlantic coast fishers. The point is that a national identity can coagulate as

I Am Canadian: Constructing a Unique Identity?

I work in the Toronto office of a multinational corporation based in the United States that bought the company from a British firm. Today I helped negotiate a contract by e-mail with someone I have never seen or spoken with. I drove home in my Japanese car and, on the way, bought a panini loaf from an Italian bakery.

My husband works for a Canadian accounting firm that does the books for a manufacturer that exports around the world but requires lots of currency transfers in US funds. On the way home, he picked up the children in his German bug (which they love), and, in the middle of our winter, he gives them a fresh peach as a snack from Chile.

For supper we had New Zealand lamb, California lettuce and tomatoes, French cheese, South African grapes, and Spanish wine. Then we watched the TV special on the three tenors from Europe.

As I nestled in my bed that night, I was so happy to be Canadian.

a result of *external relationships,* and as a consequence of this external dialogue, a society may become more aware of its internal relationships or the concerns its people share.

There is also a fourth aspect to a national identity. One perception of a national identity is merely that a distinctive identity emerges from things as they are (*descriptive*). For example, no society has quite the same relationship between anglophones and francophones as Canada does, and for better or for worse, that is what gives Canadian society its identity. But another perspective is far more *prescriptive*, suggesting vision and ideals about what Canadian society *should be.* It can be argued that by focusing on *what is*, the emphasis is more likely to be on identity problems, whereas by dreaming and working towards a new and better Canadian society, the emphasis shifts from propping up the current fragmented identity to consolidating a new societal identity. However, as we shall see, there may be considerable disagreement among opposing groups about what ought to be.

CONTRADICTIONS IN THE ANALYSIS OF CANADIAN SOCIETY

There are five key contradictions or tensions which are at the heart of debates about the nature and character of Canadian society.

1. Homogeneity vs. Heterogeneity

Is the goal the development of a society where everyone has similar traits and possesses similar loyalties or can we tolerate diversity? If diversity, how much diversity should be encouraged? What impact does an answer to this question have on immigration policy? Language policy? Does multiculturalism which promotes a plurality of ethnic identities detract from a single Canadian identity? Is a Canadian defined in a rather uniform way or should differences be tolerated, encouraged, and even fiscally supported?

2. Insularity vs. Openness

In order to develop a national consciousness, to what extent should the national borders be sealed from foreign influence? Should members of the society be discouraged from reading foreign magazines, watching foreign television, investing in foreign countries, or listening to recordings of foreign musicians? While these items may be central to our conception of individual freedom, should the government use its powers to attempt to minimize foreign influence and thereby encourage national development? The question is, how does one determine the degree of insularity necessary to encourage national development? How much openness to other societies is necessary to prevent ethnocentrism and encourage creativity, new ideas, and new social forms?

3. Legitimacy vs. Illegitimacy

Legitimacy pertains to the acceptability of those who have power to wield it over others. In general, members of Canadian society accept the rule of their democratically elected governments as legitimate and worthy of support. Yet there have been repeated challenges to national authority and objectives by those who have alternate conceptions of what the society should be like, who question the right of the central state and its agencies to make those decisions for them, or who feel that majority rule tyrannizes minorities.

When Quebec rejected the decision of the Supreme Court regarding Bill 101, it was challenging the legitimacy of the Canadian state to interfere with this aspect of Quebec life. As a result of the 1980 federal election, the West questioned the legitimacy of federal policies promoted by a government that had poor representation from that region. The election of many members of the Bloc Québécois to Parliament in the 1993 federal election also created an ironic situation of a separatist party, seeking independence from Canada, forming the official opposition in Parliament with all of the rights and privileges associated with that status. Other challenges to the legitimacy of the central state have come over Native rights, resource ownership, and even metrication.

One of the recurring complaints within Canadian society is that the actions of the central state are illegitimate because they represent specialized interests (e.g., the interests of the Golden Triangle or corporate capitalists). Should minority interest groups or hinterland interest groups be specially accommodated? How does the state wield power in the national interest when the national interest is defined in terms of a narrow interest group? Whose interests are legitimate and who is to decide whose interests are illegitimate or less legitimate?

4. Centralization vs. Decentralization

In order to build a strong Canadian society, some argue that a strong central government is needed to establish policies that promote uniformity and homogeneity throughout the society. They argue that only through strong central control is the fragmentation of the society prevented. From this point of view, one of the arguments against the Meech Lake Accord and the Charlottetown Agreement was that they strengthened the provinces by decentralizing too much authority and therefore emasculated the federal government's nation building role. Do regional or local identities strengthen the national identity or compete and distract from it? How far can we go in allowing some groups within Canada to be considered "distinct societies" or to have self-government while still being part of Canadian society? How much decentralization and regional variation can be tolerated without mocking the idea of a national society?

5. Equality vs. Inequality

All societies possess inequalities but the question is how much inequality should be tolerated within a society—especially if it is argued that the structure of the society fosters and deepens inequalities? Should one region of a society care when another region is disadvantaged? Does a prosperous region have a responsibility to a disadvantaged region? If so, how should these inequalities be addressed? Do equalization grants really help or do they merely perpetuate the inequities that already exist? And what about language, employment, and gender inequities? To what extent must the inequities that exist within the society be removed in order to create a greater sense of personal or group identification with the national society?

These dichotomous tensions remain major issues in Canadian society which are never resolved but are responded to in a variety of ways, sometimes more in one direction and sometimes more in the other direction. These responses, however, become "made-in-Canada" solutions to unique Canadian problems. For example, the particular form of bilingualism found in Canada represents a particular solution to a unique Canadian problem. Thus, it can be argued that the Canadian identity is the product of these struggles to cope with the tensions and conflicts that have emerged within the society. In that sense, the Canadian identity is not a once-for-all set-in-stone complex of traits but an evolving entity.

While in one sense, societal conflict may be viewed as problematic, there is another sense in which conflict can be viewed as the attempt to find unique compromises in which conflicting parties participate together to find solutions which may serve to reshape Canadian society. This was the perspective taken by the Task Force on Canadian Unity appointed by the federal government in the 1970s which tried to reinterpret diversity as a *national resource* rather than a societal problem.[4] Diversity was to be encouraged rather than submerged, but with the goal of harmonious coexistence. Yet merely giving a positive spin to Canada's dilemmas does not remove them or lead to quick solutions.

The most important nation-defining contradictions or tensions which preoccupy Canadian existence are the French and English clash over different conceptions of society, the contradictions between the federal centre and the regions, and the attempt to differentiate Canadian society from American society.[5] There are other tensions or contradictions (such as First Nations against Euro-Canadians), but the struggle with these key contending realities is at the heart of the evolution and development of national identity in Canada.

Conceptualizing the Contradictions: Two Perspectives

From an analytical point of view, there are two basic perspectives in assessing Canadian identity: the pan-Canadian or unitary approach and the segmentalist approach.[6] The *pan-Canadian* or *unitary approach* contends that the society is made up of *individuals* who find their collective identity in their sense of belonging to the national society. Characteristics such as a non-official language spoken at home, or other regional or ethnic loyalties, are either devalued or minimized in preference to adherence to wider allegiances to the national society. In stressing the individualist basis of society, this approach accentuates the role of the Canadian state in providing the necessary feeling of belonging.

The *segmentalist approach* focuses on the groups or communities which are founded upon regional, racial, linguistic, occupational, or cultural similarities. The segmentalist expects these *group commitments* (rather than the individual) to serve as the building blocks of Canadian society, and does not aim to dissolve these groups even when they compete with allegiances to the larger society. Anglophones, and particularly anglophones in Ontario, are more prone to prefer the pan-Canadian approach to societal unity. Francophones, Aboriginals, and some residents of hinterland regions who have other group ties are more likely to prefer the segmentalist approach to Canadian society.

It is important to understand this distinction between the pan-Canadian or unitary approach and the segmentalist approach at the outset. They represent different models of society with different outcomes, but they are both valid models of society. You may be biased towards one or the other approach in terms of what you think Canadian society should be like, but be aware that there are those who can make a strong case for the opposing model.

There was a time when it was thought that the pan-Canadian view of Canadian society would eventually win out. As immigrants were assimilated, as the continental crush of the dominant English language overwhelmed Quebec francophones, and as hinterland regions were integrated more clearly into the national economy, it was thought that commitments to the national society would become primary. Yet ethnic associations remain vital, Quebec uniqueness remains strong, First Nations commitment to self-determination is growing, and regional loyalties and grievances foster community attachments. Consequently, commitments to the national society remain diluted for at least some Canadians, thereby supporting a more segmentalized conception of society. Clearly, most of the key issues in Canadian society currently revolve around this unitary –segmentalist debate.

FACTORS IN IDENTITY FORMATION

If a national identity is not something that is immutable and unchanging or even in evolution towards a fixed form, and if there are many different versions of what it means to be a Canadian,[7] it is important to identify the central features of the evolving Canadian identity. Six features will be discussed.

1. Responding to the Colonialist Legacy

The British sponsorship of Canadian society has produced a legacy of British influence including the parliamentary system and British law. Pictures of the British royalty continue to appear on Canadian coins, and though its use is now infrequent, children are taught "God Save Our Queen" in schools as an anthem of respect towards the monarchy. The position of Governor General (the representative of the monarchy in the government) was only first filled by a Canadian in 1952 when Vincent Massey was appointed. Even though this British sponsorship has been loosened considerably, first through the creation of the British Commonwealth of Nations, and more recently through Britain's shift away from her former colonies to the European Union, a special relationship with the mother country still prevails. Members of the royal family still make regular visits to Canada, and thousands flock to see them.

There is not agreement by any means on the role of the monarchy in contemporary Canadian society. Obviously, persons of British descent are more likely to have positive feelings about this role while those of other ethnic backgrounds are more likely to prefer a more independent rather than sponsored identity. It was not until 1947 that a Canadian citizen was differentiated from a British subject, so the legacy of British ties was real for many Canadians until after World War II. Perhaps the strongest negative response to that colonialist heritage has come from the Québécois who see the symbols of the monarchy as reminders of their defeat by the British and their position as a subordinate minority. Consequently, while the colonial legacy is part of Canada's "roots," that legacy is far from a basis of pride and unity for all Canadian residents, and in fact is an issue that may divide more than it unites.

In one sense, Canada sustained her unique identity through the years as a result of this alliance with Britain.[8] On the other hand, the relationship can be viewed as essentially a maternalistic one which has shadowed the society's own expressions of independence. No issue was more symbolic of this concern than the repatriation of the constitution. The British North America Act of 1867, as an act of the British Parliament and Canada's Constitution for many years, only served as a reminder that Canadian society had never created a charter for its own existence. It also continued as a stark reminder to francophones of British dominance and the French colonial defeat. Consequently, the proclamation of the new Constitution Act, 1982 on April 17, 1982, with an amending formula and a charter of rights and freedoms, had the potential of signifying a new era in the society's independent existence. There was, however, no great outpouring of nationalist sentiment, little public enthusiasm, and perhaps more importantly, Quebec did not sign the accord.[9] Thus the document that was to be

REAL PEOPLE 7

Questioning the Taken-for-Granted

Every morning before school, nine-year-old Stephen dutifully practised for his Wednesday piano lesson. This week his teacher gave him a new song to practise and Stephen picked his way through the melody. It sounded strangely familiar.

"That's it," Stephen exclaimed. "God Save Our Queen. We sing that song at school assemblies."

Mom was in the kitchen, and had vaguely overhead Stephen's discovery over the noise of his brother yelling about what clothes to wear.

"Hey Mom," inquired Stephen. "Is the Queen the Queen of the whole world?"

"No Steve, she's the Queen of England."

There was a pause as he plunked out a few more notes.

"Hey Mom, England is another country isn't it?"

"Yes dear," his Mother assured him.

"We're on a different continent than England, right Mom?"

"Yup, you're right."

A few more notes come from the piano.

"Then how come we sing OUR Queen?"

"It's always been that way Steve. Now get ready for school."

Question To Consider: Do you think symbols of the monarchy should be more or less important in Canadian society? What are the advantages or disadvantages of their use?

---

the cornerstone for the new sense of society lacked the concurrence of one of its most significant segments.

The adoption of the new Canadian Constitution was not a moment of great celebration in Canada for it was a painful process that revealed once again some of the basic underlying struggles within the society.[10] Yet its role in the creation of a societal identity has been, and will continue to be, pivotal. That is why the absence of Quebec from the signing was so lamentable, and why the constitutional revisionism as represented by the Meech Lake Accord and the Charlottetown Agreement was a sign of hope but a hope which was eventually dashed. On the other hand, the continuing constitutional struggles represent the search by Canadians to find the mechanisms to shape their own society and thus to move even farther away from that colonial legacy.

Even though the colonial legacy continues in a form largely symbolic in nature, it reasserts old ties that some feel belong in the past and ought not to be part of the new era of independence.[11] Canada's colonial heritage is still a vestigial part of the society's identity, and the maintenance of symbolic ties seems to be a comfortable way of remaining linked to the society's roots while still building other symbols of independent identity.[12] So far, however, there have been no public discussions of cutting these ties entirely as there has been in Australia, though it is clearly implied in Quebec nationalism.

2. Proximity to the United States

The creation of a political entity on the northern portion of the North American continent which would be different from the United States is central to understanding the formation and evolution of Canadian society. In many ways, it was an economic strategy to expand the market and territory that created the political structures. The Canadian state then became the primary instrument of regulation and development for an autonomous national entity. Canada was deliberately created to be a separate unit and distinct from the United States.[13]

As we saw in Chapter Two, sharing a continent with a larger, more powerful society has always made distinctiveness a problem. At some points, such as in the 60s and 70s, it seemed that the more Canadian society became like American society, the greater were the attempts at differentiation. One analyst has referred to the amalgam of feelings between the two societies as attraction, rejection, and ambivalence.[14] Canadians feel at home in the United States where they travel in great numbers, and Americans struggle to explain subtle differences between the two societies that go beyond the metric signposts in Canada.

The interaction between the two societies is indeed considerable. However, in spite of a devalued Canadian dollar in relation to the American dollar, more Canadians visit the United States than vice versa.[15] In 1997, 50 million Canadians took trips to the United States (down from a high of 66 million in 1993). Forty million Americans took trips to Canada (up from 32 million in 1993). Canadians tended to stay longer in the United States (average length of stay 7.1 nights) than Americans stayed in Canada (3.8 nights), which primarily reflects the annual Canadian "snowbird" migration to warmer climates in the winter months. But what is particularly remarkable are the number of same-day trips (mostly by automobile) across the border. The majority of trips by Canadians to the United States are same-day trips, which suggests that intermingling is part of a daily lifestyle. Small American cities such as Bellingham, Washington, Grand Forks, North Dakota, and Plattsburg, New York are all commercially overbuilt for their size because they are border communities servicing large Canadian cities (Vancouver, Winnipeg, Montreal). Even though the exchange rate was highly unfavourable in 1997, 36 million Canadians made trips to the United States, leaving and returning on the same day (down from a high of 60.2 million trips in 1991). Eighty-four percent of all trips to the United States were for non-business reasons to vacation, visit friends and relatives, and to see events and attractions. The extent of the intermingling of Canadian and American people is revealed by the fact that 93% of Canadian residents returning from international destinations returned from the United States. Ninety percent of all international visits made to Canada in 1997 were made by American residents.

The integration of Canadian and American societies is fostered by many factors but perhaps none is more pervasive than television and popular culture. Canadians watch a large number of American television programs which are broadcast on Canadian stations, as well as on cable networks and satellites. American programming accounts for almost two-thirds of all television Canadians watch.[16]

John Meisal, the former Chairman of the Canadian Radio-television and Telecommunications Commission, has noted that Canadians feel they have a right to access American programming.[17] Because of their proximity to border stations, one of the problems has been that the majority of Canadians could receive US signals even without cable before it was available. Another problem is that American networks can amortize their programming costs over a vast domestic market and then sell these programs to foreign networks for 3–6% of their cost. Canadian producers cannot compete with these costs and therefore read-

Language and National Identity?

Which spelling is Canadian—"color" or "colour"? "neighbor" or "neighbour"? "centre" or "center"? "Or" spelling is usually identified as American and "our" spelling is identified as British.

Some people think that the British spelling is preferable because it helps Canada maintain a separate identity from the United States. Others argue that it is impractical and actually a non-issue when most Canadian newspapers, for example, use American spellings. Furthermore, we are inconsistent when we spell "favour" and "odour" with "-our" but not "horror" and "tremor."

Socio-linguists point out that both spellings have been part of Canadian usage since before Confederation. Also, there are regional differences in the predominance of one spelling over the other. Both spellings appear to be tolerated within Canadian schools. But there is some evidence that a few words such as "centre" may have an increasingly consistent usage with British spelling.

Which spelling is right? Does it matter?

Questions to Consider

Why do some people feel so strongly about this issue? Is it important for a society to have its own distinctive spellings? What does language usage tell us about our culture? What are the typical spellings in your region?

ily purchase US shows as a way to balance their budgets. Meisal also identifies a third problem as a mass-elite dichotomy. The better educated high income groups are more interested in indigenous programming whereas American programming has a more populist following. Rather than making access to American networks more difficult, the government's approach has been to control it through licensing cable companies and adding a tax to help finance Canadian programming. But the point is that Canadians have ready access to both American interpretations of the news and aspects of American popular culture.

While there is much that propels Canadian society into the American orbit, the lesson of history is certainly that Canada's existence has been predicated on differentiating itself from American society. In fact, Richard Gwyn has noted that Canadian survival has been dependent on being "not-American."[18] Gwyn claims that Canadians have become as fully North American as Americans but that they have become a distinct kind of North American. What Gwyn is arguing is that while Canadian and American societies are integrated in specific ways, Canada is still a different society primarily because it has a different political culture.

It is also not surprising that various forms of *anti-Americanism* should be present (from mild to overtly hostile) to counteract other trends which pull the two societies together.[19] Doran and Sewell have argued that anti-Americanism reflects dynamics in the perceiving nation as much as characteristics of the nation being perceived. They go so far as to assert that anti-Americanism is an important element in the cohesion of Canadian society, and "if the United States did not exist, Ottawa would have to invent it."[20] While Canadians may lament the fact that most Americans are apathetic or ignore Canada, in a curious sort of way, the United States is very important to Canadian identity.

One other aspect of American proximity that affects Canadian society is the comparison Canadians make between the Canadian "identity" and the apparent feelings about national unity and sense of destiny which exist in the United States. The American War of Independence and the succeeding events in the establishment of a new society in the United States created a pantheon of national heroes, historic documents, and a charter of ideals. For this reason it has usually been argued that, in contrast, the Canadian identity has been diffuse because Canadian society has lacked this kind of revolutionary origin.[21] While a national mythology may help differentiate a society and contribute to the arousal of patriotic feelings, it may be wrong to assume that societies are impoverished if they lack this kind of origin, or the heightened collective feelings about the society which result from such an origin. In sum, members of Canadian society are frequently affected by the ideals or practices of national unity and societal identity they observe in American society.[22]

There is no doubt that an important piece in the Canadian identity puzzle comes from both integration and resistance to the American presence. Free trade, however, and the current climate of neoconservatism are removing some of the historic barriers of differentiation. For example, the state appears no longer as willing to support and/or provide the instruments necessary to resist integration. The shift from public interventionism to market mechanisms of control mean that historic instruments of national culture such as the Canadian Broadcasting Corporation have experienced major fiscal cutbacks. The free flow of capital across borders is no longer subject to the same scrutiny and, in general, the abandonment of independent economic strategy has contributed to more and more continental convergence.[23]

At this point, it is hard to know where all this will lead but it is clear that continental integration is proceeding incrementally. One interesting study of television viewing habits shows that even though Canadians overwhelmingly prefer American programming for entertainment and relaxation, they normally choose Canadian programming for news which reflects their essential political identity.[24] Congressional politics may be irrelevant to most Canadians who prefer to hear from their own decision-makers but it is a moot point whether TV dramas and sit-coms do not also reflect American values that less consciously but pervasively affect Canadians.[25] If differentiation from the United States is an important part of the Canadian identity, then a decreasing interest in such differentiation could make the political identification of being Canadian nothing more than a regional distinction in the face of continentalism. Continental integration clearly plays a role in undermining Canadian political integration, though it has been argued that free trade is not so much the cause of this process as the culmination of a longstanding trend.[26]

3. Internal Cleavages

Another factor central to a national identity is the internal cleavages prevalent within the society. Pierre Berton has noted that the ethnic and regional loyalties which persist "hold us together as a distinctive people even as they tear us apart—a typical Canadian contradiction."[27] Language, ethnicity, and region are critical variables but it is also appropriate to add gender to this discussion.

Language not only expresses a person's identity but places the person into a larger group to which the language user belongs. Language can build bridges between people who are otherwise different or it can create barriers when the form of communication differs. The notion of two official languages can be viewed as a touchstone of national identity, but it can also be considered a "mythical unity" of two language groups for only a small majority have bilingual capacities or conduct their life in a bilingual format.[28] In fact, the French–English duality has been increasingly territorialized as official language minorities have declined outside their respective regions.[29] Furthermore, the existence of two different language broadcasting networks within the Canadian broadcasting system, for example, implies far more than the use of two different languages; it signifies two different presentations of the news (even what is considered newsworthy is different) which are targeted to two different groups.

Language can also be related to ethnic culture. Francophone Quebec is clearly articulating a new identity and, as one observer has noted, the fear of a tragic destiny for themselves as a group originated with separation from the mother country (France) much like an orphan in a trauma of infancy.[30] So if anglo-Canada perceives Canadian society as stronger because of its sponsored identity (from Britain) from which it can now become more independent, franco-Canada has had to deal with the lack of sponsorship altogether. Thus, two different agendas result from these historical origins, creating the distinctive two solitudes. While Quebec has developed this historical sense of nationhood more or less independently, anglophone Canada has its own heritage which has been diluted by decades of immigration from a diversity of sources that makes nation-building a more contemporary issue.[31] For this rea-

---

A Typology for Understanding Internal Cleavages

A *multination state* is the result of the involuntary incorporation of previously self-governing territorially concentrated cultures into a larger state. As national minorities, they wish to maintain themselves as distinct societies alongside the dominant culture and demand various forms of self-government or autonomy to ensure their survival.

A *polyethnic state* arises when immigrants arrive as individuals or families and seek to be fully accepted as members of the society in spite of their differences. They seek modifications of the dominant society in order to accommodate their own identities.

Canadian society is both multinational and polyethnic. The French and Aboriginal communities were incorporated into Canada involuntarily by the British, and at various points, they have sought ways to renegotiate their own autonomy within the broader society as national minorities (e.g., the goal of the recognition of Quebec as a distinct society in the Charlottetown Accord or the quest for Aboriginal self-government). National minorities usually feel allegiance to the larger state only insofar as the larger state recognizes and respects their distinct existence.

Canadian society is polyethnic because of its high rates of immigration. The old anglo-conformity model was replaced by a pluralistic multicultural model. Cultural distinctiveness, however, is confined more to family life and voluntary associations as ethnic subcultures, and participation in the dominant language(s) and public institutions is expected.

Question to consider:

In what ways do these two concepts of Canadian society clash?

Source: Based on Will Kymlicka, *Multicultural Citizenship* (Oxford: Oxford University Press, 1995), Chapter 2.

son, anglophone Canadians desperately want to include francophones in the nation-building process whereas Quebec vacillates between giving priority to its own objectives and participating in the Canadian entity.

It is clear that the spectre of separation from Canada by Quebec through repeated threats and divisive referendums has taken its toll on perceptions of nation-building.[32] In fact, the Quebec question has now become the most critical internal factor which has led many analysts to begin to imagine the consequences and reality of a Canada without Quebec. At some moments, this conflict appears to be pulling the national society apart, but at other times compromise, negotiation, and creativity have enabled us to perceive a revised yet distinctive Canadian character emerging from these actions.

Region has also been a factor in thwarting Canadian unity when inequities exist. Uneven economic development has sometimes caused regional feelings to coalesce around provincial governments, and this pits the sub-units of the national society against one another, or places them in opposition to the federal government, thereby arousing further animosities.[33]

It is typical in some circles to view all aspects of ethno-linguistic and regional culture as essentially negative because they imply a weak and fragmented national identity. Such conclusions, of course, are based on a unitary rather than segmentalist conception of society. While it is true that a regional or ethnic identity may be in competition with a national identity, they are not necessarily incompatible with a national identity when held simultaneously.[34]

In other words, being a Prince Edward Islander, a farmer of Scottish origin, and even a Maritimer does not necessarily exclude the broader and more distant Canadian identity. Even being Québécois may be compatible with a coexisting identification in some significant sense with other Canadians.[35] This kind of leap from local to regional to national demonstrates considerable variation between members of the society. Indications are rather strong that in spite of the diversity of reactions, some attachment to the national society is felt by most of its members. In other words, the national society is, at least in some important ways, part of every resident's frame of reference.

There is also another element in the societal identity which historically was overlooked because of the dominant position held by men. In many cases, our understanding of the role women played in Canadian life must be revised as gender bias has obfuscated the contribution of women.[36] In contemporary Canada, the feminist movement not only has challenged male conceptions of the dynamics of Canadian society but has played a key role in urging women to play a different role than they have in the past.

4. National Debate of Social Issues

Thus far we have discussed differences that are the consequence of conventional group cleavages such as ethnicity, language, and region. But there are other issues that tend to span these typical groups creating national debate based on new alignments, and initiating new forms of national dialogue.[37] These issues, in a different way, also engender discussion about what kind of society this Canadian society should be. While the issues are normally fractious and seldom yield simple agreement, the policy results of politico-legal decisions do stimulate debate about the nature of the society desired, helping to stimulate a societal identity.

One such range of issues pertains to the environment, including pollution, acid rain, resource depletion, and nuclear armaments. Another range of issues deals with gender equality, capital punishment, and abortion. The Vietnam War was an important issue in the '60s and refugees and international aid stirred controversy in the '80s. Certainly free trade has been an issue with implications far beyond the exchange of goods, and public indebtedness and deficit reduction have also been the focus of debates about what Canadians want their society to be like.

Robin Matthews has argued that at the heart of the Canadian identity is the dialectic between communitarianism and competitive individualism.[38] On the one hand, Canadians have recognized the sanctity and freedom of the individual, while on the other hand, they emphasize the values of community, social well-being, and universal justice. Historically, this dialectic has led to a blend of public and private enterprise within the society and a series of social safety nets ranging from medicare to regional equalization and concern for the disadvantaged in the community. The fact that these distinguishing features are currently under threat suggest an erosion of the basic values that have characterized Canadians over the last forty years.

The greatest emotion in the free trade debate (see Chapter Two) was generated not over whether Canada should trade with the United States, but whether in doing so, Canadian society would lose its distinctive character. Would this mean that by closer economic integration with the United States, Canada would lose medicare? Would it mean that the dialectic Matthews talked about would be sacrificed to competitive individualism? Would free trade mean that Canadian culture would be threatened? The fear was that free trade would disrupt the society's own distinctive features, and, as free trade develops, in tandem with economic conservatism, this debate is indeed occurring.

Through all of these issues, members of a society are exposed to a diversity of opinions and become attuned to the need for shaping national policies. These federal policies reflect the results of compromise and dialogue between interest groups in the society. In this way, they become uniquely Canadian resolutions to problems that may also be experienced elsewhere but are resolved differently.

5. The Evolution of Symbols of Societal Unity

Public symbols help specify the boundaries and coherence of a society as a people, rather than as just a collection of individuals, and therefore the identification of these symbols by the society is important. However, which symbols will prevail and whose interests will they represent? Competition over the specification of the *symbolic order* will occur over defining words (such as "distinct society" or "founding peoples"), language use (bilingualism, monolingualism, "non-official languages"), public policies (immigration, multiculturalism), objects (flags, monuments), special holidays (Canada Day, St-Jean Baptiste Day), or constitutional issues ("self-government", decentralization, or agreements such as the Charlottetown Accord).

For many years, Canada's identity as a political entity was shaped by its position as a *sponsored society*. The symbols of societal unity were those of the mother country, such as the use of the Union Jack as the flag, and the singing of "God Save The Queen" at public gatherings. The fact that these symbols were irritating reminders to French-Canadians of colonial defeat by the British only served to increase divisiveness rather than create symbolic unity. It has only been since 1980 that "O Canada" has had official status as the national anthem, although it had been used for many years. Perhaps even more significant is the fact that the anthem's bilingual version is not widely used. Another important symbol, the flag with the Maple Leaf, was only

The Struggle Over Societal Symbols: The Constitution

In many ways, a Constitution is a blueprint for a society. It not only establishes the institutional arrangements for the society through a structure of government, a division of powers, and judicial system (the *instrumental order*), but it also presents a set of ideals and principles on which the society is based (the *symbolic order*). These principles highlight the basic components of the social order from the role of individuals to specific groups and how they should be related to one another. For example, to state that English is the language of the country and to make the Constitution only available in English is to make a clear statement about what other language groups can expect. On the other hand, to state in the Constitution that French and English are both official languages in Canada is to make a different statement that both languages (and the people they represent) have equal status but still leaves out people who speak other languages. By placing two official languages in the Constitution, the basic principle or ideal is established against which legislation and judicial rulings are guided.

Whose ideals will be represented in the symbolic order? Disagreements over what is or is not in the Constitution, or what should be in the Constitution, or how the Constitution should be interpreted are important because of its symbolic significance. It says what Canadian society should be like, but there may be different visions for the society. It is for this reason that debate over the Constitution is so heated. People may disagree greatly over the contents of the Constitution because they have opposing ideas about what Canadian society should be like. Furthermore, the Constitution as a symbol may be interpreted as allocating status to particular groups in a society which often creates group conflict as some groups feel left out or seek to change their position.

In Chapter Five, we observed that the Canadian Constitution continues to be a problematic symbol rather than an integrating symbol. Quebec wants recognition in the Constitution as a *distinct society* on the basis that in reality they are a distinct society. From this perspective, the distinct society clause just states explicitly what already exists and serves as a form of cultural affirmation that is absurd to deny. But to others this suggests some kind of special status rather than equality and is nothing more than a claim for special powers which should be resisted. The distinct society idea then has become *a symbol of an ongoing battle* between competing factions over the place and role of Quebec within Canadian society. Putting two little words in the Constitution may seem innocent enough except that those two words have symbolic meaning to all sides in the debate about the nature of Canadian society. The fact that people give varying meanings to the term "distinct society" only complicates the problem in resolving the dilemma.

Further Reading on this issue: Raymond Breton, *Why Meech Failed: Lessons for Canadian Constitutionmaking* (Toronto: C.D. Howe Institute, 1992); and Kenneth McRoberts, *Misconceiving Canada: The Struggle for National Unity* (Toronto: Oxford, 1997).

adopted in 1965.[39] Thus, the crystallization of a national identity, rather than a sponsored identity as measured by the above-mentioned symbols, has only appeared in recent years. Vestiges of the old symbol system still remain (such as the monarchy symbols on Canadian bills and coins), but the transformation of some aspects of the symbolic order are still in process.

What happens, however, if the societal symbols are alienating to segments of a society, or if the change of existing symbols creates so much conflict that people feel alienated from their own society?[40] Francophones have been historically unhappy with British symbols, but many of the changes in the symbol system designed to make them more comfortable have now alienated anglophones who feel estranged from their own national society. If the English language was alienating francophones from English-speaking Canada (language, of course, is the most powerful symbol), so the new status of French has had an alienating effect on anglophones, to say nothing of the effect on Quebec anglophones of the mandated use of French in that province. In a similar manner, the shift away from the imperial system to the metric system, and the devaluation of British symbols in public ceremony, have created an environment in which continuity with the past is broken in favour of a transformation to a new collective identity. In the long run, these changes in the symbolic order may be significant in the production of a new societal identity, but they sometimes result in new conflict within the national society.

In fact, as societal change accelerates and creates even more ambiguities, disputes over societal symbols become even more intense. The control of symbols has become an important indicator of societal control, and therefore important symbols such as language or national policies pertaining to immigration or multiculturalism represent important struggles over the future of the society as a collectivity. Controversy over societal symbols often reflect *status anxieties* among groups who feel that they are losing power or among groups who want to gain power in the transformation of the symbol system. Breton has also argued that the failure of the constitution process occurred because there were too many different groups using the occasion to engage in socio-political bargaining over the societal symbols that were important to them.[41] It could be said, then, that Canadian society is currently in the throes of a radical symbolic transformation, and where it will lead is still unclear. A national

The Backpack Maple Leaf

While they often struggle with their national identity at home, when they travel abroad, Canadians proudly carry the maple leaf (usually in miniature) on their backpacks as they move about in countries all over the world. At first it was a way to distinguish themselves from Americans in the '60s and '70s. Now it has become a symbol that works in opening doors, establishing friendships, and even getting special treatment. It is because Canadians are often highly regarded elsewhere in the world and are seen as non-threatening.

Most of the world travels incognito but Canadians wear the flag proudly almost as part of their uniform whenever they travel overseas. Sometimes even non-Canadians are seen sporting the flag.

Question to consider:

What does this tell us about the power and meaning of a symbol?

identity crisis may exist at least partially because there is a lag between the melting down of the old symbolic order and the production of a new one.[42]

6. Globalization

It almost seems trite to say that we live in a shrinking world. No one could have anticipated how the World Wide Web has changed how we do things and how satellites and other communication/ transportation improvements make it impossible for any political state to exist as an island. As we have seen, Canadian society has always been linked to other countries (first France, then England, and then the United States), but now the range of internationalization is much broader and contacts are often mediated by international bodies and trade agreements. Whereas before, expressions of anti-Americanism played a role in a form of defensive nationalism that helped sustain a Canadian identity, globalization now minimizes that spine of societal difference.[43] The free flow of products, culture, and ideas makes it more difficult to establish and sustain a societal identity. Canadian identity was also sustained

---

Ethnic Diasporas and Transnationalism

Immigrants are often thought of as "uprooted" and "transplanted," and having stark needs to adjust and resettle in the new society. The implication is that the "old world" is left behind and the reconstruction of ethnic identity occurs in the ethnic organizations established in the "new world" as a transitional device to eventual full assimilation.

This view has increasingly become outdated by a globalized world of telecommunications and travel that allows immigrants to retain points of reference beyond the borders of their host nation—and particularly do not assume a permanent rupture with their country of origin. Immigrants who retain strong ties with their country of origin can be referred to as *diasporan* (dispersed) *communities* with complex transnational relationships. Diasporas need homelands as symbolic anchors but homelands also need diasporas in economic development or to support nationalist movements.

One ethnic group in Canada with strong transnational ties are the Croatians

who have been deeply affected by the radical changes in the former Yugoslavia. Since Croatian independence in 1990, the Croatian diaspora in Canada has been regularly solicited for support, with the result that they had considerable influence on the post-independence government in Croatia. The existence of a new Croatian state also creates mixed and complex feelings among the diasporan community with long residence in Canada that struggles to define its relationship to the homeland.

Ethnicity then needs to be understood not just in terms of its local manifestations or as cultural communities in Canada but in relation to transnational forces. Homelands can continue to play a key role among immigrants in resisting assimilation and in articulating and negotiating a unique identity in Canada.

Source: Based on Daphne N. Winland, "Our Home And Native Land? Canadian Ethnic Scholarship And The Challenge Of Transnationalism," *Canadian Review Of Sociology And Anthropology* 35(1998):555–577.

in the past by state enterprises which we have seen eroded or privatized, and distinctive public policies such as bilingualism and multiculturalism are under pressure.

Not all analysts see the impact of globalization in the same way. Rather than assuming that globalization necessarily means integration, Watson has argued that governments still have some degree of freedom and that trading with each other does not mean cultural harmonization.[44] In fact, he encourages Canadians to choose more economic integration with a smaller role for government because the impact is not as negative as presumed. Others would argue that it is government that is the backbone to societal survival for free market forces will otherwise eventually obliterate cultural distinctives. Calhoun, for example, notes that the world is too large to be one state and that independent states can become movements of democratic power that counteract other globalizing forces.[45] Whatever the result, globalization has come to play a new role in changing people's thinking about the importance of the nation-state and what role it should play in a world with porous borders. While the full impact of globalization is yet to be felt, it does undermine the significance of a single rigid national identity and potentially encourages the formation of multiple and flexible identities.[46]

Each of these six factors makes an important contribution to the articulation of a societal identity. Because the society is dynamic rather than static, considerable evidence has been given to suggest that the old sponsored society is undergoing large-scale change which is clearly producing a very different societal shape and tone. It is not that Canadian society once had an identity and lost it, or that it never had an identity and is searching for it, but that the shape and structure of that identity is changing over time.

NEGOTIATING A SOCIETAL IDENTITY

The Concept of Nationalism

The intensification of feelings about primary allegiance to the national society and its well-being is known as *nationalism*. Much like other words that end in "ism" (such as communism or capitalism), nationalism implies a set of beliefs, convictions, and a worldview pertaining to the defense and advocacy of the society contained within a political jurisdiction. It is possible to be a resident of a nation-state but yet not be nationalistic. Nationalism emerges out of strong feelings about the collectivity as a whole (rather than individuals), and the belief that the welfare of the group, as determined by established boundaries, must be a first principle in any action within the society.

A Canadian nationalist is someone who assesses the virtue of any action by its impact on the residents of Canada as a collectivity. While one person may enjoy going to a concert and then judge the music or musicians on their own merits, and leave it at that, a nationalist will ask whether it is helping Canadians develop their own unique music style. Carrying over to other fields, the nationalist will ask whether schools are promoting knowledge and love of country, or whether corporations are using their organizations to strengthen the Canadian economy and provide opportunities for Canadians. A Quebec nationalist or Dene nationalist will ask the same kinds of questions pertaining to their group. What is important to note is that some people always think in terms of this wider group while other people never do. Perhaps the most typical position is a response midway between these two extremes, as other concerns (e.g., personal gain, lifestyle preference, or personal priorities) frequently displace this concern for the larger group.

One of the biggest dilemmas with nationalism is that different definitions of the boundaries of a national group may coexist within the same country. In Canadian society, segmentalists may limit their boundaries of nationhood to a sub-territory or an ethnic group.[47] This view may challenge, or at least compete with, the pan-Canadian view of the population within all of Canada as being a national society. Furthermore, not everyone agrees that loyalty to the nation-state ought to be a priority, and they may opt for an individualistic or local group approach to life in society. Consequently, nationalist sentiment is highly variable over time; it may be widespread for a short period, or it may be adopted by interest groups who find the supporting principles personally intriguing or beneficial.

For the majority of the population, loyalty to the nation-state is one of a chain of identities (e.g., family, ethnicity, religion) they hold. The mere experience of exposure to the news, and even the weather map, for example, sensitizes persons to the national context in which they live, and leads to the assumption that a minimal level of national consciousness inevitably will be present in all residents. Particular events, e.g., the Canada-Russia hockey series, Olympic competitions, national elections, disasters or wars, or travel abroad, may also heighten one's consciousness of being part of a national fabric. The strong positive sentiments or attitudes towards one's country these experiences generate is known as *patriotism*. As love for one's country or nation-state, it is not as demanding or commanding as nationalism, which submerges other commitments by allegiance to the collective entity.

The strongest conception of nationalism assumes that individuals should subordinate all other interests and loyalties to the nation-state. This type of "full-blown nationalism" particularly lends itself to socialist societies, or to societies with a strong central government.[48] A more moderate perception of nationalism is that it is a belief in the right of societal self-determination. In this view, the society is expected to support a flexible program of actions and policies that maintain and sustain the independence and integrity of the society as a whole. Obviously, considerable differences of opinion will prevail about how flexible a national society can afford to be. Any looser conception of the nation-state (such as the concept that the state is only a framework for cultural and economic activities) suggests a more federated society such as exists in Switzerland, where only minimal societal cohesion prevails.

Patriotism or love of country is an age-old phenomenon. Most people have always identified with, and been loyal to, their place of birth or place of residence. History demonstrates that people have always been conscious of the group to which they belonged, and commitment to the group has always been valued; however, the idea that loyalty is not just to a geographic locale or a social group, but to a political state, is a more recent phenomenon. This *loyalty to the state* was first clearly expressed in the latter half of the 18th century during the French Revolution.[49] In post-revolutionary France, the state attempted to create a society or sense of nationhood out of all people living within the borders of the state, regardless of other sub-group allegiances. A single language and culture was imposed on all regions of the country, thereby breaking down barriers and aiding the creation of a single nation. Thus an ideal of the national society was established, whereby other forms of group identity were to be subsumed under a single united ideal focused on the state.

The principle that the *state now serves as the basis of society*, establishing its boundaries and blending its people into a nationality, came to be accepted as a foundation of world order. Nationality has become a part of personal identity much like gender or skin colour, and has become much more significant than earlier types of socio-political organization. Until recently, its legitimacy has hardly been questioned, though instances of ethnic groups cre-

How Important Is Citizenship?

In some counties such as Germany and Japan, citizenship is very hard to obtain. Countries such as Australia, the United States, and Canada are much more open in terms of eligibility to apply for citizenship.

Despite globalization and a shrinking world, citizenship still is an important means of classifying people:

• It is a means of categorizing individuals in a global context and giving them an identity.

• It implies loyalty and commitment to a state that in turn defines and protects individual rights and responsibilities.

• Historically, betrayal or treason of one's citizenship has been considered a most heinous crime.

• Everyone must have a citizenship. To be stateless (as are refugees) is a pitiable and unacceptable condition.

• Citizenship is both a legal and emotional concept.

• Often people have been asked to be prepared to die for their state.

Source: Based on Desmond Morton, "Divided Loyalties? Divided Countries?", 50–63; and William Kaplan, "Who Belongs? Changing Concepts of Citizenship and Nationality," 245–64, in William Kaplan, ed., *Belonging: The Meaning and Future of Canadian Citizenship* (Montreal: McGill-Queen's University Press, 1993).

ating their own states by breaking away from existing states repeatedly emerge throughout the globe. So, in contrast to the idea of "state creating nation" (i.e. states attempting to blend all residents into a single nationality), there is also the possibility of "nations creating states" (i.e., people sharing an ethnic commonality creating a new state.)[50] The former Soviet Union and Yugoslavia are but two instances of shifting boundaries between state and nation.

Alternative Explanations of Canadian Nationalism

It is clear that at the time of Confederation in 1867, there was little sense of a Canadian nationality. Many residents of Canada had little conception of a society of the nation-state because of intense local attachments, warm sentiments towards the mother country, identities more closely related to a foreign place of origin, or even an ambivalence about this new political creation known as Canada. Confederation was based on the idea that a strong central government would be needed to establish a national society, but considerable latitude was given for the expression of regional uniqueness (e.g., the church-based school system in Quebec). The "Canada First" movement of the 1870s was a short-lived campaign to forge a nationalism based on British culture.[51] In other words, a major issue for the new country was to develop some basis for unity. Nationalism became a useful tool for ethnic assimilation used by the dominant group, which wanted its ideas about what society should be like to be more widely disseminated throughout the new society. This goal was viewed with particular suspicion by francophones in Quebec who possessed a different sense of nationality.

Conflict theories of nationalism point out that it is not so much the content of nationalism that is important but who its advocates are. From this perspective, nationalism reflects power relationships. Dominant groups use nationalism to promote their objectives, though minority groups can also use their own brand of nationalism to challenge the dominant group. This kind of interpretation tends to see nationalism as an ideology to be used in the interests of particular groups within a collectivity. So nationalism, from this viewpoint, is related to domination.[52]

One type of domination has an external or foreign orientation. Powerful nations impose their will on weaker collectivities, and nationalism can be a reaction to this external control. Concern about American domination is a major impetus to nationalist thought and action in Canada, and it is for this reason that nationalism demonstrates a strong relationship with anti-Americanism.[53] But domination can also have an internal basis within a country. Members of one ethnic or territorial group may resist pan-Canadian nationalism because it thwarts their own collective interests, and they then counter that nationalism with their own nationalism (e.g., Quebec nationalism). Or, within the province of Quebec, francophones have been trying to build a political community that would transcend ethno-cultural differences, and yet some minorities have rejected that objective because of *ressentiment* about being excluded from power and have used victimhood as a strategy for minority empowerment.[54] In sum, the conflict perspective points out that nationalism is an ideology to be used by groups in a struggle for power.

Another perspective within conflict theory suggests that nationalism is related to the class structure. The issue is not just that of domination by another group but domination by a group representing specific class interests who embrace nationalism because it is supportive of their class position. For example, as representatives of the capitalist class, the Canadian Manufacturing Association was historically ardently nationalist, implying that good citizens should buy "Canadian" manufactured goods whatever the price.[55] In short, nationalism was good for business. But it has also been argued that nationalism can be a congenial ideology of the middle class. Just as the new middle class in Quebec became ardent Quebec nationalists, so it can be noted that the new middle class of young well-educated anglophones in the rest of Canada became Canadian nationalists in the 1960s and 1970s when their own interests and careers were in question.[56] Thus we see that support for a new societal identity and commitment to a nationalist position can be explained by locating such ideals within the class structure in order to determine their sources and primary proponents.

While nationalism may be explained by focusing on specific groups which become its advocates, it is also possible that nationalism may have a broad-based origin. *Integration theories* point out that nationalisms are part of larger social processes such as urbanization and industrialization that break down traditional group loyalties and draw people into larger collectivities.[57] In fact, it has been argued that nationalism is a response to the modern society that requires more centralization and a single form of communication. Nationalism is the vehicle that binds people together in order to be more competitive in the world economy and to create a more homogeneous culture.[58] Nationalism has also been linked to secularization (i.e., the decline of traditional religious attachments), so that the state becomes the new object of loyalty and devotion, almost as a form of surrogate religion. In other words, nationalism is viewed as a natural bonding process producing shared meanings and symbols that evolves over time, thereby facilitating greater unity within a political entity.

It is undoubtedly true that the industrialization of Canada and the accompanying social and cultural changes which it produced have contributed to a growing nationalist spirit. As population shifted to central Canada (particularly Ontario) because of the attractiveness of industrial growth, as new technologies brought East and West closer together, and as a consequence of higher educational levels among the population that had shifted from rural to urban residences, old attachments and ethnocentrisms slowly began breaking down.[59] Many people celebrate this trend because national unity and national pride represent important ideals to them. The nation-state, defined as pan-Canadianism, has become an important part of their personal identity, and the fact that a successful artist, athlete, or corporation is "Canadian" is important to their sense of group identity.

Ironically, the same trends that have produced a pan-Canadian nationalism have also produced competing nationalisms (such as in Quebec) within Canada. To the extent that the territorial boundaries of group identity do not encompass all of Canada, pan-Canadian nationalism is undermined. Quebec nationalists, for example, give priority to their identity as Québécois and as defined by the territory of the province of Quebec. Canadian nationalists, on the other hand, can be intolerant of new immigrants or those with a more international frame of reference. Nationalists have their own definition of what a society should be like and fear loss of control of that vision.[60] This brings us back to the conflict perspective because it raises questions about who determines the content of the nationalism being advocated.

Both conflict and integration theories provide important ideas for understanding the evolution of nationalism and the forms it has taken in Canada. Industrial change and communication technologies have brought residents of the society closer together in recent years, and have created a new environment from which a sense of a national society has developed. At the same time, a pan-Canadian form of nationalism has been resisted by Quebec nationalists and some First Nations as a coercive ideology of assimilation which they reject.

REFORMULATING AND RECONSTRUCTING THE NATIONAL IDENTITY

As a result of the conquest of the French by the English in 1759, persons of British descent thought they had a clear picture of what a <u>Canadian nationality</u> would look like; i.e., a political entity affiliated with and bearing the imprint of the mother country Britain. This view of Canada prevailed for a long time and was essentially known as *anglo-conformity*. Other views of that history were submerged but by 1960, a *two-nation view* of history entered the mainstream of Canadian thought. This was the idea that Canada had two founding nations (not just one) and that what was finally needed was a new accommodation between English and French in the structures of Canadian society. By the 1990s the two-nation view was being discredited by First Nations who argued persuasively for their prior presence which has then produced a *three-nations view* of the Canadian national community.[61] Add to this the new source non-European immigration into Canada, and concepts like multiculturalism, and suddenly it is no longer clear what the core and essentials of Canadian nationality are.

The dominance of the anglo-conformity view of nationalism is known as *hegemony* because its values and ideals are presented to societal members as taken for granted and natural and inevitable. To the extent that this is a hegemonic formation, counter-hegemonic ideas are ideas that undermine this dominance and seek to negotiate change. Québécois and Aboriginals, and more recently feminists and multiculturalists have sought to develop new strategies of inclusion.[62]

The anglo-conformity view of Canadian society had a strong centralist vision, meaning a strong federal government. It implied assimilation of all other groups to the anglo-majority. That objective has clearly not been attained after all these years among francophones in Quebec and among First Nations who have their own concepts of self-determination. Even the two-nations view is under siege as the Quebec independence movement makes a claim for statehood on behalf of Québécois as a territorially defined ethnic people. In fact, in order to prevent the incremental expansion of anglo-conformity, francophone Quebecers are motivated more by the need to make a positive affirmation of their own nationalist identity than to indicate a negative rejection of Canada. As long as Québécois nationalism exists in competition with anglo-conformity pan-Canadian nationalism, the result is a fundamental incompatibility between these two visions of society.[63] It has been argued that the popularity of sovereignty in Quebec is at least in part a response to the denial by the rest of Canada of the recognition of Quebec as a distinct society, for the essence of Quebec nationalism is to continue the struggle to exist collectively by obtaining recognition of that fact politically.[64] The fact is that anglophone Canadians have difficulty coming to terms with notions of "distinct society" whether it comes from Quebec or from indigenous peoples.[65] In many ways there has been an important paradigm shift, among both Quebec francophones and Aboriginals, from an internal colony to a nation (the former with a political structure and the latter without one) but that shift is facing considerable resistance from many other Canadians.[66] In that regard, it has been argued that the new face of Canadian nationalism in

The Search for a New Canadian Identity

If Québécois and Indigenous People have a sense of nationhood, does that leave the rest of Canada as a *no-nation*? If Quebec can be described as French Canada, does that make the rest of Canada *English Canada*?

As Quebec has numerous traits that sets it apart, there is often difficulty in knowing how to refer to the remaining parts of Canada. Perhaps the most used phrase is *Rest of Canada (ROC)*. The problem with referring to the rest of Canada as English Canada is that it can be confused with British nationality or loyalty to British institutions.

Yet, in spite of the existence of other ethnic and linguistic minorities, Resnick argues that what the ROC has in common is an overwhelming commitment to the use of the English language. Just as French is the anchor for the Québécois identity, so English provides the glue that ties ROC Canadians together and is expressed, for example, through politi-

cal and educational institutions and the media. Resnick argues that what has emerged in the ROC since Meech Lake and Charlottetown is that the Quebec question has provoked new dialogue outside Quebec about what it means to be Canadian and what kind of society we really want. In other words, English Canadians are debating with new vigour their collective identity in a manner similar to Québécois and Indigenous Peoples. And this is a good sign for, in spite of the existence of divergent opinions, it brings English-speaking Canadians together to hammer out who they are as a collectivity.

Of course, the big question is how and whether these English, French, and Aboriginal conceptions of nationhood can be joined in one political state.

Further Reading: Philip Resnick, Thinking English Canada (Toronto: Stoddart, 1994) and "English Canada: The Nation That Dares Not Speak Its Name", in Kenneth McRoberts (ed.), *Beyond Quebec: Taking Stock Of Canada* (Toronto: McGill-Queens University Press, 1995), 81–92.

English Canada is less accommodating (e.g., impatience with Quebec or multiculturalism) and more homogenizing ("One Canada" theme) in spirit.[67]

Within any political entity, and as long as Canada exists as a political entity, there will always be some pressures towards a pan-Canadian nationalism. People who define themselves in terms of their Canadian nationality will always seek to enlist the support of other residents to submerge their other identities or at least to include Canada in their chain of identities. Therefore it is not surprising that there are those who want immigrants to change their behaviour and assimilate to the majority. It is also understandable when persons who have attached their identity to symbols and values that were dominant in the past but are now eroding react in a *status preservationist backlash.*[68]

The *post-modernist perspective* suggests that contemporary society no longer has a central core and structure with which all can identify, and that society is effectively *decentred* into multiple identities and communities. Gwyn argues that Canada is the world's first post-modern state not only because it is being decentred but because it participates in a global economy with an internal population that is also globally representative.[69] Postmodernism suggests that there is little that Canadians hold in common because we celebrate our differences rather than our similarities.[70] The reassessment of societal history by groups resisting the old anglo interpretation and pointing out the faulty or biased interpretations of the past is a typical post-modern process known as *deconstructionism.*[71] The lack of a master narrative of history that would provide a single societal vision is further confused by a constant rethinking of the basic premises of the society. Much of the current conflict in Canadian society is then a struggle over the shape, form, and substance of the Canadian nationality and identity, and *post-modernism* points out the fragility, plasticity, and impermanence of political states in that context.

THE DYNAMICS OF NATION-BUILDING

Much of the analysis of this book has pointed out the difficulties the residents of Canada have in forming a national society. Amidst all the centrifugal forces, none is perhaps more fundamental to the development of a weak singular national identity than the existence of the two solitudes, the French and English segments of the population. Attempts to build bridges between these two groups were a primary objective for the federal government in the '60s and '70s, but the evidence to date is that they have had only limited success, and perhaps even have failed.[72]

However, both language groups have gone through a highly significant metamorphosis. Whereas nationality was at one time determined by ethnic characteristics, there is now a utilitarian trend to be more all-inclusive within each language group; to build a *civic nationality* based on territory.[73] For example, the civic nationality of Quebec is being built by extending the concept of belonging based on French ethnic descent to include all those in Quebec who share the French language, regardless of descent. In English Canada, this transformation occurred much earlier as non-British immigrants became part of the English-speaking community. In fact, the use of the word anglophone has become an acceptable way to speak of the unity of persons who, in spite of their ethnic differences, have found common ground in the English language. Thus, we can see that there is some nation-building occurring in both language groups.

Differing Perspectives

Structural Functionalism

Societies are indeed diverse and complex entities. But in spite of the plurality of groups, perspectives, and individual differences, the national society provides the institutions and structures which all members of the society share in order to give members a sense of collective belonging. Differences are not problems, they are assets, provided that all members of the society are conscious of the ties that bind them together in spite of these differences. So two official languages should not be perceived as a problem but as an opportunity for unilingualists to become at least partially bilingual in order to build bridges between groups. In this way, societal harmony is maintained. Building a strong sense of Canadian nationalism is the way to develop loyalty and commitment to the solidarity of the national fabric. In sum, the structures of society will ensure that unity is the ultimate goal.

Conflict

National unity is a very fragile thing in Canada because of intense social divisions particularly expressed over language, region, and ethnicity. In other words, the society is fragmented into social units that are often more competing than cross-cutting. Hostilities often seem to be never far beneath the surface and rise and wane as people are mobilized. What all of this reflects is repeated conflict over what Canadian society should

be like. Those who have the power to define the contours of the society will have ultimate control, will attempt to repress dissent, and will attempt to spread their ideals as the best for the collectivity using whatever methods possible. What we are experiencing is conflict between the old anglo-conformity concept of Canadian society and new visions of Canadian society with a different place for Québécois and indigenous groups. Those individuals or groups with traditional power or who benefit with the status quo particularly resist change.

Symbolic Interactionism

Societies are like individuals in that they seek to form their own identities and to differentiate that identity from other entities. A societal identity is also always in process and change. It depends on the creation of unique symbols such as language, literary themes, heroes, documents, songs, and flags with which members of the society can identify. It is created out of important events or characteristic activities that help societal members understand more clearly who they are. Through interaction, members of a society develop shared interpretations of the world around them and their common life together. The reformulation of old symbols of the society to new symbols, as painful as that process might be, is an evolutionary process reflecting the fact that Canadian society is redefining its collective identity.

It is frequently argued that this dualism is at the heart of the Canadian identity. How this dualism can produce a sense of unity within Canadian society continues to be a perplexing issue. But in emphasizing its divisive nature, we cannot ignore that there indeed are factors propelling all persons sharing the Canadian political entity and geographic territory towards a pan-Canadian civic nationality. This is not to suggest that countervailing forces are not as strong or stronger in the opposite direction, but to point out that there are factors that do contribute to a broader sense of nation-building. It is important that these be recognized and evaluated for their contribution to a sense of society and national identity. Five factors in nation-building will be discussed.

1. The Socialization Process

Nationality is at least partially related to place of birth. Where one is born determines in large measure one's nationality because, barring other intervening factors of personal election, place of birth usually is the basis for determining citizenship. This correlation, however, does not imply that nationality is inborn. A national identity is something that is acquired through social learning. Learning the expectations, attitudes, and behaviour demanded by a society through interaction is known as the process of *socialization*.

It is through the basic institutions of a society (i.e., school, church, government, media) that one learns about, and develops attitudes towards, the society to which one belongs. Flags, the singing of the national anthem at athletic events, reading current events in the newspaper, celebrating Canada Day, paying income tax, or obtaining a passport are all activities that remind Canadians of their civic nationality. Many of these things are taken-for-granted aspects of their life but they are implicit acknowledgments of being part of Canadian society.

The Canadian problem is not only that the society must teach its younger members about their relationship to the societal unit, but also that it must *resocialize* many of its immigrant members into identification with the national society.

Perhaps the most important socializing agent is the school system because of its key role in informing the young about the societal tradition.[74] It is here students receive a sense of societal history and geography, and an awareness of what constitutes significant societal events. School assemblies begin to develop patriotic fervor through the learning of songs that reflect the societal heritage. In addition, the classroom provides a setting in which students may acquire a sense of familiarity with other aspects of a society's culture. In other words, the school system is expected to teach not only spelling and mathematics, but all of the basics of good citizenship.

Two observations about the role of schools in inculcating this nationalist sentiment can be made. First, one of the historic problems was the lack of Canadian classroom materials in English Canada. The use of British or American materials meant that it was more difficult to create an understanding of Canadian history and culture. Since the 1960s, however, enormous developments have occurred in the publication of Canadian materials, providing students with a greater degree of societal awareness. Second, because education is a provincial matter rather than a federal matter, the basic textbooks that are used begin with an orientation to the national society through provincial eyes. Nowhere is the implication of this fact more noticeable than in Quebec, where language differences combine with Quebec nationalist views to reproduce a markedly different perception of Canadian society.

Lamy speaks of the differences in the educational experiences of English and French adolescents as "*socialization into discord*."[75] In other words, French students acquired more positive feelings towards the provincial society, whereas anglophone students were more

Are Immigrants a Threat to the Institutional Fabric of Canadian Society?

Given the fact that about 16% of the Canadian population is foreign born, it is important to find out whether there is evidence that such a large population group is problematic for the society. Are the political values and attitudes of immigrants different from those of native-born Canadians?

In a study of adults and children conducted in three Canadian cities, attitudes to authority (e.g., government, Prime Minister, Supreme Court), images of Canada (e.g., fair-unfair, friendly-unfriendly, rich-poor), and attitudes towards issues (e.g., Keeping Canada Together, Native Indians, Limiting Immigration, Gun Control) were measured.

While there may have been some differences between immigrants who had just arrived and those who have been in Canada for many years, it was found that there were few differences between native-born and foreign-born. Instead immigrants seemed to quickly adopt the political perspectives of the native-born, and the fear that immigrants are changing Canadian political values or social institutions must be discarded.

But when comparing parents with their children, there are substantial differences between the generations for both native-born and foreign born (with perhaps the exception of recently arrived immigrants).

For Discussion:

Why are generational differences more important to explain political views than in what country you were born?

Source: J.S. Frideres, "Edging Into The Mainstream: A Comparison Of Values And Attitudes Of Recent Immigrants, Their Children And Canadian-Born Adults", In W.W. Isajiw (ed.), Multiculturalism In North America And Europe (Toronto: Canadian Scholar Press, 1997), 537–561.

favourably oriented towards the federal level. One of the problems cited by the Royal Commission on Bilingualism and Biculturalism was that two different views of Canadian history were presented in the textbooks of the two languages.[76] The French language textbooks stressed the survival of French-Canadian society, with special emphasis placed on the period prior to the English Conquest. Succeeding events, including Confederation itself, were presented from the point of view of a minority facing English domination. English language textbooks, on the other hand, stressed the Conquest as a beginning rather than an ending, and glorified the historical significance of Confederation as the emergence of a new strong single entity—Canadian society. The result of this difference in socialization was that when school children were asked to identify national heroes, francophones and anglophones each identified with prominent figures of their own language group, and they shared few "reconciliation symbols."[77] Thus, schools might be viewed as perpetuating a rift in Canadian society, rather than promoting national unity. Since public school texts are frequently written for and approved by provincial educational authorities, it is not surprising that schoolchildren in Newfoundland or British Columbia will also first learn about their national society through provincial eyes.

Schools clearly have a pivotal role in creating a knowledge base about the national society, and in developing positive attitudes towards it. The influence of schools on a child begins at an early age, and it can therefore be assumed that perceptions of Canadian society established here will be formative for later life.

2. The Political Process

A second factor in nation-building emerges from the political process, particularly from politicians and political parties. Many people join political parties, take positions on national issues, and recruit people to their point of view. Others are less directly involved in the political world, but are made conscious of important political figures through the media. The media are continually soliciting reactions from politicians on virtually every issue that arises, whether that politician is part of the government or in opposition. Through the controversies articulated by political leaders, citizens are drawn into these issues and made aware of their national implications. Therefore, whether it is in electoral battle for leadership of a national or provincial party, or whether it is the articulation of positions on issues of national consequence, the political process reinforces the national context of the society in spite of disagreements or different levels of participation. In sum, political activities serve as constant reminders of the contours of Canadian society.

The political process also produces political decisions, legislation, and policies representing visions of what Canadian society should be like or compromises between competing groups. The policies of bilingualism or multiculturalism, or even minority language programs or women's programs represent attempts by the state to promote inclusiveness rather than fragmentation in order to include all of Canada's residents in the unitary sense of society.[78] The fact that these policies may not always be widely supported should not blind us to the fact that they do have an effect. Most anglophones may not be bilingual, but their exposure to French words and phrases builds a tolerance and affinity for that language quite different from the American predilection to learn Spanish as a second language. Thus, decisions taken through the political agenda, as controversial or debatable as they may be, become part of the nation-building process, and specify a uniquely Canadian means of resolving Canadian societal problems.

Other decisions by government may deliberately seek to promote and build national loyalties. For example, student exchange programs funded by government may seek to build bridges among young citizens across the country. In 1996, the government declared that February 15 was to be National Flag Day with a slogan "Canada—Take It To Heart."[79] Government funds are also set aside for celebrations of "Canada's birthday" on July First and an entertainment extravaganza is usually televised from the nation's capital. In short, politicians take actions that directly seek to engender and support nation-building, though many analysts would say that much of this is a superficial control of the masses in the light of other realities.

It is ironic that at the same time that the government pours money into nation-building at one level, at another level governments have recently withdrawn from regulating and controlling many elements of society in the name of free market principles and a less costly public service, making it harder to create national unity.[80] Whether it be support of culture or the sustenance of key sector institutions (e.g., the Canadian Broadcast Corporation), the traditional means of nation-building have been threatened with no clear replacement. In that sense, politicians themselves are responsible for the change in the role played by political processes in nation-building.

Sport as a Vehicle to Promote Nationalism

If nationhood is socially constructed rather than natural, we would expect that political leaders would use a wide variety of methods to inculcate loyalty among members of a society. In other words, leaders use methods to explicitly promote national identification rather than merely leaving it to chance or assuming that it will occur by some kind of osmosis.

In the late 1990s, the Canadian government gave the Montreal Canadiens hockey team $500 000 to display the Canada logo at centre ice in their arena and also gave $370 000 to the NHL Ottawa Senators for a similar purpose. The Montreal Expos baseball team and the Montreal Alouettes football team also received government funding for pro-

moting Canada. Rumours had it that the Canadian government had spent more than $10 million in advertising at sporting events in Quebec. The key idea was that Quebecers in particular be targetted with reminders that they were Canadian.

The government also agreed to pay the Canadian Football League for wearing Canadian flag decals on their helmets as well as other forms of advertising at more heavily watched televised games for the playoffs and the Grey Cup. The government thus became an advertiser of a product, just like corporations promote other consumer commodities, for which it sought to create greater loyalty and goodwill to the nation-state. The important idea is that this was an explicit attempt to *create* such loyalty.

3. Economic Protectiveness

A third factor in nation-building pertains to the way decisions about the economy are justified in support of national well-being. We have already seen that nationalism can be manipulated by those with vested interests. S.D. Clark has pointed out that in Canada's early years, her "most ardent patriots" were her dignitaries—business leaders, bishops, ministers of the Crown, and military officers—whose well-being and superior positions were connected to the independent existence of Canada, and to a strong Canadian society.[81] Earlier it was shown that business entrepreneurs who depend on the Canadian market may become strong economic nationalists because their livelihood depends on their survival in that market. In general, economic nationalism is most typical when business or labour groups are struggling for survival, and feel they need protection.

In the wave of nationalism of the '60s and '70s, it was the expanded middle class, or new petty bourgeoisie of salaried professionals (many of whom were working for the state), or budding professionals still in training in universities and concerned about employment opportunities, who were the most nationalistic.[82] This social class was vocally supportive of policies that protected and enhanced the national economy in matters dealing with technologies, research, management decisions, and corporate policies; i.e., matters that specifically related to white collar jobs.

Clearly there are times when specific groups feel that if their own interests are threatened, the viability and well-being of the entire national society is at stake. Whether this is untrue, partially true, or completely correct may be open to debate but, to the extent that such groups are successful in convincing public opinion and politicians, these arguments became part of the nation-building process when action is considered to protect the national society.

Ironically, the protection of the Canadian economy through nationalist thinking and action is now probably at its lowest point in Canadian history. The economic elite which had spearheaded economic protectionism for years have wholeheartedly embraced free trade and all of its implications. Primary producers such as farmers, miners, and fishers have always been oriented to international markets, though the state is sometimes asked to play a protective role. Labour unions fought free trade and invoked nationalist sentiment in the protection of jobs in Canada but their impact has been muted by the globalization of capitalism. Thus, if economic protectiveness has been an important historic basis of nationalist sentiment in Canada, it is unclear how the new economic environment will change that factor in nation-building.

4. Institutional Linkages

A fourth factor facilitating national integration comes from institutional linkages which bind the society together. These institutions such as nation-wide banks, railroads, churches, and various forms of communications, allow the member of the society to become more conscious of the boundaries of the society and aspects of the society which are held in common.[83] Not only do institutions such as the Royal Bank of Canada, CP Rail, the United Church of Canada, and the Southam newspaper chain have a high profile within the society as distinctly Canadian institutions, they also have a large number of employees and clients who support them, and this heightens a consciousness of the ties that bind members of the society together within a social and economic framework. The typical pattern of organizational structure from local to regional to national implies that whether identifying corporations (sales meetings, seminars, transfer, etc.), professional organizations, leisure clubs, or amateur sport competitions, members of the society are increasingly made aware of the national context in which their specific activity takes place.

Perhaps no institution has a more powerful role in forging national unity than that of broadcasting. While it was argued at the time of Confederation that it was to be the railroads that would provide "the ties that bind," in the modern era it is broadcasting (and particularly the Canadian Broadcasting Corporation) that can have this unique role. In spite of enormous American influences, radio and television continue to have a distinctive Canadian character as evidenced by a wide range of programming from Degrassi High, Beachcombers, The Nature Of Things, and Vision TV.[84] The print media should also not be ignored, for organizations like the Canadian Press gathers stories from all parts of the society and disseminate them daily throughout the society through newspapers. Nevertheless, radio and television broadcasting are even more pervasive because they communicate not only news but entertainment; i.e., the substance of the culture of a society through music, drama, and documentaries. Also not to be overlooked are national advertising campaigns, which frequently refer to the usage of products in a national context. Note, for example, how television weather maps acquaint the audience with the geography and weather differentials in different parts of the society. While the nationalist impetus is usually more implicit than explicit in all of these examples, their significance is that they help frame a societal or national consciousness in the minds of members of the society.

5. Cultural Products

A fifth factor contributing to nation-building is the promotion of indigenous culture. These may be forms of *popular culture* represented by Canadian television shows such as *Due South* or *North of 60*, or Canadian entertainers such as Bryan Adams, Celine Dion, or the Tragically Hip. An interesting but distinctive aspect of Canadian culture is what Acland has called *"the cult of the Canadian born,"* namely celebrating Canadians who have made it big elsewhere.[85] People such as Michael J. Fox and Kiefer Sutherland become Canadian folk heroes. It has also been argued that hockey is one of the more distinctive aspects of national unity in defining Canadianness,[86] and certainly the Grey Cup football event (at least prior to continentalization) has been an important national integrator. Popular culture both directly and indirectly can support nation-building.

The federal government has for many years played a distinct role in promoting a Canadian identity through support of cultural activity. In addition to the role of the Canadian Broadcasting Corporation there are the federally financed Canada Council which supports artists and art organizations, the National Gallery which promotes the work of Canadian artists, and the National Film Board which produces documentaries on Canadian life.[87] The idea always was to harness the arts to the process of nation-building.

Indigenous culture is also promoted by the *intelligentsia* consisting of authors, journalists, professors, or artists who help to articulate the national identity.[88] The work of historians has a special role in formulating national feeling. In researching, writing, and interpreting a society's history, historians uncover the pivotal events in Canadian history that contribute to a greater sense of awareness of the society's legacy. Literary figures write about the land and its people in novels and verse, which may develop romantic or thought-provoking images that reflect a sense of nationhood. These persons are frequently celebrated in the media, their work is cited, and a general familiarity with their work is promoted through the schools. Sometimes these writers address the nationalist sentiment indirectly, but sometimes they become leaders in directly articulating nationalist fervour. In Canada, such persons include anglophones such as Northrop Frye, Stephen Leacock, Robertson Davies, Margaret Atwood, Pierre Berton, and francophones such as Michel Brunet, Roch Carrier, Marie-Claire Blais, Fernand Dumont, Hebert Jacques Ferron, and Roger Lemelin among others. Other examples of more popular culture which reflect collective assumptions and values back to members of the society include The Royal Canadian Air Farce or even national news anchors such as Lloyd Robertson and Peter Mansbridge. Intellectuals and media commentators can also serve as critics of the society, and their work may stimulate widespread debate.

Two further observations should be made about the role of the intelligentsia. First, since literary culture is conveyed in a specific linguistic form, it is clear that the two language groups will each have their own literature which may (unless people are fully bilingual) reinforce the idea of the two solitudes. Second, since literary culture is such a critical vehicle in sustaining the nationalist sentiment, many people vociferously advocate the development of cultural nationalism. *Cultural nationalism* is the advocacy and defense of Canadian culture whether in print, in drama, or in music. Cultural nationalists feel that indigenous forms of culture should be given priority, financial support, and special recognition, perhaps even to the extreme of the exclusion or control of foreign cultural products. Clearly, this perspective creates considerable debate within the society, but at its root is the argument that the intelligentsia and the artistic community both provide invaluable service in the articulation of the national identity.[89]

How Important Is Hockey in Promoting Societal Unity?

It is often argued that what all Canadians share in common is interest in the game of hockey. If there has been little that brought Canadians together and much to divide them, then perhaps it is hockey that has helped provide the social glue that unites Canadians and helps to define the national identity. For example, the 1972 Canada–Russia hockey series (which Canada won) is often discussed as a defining moment in national unity. Professional hockey in particular has also helped to demonstrate how young boys of humble background could become national heroes.

Hockey enthusiasts (especially Canadian NHL hockey owners) have argued the point about hockey's role in the national psyche when special financial considerations are desired from the federal government. The Canadian government also accepted this logic when it bought advertising space on the side boards of the Montreal and Ottawa arenas to draw attention to the need for Canadian unity in the Quebec region.

But does hockey really play this unitive role or is it mainly illusion or romanticism?

Two studies of the role of hockey in national identity formation point out that hockey primarily became a national icon as the result of media influences (newspapers, magazine, radio, and particularly television) which created a national audience and a pseudo sense of intimacy with the game's heroes. "Hockey Night In Canada" particularly as a television production created the imagery of a nation fixated on hockey every Saturday night.

Yet the evidence is that hockey's vision of Canadian society was primarily white and male. How can a sport with such a select audience play such a pivotal role in societal unity? This is particularly a problem in recent years with the increase in non-Europeans in the Canadian population for whom hockey has not been part of their cultural tradition. Male dominance in hockey is also not congenial with the emphasis on the more pivotal role of women in public affairs. Furthermore, many of the best players are now European rather than Canadian. Lastly, hockey has become increasingly Americanized with the loss of Canadian NHL teams and the significant increase in American-based teams.

In spite of these facts, it does seem that hockey plays some kind of role in making people feel Canadian and is at least one element in Canadian collective self-understanding as a northern people. There may be some kind of nostalgia at work and it is true that many Canadians have little or no interest in hockey. Whether hockey will continue to serve a mythic role as an important part of societal unity in the future is clearly uncertain.

Source: Based on Richard Gruneau and David Whitson, *Hockey Night In Canada: Sport, Identities and Cultural Politics* (Toronto: Garamond, 1993), and Neile Earle, "Hockey As Canadian Popular Culture: Team Canada 1972, Television And The Canadian Identity," *Journal Of Canadian Studies* 30(1995):107–123.

CONCLUSION

It would be an overstatement to say that these integrating forces contributing to national unity are more compelling, or have overwhelmed disintegrating forces within the society. The previous chapters have discussed many dilemmas, conflicts, contradictions, and forces of disunity for which no immediate resolution appears attainable, and which have significant implications for the emergence of a sense of society. For example, it is debatable whether a unitary societal identity can ever crystallize without a common culture, a common language, or a common sense of history. At the same time, however, modern societies are not static homogeneous entities in which a sense of commonality will necessarily supersede individual preferences and/or local territorial identities.

One of the problems with talking about a national society is that we bring our notions of small-scale communities to discussions of national belonging. The sociologist Ferdinand Tonnies distinguished a *community* from a *society* by noting that the intensity of social relationships was much stronger in a community, and much more distant, remote, and bureaucratic, in a society.[90] When nations were smaller self-contained ethnic groups or sub-groups, it might have been possible to talk about the typical face-to-face interactions that created a sense of community. Now, however, political states are frequently formed by welding a diversity of ethnic groups together into a national polity. The result has been the creation of societies in which feelings of unity are superficial and social bonding is weak. Because the members of even the smallest modern nation will never know most of their fellow citizens, contemporary national societies are best referred to as "*imagined communities*."[91] A sense of society then begins in the mind, where the image of a level of a common identity produces an ephemeral unity that may never correspond to the hard facts of social reality. It is left to institutions such as governments, corporations, and other large organizations to give this identity a more tangible expression.

But it also needs to be said that the relationship between individual identity and collectivities is always one of negotiation and change rather than permanence and fixity. The concept of *translational identity* means that we are always trying to relate, translate, adjust, and readjust our own interpretations of reality to those around us.[92] Our "ethnic" identity, our "linguistic" identity, our "regional" identity, or our "personal" identity that emerges from our own view of the world always is in constant interaction with the identities of others. So identity is dynamic and in process, and individualistic as well as possessing its collective aspects. It is not just what is inherited or what we are at any particular point but how we change and adapt and negotiate with others around us. Similarly at the national level, identity is continuously reconstructed in relation to external and internal events and our perceptions of them and their meaning.[93]

With this framework for a national society, it should not be expected that such a society will ever be a single unified entity. In contrast to an *ethnocentric nationalism*, where exclusive power is given to the pursuit of one national ideal, and where differences and divisions are viewed as defects in the society, the Canadian experience has evidenced a greater tendency towards a *polycentric nationalism*, with a tolerance of contending ideals and identities, openness to others, and a freely self-critical spirit.[94] This has led some observers to see Canadian society as "a community of communities" where national homogeneity is rejected and decentralized community is encouraged.[95]

Ramsay Cook, a student of Canadian nationalism for many years, has argued that Canadian society is strongest when nationalism is muted.[96] And yet Raymond Breton has pointed out that with the recognition of Quebec as a distinct society in conjunction with the continentalist pressures of free trade, there is too little effort given to specifying the nature and meaning of the "Canadian" national society.[97] Is the state's role only that of providing services to people organized into smaller sub-units?[98] Or is the state to direct and embody a collective identity and commitment that members of a society feel represent their united sentiments? Responses to this question will clearly vary because there are different levels of belonging which structure the society.

It could be argued that insisting on a single national identity is old-fashioned and out of step with the times. Learning to live with more than one identity at the personal level and accepting similar conditions in the identity of others may be a more important adaptive principle in the new millennium than ever before. The dilemma for most Canadians has been stated clearly by Charles Taylor who notes that the Charter of Rights (1982) emphasized *individual rights* and equality. Yet at the same time, there are also pressures to accept *group rights* such as espoused by Québécois and native peoples.[99] Fundamentally, these two objectives are irreconcilable and reflect at root the current impasse in Canadian society in which anglophones prefer the emphasis on individual rights and francophones prefer the emphasis on collective rights. The challenge then is to allow differences to be preserved at the same time that a larger social connectedness is sustained. This can only be done if we recognize that people can hold multiple identities. In short, even people who have a strong group identity (such as Québécois or native people) can also discover the ways in which they are also Canadian. For example, the Québécois have created their own national identity by attempting to differentiate themselves from English Canadians.[100] This means the use of selected stereotypes that both groups invent to establish group boundaries, but this process is still a Canadian phenomenon in a Canadian context in which perceptions and definitions of each other are constantly changing.

The Canadian identity is currently being challenged most severely on two fronts. One is Quebec nationalism and the degree of distance that will give Quebec its sense of independence while bordered by the rest of Canada. Acronyms like ROC (Rest Of Canada) or

Identity Discourses

"You can't be a Quebecker unless you are only a Quebecker. If you feel Canadian, you don't really love Quebec"

single national identity discourse of Québécois indépendantiste

"You can't be a Canadian unless you are a Canadian first. You can be something else secondarily but must give your prior allegiance to Canada."

dominant national identity discourse of Canadian nationalist

"You can be Québécois and Canadian at the same time. Both identities as well as other identities can be held simultaneously."

multiple identities discourse of a post-modern Canadian

Question to consider:

What might the discourses look like among other groups in Canada?

CWOQ (Canada Without Quebec) struggle to define the relationship between a Canada with or without Quebec, at the same time as the acknowledgment that sheer proximity and economic realities will always require close ties implies that this relationship will always be in negotiation.[101]

The second front of critical importance to the Canadian identity is the result of globalization in what has been referred to as the *post-national state*.[102] From this perspective, national identities are becoming increasingly irrelevant as the search for commonalities of history, language, and culture are replaced by common economic interests that supersede traditional political boundaries. The need for fluidity and opportunism that is required by the process of capital accumulation supports the post-modern idea of flexibility rather than sharp boundaries in what has been called *flexible citizenship*.[103] For example, one study found that there is indeed a high level of mutual trust between Canadians and Americans and that closer economic and political ties are not being resisted by a significant number of people on this continent.[104] On the other hand, as we have seen, the state is still an important global mechanism of identity.

Perhaps the most basic dilemma, however, is that there still remain continuing tensions between unitary and segmentalized conceptions of society in Canada. The dynamics between these opposing pressures make Canadian society volatile and unstable, on the one hand, yet intriguing and vigorous on the other hand. It is because Canadians cannot take their society for granted that the quest for new solutions, innovations, and experimentation continues, making this society an exciting place in which to live.

FURTHER EXPLORATION

1. Do you think the federal government should play a more active interventionist role in building and preserving a distinct Canadian identity? What could be done? What groups would disagree with your position and why?

2. Which view of Canadian society would you prefer—unitary or segmentalist? What are the advantages and disadvantages of each?

3. In the Canadian quest for greater independence, how important is it to remove all ties with the British monarchy?

4. List the factors that make Canadian society different from and similar to American society.

5. In what way is nationalism a good thing? In what way is it suspect? Can Quebec nationalism coexist with Canadian nationalism?

SELECTED READINGS

Drache, Daniel and Roberto Perin (eds.), *Negotiating With A Sovereign Quebec*. Toronto: James Lorimer, 1992.

Earle, Robert L. and John D. Wirth (eds.), *Identities In North America: The Search For Community*. Stanford: Stanford University Press, 1995.

Kaplan, William, ed. *Belonging: The Meaning And Future of Canadian Citizenship*. Montreal: McGill-Queens University Press, 1993.

Keohane, Kieran. *Symptoms Of Canada: An Essay On The Canadian Identity*. Toronto: University Of Toronto Press, 1997.

McRoberts, Kenneth. *Misconceiving Canada: The Struggle For National Unity.* Toronto: Oxford University Press, 1997.

Taras, David, Beverly Rasporich, and Eli Mandel, eds. *A Passion for Identity.* 3rd ed. Scarborough: Nelson, 1997.

ENDNOTES

1   Keith Spicer, "Canada: Values In Search of A Vision," in Robert L. Earle and John D. Wirth (eds.), *Identities in North America: The Search for Community* (Stanford: Stanford University Press, 1995), 13–28.

2   Randy William Widdis, "Borders, Borderlands And Canadian Identity: A Canadian Perspective," *International Journal of Canadian Studies* 15(1997)49–66.

3   Stanley Morse, "National Identity from a Social Psychological Perspective: A Study of University Students in Saskatchewan," *Canadian Review of Studies in Nationalism* 7(1980): 299–312.

4   *A Future Together: Observations and Recommendations of the Task Force on Canadian Unity* (Ottawa: Minister Of Supply And Services Canada, 1979).

5   In addition to the *Task Force on Canadian Unity,* see also Herschel Hardin, *A Nation Unaware* (Vancouver: J.J. Douglas, 1974), 12.

6   This distinction was initially made by Albert Breton and Raymond Breton in *Why Disunity? An Analysis of Linguistic and Regional Cleavages in Canada* (Montreal: Institute for Research on Public Policy, 1980), 58–59 and is developed further here.

7   John Conway, "An Adapted Organic Tradition," *Daedalus* 117(1988): 388.

8   This is essentially the point of W.L. Morton, *The Canadian Identity* (Madison: University of Wisconsin Press, 1965), 111.

9   See Keith Banting and Richard Simeon, *And No One Cheered: Federalism, Democracy, and the Constitution Act* (Toronto: Methuen, 1983), chap. 1; and David Milne, *The New Canadian Constitution* (Toronto: James Lormier, 1982).

10 Keith Banting and Richard Simeon, eds., *Redesigning the State: The Politics of Constitutional Change in Industrial Nations* (Toronto: University of Toronto Press, 1985.)

11 R. Kenneth Carty and W. Peter Ward, *Entering the Eighties: Canada in Crisis* (Toronto: Oxford University Press, 1980).

12 Leon Dion argues the point that a societal identity is a combination of fragments of tradition and contemporary changes. "The Mystery of Quebec," *Daedalus* 117(1988): 307.

13 David Orchard, *The Fight for Canada: Four Centuries of Resistance to American Expansionism* (Toronto: Stoddard, 1991).

14 John Sloan Dickey, *Canada and the American Presence* (New York: New York University Press, 1975), 7.

15 International Travel, *Travel Between Canada and Other Countries,* Statistics Canada 1997, Catalogue 66–201.

16 Jeffrey Frank and Michel Durand, "Canadian Content In The Cultural Marketplace," *Canadian Social Trends,* Summer 1993, Statistics Canada Catalogue 11-008, 18–21 and Tom Gorman and Susan Crompton, "Canadian Television In Transition." *Canadian Social Trends,* Spring 1997, Statistics Canada Catalogue 11-008-XPE, 19–23. See also George Barnett and Thomas McPhail, "An Examination of the Relationship of United States Television and Canadian Identity," *International Journal of Intercultural Relations* 4(1980): 219–32.

17 John Meisal, "Escaping Extinctions: Cultural Defense of an Undefended Border," in D.H. Flaherty and W.R. McKercher, eds., *Southern Exposure: Canadian Perspectives on the U.S.* (Toronto: McGraw-Hill Ryerson, 1986), 152–68. For a good discussion of broadcasting policy and nation-building, see Jean McNulty, "Technology and Nation-building in Canadian Broadcasting" in Rowland Lormir and Donald Wilson, eds., *Communication Canada: Issues in Broadcasting and New Technologies* (Toronto: Kagan and Woo, 1988), 176–98.

18 Richard Gwyn, *The 49th Paradox: Canada in North America* (Toronto: McClelland and Stewart, 1985), 11.

19 S.D. Clark notes that anti-Americanism is frequently the means whereby this societal differentiation occurs. "Canada and Her Great Neighbor," *Canadian Review of Sociology and Anthropology* 1(1964): 193–201. See also Dallas Cullen, J.D. Jobson, and Rodney Schneck, "Anti-Americanism and its Correlates," *Canadian Journal of Sociology* 3(1978): 103–20.

20 Charles F. Doran and James P. Sewell, "Anti-Americanism in Canada," in Thomas P. Thornton, ed., *Anti-Americanism: Origins and Context, The Annals of the American Academy of Political and Social Science* 497(1988): 119.

21 See David Bell and Lorne Tepperman, *The Roots of Disunity* (Toronto: McClelland Stewart, 1979), 211–13.

22 Herschel Hardin refers to this phenomenon as American ideology-in-Canada in which Canadian objectives are coloured by American standards and patterns. *A Nation Unaware*, 55.

23 Gordon Laxer, "Constitutional Crises And Continentalism: Twin Threats To Canada's Continued Existence," *Canadian Journal of Sociology* 17(1992): 199–222.

24 Richard Collins, *Culture, Communications, and National Identity* (Toronto: University of Toronto Press, 1990), 329.

25 James Winter and Irvin Goldman, "Mass Media And Canadian Identity," in Benjamin D. Singer, ed., *Communications in Canadian Society* (Toronto: Nelson, 1995), chap. 9.

26 John N. McDougall, "North American Integration And Canadian Disunity," *Canadian Public Policy* 17(1991): 397.

27 Pierre Berton, *Why We Act Like Canadians* (Toronto: McClelland and Stewart, 1982), 12.

28 Peter Brimelow claims that the notion of bilingualism binding the two language groups together is a myth. *The Patriot Game* (Toronto: Key Porter, 1986), chap. 6.

29 Charles Castonguay, "The Fading Canadian Duality," in John Edwards (ed.), *Language in Canada* (Cambridge, Cambridge University Press, 1998), 36–60.

30 Leon Dion, "The Mystery of Quebec," 286.

31 Robert F. Harney, "So Great a Heritage as Ours: Immigration and the Survival of the Canadian Polity," *Daedalus* 117(1988): 51–97; and Neil Nevitte, "Nationalism, States and Nations," in Elliot J. Feldman and Neil Nevitte, eds., *The Future of North America: Canada, the United States, and Quebec Nationalism* (Cambridge: Center For International Affairs, 1979), 354.

32 Kenneth McRoberts, "After The Referendum: Canada With Or Without Quebec", in his *Beyond Quebec: Taking Stock of Canada* (Montreal: McGill-Queen's University Press, 1995), 403–432; and Roger Gibbins, "Canada Without Quebec: Thinking Through The Unthinkable", in David Taras and Beverly Rasporich (eds.), *A Passion for Identity*, 3rd Edition (Toronto: Nelson, 1997), 105–118.

33 James Overton discusses the neo-nationalism of regions opposing the centralization of power, "Towards a Critical Analysis of Neo-Nationalism in Newfoundland," in Robert J. Brym and R. James Sacouman, eds., *Underdevelopment and Social Movements in Atlantic Canada* (Toronto: New Hogtown Press, 1979), 219–49.

34 These ideas are an adaptation of a theme developed by Jeffrey Reitz, "Immigrants, Their Descendants, and the Cohesion of Canada," in Raymond Breton, Jeffrey G. Reitz, and Victor Valentine, *Cultural Boundaries and the Cohesion of Canada* (Montreal: Institute for Research on Public Policy, 1980), 400–406.

35 Will Kymlicka, *Finding Our Way: Rethinking Ethnocultural Relations in Canada* (Toronto: Oxford, 1998), 171–172.

36 Janice Dickin and Elspeth Cameron, " Engendering Canadian Identity," in *A Passion for Identity*, 209–224.

37 A related point has been made by Susan Crean and Marcel Rioux in *Two Nations* (Toronto: James Lorimer, 1983), 15.

38 Robin Matthews, *Canadian Identity: Major Forces Shaping the Life of a People* (Ottawa: Steel Rail, 1988), 5–6.

39 The stormy debate over the adoption of the maple leaf as the national flag is recorded in Blair Fraser, *The Search for Identity* (Toronto: Doubleday, 1967), chap. 23.

40 This discussion has benefitted enormously from the work of Raymond Breton, "The Production and Allocation of Symbolic Resources: An Analysis of the Linguistic and Ethnocultural Fields in Canada," *Canadian Review of Sociology and Anthropology* 21(1984): 123–44; and "Intergroup Competition In The Symbolic Construction Of Canadian Society", in Peter S. Li (ed.), *Race and Ethnic Relations in Canada*, Second Edition (Toronto: Oxford, 1999), 291–310.

41 Raymond Breton, *Why Meech Failed: Lessons for Canadian Constitution Making* (Toronto: C.D. Howe Institute, 1992).

42 Kieran Keohane, *Symptoms of Canada* (Toronto: University Of Toronto Press, 1997), 28.

43 Roger Gibbins, *The New Face of Canadian Nationalism* (Kingston: Queens University Institute Of Intergovernmental Relations Reflections Paper No. 14, 1995).

44 William Watson, *Globalization and the Meaning of Canadian Life* (Toronto: University Of Toronto Press, 1998).

45 Craig Calhoun, "Nationalism And Civil Society," in his *Social Theory and the Politics of Identity* (Oxford: Blackwell, 1994), 304–335.

46 Jan Penrose, "Construction, De(con)struction and Reconstruction: The Impact Of Globalization and Fragmentation On The Canadian Nation-State," *The International Journal Of Canadian Studies* 16(1997):15–49.

47 For example, see Mel Watkins, "Dene Nationalism," *Canadian Review of Studies of Nationalism* 8(1981): 101–113.

48 This concept of nationalism is developed by W. Christian and C. Campbell, *Political Parties and Ideologies in Canada* (Toronto: McGraw-Hill Ryerson, 1974). See also Chapter 6 for a good study of Canadian nationalism in historical development.

49 Anthony D. Smith, *Nationalism in the Twentieth Century* (Oxford: Martin Robertson, 1979), 1–3.

50 Richard Collins, *Culture, Communication, and National Identity*, 106. An interesting discussion using the concept of "submerged nations" has been developed by Vatro Murvar, *Submerged Nations: An Invitation to Theory* (Milwaukee: University of Wisconsin—Sociology, 1982).

51 A.G. Bailey, *Culture and Nationality* (Toronto: McClelland and Stewart, 1972), chap. 9.

52 Silvia Brucan, "The Nation-State: Will it Keep Order or Wither Away?" *International Social Science Journal* 30(1978): 9–30; and Jan Penrose, "Construction, De(con)struction, and Reconstruction: The Impact Of Globalization And Fragmentation On The Canadian Nation-State," *International Journal of Canadian Studies* 16(1997):15–49.

53 Abraham Rotstein, "Is There an English-Canadian Nationalism?" *Journal of Canadian Studies* 13(1978): 114.

54 Daniel Salee, "Quebec Sovereignty And The Challenge of Linguistic And Ethnocultural Minorities: Identity, Differences, And The Politics Of Ressentiment," *Quebec Studies* 24(1997):6–23.

55 For a discussion on the CMA and nationalist sentiment as a long-standing phenomenon, see S.D. Clark, *The Canadian Manufacturers' Association: A Study in Collective Bargaining and Political Pressure* (Toronto: University of Toronto Press, 1939).

56 Patricia Marchak, "Nationalism and Regionalism in Canada," *Canadian Review of Studies in Nationalism* 7(1980): 26. The explanation of nationalism developed here is actually built from modernization theories which point to a new educated class and their expanding influence on the rest of the society.

57 Both general theories of nationalism discussed here are elaborated in greater detail in Anthony D. Smith, *Theories of Nationalism* (New York: Harper and Row, 1971). See also Howard Aster, "Nationalism and Communitarianism," in Wallace Gagne, ed., *Nationalism, Technology and the Future of Canada* (Toronto: Macmillan, 1976), 56–63.

58 Ernest Gellner, *Nations and Nationalism* (Oxford: Basil Blackwell, 1983), 140.

59 Roger Gibbins, *Prairie Politics and Society: Regionalism in Decline* (Scarborough: Butterworths, 1980).

60 Ramsay Cook, *Canada, Quebec, and the Uses of Nationalism* (Toronto: McClelland and Stewart, 1986), 9–10.

61 Alan C. Cairns, "The Fragmentation Of Canadian Citizenship," in William Kaplan, ed., *Belonging: The Meaning and Future of Canadian Citizenship* (Montreal: McGill-Queens University Press, 1993), 181–220.

62 Jo-anne Lee and Linda Cardinal, "Hegemonic Nationalism And The Politics of Feminism And Multiculturalism In Canada," pp. 215–241 in Veronic Strong-Boag, Sherrill Grace, Avigail Eisenberg, and Joan Anderson (eds.), *Painting the Maple Leaf: Essays on Race, Gender, and the Construction of Canada* (Vancouver: UBC Press, 1998). See also Keohane, Symptoms Of Canada, 7. For an interesting comparison, see Jeffrey Lesser, *Negotiating National Identity: Immigrants, Minorities, and the Struggle for Ethnicity in Brazil* (Durham: Duke University Press, 1999) which shows how minorities from China, Japan, North Africa, and the Middle East are challenging the goal to make Brazil a European society.

63 Pierre Fournier, *A Meech Lake Post-Mortem: Is Quebec Sovereignty Inevitable?* (Montreal: McGill Queens University Press, 1991), 82.

64 Louis Balthazar, "The Faces Of Quebec Nationalism," in Alain G. Gagnon, ed., *Quebec: State and Society*, 2nd ed. (Scarborough: Prentice-Hall, 1993), 13.

65 Ken McRoberts, "English Canadian Perceptions Of Quebec," in Gagnon, *Quebec: State and Society*, 2nd ed., 116–29.

66 Augie Fleras and Jean Leonard Elliott, *The Nations Within: Aboriginal-State Relations in Canada, the United States and New Zealand*, 227.

67 Roger Gibbins, *The New Face of Canadian Nationalism*.

68 Rick Ponting, "Racial Conflict: Turning The Heat Up," in Dan Glenday and Ann Duffy, eds., *Canadian Society: Understanding and Surviving in the 1990s* (Toronto: McClelland and Stewart, 1994), 102.

69 Richard Gwyn, *Nationalism Without Walls*.

70 Stacy Churchill, *Official Languages in Canada: Changing the Language Landscape* (Heritage Canada Catalogue no. Ch3-2-7/1998), 79.

71 Robert Fulford argues that this is a key characteristic of post-modernism. "A Post-Modern Dominion," in William Kaplan, ed., *Belonging: The Meaning and Future of Canadian Citizenship*, 104–119. The Canadian preoccupation with self-questioning is discussed in David V. J. Bell, *The Roots of Disunity: A Study of Canadian Political Culture,* rev. ed. (Toronto: Oxford, 1992), chap. 3.

72 Kenneth McRoberts, *Misconceiving Canada: The Struggle For National Unity* (Toronto: Oxford, 1997).

73 The distinction between civic and ethnic nationality is made by Raymond Breton, "From Ethnic to Civic Nationalism: English Canada and Quebec," *Ethnic and Racial Studies* 11(1988): 85–102.

74 Yvonne Hebert, "Citizenship Education: Towards A Pedagogy Of Social Participation And Identity Formation," *Canadian Ethnic Studies* 29(1997)2:16–33.

75 Paul G. Lamy, "Political Socialization of French and English Canadian Youth: Socialization into Discord," in Zureik and Pike, eds., *Socialization and Values in Canadian Society*, vol, 1. Political Socialization, 263–80.

76 Report of the Royal Commission on Bilingualism and Biculturalism Book II: Education, 275.

77 Jean Pierre Richert, "The Impact of Ethnicity on the Perception of Heroes and Historical Symbols," *Canadian Review of Sociology and Anthropology* 11(1974): 156–63.

78 Leslie Pal, *Interests Of The State: The Politics of Language, Multiculturalism, and Feminism in Canada* (Montreal: McGill-Queens University Press, 1997).

79 Katarzyna Rukszto, "National Encounters: Narrating Canada And The Plurality Of Difference," *International Journal of Canadian Studies* 16(1997)150–162.

80 There are a number of very good discussions on this theme: Martin J. Morris and Nadine Changfoot, " The Solidarity Deficit: The Rise Of Neo-Liberalism And The Crisis Of National Unity", *International Journal of Canadian Studies* 14(1996)137–154; Stephen McBride and John Shields, *Dismantling a Nation*, Second Edition (Halifax: Fernwood, 1997); and John Herd Thompson, "Canada's Quest For Cultural Sovereignty: Protection, Promotion, and Popular Culture", in Stephen J. Randall and Herman W. Konrad (ed.), *NAFTA in Transition* (Calgary: University Of Calgary Press, 1995), 393–410.

81 S.D. Clark, "Canada and Her Great Neighbor," 195.

82 Philip Resnick, *The Land of Cain: Class and Nationalism in English Canada* (Vancouver: New Star, 1977), 147ff.

83 For an interesting discussion of factors promoting the integration of Canadian society, see Douglas Cole, "The Integration of Canada: An Overview," *Canadian Review of Studies in Nationalism* 7(1980): 4–13.

84 Mary Jane Miller, "Will English-Language Television Remain Distinctive? Probably", in *Beyond Quebec: Taking Stock of Canada*, 138–162; and David Taras, "The CBC And Canadian Television In The New Media Age", in *A Passion for Identity*, 265–279.

85 Charles Acland, "Cultural Survival: Sleeping with the Elephant," in Glenday and Duffy, *Canadian Society: Understanding and Surviving in the 1990's*, 234–35.

86 Richard Gruneau and David Whitson, *Hockey Night In Canada: Sport, Identities, and Cultural Politics* (Toronto: Garamond, 1993).

87 Joyce Zemans provides a good overview of these various cultural institutions and their relationship to nationhood objectives. "The Essential Role Of National Cultural Institutions," in *Beyond Quebec: Taking Stock of Canada*, 182–201.

88 For a compendium of such contributions, see David Taras, Beverly Rasporich, and Eli Mandel, eds., *A Passion for Identity*, 2nd ed. (Scarborough: Nelson, 1993); For the role of the intelligentsia, see Anthony D. Smith, ed., *Nationalist Movements* (London: Macmillan, 1976), 21–24.

89   For a discussion of the relationship between Canadian literature and national identity, see Paul Cappon, ed., *In our Own House: Social Perspectives on Canadian Literature* (Toronto: McClelland and Stewart, 1978). See also Government of Canada, Report of the Federal Cultural Policy Review Committee. (Ottawa: Department of Communications, 1981).

90   Ferdinand Tonnies, *Fundamental Concepts of Sociology* (New York: American Books, 1940).

91   Benedict Anderson, *Imagined Communities: Reflections on the Origin and Spread of Nationalism* (London: Verso, 1983), 15.

92   Sherry Simon, "National Membership And Forms Of Contemporary Belonging In Quebec", in Andre Lapierre, Patricia Smart, and Pierre Savard (eds.), *Language, Culture and Values in Canada at the Dawn of the 21st Century* (Ottawa: Carleton University Press and International Council For Canadian Studies, 1996), 121–131.

93   Daniel Latouche cautions that anglo perceptions of Quebec also needs to remember that Quebec identity is also not wooden and is changing in response to a changing North American environment. "Quebec In The Emerging North American Configuration," in Earle and Wirth (ed.), *Identities in North America: The Search for Community*, 117–139.

94   See Anthony D. Smith, Theories of Nationalism, 158–59; and S.M. Crean, *Who's Afraid of Canadian Culture?* (Don Mills: General Publishing, 1976), 277–78.

95   Lloyd Axworthy, "The Federal System—An Uncertain Path," *Daedalus* 117(1988): 141. Howard Aster uses the term "communitarian nationalism" to express the same idea. "Nationalism and Communitarianism," 66–67.

96   Ramsay Cook, *Canada and the French Canadian Question* (Toronto: Macmillan, 1966), 25. Cook argues that Canada's problem is too much, not too little, nationalism.

97   Raymond Breton, "The Concepts of 'Distinct Society' and 'Identity' in the Meech Lake Accord," in Katherine E. Swinton and Carol J. Rogerson, eds., *Competing Constitutional Visions* (Toronto: Carswell, 1988), 8–9.

98   Ramsay Cook, *The Maple Leaf Forever: Essays on Nationalism and Politics in Canada* (Toronto: Macmillan, 1971), 8.

99   Charles Taylor, "Shared And Divergent Values," *Reconciling the Solitudes: Essays on Canadian Federalism and Nationalism* (Montreal: McGill-Queens University Press, 1993), Chapter 8; Multiculturalism And The Politics Of Recognition (Princeton: Princeton University Press, 1992).

100   Daniel Latouche, "Quebec In An Emerging North America," 131.

101   For a variety of discussions on this issue, see Pierre Martin, "Association After Sovereignty? Canadian Views On Economic Association With A Sovereign Quebec," *Canadian Public Policy* 21(1995): 53–71; Dean Usher, "The Interests Of English Canada," *Canadian Public Policy* 21(1995): 72–84; Scott Reid, *Canada Remapped: How the Partition of Quebec Will Reshape the Nation* (Vancouver: Pulp Press, 1992); and David J. Bercuson and Barry Cooper, *Deconfederation: Canada Without Quebec* (Toronto: Key Porter, 1991).

102   James Laxer, *Inventing Europe: The Rise of a New World Power* (Toronto: Lester, 1991), 304.

103   Aihwa Ong, *Flexible Citizenship: The Cultural Logistics of Transnationality* (Durham: Duke University Press, 1999).

104   Neil Nevitte, "Bringing Values Back In: Value Change And North American Integration," in Donald Barry, ed., *Toward a North American Community: Canada, the United States, and Mexico* (Boulder: Westview, 1995), 185–209.

WEBLINKS

www.pch.gc.ca

The home page of Canadian Heritage is a resource for the advancement of Canadian culture, heritage, and identity.

www.cicnet.ci.gc.ca

The home page for Citizenship and Immigration Canada provides up-to-date information on policies and statistics related to Canadian immigrants and refugees.

cbc.ca/sports/hockey/

Visit the sports section of the CBC Web site to read about Canada's national sport, an integral part of our national identity. This page also features video clips from a longstanding, Saturday night Canadian tradition, Hockey Night in Canada.

www.pch.gc.ca/ceremonial-symb/english/emb.html

This section of the Canadian Heritage Web site describes some of the symbols of Canada such as the national flag, coat of arms, the maple leaf, and the beaver.

www.canadians.org

The Council of Canadians is an independent, non-partisan citizens' interest group providing a critical and progressive voice on key national issues.

Select Bibliography

Abele, F. *Gathering Strength*. Calgary: Arctic Institute of North America, 1989.

Acheson, T.W., D. Frank, and J.D. Frost. *Industrialization and Underdevelopment in the Maritimes, 1880–1930*. Toronto: Garamond Press, 1985.

Adams, I., et al. *The Real Poverty Report*. Edmonton: Hurtig, 1971.

Adams, W., ed., *The Brain Drain*. Toronto: Macmillan, 1968.

Agnew, V., *Resisting Discrimination: Women in Asia, Africa, and the Caribbean and the Women's Movement in Canada*. Toronto: University of Toronto Press, 1996.

Alexander, D. *Atlantic Canada and Confederation*. Toronto: University of Toronto Press, 1983.

Anderson, A.B., and J.S. Frideres. *Ethnicity in Canada: Theoretical Perspectives*. Toronto: Butterworths, 1981.

Anderson, F.J. *Regional Economic Analysis: A Canadian Perspective*. Toronto: HBJ Holt, 1988.

Anderson, G. *Networks of Contact: The Portuguese in Toronto*. Waterloo: Wilfred Laurier University Press, 1974.

Andrew, C. and S. Rodgers, eds. *Women and the Canadian State*. Montreal: McGill-Queens, 1997.

Anisef, P., and N. Okihiro. *Losers and Winners: The Pursuit of Equality and Social Justice in Higher Education*. Toronto: Butterworths, 1982.

Armitage, A. *Comparing the Policy of Aboriginal Assimilation: Australia, Canada, and New Zealand*. Vancouver: UBC Press, 1995.

Armstrong, P. and H. Armstrong. *The Double Ghetto: Canadian Women and Their Segregated Work*. Toronto: McClelland and Stewart, 1994.

Arnopoulos, S.M. *Voices from French Ontario*. Montreal: McGill-Queen's University Press, 1982.

Arnopoulos, S.M. and D. Clift. *The English Fact in Quebec*. Montreal: McGill-Queen's University Press, 1980.

Avery, D. *Reluctant Host: Canada's Response to Immigrant Workers 1896-1994*. Toronto: McClelland and Stewart, 1995.

Axline, A., et al. *Continental Community: Independence and Integration in North America*. Toronto: McClelland and Stewart, 1974.

Banting, K., and R. Simeon. *And No One Cheered: Federalism, Democracy, and the Constitution Act*. Toronto: Methuen, 1983.

Banting, K. and R. Simeon, eds. *Redesigning the State: The Politics of Constitutional Change in Industrial Nations*. Toronto: University of Toronto Press, 1985.

Barr, J.J., and O. Anderson, eds. *The Unfinished Revolt*. Toronto: McClelland and Stewart, 1971.

Barry, D., ed. *Toward a North American Community? Canada, the United States, and Mexico*. Boulder: Westview, 1995.

Beattie, C. *Minority of Men in a Majority Setting*. Toronto: McClelland and Stewart, 1975.

Beattie, C., J. Desy, and S. Longstaff. *Bureaucratic Careers: Anglophones and Francophones in the Canadian Public Service*. Ottawa: Information Canada, 1972.

Beaujot, R. *Population Change in Canada.* Toronto: McClelland and Stewart, 1992.

Beaujot, R. and K. McQuillan. *Growth and Dualism: The Demographic Development of Canadian Society.* Toronto: Gage, 1982.

Behiels, M.D., ed. *The Meech Lake Primer: Conflicting Views of the 1987 Constitutional Accord.* Ottawa: University of Ottawa Press, 1989.

Bell, D. *The Roots of Disunity: A Look at Canadian Political Culture.* Toronto: Oxford University Press, 1992.

Bellamy, D.J., J.H. Pammett, and D.C. Rowat, eds. *The Provincial Political Systems: Comparative Essays.* Toronto: Methuen, 1976.

Bellon, D., and Jorge Niosi. *The Decline of the American Economy.* Toronto: Black Rose, 1988.

Bercuson, D.J., ed. *Canada and the Burden of Unity.* Toronto: Macmillan, 1977.

Bercuson, D.J., and Barry Cooper. *Deconfederation: Canada Without Quebec.* Toronto: Key Porter, 1991.

Berkowitz, S.D. *Models and Myths in Canadian Sociology.* Toronto: Butterworths, 1984.

Berkowitz, S.D. and R.K. Logan, eds. *Canada's Third Option.* Toronto: Macmillan, 1978.

Berry, J.A., and J.A. Laponce, eds. *Ethnicity and Culture in Canada: The Research Landscape.* Toronto: University of Toronto Press, 1994.

Berton, P. *Why We Act Like Canadians.* Toronto: McClelland and Stewart, 1982.

Bibby, R. *Mosaic Madness: The Poverty and Potential of Life in Canada.* Toronto: Stoddart, 1990.

Bickerton, J.P. *Nova Scotia, Ottawa, and the Politics of Regional Development.* Toronto: University of Toronto Press, 1990.

Bienvenue, R.M., and J.E. Goldstein, eds. *Ethnicity and Ethnic Relations in Canada.* 2nd ed. Toronto: Butterworths, 1985.

Blake, R.B., P.E. Bryden, J.F. Strain, eds. *The Welfare State in Canada: Past, Present and Future.* Toronto: Irwin, 1997.

Bolaria, B.S. *Social Issues and Contradictions in Canadian Society.* Toronto: Harcourt Brace, 1995

Boldt, M. and J.A. Long, eds. *The Quest for Justice: Aboriginal Peoples and Aboriginal Rights.* Toronto: University of Toronto Press, 1985.

Bourgault, P. *Now or Never!: Manifesto For An Independent Quebec.* Toronto: Key Porter, 1991.

Bowles, R.T., ed. *Little Communities and Big Industries: Studies in the Social Impact of Canadian Resource Extraction.* Toronto: Butterworths, 1982.

Boyd, M., et al. *Ascription and Achievement: Studies in Mobility and Status Attainment in Canada.* Ottawa: Carleton University Press, 1985.

Brault, G.J. *The French Canadian Heritage in New England.* Montreal: McGill-Queen's University Press, 1986.

Breton, A., and R. Breton. W*hy Disunity? An Analysis of Lingusitic and Regional Cleavages in Canada.* Montreal: Institute for Research on Public Policy, 1980.

Breton, R. *Why Meech Failed: Lessons For Canadian Constitution Making.* Toronto: C.D. Howe Institute, 1992.

Breton, R., J.G. Reitz, and V.F. Valentine. *Cultural Boundaries and the Cohesion of Canada.* Montreal: Institute for Research on Public Policy, 1980.

Breton, R., W.W. Isajiw, W. Kalbach, and J.G. Reitz. *Ethnic Identity and Equality: Varieties of Experience in a Canadian City.* Toronto: University of Toronto Press, 1990.

Brimelow, P. *The Patriot Game.* Toronto: Key Porter, 1986.

Brodie, J. *The Political Economy of Canadian Regionalism*. Toronto: Harcourt Brace and Jovanovich, 1990.

_____, *Politics on the Margins: Restructuring and the Canadian Women's Movement*. Halifax: Fernwood, 1995.

_____, *Women and Canadian Public Policy*. Toronto: Harcourt Brace, 1996

Brym, R., ed. *Regionalism in Canada*. Toronto: Irwin, 1986.

_____. *The Structure of the Canadian Capitalist Class*. Toronto: Garamond, 1985.

_____. *From Culture to Power: The Sociology of English Canada*. Toronto: Oxford, 1989.

Brym, R.J., and R.J. Sacouman. *Underdevelopment and Social Movements in Atlantic Canada*. Toronto: New Hogtown Press, 1979.

Buckner, P. A., and D. Frank, eds. *Atlantic Canada After Confederation*. Fredericton: Acadiensis Press, 1985.

Burman, P. *Killing Time, Losing Ground: Experiences of Unemployment*. Toronto: Wall and Thompson, 1988.

Burrill, G., and I. McKay, eds. *People, Resources and Power*. Fredericton: Acadiensis Press, 1987.

Burt, S., L. Code, and L. Dorney, eds. *Changing Patterns: Women in Canada*. 2nd ed. Toronto: McClellend and Stewart, 1993.

Cairns, A., and C. Williams, eds. *The Politics of Gender, Ethnicity and Language in Canada*. Toronto: University of Toronto Press, 1986.

Caldwell, G., and E. Waddell. *The English of Quebec: From Majority to Minority Status*. Quebec: Institut Québécois de Recherche sur la Culture, 1982.

Cameron, D., and Mel Watkins, eds. *Canada Under Free Trade*. Toronto: Lorimer, 1992.

Cameron, D.M., ed. *Regionalism and Supranationalism*. Montreal: Insitute for Research on Public Policy, 1981.

Campbell, R.M., and L.A. Pal. *The Real Worlds of Canadian Politics*. Peterborough: Broadview Press, 1989.

Canadian Council on Social Development. *Not Enough: The Meaning and Measurement of Poverty in Canada*. Toronto: James Lorimer, 1985.

Cappon, P., ed. *In Our Own House: Social Perspectives on Canadian Literature*. Toronto: McClelland and Stewart, 1978.

Card, B.Y., ed. *Perspectives on Regions and Regionalism*. Edmonton: University of Alberta Press, 1969.

Carroll, W.K. *Corporate Power and Canadian Capitalism*. Vancouver: University of British Columbia Press, 1986.

Carty, R.K., and W.P. Ward. *Entering the Eighties; Canada in Crisis*. Toronto: Oxford University Press, 1980.

Cassidy, F., ed. *Aboriginal Self-Determination*. Toronto: Institute For Research On Public Policy, 1991.

Chodos, R., Rae Murphy, and Eric Hamovitch. *Canada and the Global Economy*. Toronto: Lorimer, 1993.

Chodos, R., and Eric Hamovitch. *Quebec and the American Dream*. Toronto: Between the Lines, 1991.

Choiniere, R. *An Overview of Demographic and Socio-Economic Conditions of the Inuit in Canada*. Ottawa: Indian and Northern Affairs Canada, 1985.

Christian W., and C. Campbell. *Political Parties and Ideologies in Canada*. 2nd ed. Toronto: McGraw-Hill Ryerson, 1983.

Clairmont, D.H., and D.W. Magill. *Africville: The Life and Death of a Black Community*. Toronto: McClelland and Stewart, 1974.

Clark, S.D. *The New Urban Poor*. Toronto: McGraw-Hill Ryerson, 1978.

———. *Canadian Society in Historical Perspective*. Toronto: McGraw-Hill Ryerson, 1976.

———. *The Social Development of Canada*. Toronto: University of Toronto Press, 1942.

———. *The Canadian Manufacturers' Association: A Study of Collective Bargaining and Political Pressure*. Toronto: University of Toronto Press, 1939.

Clement, W. *Class, Power, and Property: Essays on Canadian Society*. Toronto: Methuen, 1983.

———. *Hardrock Mining: Industrial Relations and Technological Change at Inco*. Toronto: McClelland and Stewart, 1980.

———. *Continental Corporate Power*. Toronto: McClelland and Stewart, 1977.

———. *The Canadian Corporate Elite: An Analysis of Economic Power*. Toronto: McClelland and Stewart, 1975.

———. *The Challenge of Class Analysis*. Ottawa: Carleton University Press, 1988.

———, ed. *Understanding Canada: Building on the New Canadian Political Economy*. Montreal: McGill-Queens, 1997.

Clement, W. and D. Drache. *The New Pratical Guide to Canadian Political Economy*. Toronto: Lorimer, 1985.

Clement, W. and J. Myles, *Relations of Ruling*. Montreal: McGill-Queens, 1994.

Clement, W., and G. Williams. *The New Canadian Political Economy*. Montreal: McGill-Queens University Press, 1989.

Coates, K. and J. Powell. *The Modern North: People, Politics and the Rejection of Colonialism*. Toronto: James Lorimer, 1989.

Coates, K., and William Morrison. *The Forgotten North*. Toronto: James Lorimer, 1992.

Coffey, W. J., and M. Polèse, eds. *Still Living Together*. Montreal: Institute for Research on Public Policy, 1987.

Coleman, W.D. *The Independence Movement in Quebec 1945–1980*. Toronto: University of Toronto Press, 1984.

Collins, R. *Culture, Communications, and National Identity*. Toronto: University of Toronto Press, 1990.

Comeau, P., and Aldo Santin. *The First Canadians: A Profile of Canada's Native People Today*. Toronto: James Lorimer, 1990.

Conway, John. *Debts to Pay*. Toronto: Lorimer, 1992.

Conway, J.F. *The West: The History of a Region in Confederation*. Toronto: James Lorimer, 1983.

Cook, R. *Canada, Quebec, and the Uses of Nationalism*. Toronto: McClelland and Stewart, 1986.

———. *Canada and the French Canadian Question*. Toronto: Macmillan, 1966.

———. *The Maple Leaf Forever: Essays on Nationalism and Politics in Canada*. Toronto: Macmillan, 1971.

Cox, B.A., ed. *Native People Native Land*. Ottawa: Carleton University Press, 1988.

Crean. S. and M. Rioux. *Two Nations*. Toronto: James Lorimer, 1983.

Crean, S.M. *Who's Afraid of Canadian Culture?* Don Mills: General Publishing, 1976.

Creese, G., Neil Guppy, and Martin Meissner. *Ups and Downs on the Ladder of Success: Social Mobility in Canada*. Statistics Canada Catalogue 11-612E, 1991.

Cuneo, C. *Pay Equity: The Labour/Feminist Challenge*. Toronto: Oxford, 1990.

Curtis, J., and Lorne Tepperman, eds. *Images of Canada: The Sociological Tradition*. Scarborough: Prentice-Hall, 1990.

Curtis, J. and L. Tepperman, eds. *Understanding Canadian Society*. Toronto: McGraw-Hill Ryerson, 1988.

Curtis, J., et al. *Social Inequality in Canada: Patterns, Problems and Policies*. 2nd ed. Scarborough: Prentice-Hall, 1993.

Dacks, G. *A Choice of Futures: Politics in the Canadian North*. Toronto: Metheun, 1981.

Dacks, G., ed. *Devolution and Constitutional Development in the Canadian North*. Ottawa: Carleton University Press, 1990.

Dahlie, J., and T. Fernando, eds. *Ethnicity, Power and Politics in Canada*. Toronto: Methuen, 1981.

Darling, H. *The Politics of Freight Rates*. Toronto: McClelland and Stewart, 1980.

Davis, M., and J.E. Krauter. *The Other Canadians: Profiles of Six Minorities*. Toronto: Methuen, 1978.

Dickason, O.P. *Canada's First Nations: A History of Founding Peoples From Earliest Times*. Toronto: McClelland and Stewart, 1992.

Dickerson, M. *Whose North? Political Change, Political Development, and Self Government in the Northwest Territories*. Vancouver: UBC Press, 1992.

Dickey, J.S. *Canada and the American Presence*. New York: New York University Press, 1975.

Djao, A.W. *Inequality and Social Policy: The Sociology of Welfare*. Toronto: John Wiley, 1983.

Doern, C.B., and R.W. Phidd. *Canadian Public Policy: Ideas, Structure and Process*. Toronto: Methuen, 1983.

Doern, C. Bruce, and Brian W. Tomlin. *Faith and Fear: The Free Trade Story*. Toronto: Stoddart, 1991.

Doran, C.F., and J.N. Sigler. *Canada and the United States*. Englewood Cliffs: Prentice-Hall, 1985.

Dorland, M. ed. *The Cultural Industries of Canada: Problems, Policies, and Prospects*. Toronto: Lorimer, 1996.

Dosman, E.J., ed. *The Arctic in Question*. Toronto: Oxford Univerity Press, 1976.

Doyle, M.W. *Empires*. Ithaca: Cornell University Press, 1986.

Drache, D., and Roberto Perin, eds. *Negotiating With A Sovereign Quebec*. Toronto: Lorimer, 1992.

Driedger, L., ed. *The Canadian Ethnic Mosaic*. Toronto: McClelland and Stewart, 1978.

Driedger, L. *Ethnic Factor: Identity in Diversity*. Toronto: McGraw-Hill Ryerson, 1989.

Driedger, L. *Multi-Ethnic Canada: Identities and Inequalities*. Toronto: Oxford, 1996

Duffy, A., and Norene Pupo. *The Part-time Paradox: Connecting Gender, Work and Family*. Toronto: McClelland and Stewart, 1992.

Duffy, A., N. Mandell, and N. Pupo. *Few Choices: Women, Work and Family*. Toronto: Garamond, 1989.

Dyck, N. *What is the Indian 'Problem'? Tutelage and Resistance In Canadian Indian Administration*. St. Johns: Institute of Social and Economic Research, 1991.

Earle, R.L., and J.D. Wirth, eds. *Identities in North America*. Stanford: Stanford University Press, 1995.

Edwards, J., ed. *Language in Canada*. Cambridge: Cambridge University Press, 1998.

Elkins, D.J., and R. Simeon, eds. *Small Worlds: Provinces and Parties in Canadian Political Life*. Toronto: Methuen, 1980.

Elliott, J.L., ed. *Two Nations Many Cultures: Ethnic Groups in Canada*. 2nd ed. Scarborough: Prentice-Hall, 1983.

English, H.E., ed. *Canada-United States Relations*. New York: Praeger, 1976.

Evans, P.M. and G.R. Wekerle, eds. *Women and the Canadian Welfare State: Challenges and Change*. Toronto: University of Toronto Press, 1997.

Fairley, B., Colin Leys and James Sacouman, eds. *Restructuring and Resistance: Perspectives From Atlantic Canada*. Toronto: Garamond, 1990.

Finlayson, A.C. *Fishing For Truth: A Sociological Analysis of Northern Cod Stock Assessments From 1977-1990*. St. John's: Institute For Social And Economic Research, 1994.

Feldman, E.J., and N. Nevitte, eds. *The Future of North America: Canada, The United States and Quebec Nationalism*. Cambridge: Center for International Affairs, 1979.

Flaherty, D.H., and W.R. McKercher, eds. *Southern Exposure: Canadian Perspectives on the U.S.* Toronto: McGraw-Hill Ryerson, 1986.

Flaherty, D.H., and W.R. McKercher, eds. *The Beaver Bites Back? America Popular Culture in Canada*. Montreal: McGill-Queens, 1993.

Fleras, A., and Jean Leonard Elliott. *The Nations Within: Aboriginal-State Relations in Canada, the United States, and New Zealand*. Toronto: Oxford University Press, 1992.

Fleras, A., and J.L. Elliott. *Unequal Relations: An Introduction to Race, Ethnic, and Aboriginal Dynamics in Canada*. Second Edition. Scarborough: Prentice-Hall, 1996.

Forbes, E.R. *The Maritime Rights Movement, 1919-1927: A Study in Canadian Regionalism*. Montreal: McGill-Queen's University Press, 1979.

Forcese, D. *The Canadian Class Structure*. 3rd ed. Toronto: McGraw-Hill Ryerson, 1986.

Forcese, D., and S. Richer, eds. *Social Issues: Sociological View of Canada*. 2nd ed. Scarborough: Prentice-Hall, 1988.

Foster, L. *Turnstile Immigration: Social Order and Social Justice in Canada*. Toronto: Thompson, 1998.

Fournier, M., M. Rosenberg, and D. White, eds. *Quebec Society: Critical Issues*. Scarborough: Prentice-Hall, 1997.

Fournier, P. *A Meech Lake Post-Mortem: Is Quebec Sovereignty Inevitable?* Montreal: McGill Queens University Press, 1991.

Fournier, P. *The Quebec Establishment*. 2nd rev. ed. Montreal: Black Rose, 1976.

Fraser, Blair. *The Search for Identity*. Toronto: Doubleday, 1967.

Frideres, J.S. *Native Peoples in Canada: Contemporary Conflicts*. 4th ed. Scarborough: Prentice-Hall, 1993.

Fry, J.A., ed. *Contradictions in Canadian Society: Readings in Introductory Sociology*. Toronto: John Wiley, 1984.

Fry, J.A., ed. *Economy, Class and Social Reality*. Toronto: Butterworths, 1979.

Gagnan, D.P., ed. *Prairie Perspectives*. Toronto: Holt, Rinehart and Winston, 1970.

Gagne, W., ed. *Nationalism, Technology and the Future of Canada*. Toronto: Macmillan, 1976.

Gagnon, A.G. *Quebec: State and Society*. 2nd ed. Scarborough: Prentice-Hall, 1993.

Gagnon, A.G., and M.B. Montclam. *Quebec: Beyond the Quiet Revolution*. Scarborough: Nelson, 1990.

Gardner, R.C., and R. Kalin, eds. *A Canadian Social Psychology of Ethnic Relations*. Toronto: Methuen, 1981.

Gibbins, R. *Conflict and Unity: An Introduction to Canadian Political Life*. Toronto: Methuen, 1985.

———. *Prairie Politics and Society: Regionalism in Decline*. Toronto: Butterworths, 1980.

———. *Regionalism: Territorial Politics in Canada and the United States*. Toronto: Butterworths, 1982.

Gibbins, R. and S. Arrison. *Western Visions: Perspectives on the West in Canada*. Peterborough: Broadview, 1995.

Glenday, D., and Ann Duffy, eds. *Canadian Society: Understanding And Surviving In The 1990's*. Toronto: McClelland and Stewart, 1994.

Glenday, D., H. Guindon, and A. Turowetz, eds. *Modernization and the Canadian State*. Toronto: Macmillan, 1978.

Globerman, S. and Michael Walker. *Assessing NAFTA: A Trinational Analysis*. Vancouver: Fraser Institute, 1993.

Goldenberg, S. *Men of Property: The Canadian Developers Who are Buying America*. Toronto: Personal Library, 1981.

Goldstein, J.E., and R. Bienvenue, eds. *Ethnicity and Ethnic Relations in Canada*. Toronto: Butterworths, 1980.

Grant, G. *Lament for a Nation*. Toronto: McClelland and Stewart, 1978.

———. *Technology and Empire: Perspectives on North America*. Toronto: House of Anansi, 1969.

Grant, S.D. *Sovereignty or Security? Government Policy in the Canadian North 1936-1950*. Vancouver: University of British Columbia Press, 1988.

Gray, Earle. *Super Pipe: The Arctic Pipeline*. Toronto: Griffin House, 1979.

Grinspun, R., and Maxwell A. Cameron. *The Political Economy of North American Free Trade*. Kingston: McGill-Queens University Press, 1993.

Gruneau, R., and David Whitson. *Hockey Night in Canada: Sport, Identities, And Cultural Politics*. Toronto: Garamond, 1993.

Guindon, H. *Quebec Society: Tradition, Modernity, and Nationhood*. Toronto: University of Toronto Press, 1988.

Gunderson, Morley, Leon Muszynski, and Jennifer Keck. *Women and Labour Market Poverty*. Ottawa: Canadian Advisory Council on The Status of Women, 1990.

Gwyn, R. *The 49th Paradox: Canada in North America*. Toronto: McClelland and Stewart, 1985.

Gwyn, R. *Nationalsim Without Walls*. Toronto: McClelland and Stewart, 1995.

Haemlin, L.E. *Canadian Nordicity*. Montreal: Harvest House, 1979.

Halli, Shiva S., Frank Trovato, and Leo Driedger, eds. *Ethnic Demography: Canadian Immigrant, Racial And Cultural Variations*. Ottawa: Carleton University Press, 1990.

Hamilton, R., *Gendering the Vertical Mosaic*. Toronto: Copp Clark, 1996.

Hardin, H. *A Nation Unaware*. Vancouver: J.J. Douglas, 1974.

Harp, J., and J.R. Hofley, eds. *Structured Inequality in Canada*. Scarborough: Prentice-Hall, 1980.

Harrison, Trevor. *Of Passionate Intensity: Right Wing Populism and the Reform Party of Canada*. Toronto: University of Toronto Press, 1995.

Hartz, L. *The Founding of New Societies*. New York: Harcourt, Brace and World, 1964.

Harvey, D. *Christmas Turkey or Prairie Vulture An Economic Analysis of the Crow's Nest Pass Grain Rates*. Montreal: Institute for Research on Public Policy, 1980.

Hawkes, David C., ed. *Aboriginal Peoples and Government Responsibility: Exploring Federal and Provincial Roles*. Ottawa: Carleton University Press, 1989.

Hawkins, F. *Canada and Immigration: Public Policy and Public Concern*. 2nd ed. Montreal: McGill-Queens University Press, 1988.

————. *Critical Years in Immigration: Canada and Australia Compared*. Montreal: McGill-Queens University Press, 1989.

Heap, J.L., ed. *Everybody's Canada: The Vertical Mosaic Reviewed and Re-examined*. Toronto: Burns and MacEachern, 1974.

Helmes-Hayes, Rick, and James Curtis (eds.). *The Vertical Mosaic Revisited*. Toronto: University of Toronto Press, 1998.

Henderson, M.D., ed. *The Future on the Table: Canada and the Free Trade Issue*. North York: Masterpress, 1987.

Henry, Frances. *The Caribbean Diaspora In Toronto: Learning To Live With Racism*. Toronto: University of Toronto Press, 1994.

Henry, F. *Forgotten Canadians: The Blacks of Nova Scotia*. Don Mills: Longmans, 1973.

Henry, Frances, Carol Tator, Winston Mattis, and Tim Rees. *The Colour of Democracy: Racism in Canadian Society*. Toronto: Harcourt Brace, 1995.

Herberg, E.N. *Ethnic Groups in Canada: Adaptations and Transitions*. Scarborough: Nelson, 1989.

Higgins, B. *The Rise and Fall of Montreal?* Moncton: Canadian Institute for Research on Regional Development, 1986.

Hiller, H.H. *Society and Change: S.D. Clark and the Development of Canadian Sociology*. Toronto: University of Toronto Press, 1982.

Hiller, J, and P. Neary. *Newfoundland in the Nineteenth and Twentieth Centuries: Essays in Interpretation*. Toronto: University of Toronto Press, 1980.

Hillmer, N., ed. *Partners Nevertheless: Canadian American Relations in the Twentieth Century*. Toronto: Copp Clark Pitman, 1989.

Himmelfarb, A., and C.J. Richardson. *Sociology for Canadians: Images of Society*. Toronto: McGraw-Hill Ryerson, 1982.

Hindley, M.P., G.M. Martin, and J. McNulty. *The Tangled Net: Basic Issues in Canadian Communications*. Vancouver: J.J. Douglas, 1977.

Holmes, J.W. *Life With Uncle: The Canadian-American Relationship*. Toronto: University of Toronto Press, 1981.

Honderich, J. *Arctic Imperative: Is Canada Losing the North?* Toronto: University of Toronto Press, 1987.

House, J.D. *The Challenge of Oil*. St. John's: Institute for Social and Economic Research, 1985.

House, J.D., ed. *Fish vs. Oil: Resources and Rural Development in North Atlantic Societies*. St. John's: Institute for Social and Economic Research, 1986.

Hughes, D.R., and E. Kallen. *The Anatomy of Racism: Canadian Dimensions*. Montreal: Harvest House, 1974.

Hunter, A.A. *Class Tells: On Social Inequality in Canada*. 2nd ed. Toronto: Butterworths, 1986.

Hutcheson, J. *Dominance and Dependency*. Toronto: McClelland and Stewart, 1978.

Innis, H.A. *The Cod Fisheries*. Toronto: University of Toronto Press, 1940.

———. *The Fur Trade in Canada*. Toronto: University of Toronto Press, 1930.

———. *Problems of Staple Production in Canada*. Toronto: Ryerson Press, 1933.

————— *Nationalism Without Walls*. Toronto: McClelland and Stewart, 1995.

Inglehart, R., N. Nevitte, and M. Basanez. *The North American Trajectory: Cultural, Economic, and Political Ties Among the United States, Canada, and Mexico*. New York: Aldine DeGruyter, 1996.

Irving, J.A. *The Social Credit Movement in Alberta*. Toronto: University of Toronto Press, 1959.

Isajiw, W.W., ed. *Multiculturalism in North America and Europe*. Toronto: Canadian Scholar's Press, 1997.

Jabbra, J.G., and R.G, Landes. *The Political Orientation of Canadian Adolescents: Political Socialization and Political Culture in Nova Scotia*. Halifax: St. Mary's University, 1976.

Jackson, E., ed. *The Great Canadian Debate: Foreign Ownership*. Toronto: McClelland and Stewart, 1975.

James, C.E. *Seeing Ourselves: Exploring Race, Ethnicity, and Culture*. Toronto: Thompson, 1995.

Jenson, Jane, Elisabeth Hagen, and Ceillaigh Reddy, eds. *Feminization of the Labour Force: Paradoxes and Promises*. New York: Oxford, 1988.

Jones, R. *Community in Crisis: French-Canadian Nationalism in Perspective*. Toronto: McClelland and Stewart, 1972.

Joy, R. *Languages in Conflict: The Canadian Experience*. Toronto: McClelland and Stewart, 1972.

Kalbach, M.A. and W.E. Kalbach, eds. *Perspectives on Ethnicity in Canada*. Toronto: Harcourt Brace, 2000.

Kalbach, W.E., and W.W. McVey. *The Demographic Basis of Canadian Society*. 2nd ed. Toronto: McGraw-Hill Ryerson, 1979.

Kallen, E. *Ethnicity and Human Rights in Canada*. Toronto: Gage, 1982.

Kaplan, William, ed. Belonging: *The Meaning And Future of Canadian Citizenship*. Montreal: McGill-Queens University Press, 1993.

Keohane, K., *Symptoms of Canada: An Essay on the Canadian Identity*. Toronto: University of Toronto Press, 1997.

Krahn, Harvey and Graham Lowe. *Work, Industry and Canadian Society*. 2nd ed. Toronto: Nelson, 1993.

Kymlicka, W. *Finding Our Way: Rethinking Ethnocultural Relations in Canada*. Toronto: Oxford, 1998.

Lachapelle, Guy, Gérald Bernier, Daniel Salée, and Luc Bernier. *The Quebec Democracy: Structures, Processes, And Policies*. Toronto: McGraw-Hill Ryerson, 1993.

Laczko, L. *Pluralism and Inequality in Quebec*. Toronto: University of Toronto Press, 1995.

Langlois, Simon, et al. *Recent Social Trends in Quebec 1960-1990*. Montreal: McGill-Queens University Press, 1992.

Lanning, R. *The National Alabum: Collective Biography and the Formation of the Canadian Middle Class*. Ottawa: Carleton University Press, 1996.

LaPierre, A., P. Smart, and P. Savard. *Language, Culture, and Values in Canada at the Dawn of the 21st Century*. Ottawa: Carleton University Press, 1996

LaPierre, L., ed. *If You Love This Country: Fact and Feelings on Free Trade*. Toronto: McClelland and Stewart, 1987.

Lavoie, Y. *L'émigration des Canadians aux Etats-Unis avant 1930*. Montreal: University of Montreal Press, 1982.

Laxer, G. *Open For Business: The Roots of Foreign Ownership in Canada*. Toronto: Oxford University Press, 1989.

Laxer, J. *Leap of Faith: Free Trade and the Future of Canada*. Edmonton: Hurtig, 1986.

Levine, M., and C. Sylvester. *Foreign Ownership*. Toronto: General Publishing, 1972.

Levine, Marc V. *The Reconquest of Montreal: Language Change and Social Policy In A Bilingual City*. Philadelphia: Temple University Press, 1990.

Li, P.S. *Ethnic Inequality in a Class Society*. Toronto: Wall and Thompson, 1988.

Li, P.S., ed. *Race and Ethnic Relations in Canada*. Toronto: University of Toronto Press, 1990.

_____ *The Chinese of Canada*, Second Edition. Toronto: Oxford, 1998.

_____ *The Making of Post-War Canada*. Toronto: Oxford, 1996.

Li, P.S., and B.S. Bolaria, eds. *Racial Minorities in Multicultural Canada*. Toronto: Garamond Press, 1984.

Lipset, S.M. *Agrarian Socialism: The Co-operative Commonwealth Federation in Saskatchewan*. New York: Doubleday, 1968.

———. *Revolution and Counter-Revolution: Change and Persistence in Social Structure*. rev. ed. Garden City: Doubleday, 1971.

———. *Continental Divide: The Values and Institutions of the United States and Canada*. New York: Routledge, 1990.

Little Bear, L., M. Boldt, and J.A. Long, eds. *Pathways to Self-Determination: Canadian Indians and the Canadian State*. Toronto: University of Toronto Press, 1984.

Litvak, I.A., and C.J. Maule. *The Canadian Multi-Nationals*. Toronto: Butterworths, 1981.

Lorimer, R., and D. Wilson, eds. *Communication Canada: Issues in Broadcasting and New Technologies*. Toronto: Kagan and Woo, 1988.

Lucas, R. Minetown, *Milltown, Railtown: Life in Canadian Communities of a Single Industry*. Toronto: University of Toronto Press, 1971.

Lumsdem, I., ed. *Close the 49th Parallel: The Americanization of Canada*. Toronto: University of Toronto Press, 1970.

Lustig, N., B.P. Bosworth, and R.Z. Lawrence, eds. *North American Free Trade: Assessing the Impact*. Washington, D.C.: The Brookings Institute, 1992.

Luxton, M., and H. Rosenberg. *Through the Kitchen Window: The Politics of Home and Family*. Toronto: Garamond, 1986.

Mackie, M. *Exploring Gender Relations In Canada: Further Explorations*. Toronto: Butterworths, 1991.

Macpherson, C.B. *Democracy in Alberta: Social Credit and the Party System*. Toronto: University of Toronto Press, 1953.

Mandel, E., and D. Taras, eds. *A Passion for Identity*. Toronto: Methuen, 1987.

Marchak, P. *Green Gold: The Forest Industry In British Columbia*. Vancouver: UBC Press, 1983.

Marchak, M.P. *Ideological Perspectives on Canada*. 3rd ed. Toronto: McGraw-Hill Ryerson, 1988.

———. *In Whose Interests: An Essay on Multinational Corporations in a Canadian Context*. Toronto: McClelland and Stewart, 1979.

Marsden, L.R., and E.B. Harvey. *Fragile Federation: Social Change in Canada*. Toronto: McGraw-Hill Ryerson, 1979.

Matthews, R. *The Creation of Regional Dependency*. Toronto: University of Toronto Press, 1983.

———. *There's No Better Place Than Here: Social Change in Three Newfoundland Communities*. Toronto: Peter Martin, 1976.

———. *Canadian Identity: Major Forces Shaping the Life of a People*. Ottawa: Steel Rail, 1988.

Matthews, R., and J. Steele. *The Struggle for Canadian Universities*. Toronto: New Press, 1969.

McBride, S., and J. Shields. *Dismantling a Nation: Canada and the New World Order*. Halifax: Fernwood, 1993.

McCann, L. and A.M. Gunn. *Heartland and Hinterland: A Regional Geography of Canada,* Third Edition. Scarborough: Prentice-Hall, 1998.

McCrorie, J.N., and M. L. McDonald, eds. *The Constitutional Future of the Prairie and Atlantic Regions of Canada*. Regina: CPRC, 1992.

McDaniel, S. *Canada's Aging Population*. Toronto: Butterworths, 1986.

McRae, K.D. *Conflict and Compromise in Multilingual Societies: Belgium*. Waterloo: Wilfrid Laurier University Press, 1986

———. *Conflict and Compromise in Multilingual Societies: Switzerland*. Waterloo: Wilfrid Laurier University Press, 1983.

McRoberts, K. *Quebec: Social Change and Political Crisis*. 3rd ed. Toronto: McClelland and Stewart, 1988.

McRoberts, K., ed. *Beyond Quebec: Taking Stock of Canada*. Montreal: McGill-Queens, 1995.

McRoberts, K. *Misconceiving Canada: The Struggle for National Unity*. Toronto: Oxford University Press, 1997.

McVey, W. W. and W.E. Kalbach. *Canadian Population*. Scarborough: Nelson, 1995.

Milne, D. *The New Canadian Constitution*. Toronto: James Lorimer, 1982.

Milner, H. *Politics in the New Quebec*. Toronto: McClelland and Stewart, 1978.

Milner, S.H., and H. Milner. *The Decolonization of Quebec*. Toronto: McClelland and Stewart, 1973.

Monahan, P. and Ken McRoberts. *The Charlottetown Accord, the Referendum, And the Future of Canada*. Toronto: University of Toronto Press, 1993.

Monière, D. *Ideologies in Quebec: The Historical Development*. Toronto: University of Toronto Press, 1981.

Morse, B.W. *Aboriginal Self-government in Australia and Canada*. Kingston: Queen's University Institute of Intergovernmental Relations, 1984.

Morton, W.L. *The Canadian Identity*. Madison: University of Wisconsin Press, 1965.

———. *The Progressive Party in Canada*. Toronto: University of Toronto Press, 1957.

Murray, J., ed. *Canadian Cultural Nationalism*. New York: New York University Press, 1977.

Nakhaie, M.R., ed. *Debates on Social Inequality: Class, Gender, and Ethnicity in Canada*. Toronto: Harcourt Brace, 1999.

Nelson, E.D., and Augie Fleras. *Social Problems in Canada*. Scarborough: Prentice-Hall, 1995.

Nelson, E.D., and B.W. Robinson, *Gender in Canada*. Scarborough: Prentice-Hall, 1999.

Nevitte, N., *The Decline of Deference*. Peterborough: Broadview, 1996.

Niosi, J. *Canadian Multinationals*. Toronto: Between the Lines, 1985.

———. *The Economy of Canada: Who Controls It?* 2nd rev. ed. Montreal: Black Rose, 1982.

———. *Canadian Capitalism: A Study of Power in the Canadian Business Establishment*. Toronto: Jame Lorimer, 1981.

Noel, S.J.R. *Politics in Newfoundland*. Toronto: University of Toronto Press, 1971.

Olsen, D. *The State Elite*. Toronto: McClelland and Stewart, 1980.

Orchard, D. *The Fight For Canada: Four Centuries of Resistance To American Expansionism*. Toronto: Stoddard, 1991.

Ossenberg, R.J. *Canadian Society: Pluralism, Change and Conflict*. Scarborough: Prentice-Hall, 1971.

Ossenberg, R.J., ed. *Power and Change in Canada*. Toronto: McClelland and Stewart, 1980.

Ostry, S., ed. *Canadian Higher Education in the Seventies*. Ottawa: Economic Council of Canada, 1972.

Page, R. *Northern Development: The Canadian Dilemma*. Toronto: McClelland and Stewart, 1986.

Pal, L. *Interests of the State: The Politics of Language, Multiculturalism, and Feminism in Canada*. Montreal: McGill-Queens University Press, 1997.

Palmer, H., ed. *The Settlement of the West*. Calgary: University of Calgary Press, 1977.

Panitch, L., ed. *The Canadian State: Political Economy and Politcal Power*. Toronto: University of Toronto Press, 1977.

Paterson, D.G. *British Direct Investment in Canada 1890-1914*. Toronto: University of Toronto Press, 1983.

Peacock, D. *People, Peregrines, and Arctic Pipelines*. Vancouver: J.J. Douglas, 1977.

Peitchinis, S.G. *Women at Work: Responses and Discrimination*. Toronto: McClelland and Stewart, 1989.

Perry, R.L. *Galt U.S.A.: The American Presence in a Canadian City*. Toronto: Maclean-Hunter, 1971.

Phillips, P. *Regional Disparities*. Toronto: James Lorimer, 1982.

Phillips, P., and E. Phillips. *Women and Work: Inequality in the Labour Market*. Toronto: James Lorimer, 1993.

Ponting, J.R., ed. *Arduous Journey: Canadian Indians and Decolonization*. Toronto: McClelland and Stewart, 1986.

Ponting, J.R., and R. Gibbins. *Out of Irrelevance: A Socio-Political Introduction to Indian Affairs in Canada*. Toronto: Butterworths, 1980.

Porter, J., M. Porter, and B.R. Blishen. *Stations and Callings: Making it Through the School System*. Toronto: Methuen, 1982.

Porter, J. *The Vertical Mosaic*. Toronto: University of Toronto Press, 1965.

Pratt, L., and G. Stevenson, eds. *Western Separatism: The Myths, Realities, and Dangers*. Edmonton: Hurtig, 1981.

Purich, D. *The Inuit and Their Land: The Story Of Nunavut*. Toronto: James Lorimer, 1992.

Purich, D. *Our Land: Native Rights in Canada*. Toronto: James Lorimer, 1986.

Putnam, D.F., and R.G. Putnam. Canada: *A Regional Analysis*. Toronto: J.M. Dent, 1970.

Ramcharan, S. *Racism: Non-Whites in Canada*. Toronto: Butterworths, 1982.

Randall, S., and Roger Gibbins eds. *Federalism and the New World Order*. Calgary: University of Calgary Press, 1994.

Rawlyk, G.A., ed. *The Atlantic Provinces and the Problems of Confederation*. St. John's: Breakwater, 1979.

Rea, K.J. *The Political Economy of the Canadian North*. Toronto: University of Toronto Press, 1968 .

Reid, S. *Canada Remapped: How The Partition Of Quebec Will Reshape The Nation.* Vancouver: Pulp Press, 1992.

Reitz, J.G. *The Survival of Ethnic Groups.* Toronto: McGraw-Hill Ryerson, 1980.

Report of the Federal Cultural Policy Review Committee. Ottawa: Department of Communications. 1981.

Report of the Task Force on Broadcasting Policy. Ottawa: Minister of Supply and Services, 1986.

Resnick, P. *The Land of Cain: Class and Nationalism in English Canada.* Vancouver: New Star, 1977.

Richards, J., and L. Pratt. *Prairie Capitalism: Power and Influence in the New West.* Toronto: McClelland and Stewart, 1979.

Richmond, A. *Post-War Immigrants in Canada.* Toronto: University of Toronto Press, 1970.

Riggs, A., and T. Velk, eds. *Beyond NAFTA: An Economic, Political, and Sociological Perspective.* Vancouver: Fraser Institute, 1993.

Rinehart, J., C. Huxley, and D. Robertson. *Just Another Car Factory? Lean Production and its Dissidents.* Ithaca: ILR Press, 1997.

Rioux, M., and Y. Martin, eds. *French-Canadian Society.* Vol. I. Toronto: McClelland and Stewart, 1971.

Ross, D.P., and R. Shillington. *The Canadian Fact Book on Poverty 1994.* Ottawa: Canadian Council on Social Development, 1994.

Rotstein, A., and G. Lax. *Getting it Back: A Program for Canadian Independence.* Toronto: Clarke Irwin, 1974.

Rousseau, M.O., and R. Zariski. *Regionalism and Regional Devolution in Comparative Perspective.* New York: Praeger, 1987.

Ryan, T.J. *Poverty and the Child: A Canadian Study.* Toronto: McGraw-Hill Ryerson, 1972.

Sardo, C. *Poverty In Canada.* Vancouver: Fraser Institute, 1992.

Satzewich, V., ed. *Deconstructing A Nation: Immigration, Multiculturalism, And Racism In 90's Canada.* Halifax: Fernwood, 1992.

Satzewich, V., ed. *Racism and Social Inequality in Canada.* Toronto: Thompson, 1998.

Savoie, D. J., *Governing from the Centre: The Concentration of Power in Canadian Politics.* Toronto: University of Toronto Press, 1999.

Schwartz, B. *Fathoming Meech Lake.* Winnipeg: University of Manitoba Legal Research Institute, 1987.

Schwartz, M. *Politics and Territory: The Sociology of Regional Persistence in Canada.* Montreal: McGill-Queen's University Press, 1974.

Shapiro, D.M. *Foreign and Domestic Firms in Canada.* Toronto: Butterworths, 1980.

Sinclair. P.R., ed. *A Question Of Survival: The Fisheries And Newfoundland Society.* St. John's: Institute For Social And Economic Research, 1988.

Singer, B.D., ed. *Communications In Canadian Society.* Toronto: Nelson, 1995.

Sitwell, O.F.G., and N.R.M. Seifried. *The Regional Structure of the Canadian Economy.* Toronto: Methuen, 1984.

Smiley, D. *Canada in Question: Federalism in the Seventies.* 2nd ed. Toronto: McGraw-Hill Ryerson, 1976.

Smith, D.E., Peter MacKinnon, John C. Courtney, eds. *After Meech Lake: Lessons For The Future.* Saskatoon: Fifth House, 1991.

Smith, M.G., and F. Stone, eds. *Assessing the Canada-U.S. Free Trade Agreement*. Halifax: Institute for Research on Public Policy, 1987.

Smith, P.H., ed. *The Challenge Of Integration: Europe And The Americas*. New Brunswick, N.J.: Transaction, 1993.

Sobel, D., and S. Meurer. *Working At Inglis: The Life And Death Of A Canadian Factory*. Toronto: Lorimer, 1995.

Stairs, D., and G.R. Winham, eds. *The Politics of Canada's Economic Relationship With The United States*. Toronto: University of Toronto Press, 1985.

Stanley, G.F.G. *The Birth of Western Canada: A History of the Riel Rebellion*. Toronto: University of Toronto Press, 1978.

Starks, R. *Industry in Decline*. Toronto: James Lorimer, 1978.

Stevenson, G. *Unfulfilled Union: Canadian Federalism and National Unity*. rev. ed. Toronto: Gage, 1982.

Stone, L. *Migration in Canada: Regional Aspects*. Ottawa: Statistics Canada, 1969.

Strong-Boag, V., S. Grace, A. Eisenberg, and J. Anderson, eds. *Painting the Maple Leaf: Essays on Race, Gender, and the Construction of Canada*. Vancouver: UBC Press, 1998.

Swinton, K.E., and C.J. Rogerson, eds. *Competing Constitutional Visions*. Toronto: Carswell, 1988.

Taras, D., B. Rasporich, and E. Mandel, eds. *A Passion For Identity*. 2nd ed. Scarborough: Nelson, 1993.

Teeple, G., ed. *Capitalism and the National Question in Canada*. Toronto: University of Toronto Press, 1972.

Teeple, G. *Globalization And The Decline Of Social Reform*. Toronto: Garamond, 1995.

Tepperman, L., and J. Curtis, eds. *Readings in Sociology: An Introduction*. Toronto: McGraw-Hill Ryerson, 1988.

Thomas, D., ed. *Canada and the United States: Differences that Count*. Peterborough: Broadview, 1993.

Thomson, D.C., ed. *Quebec Society and Politics: Views from the Inside*. Toronto: McClelland and Stewart, 1973.

Tupper, A., and G.B. Doern, eds. *Public Corporations and Public Policy in Canada*. Montreal: Institute for Research on Public Policy, 1981.

Ujimoto, V., and G. Hirabayashi. *Visible Minorities amd Multiculturalism: Asians in Canada*. Toronto: Butterworths, 1980.

Vallieres, P. *White Niggers of America*. Toronto: McClelland and Stewart, 1971.

Veltmeyer, H. *The Canadian Class Structure*. Toronto: Garamond, 1986.

Wade, M. *Regionalism in the Canadian Community, 1867-1967*. Toronto: University off Toronto Press, 1969.

Walsh, B. *More Than a Poor Majority: The Story of Newfoundland's Confederation With Canada*. St. John's: Breakwater, 1985.

Wardhaugh, R. *Language and Nationhood: The Canadian Experience*. Vancouver: New Star, 1983.

Warkentin, J. *Canada: A Geographcial Interpretation*. Toronto: Metheun, 1968.

Warnock, J.W. *Free Trade and the New Right Agenda*. Vancouver: New Star, 1988.

Watkins, M., ed. *Alternatives to the Free Trade Agreement*. Ottawa: Canadian Centre for Policy Alternatives, 1988.

Watkins, M. *Dene Nation: The Colony Within*. Toronto: University of Toronto Press, 1977.

Watson, W. *Globalization and the Meaning of Canadian Life*. Toronto: University of Toronto Press, 1998.

Weston, A., A. Piazze-McMahon, and E. Dosman. *Free Trade With A Human Face? The Social Dimensions of CUFTA and NAFTA*. Ottawa: North South Institute, 1992.

White, J. *Sisters and Solidarity: Women And Unions In Canada*. Toronto: Thompson, 1993.

Wigdor, B.T., and D.K. Foot. *The Over-forty Society: Issues for Canada's Aging Population*. Toronto: James Lorimer, 1988.

Wilson, S.J. *Women, the Family and the Economy*. 3rd ed. Toronto: McGraw-Hill Ryerson, 1991.

Wotherspoon, T. and V. Satzewich. *First Nations: Race, Class, And Gender Relations*. Scarborough: Nelson, 1993.

Yeates, M. *Main Street: Windsor to Quebec City*. Toronto: Macmillan, 1975.

Zimmerman, C.C., and G.W. Moneo. *The Prairie Community System*. Ottawa: Agricultural Economics Research Council of Canada, 1970.

Zureik, E., and R.M. Pike, eds. *Socialization and Values in Canadian Society*. Vol. I., *Political Socialization*. Toronto: McClelland and Stewart, 1975.

Index

Lannie Gordon - Gonna catch you
Derek B - you've got to lock up